Neil Gerard McCluskey, S.J.

Public Schools AND

Moral Education

The Influence of HORACE MANN

WILLIAM TORREY HARRIS and

JOHN DEWEY

1958

Columbia University Press   New York

This book is for
Mary G. and Patrick J., Moral Educators
From one who is grateful for
having fallen under their
benign influence

PREFACE

. The preface of a book of this kind is like the master's den
in a meticulously kept mansion. Outside the den door the author may
leave his *wissenschaftlich* apparatus and tools, and relax within while
writing a few simple lines of thanks and explanation.

The extent of the present explanation is to identify the author as a
Catholic priest and a Jesuit, and to mention how this book came to be
written. Nearly ten years ago a group of theological students in California met in seminar to discuss the Church-State aspects of the controversy over the decisions of the U.S. Supreme Court in the *Everson*
and *McCollum* cases. One by-product of the seminar sessions was a
firmer conviction in the author's mind that the fervor of the controversy
could be accounted for only by something deeper than the arguments
aired in public. Two basic value systems seemed to be contesting a narrow passageway with neither position yielding a step. A few years later,
firsthand acquaintance with the school systems in several European
countries which seemed to have somewhat resolved similar problems
raised higher the question as to why the American impasse remained.
Later still, participation in a series of lively seminars at Columbia University's Teachers College finally brought to a writing point the ideas of
the present study.

The author is beholden to many people and many institutions. Academic amenities would be flouted if some names at least were not mentioned. Gratitude and appreciation are expressed to these members of the Columbia Graduate School of Philosophy and Teachers College faculties: to Professors Dumas Malone and Henry Steele Commager, whose cultural stress in lecturing upon nineteenth-century American history was invigoratingly luminous; to Professors Jacques Barzun and Lionel Trilling, in whose exacting seminar several chapters of the study were hammered out; to Professor Philip H. Phenix, for encouragement and thoughtful criticism; to Professor Lawrence A. Cremin, whose brilliantly led seminars overflowed into hours of delightful discussion beyond the call of duty; to Professor R. Freeman Butts, for painstaking assistance and unswerving loyalty to the academic law which says that even basic disagreements can be made profitable for all concerned.

A formal acknowledgment is only a slender symbol of appreciation to the men and women of the library world, without whom mining in academic piles would cease. The author extends his sincere thanks to the staffs of these libraries: first and foremost, the libraries of Columbia University, especially the Butler Library and the Teachers College Library; the Library of the Fordham University School of Education; the New York Public Library; the Library of the New York Academy of Medicine; the Library of the Union Theological Seminary of New York; the America Press Library; the Archives of the Massachusetts Historical Society; the Boston Public Library; the St. Louis Public Library; the Archives of the Missouri Historical Society; the Library of the School of Philosophy of the University of Southern California; the Library of Seattle University; the Library of the National Education Association; the Library of the U.S. Office of Education; the Library of Congress.

The author's gratitude and appreciation also extend to Mrs. John Dewey for permission to publish letters from her husband to William Torrey Harris; to Miss Edith Davidson Harris for permission to use correspondence from her father to John Dewey; to Robert L. Straker, whose lifelong study of Horace Mann made his criticisms invaluable; to several of the author's associates on the editorial staff of *America* for suggestions and criticism; to Rev. Charles Keenan, S.J., of Gonzaga University, Spokane, Washington, who read the book in manuscript.

Acknowledgment is also made to the following publishers for permission to quote from copyrighted works: Henry Holt and Company, from R. Freeman Butts and Lawrence Cremin, *A History of Education in American Culture,* and John Dewey, *The Influence of Darwin on Philosophy, Reconstruction in Philosophy, Human Nature and Conduct,* and *Logic;* G. P. Putnam's Sons, from John Dewey, *The Quest for Certainty* and *Freedom and Culture;* Allen and Unwin, Ltd., from *Contemporary American Philosophy,* edited by G. P. Adams and W. P. Montague.

NEIL GERARD MCCLUSKEY, S.J.

Campion House
New York City
September, 1958

CONTENTS

CONTENTS

PART FIVE: CONCLUSION

PUBLIC SCHOOLS AND MORAL EDUCATION

PART ONE

INTRODUCTION

I. THE PROBLEM

This is the history of a problem and the solutions to it proposed by three men. From the origin of the American public school in the early decades of the nineteenth century down to the present day, educators have tried to state what values should govern the school in its effort to form character and to inculcate value judgments. These attempts at a philosophy of values have been complicated by the shifting and highly dynamic religious pluralism of American society.

Often enough discussions of values in public education fail to touch the central problem: the limitations inherent in the idea of a *common* school serving a pluralistic society. The coexistence within a society of groups holding fundamental differences regarding the nature and destiny of man makes the approach to education through one common school a delicate matter. For in the final analysis values are rooted in what men hold as ultimate or supreme in life—in what may be taken in a broad sense as "religion." Only in an ideal society, wherein men agree freely and completely about ultimate values, can there be a successful common approach to the moral side of education. Nevertheless, groups of citizens in any society, despite differences that may originate in conflicting cultural and social backgrounds, do share some

basic values and ideals. For instance, they must agree to live peace-
fully and to work together for the essential temporal goals of the community of which they are a part. They must give at least implicit
allegiance to the framework of legal sanctions which protects the
exercise of individual rights, resolves conflicts of rights, and oversees
the discharge of obligations. Such a system of agreed-upon values,
ideals, and sanctions can be called a "public philosophy." [1] Evidently
without the cement of a shared public philosophy no society can long
maintain the required degree of cohesion.

It is to the schools that we particularly look to communicate the
heritage of the American public philosophy. Historically the common
school has been one of the most effective forces in building a sense of
the American "community." Indeed, the melting-pot metaphor is both
a description and praise of the important function performed by the
common school during the periods of the great immigrations. These
schools helped give immigrant children and the children of immigrants
love for a common country and taught respect for difference in background. The same respect for the cultural diversity in our national
unity is a vital part of the Americanizing process in today's school,
whereby we are *made e pluribus unum*—in John Courtney Murray's
rendition, "one society subsisting amid multiple pluralisms." [2]

But here we are immediately face to face with a question of balance.
To what degree can pluralisms flourish before they weaken the bonds
of national unity? How much unity can be had without sacrificing
the richness of diversity? No rule-of-thumb measure has yet been discovered. Except for a few wild oscillations, usually during periods of
national hysteria, the good sense of the American people has followed
a steady middle course between the extremes of totalitarian uniformity
and chaotic individualism.

Like compunction, a public philosophy is better lived than defined.
In fact, definition can be both hazardous and unrewarding. In those
social areas where friction can readily develop between different ethnic
or religious groups, arrangements for joint procedures are come by

[1] For an elaboration of this idea see Lippmann, *The Public Philosophy*, Chapters
8–12.
[2] "The Problem of Pluralism in America," *Thought*, XXIX (Summer, 1954),
166.

more easily than joint statements of policy. In such areas men follow
a tendency to found agreement on a penultimate level rather than upon
a basis of ultimate principles. As one writer has put it:

> If men in their temporal affairs can agree to obey the laws, albeit one is
> following the will of God, a second, the command of reason, and a third,
> the dictates of expediency, that should be enough for Caesar. Ultimacies,
> as far as the state is concerned, remain the realm of the private.[3]

On the political level this holds true—Caesar need not scrutinize the
hearts that conform outwardly to his bidding. How far Caesar as educator can follow the same principle is a more involved question.

For a long period in American history there was pretty general
agreement on the basis of our public philosophy. Despite Protestant-
Catholic tensions which drew agonizingly taut during certain years,
the Old World inheritance of Greco-Roman natural law and of many
of the central religious concepts of the Judaeo-Christian tradition was
universally accepted and widely operative in American society. This
condition also favored agreement regarding the basis and content of a
 philosophy of character education for the common school. However,
even during this period the fissures steadily widened and new ones
began to appear. The further fragmentation of the Protestant churches
multiplied differences over dogma both among Protestants themselves
and with the Catholics, whose numbers were steadily increasing. Non-
European religious groups established themselves. New groups arose
whose ultimates derived from a secular and humanist, rather than a
Christian, tradition. All these factors entered into the historical process
which resulted in the secularization of American public education. They
have also contracted the area governed by the public philosophy and
have had profound repercussions upon the philosophy of character
education for the common school.

It is perhaps repeating a truism to remark that the less the agreement
in society over ultimate values, the less its common school can reflect
a unified philosophy of values. We have a political consensus enshrined in the Constitution and Bill of Rights which our founding fathers based upon their understanding of natural law and natural

---

[3] Cremin, "The Public School and the Public Philosophy," reprint from *Teachers
College Record* (March, 1956), pp. 2–3.

rights.[4] Although this basis is no longer universally accepted, the impetus given by the initial consensus still enables us to agree that certain principles of the moral and spiritual sphere should have place in our common schools. In 1951 the Educational Policies Commission of the National Education Association and the American Association of School Administrators published a document listing ten of these basic moral and spiritual values:[5] the supreme importance of the individual personality, the moral responsibility of each individual, institutions as the servants of men, common consent, devotion to truth, respect for excellence, moral equality, brotherhood, the pursuit of happiness, and spiritual enrichment.

At an earlier period in American history, these moral and spiritual values were generally assumed to be closely related to traditional religious value-systems; so much so that religion was considered their solid guarantee. It was in this vein that George Washington warned his countrymen in his Farewell Address:

And let us with caution indulge the supposition that morality can be maintained without religion. Whatever may be conceded to the influence of refined education on minds of peculiar structure, reason and experience both forbid us to expect that national morality can prevail in exclusion of religious principle.[6]

Another prominent example of this linking of morality to religion can be found in the phrasing of the Northwest Ordinance of 1787 and of the Southwest Ordinance of 1790, both of which contain an article stating: "Religion, morality and knowledge, being necessary to good government, and the happiness of mankind, schools and the means of education shall forever be encouraged."[7] Moreover, "religion" was set forth specifically as one of the aims of education in many of the original state constitutions.[8]

The inclusion of these values within a universally accepted religious

[4] Clinton Rossiter has an enlightening treatment of this point in *Seedtime of the Republic*.

[5] National Education Association, *Moral and Spiritual Values in the Public Schools*.

[6] Richardson, *A Compilation of the Messages and Papers of the Presidents,* I, 212.

[7] Stokes, *Church and State in the United States,* I, 480–82.

[8] See Dunn, "The Decline of the Teaching of Religion in the American Public

framework, however, is no longer feasible. When the attempt is made
to formulate a religiously based statement of values, many groups in
American society find they can no longer give their assent. The reason
is not far to seek. Although most Americans continue to avow belief
in God, their ideas of the nature of divinity and of the implications of
religious belief for conduct run to every shade of the spectrum. For
the traditional orthodox believer God is still an absolute, eternal, transcendent, personal—and for Christians, triune—Being. Yet each of
these attributes has been the occasion for religious division, separating
groups of Americans into different sects. Today the common school
serves children who come from families divided into more than 250
different religious bodies. The question, then, as the NEA statement
sees it, is expressed as follows:

> The public schools faithfully reflect the religious diversity and tolerance
> which have helped to make our nation strong. In view of differing religious
> faiths, a common education consistent with the American concept of free-
> dom of religion must be based, not on the inculcation of any religious
> creed, but rather on a decent respect for all religious opinions.[9]

✦

The present study undertakes to set forth the treatment by three
prominent educators of the problem of religious pluralism and of the
public school philosophy of values, so as to indicate to some extent
the influence of their thinking upon the formulations of modern policy
statements like that which appeared in the 1951 report of the Educational Policies Commission, *Moral and Spiritual Values in the Public
Schools*. The three men selected for study roughly span the history
of the American public school. They are Horace Mann (1796–1859),
William Torrey Harris (1835–1908), and John Dewey (1859–1952).

The study is grounded on the following assumptions: (1) that
American society has insisted historically, and continues to insist, that
the common school take a proper responsibility for the character forma-

---

Elementary School in the States Originally the Thirteen Colonies, 1776–1861"
(unpublished Ph.D. dissertation, Dept. of Education, Johns Hopkins University,
1956).

[9] *Moral and Spiritual Values in the Public Schools*, p. 6.

tion of its children; (2) that the thinking of these three men on the problem of values has had a profound influence on the conception of character education in the common school; (3) that the 1951 NEA Educational Policies Commission statement is peculiarly representative of the thinking of important agencies which formulate, apply, and administer policies for the common schools, and which are today trying to define the role of the common school for character education in a religiously pluralistic society.

The choice of these three men hardly requires justification. The consensus among historians of education and students of social thought clearly indicates that Horace Mann, William Torrey Harris, and John Dewey can be considered the triumvirate whose thought has most affected the creation and development of the present philosophy of the American public school. A few other names, like those of Henry Barnard, Calvin Stowe, Francis Parker, John Swett, Samuel Lewis, Calvin Wiley—all educators of the first rank—might come to mind as a challenge to the above selection. However, with the exception of Barnard, who in addition to his pioneer work in Connecticut and Rhode Island was the first U.S. Commissioner of Education, the others labored on a regional level. Henry Barnard could have been a fourth figure in this study, but since much of his career paralleled Mann's, and since his ideas on the function of the common school were so close to those of his Massachusetts colleague, his inclusion would have entailed considerable overlapping.

The three principals selected are assumed to have had paramount influence on the development of the value philosophy underlying the 1951 NEA statement, and yet it must not be supposed that they are the only influences. It is usually a formidable task to attempt the establishment of direct causal connections between a given theory in education and its concrete embodiment in a later policy statement prepared by other hands. There is no certainty that the progenitors would recognize, or own to, what was supposedly prepared from their own works.

We add a further caution. Indirect influence, as it is usually more pervasive than direct, is sometimes more important. Once an idea has been put into practice, it is continually adopted (and adapted) by others who need never advert to its source. The distinguished group of citizens and educators who prepared the 1951 statement on values need not have been directly aware that much of what they assembled consisted of ideas originally propounded by Mann, or Harris, or Dewey.[10]

The 1951 document, for example, states a cardinal principle which Mann first defended:

As public institutions, the public schools of this nation must be non-denominational. They can have no part in securing acceptance of any one of the numerous systems of belief regarding a supernatural power and the relation of mankind thereto.[11]

In another passage the document insists, as did Mann, Harris, and Dewey, that "the public schools have a highly significant function in teaching moral and spiritual values."[12] Harris made current the idea of the 1951 statement that

although these declarations [i.e., of moral and spiritual values] are not couched in terms of rituals or other religious forms, the major religious groups can discover in their respective Bibles and creeds many statements which support them.[13]

And here is an instrumentalist principle which Dewey has laid down, to be used when efforts at reconciling conflicts in values are unsuccessful:

But when no such reconciliation can be found, the choice of a course of action can be made only in terms of the anticipated consequences—whether they are temporary or lasting, whether they affect many people or few. Out of some such moral calculus emerges a judgment as to which course of action, all things considered, is the ethical imperative.[14]

The very definition of moral and spiritual values in the document is that of John Dewey:

By moral and spiritual values we mean those values which, when applied in human behavior, exalt and refine life and bring it into accord with the standards of conduct that are approved in our democratic culture.[15]

[10] Appointed members of the commission were: John K. Norton, chairman; George A. Selke, vice-chairman; Ethel J. Alpenfels, Ruby Anderson, Sarah C. Caldwell, James B. Conant, Dwight D. Eisenhower, Alonzo G. Grace, Eugene H. Herrington, Henry H. Hill, William Jansen, Galen Jones, N. D. McCombs, T. R. McConnell, Mae Newman, Lee M. Thurston. Ex-officio members were: Willard E. Givens, Worth McClure, Corma A. Mowrey, Warren T. White. William G. Carr was secretary; Wilbur F. Murra, assistant secretary.
[11] *Moral and Spiritual Values in the Public Schools*, p. 4.   [12] *Ibid.*
[13] *Ibid.*, p. 18.   [14] *Ibid.*, p. 32.   [15] *Ibid.*, p. 3.

✦

The present study is not an evaluation of the total contribution to education by these three men. If it were such, more would have to be written about Mann's role in the introduction to American schools of the best teaching and administrative practices of the Prussian schools, about Harris's broadening of the curriculum to make high school possible for all children, about Dewey's demands for a pedagogy accommodated to a modern industrial democracy and his part in the progressive-education movement.[16]

There is always the danger of distortion in selecting one idea and tracing its development in a man's writings. Yet this seems to be a calculated risk taken by those who put their hand to writing the history of ideas. We have tried to lessen the risk here by beginning each of the three sections of the study with a background chapter. What the three principals have themselves written on the topic of moral and spiritual values is the primary material used in the study. This has of course been supplemented by biographical matter, contemporary records, social and intellectual history, to the extent needed for a full understanding of each man's conception of values.

From one point of view the nature of education is such that the sheer communication of knowledge can generally prescind from the personal value-philosophies or religious commitments of either master or disciple. On the other hand, there is a peculiar moral dimension to education which is inevitably conditioned by one's moral and religious principles. There is good reason then for interest in an educator's personal philosophy, at least to the extent that this noticeably colors his work. No adequate understanding of a man's educational theory or work, therefore, can be had by totally prescinding from his personal views. If, in addition, these views are a departure from generally accepted standards so that they ignite controversy in the community, there is all the more reason to scrutinize them. This is the lot, for good

---

[16] The term "progressive education" is a semantic booby trap. With the unmourned demise of the Progressive Education Association in 1957 did not pass many older and more comprehensive ideas which have made for solid progress in education. Says one scholar, "Progressive education in this country, if it has done nothing else, should forever be honored and given thanks for insisting on genuine, hand-to-hand teaching, as against the giving out of predigested hokum." Barzun, *Teacher in America*, p. 27.

or ill, of public servants in general and of those associated with *public* education in particular.

In presenting the personal views of these three men this study has tried to follow this sage counsel:

To refuse a man the right to inform us of what he thinks and to arrogate to oneself the right to understand him, not as he understands himself but "as he *ought* to be understood," is a very subjective principle of exegesis. The principle is not, perhaps, completely false, but it is at least dangerous. It is particularly arbitrary when the thing to be judged is not just a system of concepts, but a faith—and a faith which is amply, richly expressed: whatever the preliminaries may be, should not such a faith be judged first of all in itself? [17]

When honesty and sympathy are brought to the judging of a faith, history is always the gainer. The complete presentation from its sources of these three men's thought—and the chief formative factors that went into it—cannot fail to clarify an important cultural problem which is very much with us today.

[17] Lubac, *The Drama of Atheist Humanism*, p. 58.

PART TWO

HORACE MANN

1796–1859

II. THE SHAPING OF A PHILOSOPHY

With the appointment of Horace Mann in 1837 as secretary of the newly formed State Board of Education for the Commonwealth of Massachusetts, there opened a new phase in the history of American education. The shoots that had been planted two centuries earlier by sturdy Puritan hands were about to burst into bloom.[1] In 1635 the town of Boston had opened the Latin School. Four years later Dorchester levied a land tax for the support of a free school, an action generally cited by historians as the first example in American history of general taxation for common schools. In 1641 the General Court of the commonwealth resolved "that all masters of families, do once a week (at the least) catechise their children and servants in the grounds and principles of religion." [2] An act in 1642 made education compulsory for all children but contained no provision for schools or teachers.

[1] For a full treatment of this pioneer period in public education, see Hinsdale, *Horace Mann and the Common School Revival;* Cubberley, *Public Education in the United States;* Butts and Cremin, *A History of Education in American Culture.*

[2] *The Colonial Laws of Massachusetts* (Boston, 1889). Reprinted from the edition of 1660, with the Supplements to 1672. Containing also, the Bodies of Liberties of 1641. Published by the order of the City Council of Boston, under the supervision of William H. Whitmore.

Finally in 1647 Massachusetts passed the pioneer general school law in the nation. This was the famous "Old Deluder" Act which reminded the citizenry:

It being one chief object of that old deluder, Satan, to keep men from the knowledge of the Scriptures, as in former times by keeping them in an unknown tongue, so in these latter times by persuading from the use of tongues . . .[3]

so this present act would thwart the "deluder" by having every township, "after the Lord hath increased them to the number of fifty householders," appoint a teacher and provide a school.

In the following decades schools multiplied, but their number and quality varied considerably in the different quarters of the commonwealth. Many factors prevented the realization of the ideal behind the act of 1647, among them the vicissitudes of Indian warfare and the long Revolutionary War. A law of 1789, which authorized towns to divide themselves into districts, proved to be a mixed blessing. In fact, this piece of legislation was afterwards stigmatized by Mann as "the most unfortunate law on the subject of Common Schools, ever enacted in the State." [4] For although the development of the autonomous local school district weakened the control of the established Congregationalist Church over the schools—which by many Massachusetts citizens was considered a gain—it made for an unbalanced school development in the commonwealth. Some districts (often the wealthier ones) faced their responsibilities and provided well for the schools. Other districts did little or nothing. At the opening of the nineteenth century, the growing industrial development and consequent demand for cheap labor put pressure upon parents to divert their children from schoolhouse to factory or mill. The first great step toward ordering the school chaos was the 1837 law creating the State Board of Education and providing for a secretary.

[3] *Ibid.*, 1647. For ease in reading we give a modern spelling. See Knight, *Education in the United States*, p. 105.

[4] Horace Mann, *Tenth Annual Report of the Secretary of the Board*, facsimile ed., p. 130. Ordinarily all references to the Mann reports will be to the *Life and Works*, ed. by Mary Mann and George Combe Mann, 5 vols. For the *Seventh, Tenth,* and *Twelfth Reports,* however, the references will be to the facsimile editions, for several important sections of these reports do not appear in the *Life and Works*.

✦

The immediate challenge which confronted any reformer who in 1837 might be emboldened to lead his people forward in the cause of education was the sectarian problem. Some understanding of the religious situation is needed in order to understand Horace Mann himself and the problems which he had to face as secretary.

Religion was the principal motivating force that had brought the Puritans to the shores of the New World. For generations religion had been food, strength, and light to the settlers and their descendants. They had labored long to build a theocracy. The dawning light of the nineteenth century, however, showed the monolith of Puritan Congregationalism to be badly cracked.[5] Differences over dogma had divided not only Liberal believer from Orthodox but had split this latter group into "Old Calvinists" and "New Light Calvinists." Both of these Orthodox groups taught the doctrine of the Trinity, the divinity and redemption of Jesus Christ, and the direct inspiration of the sacred scriptures. They further agreed on certain basic tenets of John Calvin: that through Adam's sin human nature had become totally depraved; that mankind's single hope for salvation was the grace imputed to man by Christ's redemption; that this grace was a pure gift, arbitrarily bestowed by God in an irresistible fashion upon the predestined elect, but withheld from those predestined to damnation.

The "New Light" school spoke of a return to true Calvinism. Hence this party was also known as "Strict Calvinists" or "Consistent Calvinists." They pushed the doctrine of man's utter depravity further toward its logical conclusion than the Old Calvinists. The New Lights held that the attempt to use any means whatsoever to render God propitious was nothing but sinful self-love. Jonathan Edwards, Samuel Hopkins, and Nathanael Emmons—a man whose influence loomed large in the life of Horace Mann—are the names most closely associated with this revival of rigid Calvinism. The practical application of such an understanding of human nature would evidently have wide-sweeping consequences for education. In attacking the application, Horace Mann throughout his career was forced to attack the theological principle which supported it.

[5] For a detailed listing of all the churches throughout this period see Clark, *Historical Sketch of the Congregational Churches in Massachusetts.*

Opposed to both types of orthodoxy were the Liberal Congregationalists. Though differing among themselves regarding Christ's nature and His office toward mankind, the Liberals were united in rejecting the sometimes overdrawn Trinitarianism of the Orthodox, which they contemptuously called "Tritheism." The Liberals likewise were one in rejecting the Calvinist doctrine of human depravity and consequent need for human regeneration. They resented the favored position accorded by law to the established Congregational—usually Orthodox—churches.

The march of events quickly brought the religious situation to a head, and at length resulted in the separation of the Orthodox and the Liberals in the New England Congregational churches. But as one historian has said:

A reverence for the sacred history and traditions of their common fellowship caused each group to postpone the definite split in the constant hope that the other would be converted. But, instead of conversion, the lines of demarcation grew more clearly defined largely because of the insistent demands of the Orthodox.[6]

It had long been customary among the pastors to exchange pulpits in sign of fraternal unity. Now, however, the two Orthodox groups began pointedly to exclude pastors with the Liberal taint. Schisms occurred in scores of parishes. A group in a congregation would rebel against the pastor and betake themselves to a congregation whose views were more akin to their own. Or if a majority in a congregation voted a pastor out, he and his loyal followers would set up a new church where the true faith, be it Orthodox or Liberal, could be maintained in quiet unanimity. Lockouts and lawsuits commonly marked these family quarrels.

The irreparable break between Liberal and Orthodox was occasioned by a 48-page pamphlet which appeared in Boston in 1815. Thomas Belsham, a leader of the British Unitarians, had written *Memoirs of the Life of Theophilus Lindsey,* which included an account of Unitarianism in the United States. This section of the Belsham work was published by Jedidiah Morse, the Orthodox pastor of the Charlestown Congregational church, under the title *American Unitarianism, or a Brief History of the Progress and Present State of the Unitarian Churches*

[6] Morse, *Jedidiah Morse,* p. 121.

in America.[7] Its publication was a shrewd move designed to smoke out the Liberals, for it carried an unfriendly preface showing the identity of the American Liberals with the British Unitarians and demanding that the Liberals drop all hypocrisy and separate themselves from the Congregationalist communion. The Boston press leaped into the fray and the "Unitarian Controversy" took its inevitable course. Pamphlets, sermons, letters, and denunciations flowed from pen and pulpit. Finally, under the leadership of William Ellery Channing and others, the Liberals came to separate themselves formally from the established Congregationalist Church and to accept the title "Unitarian."[8] In 1825 the American Unitarian Association was formed. The process of separation continued for the next few decades, during which all the leading churches of Boston, with the exception of Old South Church, went over to the Liberals. The Congregationalist Church was legally disestablished in 1833.

Such was the atmosphere, charged with sectarian strife, in which Horace Mann came to adulthood and which hung over his career as secretary of the State Board of Education. Throughout his twelve years in this office, as well as during his later educational work at Antioch College, Mann's own views on character training and religious education were under almost constant attack.[9]

The dates and occasions of controversy may have varied, but the point at issue—no matter who the antagonists—was always the same: the place of religious education in the common schools. This is not to oversimplify matters. It is true that there was political by-play during Mann's

[7] See *ibid.*, Chapter IX, "The Split in the Congregational Fellowship," pp. 121-49.

[8] Channing (1780–1842) preached a sermon in Baltimore in 1819 in which he stated the beliefs generally acceptable to those Congregationalists who denied the Trinitarian doctrine. It is the general agreement that this marks the beginning of Unitarianism as an independent denomination. Stokes, *Church and State in the United States,* I, 763.

[9] In 1853 Mann accepted the post of president of Antioch College in Ohio, founded on prayer and hope by a sect called the Christian denomination. Antioch was one of the pioneer coeducational and nondenominational colleges of the country. Supplementary use has been made of Mann's Antioch writings to clarify his position during the controversies over religion in the schools. For even though written after the controversies, they are a reaffirmation and clarification in the full sunset of his life of many of the principles he left as a legacy to American public school education.

term of office, notably the attempts to abolish the school board, for Whigs and Democrats continually used school issues against one another to suit party purposes. The changing economic and demographic pattern of the Massachusetts community also figured indirectly in the common school disputes. Nonetheless, the religious education issue was central, and it is a unifying theme for all the controversies in which Mann was involved.

✦

Horace Mann was born May 4, 1796, into a farming family of modest means in Franklin, Massachusetts. Like many another Franklin youngster of devout Puritan stock, Horace might have grown into the rigid orthodoxy of his patriarchal pastor, the redoubtable Nathan l Emmons, but for a tragic event which took place in 1810.[10] That year his seventeen-year-old brother and bosom companion Stephen drowned. In the church's eyes the youth had not yet passed through the Orthodox experience of conversion. Like the angel of the flaming sword posted at Eden's gate, the Reverend Dr. Emmons in his funeral address dolefully pointed out the penalty for death without conversion. The sensitive fourteen-year-old Horace never forgot his mother's groan. Then and there he conceived a hatred of Calvinism which never left him.

Three years before his own death, Mann could still write with bitterness of "what an unspeakable calamity a Calvinistic education is." Although his early association with Emmons and Calvinistic training had not succeeded in making him "that horrible thing, a Calvinist," he wrote, "it did succeed in depriving me of that filial love for God that . . . it is natural the child should feel towards a Father who combines all excellence." [11] Mann said that his Calvinistic background had robbed him of other things too. In one of the first entries in his private journal he said:

In my early life I was accustomed to hear all doctrines, tenets, creeds, which did not exactly conform to the standard set up, denounced as heresies, their believers cast out from fellowship in this life and coolly consigned to

[10] Mann's brother Stephen was born Dec. 23, 1792, and was drowned July 22, 1810 (not 1808 as many biographers have stated). He was Horace's senior by three years.

[11] Letter to Mr. Craig, January, 1856, in Mann Papers, Mass. Hist. Soc. archives. Cf. *Life and Works,* I, 480.

eternal perdition in the next. I think it would have made an immense difference, both in my happiness and character, had the genial, encouraging, ennobling spirit of liberality been infused into my mind when its sentiments were first capable of being excited on that subject.[12]

In giving vent to his severe strictures on the Orthodox, as he did from time to time, Mann had before his eyes the memory of a straitened adolescence over which hung the shadow of Dr. Emmons, whom he once described in these words:

He was an extra- or hyper-Calvinist, a man of pure intellect, whose logic was never softened in its severity by the infusion of any kindliness of sentiment. He expounded all the doctrines of total depravity, election, and reprobation, and not only the eternity, but the extremity of hell-torments, unflinchingly and in their most terrible significance.[13]

Mann never quite succeeded, though, in emancipating himself from Calvinism. Despite the scorn he heaped upon the Calvinist doctrines, his spirit remained true to the fundamental theology he attempted to disown.[14] His wife, Mary Peabody Mann, wrote that

he could have said with another remarkable man who emerged from the gloom of Orthodoxy into the light and life of religious liberty, "My heart is Unitarian; but my nerves are still Calvinistic." [15]

Horace Mann has been likened by some biographers to a Hebrew prophet of the Old Testament.[16] Certainly duty and destiny loomed

[12] Journal, July 2, 1837. This intimate diary contains entries irregularly over a six-year interval. Mann considered it the sacred repository of his inmost thoughts and emotions. In the opening entry he writes: "It is my belief, that each individual will hereafter remember all that he has ever *done, said* or *thought*. That is the *Book of Judgment*. May that volume be so filled, that it may in after periods of existence, be unrolled and inspected with pleasure, and may this volume be a transcript of that." Entry of May 4, 1837, quoted in *Life and Works*, I, 65.

[13] Letter to a friend, *Life and Works*, I, 13.

[14] Theodore Parker said: "I know no politician who so hated Calvinism; none who used its language so much, or who, to the public, appeared so much the friend of the ecclesiastic theology of which it is the poison-flower." Weiss, *Life and Correspondence of Theodore Parker*, II, 342. Cf. Morgan, *Horace Mann at Antioch*, p. 52. Also see Hinsdale, *Horace Mann and the Common School Revival*, p. 75.

[15] *Life and Works*, I, vii. Mary Peabody Mann was one of the Peabody sisters of Salem. One sister married Nathaniel Hawthorne. Another, Elizabeth, became famous in her own right as an educator and leader in the transcendentalist movement.

[16] William Torrey Harris frequently uses this comparison. Young Harris used to paste speeches of Mann in his scrapbook.

large in his life as he followed what he referred to as the call to be a "missionary of the popular education." [17] Once he had set forth on his mission he would brook no interference and, in his prophetic role, considered himself above criticism. Almost any criticism of himself and the school board he was quick to dismiss as something evil, inspired by narrow sectarian interests—which frequently enough it was.[18]

Mann stood aloof from the churches, was virulently anticlerical and antisectarian, but was withal a deeply religious person.[19] He had a strong faith or conviction in the existence of a personal God who had created the world and governed it through His benevolent laws. He had nothing but scorn for all species of atheism and he reacted most sensitively to the accusation which insinuated that he was a promoter of atheism or irreligion in the schools.[20] He held rigidly to the necessity of religion for all men. He believed in personal moral responsibility, in the immortality of the human soul, and in a day of judgment. He esteemed the Bible as the recorded word of God. He spoke frequently of heaven, though rarely of hell and retribution. His writings contain references to the traditional Christian angelology. From the hundreds of biblical quotations and figures with which his writings are interlarded one can surmise Mann's love and respect for the Bible. He speaks regularly of the person of Jesus Christ and His mission to mankind in the loftiest of terms.

[17] Journal, July 4, 1837.   [18] See especially Chapter IV.

[19] To the extent that Mann was formally affiliated with any church group he was Unitarian. During his Boston residence he attended the Federal Street Church, whose minister was his close friend, William Ellery Channing. In 1848 he helped establish the First Unitarian Church in Newton. When he went to Ohio he joined, to the displeasure of many of his Unitarian friends, the "Christian Church," the new sect which brought Antioch College into existence. Writing from there to a friend he said: "We are in the midst of a great community, ferociously Orthodox. In this great State of Ohio, already having a population of more than two millions and a half, there are but four Unitarian churches. Calvinism has terrible sway, and its whole artillery is levied against us. We take it broadsides, and work on. If we can go on, we will make a breach in the Chinese Wall, and let in the light." Life and Works, I, 519.

[20] Theodore Parker, a lifelong friend, said of Mann that "in his reactionary swing from Dr. Emmons' Calvinism, he went about as near Atheism as an intellectual man can go." (Weiss, Life and Correspondence of Theodore Parker, II, 342.) If this is true, such a state did not last for any length of time. Parker is probably thinking of the numbing effect upon Mann of the loss of his first wife, Charlotte Messer Mann.

Mann rejected the pessimistic doctrines of Calvinism, and most emphatically the extreme version of the fall of man. However, Mann does speak of a "fall" but seems to define it with reference to a natural punishment which overtakes man when he acts in ignorance or in defiance of the laws of God.[21] The core of his religious philosophy was his firm belief in the infinite perfectibility of mankind through the process of education.

✦

In college Mann was drawn to deism because of his interest both in the humanism of the classical writers, particularly Cicero, and in the philosophy of John Locke, then still the vogue at Brown and other American colleges.[22] Lockian philosophy fitted him well. It was highly moralistic and practical and aimed at building a better society. By the close of the seventeenth century natural religion had become widely accepted among the English upper classes. There were, however, two distinct categories among them. The Deists or radical group rejected all revealed religion, holding for the sufficiency of natural religion discoverable by the unaided human reason. The conservative group agreed with the Deists that the core of religion could be established by man's unaided reason but held further that supernatural revelation (as long as it was consonant with reason) complemented the religion of nature. John Locke was one of the leaders of these supernaturalist rationalists.[23]

Nevertheless, this English thinker, whom Merle Curti has called in the title of a monograph, "America's Philosopher, 1783–1861," provided powerful ammunition in his writings for the attack on super-

[21] "Were children born with perfect natures, we might expect that they would gradually purify themselves from the vices and corruption which are now almost enforced upon them by the examples of the world. But the same nature by which the parents sunk into error and sin pre-adapts the children to follow in the course of ancestral degeneracy." (*Ninth Annual Report*, in *Life and Works*, IV, 5.) See also Antioch Inaugural Address, *Life and Works*, V, 332–33.

[22] John Locke (1632–1704) was one of the founders of British empiricism. To Mann, Locke was the criterion of perspicacity in the philosophy of education. He wrote during the debate with the Boston schoolmasters: "Miss Edgeworth, universally acknowledged to have been the ablest writer on education after John Locke . . ." (*Reply to the "Remarks,"* p. 8). See also *Life and Works*, II, 255.

[23] The three central propositions of this group were: "There is an omnipotent God, he demands virtuous living on the part of man in obedience to his will, and there is a future life in which he will reward the virtuous and punish the wicked.

naturalism that was to come.[24] Locke affirmed in his famous essay on
miracles the higher certainty of natural knowledge over the knowledge
of faith. In writings like *The Reasonableness of Christianity* and *An
Essay for the Understanding of St. Paul's Epistles* he further developed
a thoroughly naturalist theology. In the *Essay concerning Human
Understanding* Locke argued for reliance on the data of sense and reflection in place of innate ideas. All this served to rub out the line
demarcating the world of matter from the world of spirit, the natural
world and the supernatural world. Despite his insistence that divine
revelation did confirm reason and experience, Locke became the patron
of the more radical deistic school. Many features of Locke's religious
thought were anticipatory of central doctrines maintained a hundred
years later by the early Unitarians.

Young Horace Mann must have found Locke and deism a refreshing
change after the "New Light" theology of the earnest Dr. Emmons.
The primacy of human reason, the unbounded perfectibility of the race,
the untrammeled freedom of inquiry, the certainty of natural science,
the uniformity of natural and divine law—all these became more deeply
imprinted upon his mind. Shortly before taking up the post of secretary,
Mann recorded in his journal his impressions of an article discussing
Lord Brougham's *A Discourse of Natural Theology*. He writes:

For myself Natural Religion stands as preeminent over Revealed Religion
as the deepest experience over the lightest hearsay. The power of Natural
Religion is scarcely begun to be understood or appreciated. The force
and cogency of the evidence, the intensity and irresistibleness of its power,
is not known. It gives us more than an intellectual conviction, it gives us
a feeling of truth. And however much the light of Revealed Religion may
have guided the generations of men amid the darkness of mortality, yet I
believe the time is coming when the light of Natural Religion will be
[to] that of Revealed as the rising sun is to the day-star that preceded it.[25]

To Mann all nature was full of divine revealings, "revealings of beneficent laws, of overflowing love." His wife said that

---

Man employing his faculty of drawing conclusions from given premises, will
thus see the advantages of living a righteous life, and will rationally order his
life to attain a reward in heaven." (See Randall, *The Making of the Modern Mind*,
pp. 286–87.)

[24] *The Great Mr. Locke: America's Philosopher, 1783–1861*, p. 114.

[25] Journal, May 8, 1837.

while he loved with an unutterable love the beauty God had made, the revelations of science were scarcely less sacred to him than the revelations of moral truth; and they were illustrative of each other in his teachings. This conception of the universe was not given to his childhood . . . [but Mann] wished it to remain *the birthright of all who came under his influence,* rather than that it should be wrested from their experience as it had been from his own.[26]

Near the close of his life, Horace Mann was still firm in his conviction that man's duty is to follow the revelation of nature by obeying God's laws therein. From Antioch he professed his belief

not only in the Ten Commandments. But in ten thousand. God lives and rules by law; and, therefore, wherever He lives, and wherever He rules, there is law and a law of God is a command. All the kingdoms of nature around us—the inorganic which exists, and the organic which lives, and the sentient which feels—are pervaded by God's laws. We also in all our powers, faculties, and susceptibilities, are the subjects of God's laws.[27]

After his graduation from Brown, where he was class valedictorian,[28] Horace Mann tutored at the same institution for two years and then turned to the law. In 1823 he was admitted to the bar and opened an office in Dedham. His legal acumen and personal integrity quickly established his reputation and in 1827 he was elected by the townspeople to the commonwealth legislature. Mann's world turned to ashes with the death of his first wife, Charlotte Messer Mann, in 1832.[29] They had been married only two years and her loss was a blow from which Horace never really recovered. His friends, fearing for his health, urged the grief-stricken young lawyer to remove to Boston, which he did.[30] The next year he was sent to the State Senate from Suffolk, serv-

[26] *Life and Works,* I, vii (emphasis added).

[27] Antioch Sermon: "God's Being, the Foundation of Human Duty," in *Twelve Sermons Delivered at Antioch College,* p. 12. See also the latter part of Chapter IV.

[28] The subject of his oration was the "Progressive Character of the Human Race." Mary Mann calls this "his favorite theme all through life, the basis of all his action in education and in politics." (*Life and Works,* I, 28.)

[29] Charlotte Messer was the daughter of the president of Brown. Mann wrote his sister years later and described his feelings then: "I have looked at the world from the side of a grave that has swallowed up my happiness. For months afterward, I daily and hourly yearned for death as much as ever a famishing infant yearned for the breast of its mother." (*Life and Works,* I, 51.)

[30] In Boston he boarded at the home of a Mrs. Clarke, as did the three Peabody sisters. Louise Hall Thorpe in two books—*The Peabody Sisters of Salem* and

ing as president in 1836 and in 1837.[31] From this position he resigned in order to take up the secretaryship of the State Board of Education.

At the age of forty-one Horace Mann had already made his mark both in the legal world and in the politics of his state. Why should he have turned aside from a lucrative and honorific career to embark upon the uncharted seas of common school education? His motives are not secret. In his private journal Mann records his feelings during this period of decision.

His election to the position was due mainly to the effort of Edmund Dwight, a wealthy Springfield philanthropist, who had interviewed him and was urging him to accept the position. On May 18, 1837, Mann writes:

Mr. Dwight again urged upon me a consideration of the subject of my being Secretary of the Board. Ought I to think of filling this high and responsible office? Can I adequately perform its duties? Will my greater zeal in the cause than that of others supply the deficiency of talent and information? [32]

On June 30 Mann communicated to Dwight and the board his acceptance of the office. With a sense of dedication proper to a crusader Horace Mann accepted this challenging, underpaid post [33] in the most literate and religious corner of the United States. "Henceforth," he wrote, "so long as I hold this office, I devote myself to the supremest welfare of mankind upon earth. . . . *Faith* is the only sustainer. I have faith in the improvability of the race—in their accelerating improvability." He apparently suspected opposition ahead, but he was certain that his strong love for humanity would bring things to a triumphant close. The future could be full of battles with the Smiths, Brownsons,

---

Until Victory: Horace Mann and Mary Peabody—has skillfully re-created this period in Mann's life. However, Robert L. Straker's remark that these books are better read as fiction than history has merit. For his strictures see "A Gloss upon Glosses," an unpublished manuscript, copies in the New York Public Library and in the Mass. Hist. Soc. archives.

[31] It is clear from the election returns, the membership rolls of the General Court, and from other sources that Mann first sat as State Senator on Jan. 7, 1835. He was elected on Nov. 10, 1834, and could not have sat in 1833—his own statement to the contrary. I am indebted to Robert L. Straker for this clarification.

[32] Journal, May 18, 1837.

[33] His salary from the state was $1,500. Edmund Dwight added another $500.

and Packards, but "a spirit mildly devoting itself to a good cause,"
records Mann, "is a certain conqueror—Love is a universal solvent." [34]

✦

It was about this same time that phrenology, an important influence
upon Horace Mann's philosophy of education, came into his life.[35] Of
equal importance was the beginning of Mann's long acquaintanceship,
and later close friendship, with the Scottish phrenologist George
Combe.[36] Many of Mann's biographers have had almost nothing to
say about phrenology.[37] Several writers who do treat it do so in an apolo-

[34] Journal, June 30, 1837.

[35] Phrenology was a primitive behavioristic psychology united to a theory of
localized brain functions. Its four basic principles:

1. Anatomical and physiological characteristics have a direct influence upon
mental behavior.

2. The mind is made up of 37 independent and ascertainable faculties. These
were charted and labeled, e.g., "Veneration," "Causality" (see Life and Works,
I, 14), "Human Nature," "Alimentativeness," "Philoprogenitiveness," etc.

3. These aptitudes or faculties are localized in different organs or regions of the
brain.

4. The development of these 37 organs affects the size and contour of the
cranium, so that a well-developed region of the head indicates a correspondingly
well-developed faculty.

As a result, it was believed that moral and intellectual traits could be analyzed by
studying the shape of the head in conjunction with some knowledge of tempera-
ment. The phrase "the bump of knowledge" is a phrenological relic surviving in
our language. Added to this theory of brain structure were the postulates of a
behavioristic psychology.

[36] No other single topic in the bulky correspondence between Mann and Combe
is treated as fully or as frequently as phrenology. Mann felt deeply indebted to
Combe, after whom he named one of his three sons. Once, writing to apologize
for having neglected his duty of correspondence, Mann paid him this tribute:
"How can I forget you, who have done my mind more good than any other
living man—a hundred times more? I not only think of you, remembering you,
but in a very important and extensive sense, I am you" (Life and Works, I,
484). In another letter: "There is no man of whom I think so often; there is
no man of whom I write so often; there is no man who has done me so much
good as you have. I see many of the most valuable truths as I never should have
seen them but for you, and all truths better than I should otherwise have done"
(ibid., p. 518). See also ibid., pp. 131–32. Both men were trained in the law and
were disciples of Locke. This would explain much of their affinity.

[37] Culver, who has produced the most extensive study of Mann and the religious

getic manner, showing obvious embarrassment over what they seem to have judged a shameful quirk in Mann's character. This attitude is strange. Mann's work in education, particularly the philosophy of character education which he bequeathed to American society, is hardly understandable without some knowledge of the place of phrenology in his life.[38] For phrenology gave a distinctive coloring to the Lockian deism which in great measure had filled the vacuum left by the expulsion of his boyhood Calvinism. Moreover, phrenology enjoyed a respectable reign among American intellectuals [39] during the early decades of the nineteenth century before it fell into the hands of quacks and charlatans.

Hinsdale, in a work first published in 1898, speaks of "Mr. Mann's enthusiastic adhesion to the quasi-science, and its extraordinary influence upon his mind and work." [40] He writes further: "Just as he [Mann] was about to take the public schools of Massachusetts for his province, he was converted to phrenology by reading George Combe's *Constitution of Man.*" [41] In a recent study of the phrenology movement Davies writes that Mann "regarded phrenology as the greatest discovery of the ages and built all his theories of mental and moral improvement upon the ideas which it had furnished him." [42]

The distinguished French educator and historian François Pécault

---

education question in Massachusetts, has one small footnote (p. 123). See Culver, *Horace Mann and Religion in the Massachusetts Public Schools.*

[38] This is Merle Curti's judgment, too, when he says that "to understand Mann's educational and social philosophy one must bear in mind the fact that . . . he [Mann] became a convert without qualification to the doctrines of phrenology." *Social Ideas of American Educators,* p. 110.

[39] Amongst others, Ralph Waldo Emerson, Walt Whitman, William Ellery Channing, Charles Sumner, Henry Ward Beecher—in varying degrees.

[40] Hinsdale, *Horace Mann and the Common School Revival,* p. 96.

[41] *Ibid.,* p. 94. Mann regarded this book as one of the greatest books ever written. On the back of its title page appears this printed endorsement: I LOOK UPON PHRENOLOGY AS THE GUIDE OF PHILOSOPHY, AND THE HANDMAIDEN OF CHRISTIANITY. WHOEVER DISSEMINATES TRUE PHRENOLOGY IS A PUBLIC BENEFACTOR . . . HORACE MANN. This endorsement presumably was carried only in the American editions.

[42] Davies, *Phrenology,* p. 85. This is an excellent introduction to phrenology. To get the racy flavor of the movement, however, nothing is a substitute for the works of the phrenologists themselves. Combe's *Constitution of Man* and his two-volume *Notes,* along with Gibbon's two-volume *Life of George Combe,* are a good start.

made an observation after Mann's death which is peculiarly significant for this present study:

He [Mann] had hoped, with other generous spirits, that the doctrine of Combe—a doctrine both scientific and religious, speculative and practical —might serve as a basis of moral education in the public schools, and that all the churches of the country would rally to this common ground. To this was to be added the reading of some beautiful passages from the Scriptures.[43]

These few lines are perspicacious, indeed. For despite the cumbersome scientific nomenclature in which it was decked out, Combe's phrenology was a kind of religious philosophy, or philosophical religion, wonderfully in keeping with the spiritual ferment of the times. Phrenology for many of its enthusiasts amounted to a cult, a substitute for the old orthodoxy. With its unbounded faith in the improvability of humanity it was an invigorating antidote to Calvinism's pessimistic doctrines of original sin and total corruption.[44]

The Davies study points out how in its vocabulary and propaganda phrenology took over the "logic and techniques of evangelical Protestantism." Typical of this turn is a lengthy letter, dated March 25, 1839, that Mann wrote to Combe:

There have been some striking conversions, since you were here, to the religious truths contained in your "Constitution of Man." Some of these have happened under my own ministry.[45]

He goes on to tell how a young college graduate interested in a teaching career had approached him to solicit advice on how to prepare himself. Mann gave him a list of books headed by the *Constitution of Man*. The young man, with his orthodoxy more and more shaken, reported back several times. Once he spent an entire evening with Mann, who

[43] François Pécault wrote a review in *Revue Pedagogique*, March, 1888, of *The Work and Writings of Horace Mann*, by M. J. Gaufrès, published by the Musée Pedagogique, Vol. 39 of the "Educational Memoirs and Documents" (Paris: Delagrave & Hachette, 1888). An English translation of the Pécault review appears as an appendix in *Life and Works*, V, 540.

[44] Davies, *Phrenology*, p. 163. Henry Ward Beecher proclaimed that phrenology underlay his whole ministry and recommended as the best preparation for a Christian "a practical knowledge of the human mind as is given by phrenology" (Capen, *Reminiscences*, p. 157). Cited in Davies, *Phrenology*, p. 163.

[45] *Life and Works*, I, 112–13.

explained to him that Combe's system "contained all there is of truth in orthodoxy." Finally, reported Mann, "he adopted my views on the subject, and is now, I believe, a convert beyond the danger of apostasy."

Some looked upon George Combe as a latter-day Messiah. Combe himself may well have come to this belief. In any event he records in his diary how the New York philanthropist James Wadsworth said to him:

> Are you aware that in the *Constitution of Man* you have given a new religion to the world: I replied, "No; I am not conscious of having done so, and certainly did not intend it." He said, "But you *have* done so. The views of the Divine government there unfolded will in time subvert all other religions and become a religion themselves." He added, "I call it Combeism." [46]

Combe concludes the entry: "I have never mentioned this conversation except to members of my own family; but it set me on a new track of thought, and finally produced this work." [47]

Horace Mann himself wrote Combe after the start of his lecture tour in 1839: "We are all very glad to hear of your success and acceptability where you have been. . . . We see that there will be a new earth, at least, if not a new heaven, when your philosophical and moral doctrines prevail." In the same letter he added these words: "It has been a part of my religion for many years that the earth is not to remain in its present condition forever. You are furnishing the means by which the body of society is to be healed of some of its wounds heretofore deemed irremediable." [48]

Through the liberally minded clergy Mann hoped that phrenology would exorcise the wonder-working God of Calvinism and restore Him as a divinity who abided by the natural laws of causality. [49] Phrenology as it developed on American shores, however, did not make a frontal attack upon the traditional religious beliefs based on oral or written

---

[46] Gibbon, *Life of George Combe*, II, 356.

[47] *Ibid*. The work referred to was a volume entitled *The Relation between Science and Religion*. One of Combe's phrenological works was placed on the *Index Librorum Prohibitorum*. The 1940 French edition calls it *Nouveau manuel de phrénologie*, traduit de l'Anglais et augmenté d'additions nombreuses et de notes par J. Fossati (Decr. 14 fév. 1837). This work is the only one of Combe's books on the list by name. Davies (*Phrenology*, p. 156) is incorrect in stating that all of Combe's works are on the *Index*.

[48] *Life and Works*, I, 111.   [49] *Ibid*., p. 155.

revelation. It did, nevertheless, urge what it called a more "scientific" approach to all religion. Phrenology, like Lockian philosophy, aimed at adapting Christianity to the new scientific age. The Christianity it concerned itself with was the Christianity of the Ten Commandments, the Golden Rule, the Beatitudes, the ethical example of Christ and other biblical characters. In other words, it was the moral and ethical aspect of the revealed Christian religion that the phrenologists hoped to salvage. The laws of science governed nature, and man himself was part of nature. An analysis of man himself, therefore, and of his relation to all exterior objects would provide the foundation of correct living. In fact, George Combe's famous book carried the full title *The Constitution of Man Considered in Relation to External Objects*. This, as Pécault shrewdly observed, was the substance of the natural religion which Mann championed all during his career.

To those who were scientifically bent phrenology pointed out how man himself could be brought within the purview of science. From the days of Aristotle psychology had been considered an introspective science, a branch of metaphysics, with little seeming relation to the measurable phenomena of the objective order. Phrenology now made the mind a subject for scientific experiment and measurement. Thus, in foreshadowing experimental psychology, phrenology was a step forward in the march of science.

Phrenology was not, of course, the original source of many of the philosophical and religious ideas which it purveyed to an eager American public. Doctrines like those concerning the infinite perfectibility of man, the goodness of all nature, the reasonableness of religion, the universal efficacy of science and its methods—all these in a variety of packages had been served up by other movements of the eighteenth and nineteenth centuries, some of which also took their inspiration from the Enlightenment.

What at least partially distinguished phrenology from kindred movements was its bizarre biological basis and the extreme twist it gave to the Newtonian understanding of law.[50] The machinelike world con-

[50] Some Mann apologists insist that his phrenology was nothing more than Lockianism. Yet Benjamin Franklin and Joseph Priestley, who were both decidedly influenced by Locke's philosophy, advocated educational theories in marked contrast to Mann's.

structed by Newton's Great Mechanic operated according to the most inexorable of laws which thereby ruled out any evolutionary development or supernatural intervention. By using his intelligence and by co-operating with science man could avoid all physical and moral evil simply by obedience to these laws. All disorders in society grew out of violations of the laws. Hence the proclivity of the phrenologists to enlist under any passing banner marching against liquor, tobacco, confining dress, poor ventilation, crowded prisons, sectarianism, etc., etc.[51] All these things contravened the moral order and natural constitution established in nature by God. But knowledge of the laws would eliminate all disorder from life here below, and this was the mission of the schools.

Another appeal that phrenology had was educational. The phrenologists built an extensive system of education upon the interpretation of their findings. This, perhaps more than any other single reason, explains its fascination for Horace Mann. As he wrote to his sister Lydia, he considered the philosophy of phrenology "the only practical basis of education." Combe himself looked upon his *Constitution of Man,* "in one sense, as an essay in education. If the views unfolded in it be in general sound, it will follow that education has scarcely yet commenced." [52]

In his annual reports Mann is careful not to speak of phrenology by name, although he does, on occasion, cite the works of George Combe and his brother Andrew. The twelve reports, however, do contain doses of phrenological doctrine. In fact the *Sixth Annual Report* has been called a "vast gloss" on the *Constitution of Man.* This is the report on the study of physiology in the school, and its appearance in 1843 scandalized some readers. Moreover, its undisguised phrenological tone damaged Mann's reputation among many of the teaching fraternity, thus preparing the way for his controversy with the Boston schoolmasters over the *Seventh Annual Report.*

Theodore Parker wrote to Samuel G. Howe that Mann "took phrenology for his scheme of metaphysics and knew no psychology but physiology." This Parker bluntly called "materialism" and "a great

[51] E. D. Branch in *The Sentimental Years* describes this in a wonderful chapter on "Pure Science and Some Others."

[52] Combe, *Constitution of Man,* p. 390.

hindrance to him in his educational schemes" because "it narrowed his views of human nature." [53]

To what extent did Horace Mann believe in the "bumps"? This is the skeleton which many of Mann's biographers seem to have preferred to leave quiescent in his phrenological closet. One apologist argues that "Mann was in no sense a believer in the occult, and he specifically denied any interest in cranial topography." [54]

The denial referred to is based upon a letter that Horace wrote his ailing sister Lydia, dated November 9, 1838, telling his intention of sending her Combe's book. In the letter Mann urges her

to read something of Phrenology, not that you may become a believer in that part of it which treats of the correspondence between the powers of the mind and the external development of the head, but that you may study thoroughly and become complete master of that system of mental philosophy which is maintained by the phrenologists.[55]

He tells her further that no other study can be more useful to her "after knowing how to take care of her health." "Its philosophy," he concludes, "is the only practical basis of education."

His letter, however, is not necessarily a denial of a personal interest in cranial topography. Mann could be merely omitting this as a motive for his sister's reading Combe. A reason for this precaution might have been concern lest this controversial aspect of the movement prejudice her against the entire thing. His words neither affirm nor deny his own belief in the "bumps." [56]

[53] Weiss, *Life and Correspondence of Theodore Parker,* II, 342. Of such criticisms Mann once wrote: "I could never discover the slightest ground for this objection. Instead of tending to infidelity, I think it tends to fidelity, both to God and to man; and its only semblance to materialism consists in the solid basis which it supplies for natural religion." (Letter to a young lawyer of Dansville, N.Y., July 23, 1852. Reprinted in Dansville paper. On file with Mann Papers.)

[54] Straker, *The Unseen Harvest,* p. 15. Mr. Straker is a leading authority on Mann. His typescript of "Mann-ia" on deposit at the Antioch College library runs to fourteen thousand pages. Mr. Straker kindly assisted the present study with his critical reading of portions of the manuscript.

[55] *Life and Works,* I, 287.

[56] As a matter of fact, Horace Mann had more than a casual interest in "bumps." In the *Common School Journal,* Mann once warned of the consequences of neglecting physical education: "In a word, the forces of the soul will retreat from the fore-head to the hind-head, and the brow, that 'dome of thought, and palace of the soul,' will be narrow and 'villainously low'; for it is here that Nature

It is hardly necessary to add that Horace Mann's belief in "bumps" need take nothing from him or his work. Mann was not the first, nor will he be the last highly intelligent person to give credence to "scientific" explanations of reality which later true science shows up as myths or fables.

Mann had suggested Combe's book to an inquirer as the finest pedagogical textbook to prepare him for a career as a teacher. And the book does contain snatches of wisdom.[57] In fact many of the educational maxims of the phrenologists contained a good dose of common sense and contributed to solid school reform. By the close of the century, many of these ideas, detached from their discredited source, were put to work in the schools by Francis Parker, William Torrey Harris, G. Stanley Hall, and John Dewey: the body must receive careful attention as well as the soul; physical health is essential to efficiency, usefulness, and happiness; food and clothing are moral factors as well as books, studies, schools, and sermons; man must be considered in his environment and not merely in himself. We have come to accept

---

sets her signet, and stamps her child a philosopher or a cretin. Here she will not suffer signatures to be counterfeited, for neither tailors nor mantua-makers can insert their cork or padding beneath the tables of the skull." (*Life and Works,* V, 49.)

During his congressional interlude (Mann served in Congress as a Representative from 1848 to 1852), Mann wrote enthusiastically to his wife, describing Henry Clay: "Half an hour ago, Mr. Clay came into the House, and took a seat near mine. I have been studying his head—manipulating it with the mind's fingers. It is a head of very small dimensions. Benevolence is large; self-esteem and love of approbation are large. . . . His benevolence prevents his self-esteem from being offensive; and his intellect controls the action of his love of approbation, and saves him from an excessive vanity. . . . Considering the volume of the brain, or size of the head, it has the best adjusted faculties I have ever seen." (*Life and Works,* I, 282.)

In his inaugural address as president of Antioch College in 1853, Mann reminded his audience that "the British government lowered the forehead of the Irish Catholic peasantry two inches, by making it an offence punishable with fine, imprisonment, and with a traitor's ignominious death, to be the teacher of children in school; and by her cruel administration of her cruel laws she transposed their brain from the intellectual fore-head to the animal hind-head." (*Life and Works,* V, 321.)

[57] Channing's statement, "The common remark . . . is that the book is excellent in spite of its phrenology," corroborates the impression that many people distinguished phrenology as a *philosophy* from phrenology as a *science*. (Channing is quoted in Gibbon, *Life of George Combe,* I, 22.)

these principles of pedagogy as ordinary common sense, but when first proposed they sounded startling indeed.

It is to the credit of the phrenologists and other nineteenth-century reformers that they did focus society's attention upon some of the more glaring abuses in the current system of education. The system was vicious, according to the phrenologists' way of viewing things, because it was out of harmony with the laws of nature, and hence did not properly develop the physical, intellectual, and moral nature of man. These ideas formed the burden of several of the Mann reports and were integral to his philosophy of character education.

III. THE MANDATE FOR CHRISTIAN PIETY

The law establishing the office of secretary of the Massachusetts State Board of Education had defined the occupant's duties only in a general way. Mann began to familiarize himself with the state of the schools. He pored over the district school reports, read books on education, visited scores of schools, consulted people interested in improving them, and between August 28 and November 15 "met conventions of the friends of education in every county in the State except Suffolk."[1] On January 1, 1838, Mann had his *First Annual Report* ready to present to the board.[2]

It was toward the close of this report that Mann turned to the topic of moral instruction in the common schools. The secretary expressed his concern over the want of such instruction, calling it a singular and alarming phenomenon. But there existed a dilemma, one which would plague him all through his career. We have a statute, he recalls, which makes special provision that no school books should be used in any

[1] *Life and Works,* II, 385.
[2] Several of the Mann reports are classic documents. The *Fifth Annual Report* was the first to arouse international interest. It was printed and distributed at public expense in Germany and England.

of the public schools "calculated to favor any particular religious sect or tenet." [3] This measure was provided in 1826, he wrote, "to prevent the school from being converted into an engine of religious proselytism; to debar successive teachers in the same school from successively inculcating hostile religious creeds, until the children in their simple-mindedness should be alienated, not only from creeds, but from religion itself." [4]

Horace Mann was one of that small band of seers who early saw that the peculiar character of the American form of republican government demanded a broad basis of education among its citizenry. He was among the first to propose the *common* school as the peculiar instrument for preparing children—no matter the class or creed—for common citizenship in the great New World republic. Although the object of the common school could never be for Mann the preparation of communicants for some religious sect, its object could be and was for him "to give every child in the Commonwealth a free, straight, solid pathway, by which he could walk directly up from the ignorance of an infant to a knowledge of the primary duties of man; and would acquire a power and an invincible will to discharge them." [5] That pathway in Mann's mind was full, intelligent participation in American democratic life. Part of that life was an ethical and moral commitment for which in its wisdom Massachusetts law had made provision in the schools.

But the legal exclusion of sectarian books, the secretary finds, has brought about an almost complete dearth of books fit for use in the schools. This, in turn, means that a more ancient statute, a provision for instruction in "piety" which was passed in 1789 and reenacted in

[3] *The General Laws of Massachusetts, from June 1822, to June 1827,* ed. by Theron Metcalf (Boston: Wells and Lily, 1827), III, 183: March 10, 1827, ch. 143, sec. 7. This law is for some writers the "law of 1826" and for others the "law of 1827." Both are correct. The Massachusetts legislative year began May 31, 1826, and concluded March 10, 1827, but the enumeration of bills passed into law is by chapter, consecutively, from 1 to 145. The law in question is in chapter 143. In this text we shall call it the "law of 1827." See Culver, *Horace Mann and Religion in the Massachusetts Public Schools,* p. 22.

[4] *First Annual Report,* in *Life and Works,* II, 423.

[5] *Ibid.,* pp. 387–88. See also the Prospectus of Mann's *Common School Journal* (Vol. I, No. 1, November, 1838).

1827, is being violated. Since this statute and its interpretations were to become a field of battle for Mann and his opponents, we cite it here.

It shall be, it hereby is, made the duty of the President, Professors, and Tutors, of the University at Cambridge, and of the several Colleges in this Commonwealth, Preceptors and Teachers of Academies, and all other Instructors of Youth, to take diligent care, and to exert their best endeavors to impress on the minds of children, and youth, committed to their care and instruction, the principles of piety, justice, and sacred regard to truth, love to their country, humanity, and universal benevolence, sobriety, industry, and frugality, chastity, moderation, and temperance, and those other virtues, which are the ornament of human society, and the basis upon which the Republican Constitution is founded.[6]

Accordingly, it was clear that all those charged with education in the commonwealth had a mandate to form character. However, it was the same 1827 amendment to this statute which warned "that said committee shall never direct any school books to be purchased or used, in any of the schools under their superintendence, which are calculated to favor any particular sect or tenet." [7]

It was stated in the preceding chapter that the common denominator of the controversies which centered about Horace Mann and his school work was the place of religious education in the public schools. It can as truly be stated that in his mind all the controversies had common boundaries. On the one side was sectarianism, an evil to be avoided at

[6] *Laws of Mass.*, March 10, 1827, ch. 143, sec. 3. The revision of 1789 (a codification of the original constitution of Massachusetts framed eight years earlier) differs only slightly in wording from the 1827 law. In its education law, however, the constitution refers specifically to "public protestant instructors in piety, *religion* [emphasis added], and morality." This occurs in Article III of the Declaration of Rights and reads: "As the happiness of a people, and the good order and preservation of civil government, essentially depend on piety, religion and morality; and as these cannot be generally diffused through a community, but by the institution of the public worship of God, and of public instructors in piety, religion, and morality: Therefore . . . the people of this commonwealth have a right to invest their legislature with power to authorize and require . . . the several towns, parishes, precincts and other bodies politic, or religious societies, to make suitable provision, at their own expense, for the institution of the public worship of God, and for the support and maintenance of public protestant teachers of piety, religion and morality, in all cases where such provision shall not be made voluntarily." *American Antiquarian Society Pamphlets*, p. 312: cited in Sherman M. Smith, *The Relation of the State to Religious Education in Massachusetts*, p. 71. Mann quotes the more liberal 1827 law. See *Life and Works*, II, 421.

[7] *Laws of Mass.*, March 10, 1827, ch. 143, sec. 7.

all cost; on the other was irreligion or infidelity, equally to be deplored and avoided. Beginning with the dispute over books for the school district libraries in this initial year of office, Mann attempted to steer his course so as to avoid either horn of the dilemma. The central issue now, as well as later, would be how the common school could give religious training as ordered by law, without at the same time making it sectarian. How could piety be inculcated in the schools without favoring piety as interpreted by one or another particular church group through its beliefs and practices?

As a result of the law concerning libraries, no books "expository of religion" had been found, Mann reported, which would qualify them for recommendation by the committees and allow them to be introduced into the common schools. Mann's official report continues:

Independently, therefore, of the immeasurable importance of moral teaching in itself considered, this entire exclusion of religious teaching, though justifiable under the circumstances, enhances and magnifies a thousand fold, the indispensableness of moral instruction and training.[8]

The remark about circumstances justifying the present exclusion of religious teaching could hardly have been received as anything but an affront by the Orthodox religious groups. But Mann's next sentences were to draw down upon his head their full wrath.

Entirely to discard the inculcation of the great doctrines of morality and of natural theology has a vehement tendency to drive mankind into opposite extremes; to make them devotees on one side, or profligates on the other; each about equally regardless of the true constituents of human welfare. Against a tendency to these fatal extremes, the beautiful and sublime truths of ethics and of natural religion have a poising power. Hence it will be learned with sorrow that of the multiplicity of books used in our schools, only three have this object in view; and these three are used in only six of the two thousand nine hundred and eighteen schools, from which returns have been received.[9]

[8] *Life and Works,* II, 424.

[9] *Ibid.* There never was any question for Mann about the fact that religion belonged in the common schools. He writes in the *Twelfth Annual Report:* "But such is the force of the conviction to which my own mind is brought by these general considerations, that I could not avoid regarding the man, who should oppose the religious education of the young, as an insane man; and were it proposed to debate the question between us, I should desire to restore him to his reason, before entering upon the discussion." (Facsimile ed., p. 103.)

These words, taken at their face value and detached from other expressions of Mann, would seem to put him on the record in favor of excluding all teaching of "supernatural" religion from the schools and arguing instead for "moral instruction and training," that is, "the truths of ethics and of natural religion." That his position is not quite so simple will become clear when we take up the matter in detail. Here it might be pointed out that even in the present context, Mann is necessarily making reference to *sectarian* religion when he speaks of this exclusion of religious teaching. In other words, the opposition is not between *natural* and *supernatural* religion; Mann is opposing *natural* religion, which he sometimes calls "the religion of heaven," to *sectarian,* or what he calls "man-made" religion. In fact, the circumstances which he says presently justify this entire exclusion are precisely the sectarian bias of the books available to the committees for selection and recommendation to the schools. Later we shall see more in detail what Mann means by religion.

Mann had no sympathy for any sectarian interpretation of common religious truths. At the same time he did have his own religious convictions and commitments. As a policy-maker for the common public school, however, he confronted the practical problem of what to do about forming "piety" in the breasts of Massachusetts children—Congregationalist, Methodist, Unitarian, Baptist, Episcopalian—whose parents and ministers were peering over his shoulder. The central theses of Mann's philosophy of character education must be understood against the background of Mann's understanding of the educational process. Horace Mann followed the traditional division of education into three areas which, he insisted, sound pedagogy must heed. In the *Eleventh Annual Report* he discusses this division:

First, as embracing the proper care and training of the body, that its health and longevity may be secured.

Second, as cultivating the faculties by which we perceive, compare, analyze and combine, remember, reason, and perceive natural fitness and the beauty of things, so that we may know more of the world in which we are placed and of the glorious attributes of its Maker, and so that, by more faithfully harmonizing our conduct with its laws, we may the better enjoy its exquisite adaptations to our welfare.

Thirdly, as fashioning our moral nature into some resemblance to its divine original—subordinating our propensities to the law of duty, expanding our benevolence into a sentiment of universal brotherhood, and lifting our hearts to the grateful and devout contemplation of God.[10]

Mann is clear and consistent in his understanding of education on the first, or physical, level: the training and harmonious development of the body was important and necessary as the foundation for intellectual and moral education. In his understanding of the relation between the second and third areas, however, there is some ambiguity, complicated by his phrenological background, which it is difficult to resolve.

In the second paragraph Mann says that the intellectual faculties are cultivated so that we may know God's attributes and His world and harmonize our conduct with its laws. But how is this natural knowledge of God and consequent conduct on the level of *intellectual* nature related to the knowledge of God and conduct on the third level of the *moral* nature? Is one of the "natural" religious order and the other of the "supernatural" religious order? Very unlikely.[11] Is one equivalent to the modern phrase "moral values" and the other to the modern phrase "spiritual values"? This, too, is extremely unlikely. Mann does distinguish two distinct levels but fails to indicate any real differences between the knowledge of deity and accompanying ethical behavior of which both paragraphs speak. In any event, moral training has the primacy in education. Horace Mann affirms this central thesis almost to the point of monotony. In fact, morality for him is "the central point of this earthly universe."[12]

Mann goes further. "A man is not educated," he insists, "because he buys a book; nor is he educated because he reads a book; though it should be the wisest book that ever was written, and should enumerate and unfold all the laws of God. *He* only is educated, who practises according to the laws of God."[13] To a letter from a school committee

[10] *Eleventh Annual Report*, in *Life and Works*, IV, 142–43.

[11] It is doubtful if Mann accepted the duality of "natural" and "supernatural." He did not believe in the miraculous, nor in the divinity of Christ. Once, however, he speaks of two kinds of truth: "natural" and "spiritual." See *Life and Works*, V, 388.

[12] Journal, May 16, 1837. See also: *Common School Journal*, III, No. 1 (Jan. 1, 1841), 10. Also, *Life and Works*, V, 27. Future references to the *Common School Journal* will be indicated by *CSJ*.

[13] *CSJ*, VIII, No. 1 (Jan. 1, 1846), 6. Also, *Life and Works*, V, 148–49.

inquiring of him whether literary qualifications alone were sufficient
for hiring a teacher, Mann replied that "in my opinion, they are not.
Moral qualifications, and ability to inculcate and enforce the Christian
virtues, I consider to be even of greater moment than literary attain-
ments." [14]

What were the functions of the moral nature and how was it related
to the physical and intellectual natures? These passages throw light on
the point. Mann explains that to the moral nature

belong the awe-inspiring ideas of duty and destiny, and the awe-stricken
sentiments of wonder and adoration. Here our contemplations rise from
the mighty genius who can draw down lightnings from the lower heavens,
to the hallowed genius who can draw down sanctities and beatitudes from
the upper heavens. It is through moral and spiritual power that the
rivers of thought and feeling are to be turned, as men now turn the rivers
of water.

The moral and religious part of man's nature is the highest part. Of
right it has sovereignty and dominion over all the rest. Some of our faculties were bestowed for a temporary purpose. This was given for an eternal
one.[15]

These lines, incidentally, contain one of Mann's rare uses of the phrase
"moral and spiritual." It is clear, though, that he is using the phrase
interchangeably with the later phrase "moral and religious." It is also
plain that he calls this third nature the moral *and* religious part of
man.

Resolution or reformation is another function of the moral nature,
which Mann calls "that portion of our complex nature, respecting
which we are most emphatically bound to 'begin once more' or to 'try
again,' and to see if something better cannot be done with the *new*
than was done with the *old*." [16]

The unity and harmony of the three natures he describes thus: "If
the appetites govern, they bring the whole physical system to sudden
ruin. But if the spiritual nature enlightened by the intellect governs,
then the bodily system runs rejoicing to its goal." [17] He argues that the
whole scheme of creation—man and nature—was based upon the su-

[14] Letter to Rev. D. Wight, Jr., April 28, 1848, in *Life and Works*, I, 262.
[15] Antioch Inaugural Address, *Life and Works*, V, 367–68.
[16] *CSJ*, VII, No. 1 (Jan. 1, 1845), 12. Also, *Life and Works*, V, 128.
[17] Antioch Inaugural Address, *Life and Works*, V, 368.

premacy of the moral faculties, and assures his auditors: "Let but the laws of God be understood and obeyed, and justice and love will reign over all the earth, and man will be restored to his Eden of happiness." [18]

✦

Whether Mann called it the "moral" or "spiritual" or "religious" (even at times the "intellectual") nature, he had in mind this "third" nature of man. Most of the time, however, he does call this the "moral nature." But when he speaks of "piety" and "religion," what does he mean? Is he indicating anything more than a theistically based natural-law morality, that is, a belief in God and the natural law arrived at through man's reason independently of any supernatural revelation from God?

Voltaire wrote: "J'entends par religion naturelle les principes de morale communs au genre humain." [19] Horace Mann would not have been satisfied with this definition. He would have added to it. The deistic influence in his own life was more akin to that of the British empiricists than to that of the continental freethinkers.[20] Locke and Bolingbroke, the two most influential of the English school, did not intend to cut themselves off completely from the Western Christian tradition. They did not openly reject Christianity. What they claimed to be pleading for was a more reasonable approach to religion, one more in conformity with the newly discovered truths of science, and hence one becoming to man's rational nature.

Horace Mann held the existence of a natural law as defined and interpreted through the scholastic tradition from Aristotle to John Locke,

[18] *Ibid.*

[19] Voltaire, *Oeuvres Complètes,* XXII, 419. Voltaire professed complete apostasy from Christianity: "Je conclus que tout homme sensé, tout homme de bien, doit avoir la secte chrétienne en horreur. *Le grand nom de théiste, qu'on ne révère pas assez,* est le seul nom qu'on doive prendre. Le seul Évangile qu'on doive lire, c'est le grand livre de la nature, écrit de la main de Dieu, et scellé de son cachet. La seule religion qu'on doive professer est celle *d'adorer Dieu et d'être honnête homme.* Il est aussi impossible que cette religion pure et éternelle produise du mal qu'il était impossible que le fanatisme chrétien n'en fit pas." "Bolingbroke," in *Oeuvres Complètes,* XXVI, 298.

[20] For good background material here see Haraszti, *John Adams and the Prophets of Progress,* and Becker, *The Heavenly City of the Eighteenth Century Philosophers.*

but this he usually distinguished from religion. In the *Tenth Annual Report*, which contains his oft-quoted argument for the natural right of every child to an education, his premise is:

I believe in the existence of a great, immutable principle of natural law, or natural ethics,—a principle antecedent to all human institutions and incapable of being abrogated by any ordinances of man,—a principle of divine origin, clearly legible in the ways of Providence as those ways are manifested in the order of nature and in the history of the race.[21]

Mann follows, of course, the common distinction between the moral and religious interests of mankind. However, does he advocate the *separation* of moral training from religion? Or a moral training in school *separated* from all religious training? Does he conceive of intellectual, moral, and religious training as three distinct things? Let us see.

In the *Common School Journal* he says that it is to be deplored that "the intellect, uncultivated as it is, is still more adequately cared for than the moral nature of children." The schools spend hours in instructing the head but only minutes in purifying the heart. The strictly religious interests of mankind receive paternal care and supervision, for numerous shepherds are appointed to feed the souls of men. And then he writes:

But between the intellectual and the strictly religious concernments of men, there, is the lair of appetites more ferocious than those which madden the wild beasts of the forest, and there, is the home of passions more relentless than the vulture's when she swoops upon her prey. It is true, that intellectual culture has some favoring relations and affinities with moral culture; and, it is also true that the citadel of religion is never secure unless the outworks of virtue are safe.[22]

But why does the race languish and fade? Mann explains that the clergy, to whose care such things are confided, have been so unsuccessful in improving mankind because

by tradition and the usages of the age our spiritual guides address but a small part of the various faculties of the human mind. They speak only from one set of faculties in their own minds, and to one set only in the minds of their hearers; and thus, without any fault of their own, but in accordance with the practice of the times, they sometimes leave a feeling

[21] *Life and Works*, IV, 112.
[22] *CSJ*, VII, No. 2 (Jan. 15, 1845), 20. Also, *Life and Works*, V, 142.

of want or incompleteness, which seeks for relief elsewhere, and often, in improper gratifications. The many-toned soul is not satisfied, when the performer strikes but a few of the numerous strings which make its music.[23]

The phrenologists sharply differentiated between morality and religion but based the distinction upon the difference in faculties.[24] Regardless, however, of the basis for the distinction, Mann is perfectly correct when he points out the fact that mankind has considered the area of morals distinct from that of strict religion or "faith," even to the point that morality is cultivated far less than strict religion or "faith." But nowhere in his writings does Horace Mann argue for an education based upon a morality of pure nature or natural ethics. He speaks of the distinction between religion and morality as "somewhat vague and only partially correct"—namely, that "the former comprises the relations between man and his Maker, and the latter the relations between man and his fellow-men." [25] He goes on to lament that in the practical order the energy of the church is "principally devoted to religious, as contradistinguished from moral teachings."

But in defining education Mann invariably included some reference to religion, i.e., elements clearly transcending pure ethics. In one of his earliest lectures on education he concluded his definition: "And finally, by the term Education I mean such a culture of our moral affections and religious susceptibilities, as, in the course of Nature and Providence, shall lead to a subjection or conformity of all our appetites, propensities, and sentiments to the will of Heaven." [26]

Writing in the introduction to the eighth volume of the *Common*

[23] *CSJ*, IV, No. 7 (April 1, 1842), 101. Also, *Life and Works*, V, 211.

[24] Mann's great friend, George Combe, wrote: "There is a distinction in nature between morals and religion. The organs of Conscientiousness and Benevolence are the foundations of morals. When they are predominantly large, they produce the tendency to do justly, and to act kindly, towards all men; but if the organs of the religious sentiments be deficient, there will not be an equal tendency to worship. Thus we meet with many men who are moral, but not religious. In like manner, if the organs of the religious sentiments be large, and those of Conscientiousness and Benevolence be deficient, there may be a strong tendency to perform acts of religious devotion, with a great disregard of the duties of brotherly love and honesty. We meet with such characters in the world." Combe, *Moral Philosophy*, Lecture XVII, p. 106, "Religious Duties of Man."

[25] *CSJ*, VII, No. 2 (Jan. 15, 1845), 20. Also, *Life and Works*, V, 143.

[26] 1838 Lecture III, *Life and Works*, II, 144.

School Journal, he inquires: "Can any rational or religious man believe that the kingdom of heaven will ever come upon earth until a moral and religious education shall have prepared the human
family to understand and receive it?" [27]

In the summer of 1846 he penned his beautiful letter to the school
children of Chautauqua, New York, in which he told them: "You
were made to be moral and religious. Morality consists primarily in
the performance of our duties to our fellow-men; religion in the performance of our duties to God." [28] And in another passage of the letter
he phrased his thought this way: "You must be religious; that is, you
must be grateful to God, obey his laws, love and imitate his infinite
excellences." In a speech given a few years later he further defined
religion: "By religion, I mean the great ideas and affections pertaining
to human brotherhood and to practical obedience to the precepts of the
Gospel of Jesus Christ." [29]

Commenting upon the first Packard letter against the board, Mann
made St. James's definition his own. The letter, which was printed in
the *New York Observer,* professed to inquire into the bearings of the
action of the board in regard to religious teaching in the schools. Mann's
dry comment is:

Probably they will have no difficulty in making out that the Board is
irreligious; for with them religion is synonymous with Calvin's five points.
As for St. James' definition of it, "Pure religion and undefiled is to visit
the fatherless and widows in their affliction," etc.; and that other definition, "Do justly, love mercy, and walk humbly with thy God,"—the
Orthodox have quite outgrown these obsolete notions, and have got a religion which can at once gratify their self-esteem and destructiveness. They
shall not unclinch me from my labors for mankind.[30]

The next Mann statement is important because it comes after nearly a
decade of his service as secretary:

Directly and indirectly, the influences of the Board of Education have been
the means of increasing, to a great extent, the amount of religious instruc-

[27] *CSJ,* VIII, No. 1 (Jan. 1, 1846), 2. Also, *Life and Works,* V, 144.
[28] *Life and Works,* V, 271.
[29] Lecture, "Demands of the Age on Colleges," delivered before the Christian
Convention at Cincinnati, Oct. 5, 1854. *Life and Works,* V, 425.
[30] Journal, Oct. 27, 1838; *Life and Works,* I, 107. "Self-esteem" and "Destructiveness" were two of the 37 faculties tabulated by the phrenologists.

tion given in our schools. Moral training, or the application of religious principles to the duties of life, should be its inseparable accompaniment. No community can long subsist, unless it has religious principle as the foundation of moral action, nor unless it has moral action as the super-structure of religious principle.[31]

These statements, and the following, leave no room for doubt that for Mann morality and religion are inseparable:

But, it will be said that this grand result, in Practical Morals, is a con-summation of blessedness that can never be attained without Religion; and that no community will ever be religious, without a Religious Educa-tion. Both of these propositions, I regard as eternal and immutable truths.[32]

Summarizing Mann's thought to this point, we can now state these conclusions:

1. Moral or character education has the primacy in education.
2. "Piety" and "religion" include more than theistically based natural ethics.[33]
3. There is a distinction between moral and religious education.
4. Moral training and religious training should not be separated in education.

In addition to these conclusions, many elements, both positive and negative, belonging to Mann's concept of religion have emerged. It is clear that Mann did not identify religion with any kind of creed or covenant (especially Calvin's five points). Nor did it include reliance upon blind authority, nor belief in miracles, nor attendance at church services, nor persecution of others, nor denial of full liberty to (almost) all others.[34] It is important to keep in mind that "natural" religion or

[31] *Ninth Annual Report*, in *Life and Works*, IV, 103.

[32] *Seventh Annual Report*, p. 98.

[33] Religion and piety for Mann are associated with many ideas not arrived at solely through a study of the evidences in the physical universe. These "super-natural" elements include the subjection of all our appetites and propensities to the will of heaven; the arrival of the kingdom of heaven; practical obedience to the precepts of the Gospels of Jesus Christ; fulfillment of St. James's injunction to visit the orphans and widows and the biblical admonition to "do justly, love mercy, and walk humbly with thy God."

[34] Mann shared the general American disdain for the Mormons. See *Life and Works*, V, 444 and 479–80.

the religion of nature did not mean for Mann a natural religion in the literal sense. Neither personally nor in his official capacity did he believe in or advocate natural religion.

Mann reverenced Christianity and looked upon himself as a devout Protestant Christian, but he tended to describe Christianity in terms as broad as creation. Tertullian referred to the *"anima naturaliter Christiana"* and in somewhat the same sense Mann continually interchanged the terms "Christianity," "religion," "civilization," "education," and "morality." [35]

"Oh how beautiful and divine the work," writes Mann, "by which the jungles of society that calls itself civilized, can be cleared from the harpies, the wild beasts, and the foul creeping things which now dwell therein! This is the work of civilization and Christianity." [36] In the introduction to the eighth volume of the *Common School Journal* he says: "He who is ignorant is almost necessarily superstitious. But a Christian education lifts off the whole, black, iron firmament of superstition from the soul, and brings life and immortality to light." [37]

In the peroration of this introduction, Mann assures his readers:

All those who are worthily laboring to promote the cause of education are laboring to elevate mankind into the upper and purer regions of civilization, Christianity, and the worship of the true God; all those who are obstructing the progress of this cause are impelling the race backwards into barbarism and idolatry.[38]

Elsewhere, Mann contends that "a people who tolerate great national sins are not entitled to be called Christian or morally civilized." And that "among whatever people the law of caste prevails, or the fact of caste without the law, that people has no right to call itself civilized or Christian." [39]

✦

[35] Tertullian's argument was that the human spirit was naturally disposed to receive the revelation of Christianity, that a harmonious continuity existed between God's first revelation (creation) and His second (Christianity).

[36] *CSJ*, IV, No. 7 (April 1, 1842), 103. Also, *Life and Works*, V, 215. (See also *CSJ*, VIII, No. 1 [Jan. 1, 1846], 15.)

[37] *CSJ*, VIII, No. 1 (Jan. 1, 1846), 15.   [38] *Ibid.*

[39] Antioch Inaugural Address, *Life and Works*, V, 371 and 373. See also *Life and Works*, IV, 4.

On the other hand, Christianity and religion, according to Mann's convictions, became distorted in sectarian form. While Mann would not interfere with anyone's freedom to subscribe to almost any form of Christianity, he did insist that creeds and sects be kept completely away from the common schools. In the *Second Annual Report,* he defends the action of the school committees referred to in the preceding year's report. These committees had excluded books "which, but for their denominational views they would have been glad to introduce." [40] But, he continues, "No candid mind could ever, for a moment, accept this as evidence of an indifference to moral and religious instruction in the schools; but only as proof that proper manuals had not been found, by which the great object of moral and religious instruction could be secured, without any infringement of the statutory regulation." [41] Many of Mann's adversaries seem to have been lacking in the "candid" mind.

Their intransigent attitude puzzled Mann but did not budge him. In a private diary entry under date of January 20, 1839, he wrote:

Both Reports in. Some efforts making by disappointed Orthodoxy to disaffect the public with the Board. They want, at least some of them, their doctrines introduced. This cannot be, neither theirs, or those of any others, considered as sects—mainly. The fundamental principles of Christianity may and should be inculcated. This should be done thro' the medium of a proper text book to prevent abuses. After this, each denomination must be left to its own resources, for inculcating its own faith or creed.

That Voltaire's definition of natural religion as common ethics was not that of Mann is again made clear when we consider that the manuals called for in the report were, in Mann's planning, to become the *means* of bringing back to the common school the very moral and religious instruction whose absence he had deplored. These books of course had to emphasize ethical rather than the creedal aspects of religion. Most of all, however, they had to be free of sectarianism. Horace Mann never seemed to appreciate the practical impossibility of such a procedure, and consequently when Orestes Brownson and other opponents in the school library controversy pointed out this impossibility, he failed to give it consideration. This we shall see later in detail.

[40] *Ibid.,* II, 561. [41] *Ibid.*

Mann was not content to have merely ethics and natural law theism taught in the schools, nor would he allow sectarianism to interfere with the liberty of a child. Yet he did very much want Christianity—as he personally understood it—to be in the common schools.

As educators, as friends and sustainers of the Common School system our great duty is to . . . keep them [the pupils] unspotted from the world, that is, uncontaminated by its vices; to train them up to the love of God and the love of man; to make the perfect example of Jesus Christ lovely in their eyes; and to give to all so much religious instruction as is compatible with the rights of others and with the genius of our government—leaving to parents and guardians the direction, during their school days, of all special and peculiar instruction respecting politics and theology, and at last, when the children arrive at years of maturity, to commend them to that inviolable prerogative of private judgement and of self-direction, which, in a Protestant and a Republican country, is the acknowledged birthright of every human being.[42]

In the above passage there is introduced another notion of Mann's, that there existed some common core of Christian religious beliefs which could conveniently be taught in the common school without infringing anyone's liberty, while leaving the home and church free to embroider their own peculiar tenets upon this common framework. "The diversity of religious doctrines prevalent in our community," he writes, "would render it difficult to inculcate any religious truths, through the pages of a periodical designed for general circulation, were it not for two reasons." [43]

The first reason he brings forth is "that the points on which different portions of a Christian community differ among themselves are far less numerous than those on which they agree." It is hard to escape the conclusion here that Mann's zeal for his cause blinded him to the facts. It is inconceivable that he could have seriously thought men like Nathanael Emmons or Matthew Hale Smith had much in common religiously with William Ellery Channing or Theodore Parker. Mann's

[42] 1840 Lecture V: "An Historical View of Education: Showing Its Dignity and Its Degradation." *Life and Works*, II, 289–90.

[43] *CSJ* Prospectus, I, No. 1 (Nov., 1838), 14. Reprinted in *Life and Works*, II, 29–30. Although referred primarily to a common school journal, the argument is equally applicable to the common school itself. See also the Jan. 20, 1839, entry of Mann's diary.

second reason is "that a belief in those points in which they all agree, constitutes the best possible preparation for each to proceed in adding those distinctive particulars, deemed necessary to a complete and perfect faith." [44]

In the preceding chapter some of the factors explaining Mann's attitude toward sectarianism have been recounted. Mann rebelled as a youngster, and for that matter throughout his adult life, against the threat to religious freedom which he saw as inherent in the sectarian approach to religion. He welcomed, for that reason, the vast liberty which deism (and phrenology) offered. The greatest curse of sectarianism was that it deprived the child of his God-given freedom to grow in a natural way into knowledge of God and the beautiful laws of creation. He constantly complained that "all the Christian sects, and almost all Colleges and private schools, at this day, are training children and youth under their care to be incapable of impartial thought." [45] This was done "by stamping the peculiarities of their own faith as early and as deeply as possible upon the unformed mind, as though that faith were infallibly true, and by stigmatizing all conflicting ones as certainly false."

In contrast, Mann's philosophy was "to produce intelligent and virtuous, not partisan minds," and this should be the aim of "every one who believes in the Divine Being, and in human responsibility." [46] Despite long-standing practice the colleges, instead of aiming "to indoctrinate their students into special denominational tenets," should strive to establish "the great principles of practical morality" and to secure obedience to them. Otherwise they would be ignoring the everlasting truth that "man's creed grows out of his life a thousand times more than his life out of his creed." [47]

Mann's distaste for sectarianism extended principally to the Ortho-

[44] *CSJ* Prospectus, I, No. 1 (Nov., 1838), 14.

[45] Baccalaureate Address of 1857, *Life and Works*, V, 491.

[46] *CSJ*, III, No. 1 (Jan. 1, 1841), 9. Also, *Life and Works*, V, 24.

[47] Baccalaureate Address of 1857, *Life and Works*, V, 488–89. Prime offenders were the Jesuits' colleges, which "were founded in Europe . . . for the purpose of holding more closely to the eye of the pupils the painted glass of a creed, and of substituting, in their delineations of Divine power and wisdom, the feeble and distorted sketches of men for the transcendent proportions and coloring of the original." (*Life and Works*, V, 18–19.)

dox Calvinists, whose dogmas and ministers he frequently ridiculed in his private diary. In one entry he says waspishly: "If religion consists in going to meeting, I have been non-religious today. The truth is that hearing common sermons gives my piety the consumption. Ministers seem to me to care not half as much about the salvation of mankind, as I do about a justice's case." [48]

When Horace Mann assumed the office of secretary in 1837, there was no "Catholic problem" as far as the schools were concerned for the simple reason that there was not yet a considerable number of Roman Catholics in New England.[49] Mann could have had only the slightest direct contact with American Catholics. His private journal and his correspondence give no indication that he had Catholic friends or acquaintances. The Catholic religion, nonetheless, was regularly included in his general criticism of sectarianism. His unflattering comments upon that religion were, it must be remembered in fairness, voiced by a man conditioned by the religious mentality of his day. Hatred and fear of "Popery" or "Romanism" were imbibed with the milk a God-fearing Protestant child drew from its mother's breast. God had led the Pilgrim Fathers to a Protestant Canaan away from the tyranny of the Stuart Pharaohs. "Guy Fawkes," "Titus Oates," and the "Glorious Revolution" were as much religious as civic celebrations in New England towns. It is little to be wondered at if good men like Horace Mann took a rather jaundiced view of the Mother Church and the faith against which their own belief was a protest.

During his trip to Europe in 1843 Mann visited Catholic institutions in several foreign lands and recorded his impressions in a special journal kept for the trip. In Brussels, after having visited a number of churches, he writes: "Here I saw many Catholics worshipping in the churches; and everything which I have seen of them, here and elsewhere, impresses me more and more deeply with the baneful influ-

---

[48] Journal, June 4, 1837. His general condemnation of the ineffectiveness and unrealism of ministers was usually qualified with this kind of remark: "Let me always except, however, in this city, Dr. Channing and good old Father Taylor." (*Ibid.*) An entry under May 29, 1838, calls Father Taylor the "noblest *man* I have ever known."

[49] Mann himself estimated the Catholic population of his state to be 30,000. The first Catholic mission was established in Boston in 1790, though Mass had been offered there two years earlier.

ence of the Catholic religion upon the human mind." [50] The phrenologist in Mann penned the next words: ". . . and not upon the mind only, but even upon the body. The votaries are not degraded only but distorted; not only debased; but deformed."

He mentions in the same entry of the journal that he had visited "some *Salles d'Aube* or Infant Schools" and other schools for larger children kept by the Brothers of the Christian Schools, a teaching order of Catholic men. Here in these schools, in Mann's eyes, was sectarianism at its blackest:

The intellectual training seems to be deficient, & the religious training intensely Catholic. The number of prayers which the children are obliged to make, the frivolous forms they are compelled to observe, the profusion of pictorial representations of objects connected with their faith, the sectarian book which they regularly read,—all these prove the intensity of the zeal which is exerted to [forestall] the opinions of children on this sacred subject, before they arrive at an age when they can form an opinion for themselves, even to shut out all desire on their part, of ever forming an independent opinion.[51]

On the other hand, when Horace Mann encountered a Catholic who impressed him favorably, he could rise above his prejudices to pay a tribute. In the European journal he tells of his meeting with the "Hofprediger Ammon, a Catholic priest, the keeper of the king's conscience" and says of him:

I found him a most delightful man; full of generosity; a noble figure, fine head, the most charming expression of countenance; and, when anything was said that particularly interested or pleased him, he would seize the speaker by the hand, and evince the liveliness of his satisfaction by a hearty shake. He inquired very particularly about the Germans in America, —their civil, social, and political condition; and exhibited the warmest interest in every thing that concerned the welfare of man. If such a man can grow up under the influence of Catholicism, what would he be under a nobler dispensation? [52]

[50] European Journal, Sept. 12, 1843, in Mass. Hist. Soc. archives. Compayré (*Horace Mann and the Public School,* p. 46) quotes from a Mann letter to Combe following upon the *coup d'état* of Napoleon III: "What do you think of France? Frivolity, sensualism, Catholicism—from these three causes united, what may not be the issue debasing to humanity?"

[51] European Journal, Sept. 12, 1843. The bracketed word is almost illegible.

[52] Entry for Aug. 7, 1843.

But when it came to the question of religious freedom, Mann fought for that freedom for those with whose beliefs he radically disagreed. While on the one hand he may have hoped to educate Roman Catholic immigrants out of their superstitions,[53] on the other hand he served as legal counsel for the public committee of protest against the burning of the Ursuline Convent in Charlestown.[54]

For this period Mann was, on the question of civil rights, far in advance of most of his generation. It must be remembered that New England at this time looked upon the common schools as Protestant terrain.[55] Yet when Rev. D. Wight, Jr. wrote Mann to ask whether school committees were bound to approve Roman Catholics as teachers, Mann replied that, if a candidate possessed all the other qualifications, he could not be "disfranchised, or held to be disqualified for the office of a teacher, merely because he is a Catholic." [56] His esteem for individual Catholic educators evokes these next lines: "Would Père la

[53] Cremin, in *The American Common School,* p. 46, has made the point that: "Very much as Protestant Christianity was related to nationalism as a conservative and morally guiding influence, so was it related to the prevailing conception of how to Americanize immigrants." The Bible was definitely a patriotic symbol and in the context of the 1840s the Bible meant Protestantism. The Boston religious journals regularly carried accounts of the "conversion" of benighted Irish immigrants to Americanism, i.e., Protestantism.

[54] On two successive nights in August of 1834 a mob of some 40 or 50 men, incited by lurid tales of immorality in the Ursuline Convent of Charlestown, broke into the buildings. They burned everything, Stokes says, including the trees and fences on the property, while town officials stood by. The mob action was condemned on all sides. The next day in Faneuil Hall, a mass meeting of Protestants presided over by the mayor denounced the burning and resolved: "That we, the Protestant citizens of Boston, do pledge ourselves individually and collectively to unite with our Catholic brethren in protecting their persons, their property and their civil and religious rights." (See Stokes, *Church and State in the United States,* I, 818–22.) See Mann's "Fourth of July Oration, 1842," *Life and Works,* IV, 390.

[55] Mann wrote in the Prospectus for the *Common School Journal:* "It may, indeed, be said, that it was freedom of thought, constituting, as it did, the main element of Protestantism, which has given superiority to the communities where common schools have flourished. But if Protestantism, from which systems of public instruction emanated, has always tended towards free institutions, yet could Protestantism itself have survived without the alliance of a system of public instruction?" (*Life and Works,* II, 3.)

[56] Letter of April 28, 1848, in Mass. Hist. Soc. archives. (Also see *Life and Works,* I, 262.)

Salle, Fénelon, or Bishop Cheverus, be disqualified, by the fact of their faith alone, to keep a school in Massachusetts?" [57]

But Mann goes on to point out that in this kind of case "there are some other points which I should think it lawful to consider and act upon. For instance, I have always and under all circumstances held that the Bible is a book which should be introduced into our schools. Protestant parents have an undoubted right to have their child read the Protestant version, and be instructed from it." However, he suggests as a precaution that the Catholic candidate be asked if "he would use the Bible in school in such a way as the committee should direct," and whether "he would use the Protestant version for a Protestant school." Mann, finally, would demand some assurance that the Catholic would feel obliged "to abstain, on all occasions, from obtruding his peculiar or sectarian views upon the scholars." [58]

Another of Mann's central theses was that the common school is the most perfect agency for training the child in proper religion and morality. Mann made no secret of his opinion that the clerically dominated sectarian education had failed, an opinion which did not increase his popularity with a certain class in Massachusetts society. In his *Ninth Annual Report* he put it most frankly when he said that "for sixteen centuries, the anointed ministers of the gospel of Christ were generally regardless of the condition of youth." [59] Since then the clergy in three or four Christian countries had done a slightly better job, but "by far the greater part, even of these, must be excepted from the exception."

He is somewhat gentler on the clergy in a long article in the *Common School Journal* where he makes some excuse for clerical ineffectiveness. [60] First of all, at least one half of the whole community lies outside the reforming influences of the church, and secondly, the

---

[57] John Baptist de la Salle (1651–1719), founder of the Brothers of the Christian Schools, would be known to Mann as the originator of the normal school. Fénelon (1651–1715) wrote several treatises on education. The saintly Bishop Cheverus (1768–1836), first bishop of Boston, was admired and loved as much by Protestants as by Catholics of New England.

[58] Letter of April 28, 1848. Mann never realized that others might with good reason consider his own views as "peculiar" and "sectarian."

[59] *Life and Works*, IV, 6–7.

[60] "The Legislature of 1842," *CSJ*, Vol. IV, No. 7 (April 1, 1842). Also, *Life*

church addresses itself principally to men, to adults, to those "whose
habits of thinking and acting are established." He feels that "the
clergy, as clergy, do but little to guide the stream of infant thought
and feeling as it gushes clear from the spring, at a time when the
direction of its channel might be turned by a motion of the hand."
Mann concludes from this clerical failure that

the only instrumentality left is that of Public Schools. This institution, like
the law, takes cognizance of outward actions. Like the church, it enters into
the sanctuary of the soul, and inquires there what are its motives, affections, purposes,—whether they flow out into action, or are indulged only
in the secret recesses of thought.[61]

The public school possesses, says Mann, "two grand, fundamental
attributes, peculiar to itself," which give it its superiority "as a means
of reclaiming the world," the qualities wherein "it is super-eminent
over all others." [62] It has universality, "for it is capacious enough to
receive and cherish in its parental bosom every child that comes into
the world." [63] Its second great attribute is its timeliness in influencing
the malleable child, for "every effort made here propagates its influence
over the whole life," and thus "in these circumstances, then, lies the
superiority of schools over all other human agencies." [64]

Mann holds up the common school as the antidote to the evil of
society. This eloquent passage is from the *Ninth Annual Report* and
must have set some teeth to gnashing in Copley Square:

If there must be institutions, associations, combinations amongst men,
whose tendency is to alienation and discord; to whet the angry feelings of
individuals against each other; to transmit the contentions of the old to the
young, and to make the enmities of the dead survive to the living;—if
these things must continue to be, in a land calling itself Christian;—let
there be one institution, at least, which shall be sacred from the ravages
of the spirit of party,—one spot, in the wide land, unblasted by the fiery
breath of animosity.[65]

<hr>

and Works, V, 210. For other and gentler remarks about the clergy, see *ibid.,* II,
185; IV, 394-95; V, 215-45.
[61] *CSJ,* Vol. IV, No. 7 (April 1, 1842), 102. Also, *Life and Works,* V, 210.
[62] *CSJ,* III, No. 1 (Jan. 1, 1841), 15. Also, *Life and Works,* V, 37.
[63] *CSJ,* III, No. 1 (Jan. 1, 1841), 15.
[64] *Ibid.,* IV, No. 7 (April 1, 1842), 102. Also, *Life and Works,* V, 212.
[65] *Life and Works,* V, 36-37.

His enthusiasm then calls forth this encomium: "This institution is the greatest discovery ever made by man;—we repeat it, *The Common School is the greatest discovery ever made by man.*" And in the same vein he writes: "There never was but one greater innovation upon the practice and doctrines of all former times, than the establishment of Free Schools themselves; and this greatest, most offensive, and most violently resisted innovation, since the world began, was the introduction of Christianity." [66]

It is not to be wondered at, after hearing Mann express such convictions, that he wanted every child to come under the influence of the common school system. This he calls one of the dearest ambitions of his life.[67] In order to abolish the vicious sentiments and noxious habits into whose midst so many children are born, Mann says, "every child should pass into life through their avenue; and I believe this country will soon see the necessity of requiring that every child, not voluntarily educated by its parents, shall be compulsorily educated by the State." [68]

The above statement about compulsory state education, though, must be read along with another statement in which he gives a more qualified view.

Let me not, however, be understood as censuring those parents, who, *after having conscientiously and perseveringly done everything in their power,* to improve the character of their own schools, and still finding them to be places of intellectual or moral dearth or danger, seek for those benefits in private establishments which are denied them in the public ones.[69]

This was only a concession grudged to necessity, for Mann was no friend to private schools. He spoke strong words about their rivalry

[66] "Practice *Against* Theory. Theory *and* Practice." *Life and Works,* V, 283.

[67] In the letter quoted on page 50 Mann makes a curious aside which is seemingly inconsistent with his general attitude regarding the function of the *common* school. He writes: "The city of Lowell presents the most striking case that has come to my knowledge. There, several years ago, a very intelligent committee, consisting of clergymen and laymen, entered into an arrangement with the Catholic priests and parents, by which it was agreed that the teachers of their children should be Catholics. They were, however, to be subject to examination, and their schools to visitation, by the committee, in the same manner as other teachers and schools." He refers his correspondent to the last April number of the *New Englander* "for a minute and interesting account of the whole proceeding." (*Life and Works,* I, 262.)

[68] *Life and Works,* V, 477.   [69] *Eighth Annual Report,* in *ibid.,* III, 421.

with the common schools for support and attendance.[70] His real objection, however, was the sectarian nature of private schools. In his very first report he warned that the private school system tended to make American modes of education like those of England, where each sect maintained separate schools in which children were taught from their tenderest years "to wield the sword of polemics with fatal dexterity; and where the gospel, instead of being a temple of peace, is converted into an armory of deadly weapons, for social, interminable warfare." [71]

✦

The members of the State Board of Education agreed with the secretary that books were needed to teach morality and the religious principles common to the different sects. Plans for the selection of books for the school district libraries were discussed and approved. In order to obviate the danger of sectarian bias appearing in any book, it was prescribed that unanimous approval of the board should be required for each book to be recommended.[72] By September of 1839 these books were in use:

Life of Columbus by Washington Irving
Paley's Natural Theology, Adapted for the School Library by Elisha Bartlett, M.D. (2 vols.)
Lives of Eminent Individuals, Celebrated in American History (3 vols.)
The Sacred Philosophy of the Seasons, by Rev. Henry Duncan, D.D., of Scotland, Adapted by Rev. F. W. P. Greenwood, D.D., of Boston (4 vols.)

These were books that according to the mind of the board could be used in the common schools to inculcate "piety" without favoring any particular sect. These selections definitely did not favor any sect. In fact, they could hardly be said even to have favored the Christian re-

---

[70] See *First Annual Report.*   [71] *Life and Works,* II, 419.
[72] Mann also opposed books written for a class society, notably that of Great Britain, books that "suppose and represent a state of society where wealth outranks virtue, and birth takes precedence of talent, except in extraordinary cases of mental endowment or attainment." (*Life and Works,* III, 30.)

ligion. In Paley's classic work, for example, the words "Christ," "Christian," "Bible," and "Church" do not appear.[73]

The work consists of 27 chapters, of which 22 are concerned with a proof for the existence of a Creator through the design in nature. Dr. Paley, who is frequently quoted and paraphrased by Horace Mann,[74] gives the thesis of the book in the 23rd chapter:

Upon the whole; after all the schemes and struggles of a reluctant philosophy, the necessary resort is to a Deity. The marks of *design* are too strong to be gotten over. Design must have had a designer. That designer must have been a person. That person is GOD.[75]

The defenders of Christian orthodoxy were not slow in attacking the school board's policy in the selection of library books. There enters the scene now one Frederick A. Packard, who directly and indirectly agitated for years against the board and its secretary.[76] The American Sunday School Union, an interdenominational organization, had engaged Packard as recording secretary and editor of its publications. The Union had selected a group of 121 volumes from its published list to form a library for the common schools, and Packard was charged with promoting it.

Mann records in his diary his first contact with Packard. The latter had inquired if Abbott's *Child at Home,* a Union school text, would be admitted into school district libraries in Massachusetts. Mann says that he wrote Packard a long letter "condemning the book *in toto* so far as the views of a great portion of our people are concerned. For my part, I should rather no District Library should ever be formed, than to have them, if they must be composed of such books as that." [77]

[73] In his prefatory dedication Paley explained that the present work was part of a series: "The following discussion [*Natural Theology*] alone was wanted to make up my works into a system; . . . the evidences of Natural Religion, the evidences of Revealed Religion, and an account of the duties that result from both." Paley, *Works,* one-volume edition of complete works, p. 387, Preface to *Natural Theology.*

[74] Compare *Life and Works,* V, 162, with Paley, *Works,* p. 485.

[75] Paley, *Works,* p. 468.

[76] The extant Mann-Packard correspondence has been published as an appendix to Culver's study, *Horace Mann and Religion in the Massachusetts Public Schools.*

[77] Journal, March 18, 1838.

Mann was frank in his reply, almost too frank, for he put ammunition in Packard's hands which would be long used against him and the board. These lines of Mann's letter give his chief objections:

The book would be in the highest degree, offensive to the Universalists. In this State, we have about 300 towns; & there are more than one hundred *societies* of Universalists; & besides, very many of that denomination are scattered all over the State amongst other denominations.[78]

Moreover, the letter continues, "the whole scope and tenor of the book would ill accord with the views of Unitarians, whether clergymen or laymen."

Packard's reply, under date of March 28, 1838, is courteous and conciliatory.[79] He is perfectly aware that many passages in the book would be offensive to Universalists and others but fails to see how piety can be inculcated without the theology upon which Abbott's book is based. He is convinced that the majority would not bridle at this type of book, and, as he will frequently argue, has not the majority the right to decide what kind of religion should be taught in the schools? When Mann did not reply, the Union's secretary sent him a spelling book and primer for his opinion. This time Packard got a long answer. Mann pointed out again certain passages which would exclude such books from Massachusetts schools. One reading lesson, for example, which came in for a vigorous denunciation, referred "the common events of life to Divine interposition." And Mann continues:

It seems to me the most dangerous of all teaching,—tending more than anything else to unsettle all sound notions, respecting the constitution of the system in which we are placed,—which is a system of fixed, unrepealed, unsuspended laws, & whoever transgresses them, or comes in collision with them, knowingly, or ignorantly, be he saint or sinner, must suffer the consequences.[80]

Mann repeated his earlier objections and concluded the letter with some plain words on the inability of a mere creed to uplift human nature from its baser propensities. The letter as a whole is an eloquent expression of Unitarian optimism in face of the old Calvinistic pessimism about human nature.

[78] Culver, *Horace Mann and Religion in the Massachusetts Public Schools,* Appendix A: Letter 2, March 18, 1838, p. 241.
[79] *Ibid.,* Letter 3, pp. 243–45.   [80] *Ibid.,* Letter 5, June 23, 1838, p. 247.

The basic issue between the two men is one that has never yet been settled. What *is* sectarianism? The American Sunday School Union had an examining committee to pass on books. The committee consisted of two Methodists, two Baptists, two Episcopalians, and two Presbyterians.[81] For Packard this was a "nonsectarian" process of selection. This was "nonsectarianism." Mann, however, insisted that the term had to cover the nonevangelical sects, like the Unitarians and Universalists, as well as the evangelical ones.

Mann's final letter to Packard was written July 22, 1838.[82] It is a clear and vigorous defense of his own position and an effort to correct some of Packard's erroneous impressions. Confirmation of some of our earlier analysis of Mann's thought on the relation of creedal religion to natural religion is found in the letter. "Conscience, duty, truth, oblige me," says Mann, "to meet with an unqualified denial" Packard's allegation "that the mind of a child should not be influenced on religious subjects until its judgment is sufficiently matured to weigh the evidence, and arguments for itself." [83] He continues:

Such a notion conflicts with my whole theory of the nature, and character of a child's soul. What I said was, that "Creeds," the abstruse points, which divide one set of Christians from another, "ought not to be taught to children" . . . and my conclusion was, that the Religion of Heaven should be taught to children, while the creeds of men should be postponed until their minds were sufficiently matured to weigh evidence, and arguments.[84]

Mann finally turns to a related charge, in which he was reported by Packard to have said *"generally, and without exception,* that 'the doctrines of revealed religion, could not be safely connected with a course of public instruction.'" This he dismisses as "too erroneous to be credited a moment by anyone." [85]

Packard came back with a 21-page reply. He labels Mann's interpretation of the "wise, necessary, wholesome" law of 1827 as "monstrous, forced, mischievous, absurd." [86] Here and there amidst the

---

[81] *New York Observer,* XVI (March 17, 1838), 11.

[82] Packard acknowledged this letter as "your communication of July 26th" and said he did not receive it until September 5. His "Verax" article in the *New York Observer* was dated August 18.

[83] Culver, *Horace Mann and Religion in the Massachusetts Public Schools,* Appendix A: Letter 10, July 22, 1838, p. 266.

[84] *Ibid.*   [85] *Ibid.,* p. 267.   [86] *Ibid.,* Letter 11, Sept. 19, 1838, p. 270.

bombast Packard strikes a telling blow. For example, when he asks
Mann point-blank:

And pray who but men are to determine what is "the religion of Heaven."
Does it include the holiness of God, the corruption of the human heart—
the sacrifice of Christ for sin—the eternal punishment of the finally im-
penitent &c. &c.? No, you will say, these belong to the "creeds of men" &
must be postponed until the pupil's mind is sufficiently matured to weigh
evidence & argument. The "religion of heaven" you will say is "a religion common to all— Its doctrines are revealed in the skies & the flowers,
in the ocean & the landscape— These, children can understand— There is
nothing in them to confuse & perplex & divide their innocent minds." [87]

The traditional meaning of "natural" religion, i.e., theistically based
ethics, must have been in Packard's mind when he asked Mann: "What
doctrines of revealed religion will remain to be connected with a system of public instruction, after subtracting those about which there
are conflicting creeds among men?" [88]

In his letter Packard is only one of the first to throw up this difficulty inherent in Mann's solution:

The simple truth is disclosed in your report & it will finally be seen in
your operations—that your theory of public instruction excludes the doctrines of revealed religion & sends the pupil to the religion of nature as it
is called—or to the religion of Socrates & Plato, to learn his origin, character & destiny.[89]

The Union secretary several times in his concluding pages states
that he is convinced now that according to Mann's policy "the Christian religion" will not be recognized as the basis of the system of public
instruction in Massachusetts.[90] Mann's "great idea," he concludes, "is a
grand instrument in the hands of freethinkers, atheists & infidels for
the accomplishment of their purposes. They would shut out every ray
of light from the Bible." [91] But opposing Mann's idea is another "great
idea," viz., that a book may "illustrate the prominent doctrines of the
Christian faith & still not be objectionable on account of sectarianism—
This idea you will find is & has been held, by men of the most enlightened & elevated minds." This exchange closed the private corre-

87 *Ibid.*, pp. 277–78.   88 *Ibid.*, p. 278.   89 *Ibid.*
90 *Ibid.*, p. 281.   91 *Ibid.*, p. 283.

spondence between the two men but did not conclude their controversy. Frederick Packard now turned to the public press.

✦

The opening salvo in the new phase of the battle was an article in the *New York Observer* for August 18, 1838, which bore the signature "Verax." The author, it has been established, was Frederick A. Packard. The article quotes from Mann's *First Annual Report* the lines concerning the lack of appropriate books to inculcate ethics and natural religion, and charges that such a policy is a "triumph of infidelity." The article further claims that this can only be "the artful movement of a few minds hostile to all the great doctrines of the Bible" and "another of the bold efforts of the day to banish the gospel from the world." [92]

In the same journal for October 20, 1838, appeared the first of a series of anonymous letters addressed to the president of Amherst College, the Reverend Dr. Heman Humphrey.[93] A second letter appeared and then the series abruptly stopped, but at the end of the year there appeared in Boston in pamphlet form these two letters along with a third and a fourth, all addressed to Dr. Humphrey. Their anonymous author was Packard.[94]

The first letter is mild. Its writer warns of the potential for good or evil in the powers of the Massachusetts board and concludes with this single question: "Will the Christian religion be recognized by your Board as the basis of the system of public instruction?" [95]

The second letter of the series contains much of the same polemic that Packard used in his letters to Mann. He quotes the same passages from the *First Report,* and insists:

There is no room here for doubt or misconception. It is plainly declared, in so many words, not only that the Christian religion has ceased to be the basis of public instruction, but that RELIGIOUS TEACHING IS EN-

[92] *New York Observer,* XVI (Aug. 18, 1838), 129.

[93] As a highly respected member of the community and president of the Orthodox Amherst College, Dr. Humphrey was a person to be reckoned with.

[94] Packard, *The Question.* A copy of this pamphlet is in the library of Teachers College, Columbia.

[95] *Ibid.,* Letter 1, p. 6.

TIRELY EXCLUDED BY LAW; and that this entire exclusion of religious teaching is, in the Secretary's opinion, "justifiable under the circumstances" of the case.[96]

The Sunday School Union secretary ridicules Mann's proposal to introduce the sublime truths of ethics and natural religion, as a sort of poising power between bigotry and profligacy, and his statement that this poising power is found at present in only six out of nearly three thousand schools. This law, says Packard, has been in force for twelve years already, which must mean that boys and girls trained up in the schools during this interval, who are now between eighteen and thirty years of age, would not have had even this poising power to preserve them from bigotry or profligacy, except in only one out of every five hundred schools! His ironic exclamation is: "Who would have believed that the Massachusetts schools had sunk so low?"[97] Packard then insinuates that the board's policy of exclusion also embraces the Bible itself, and he quotes figures to prove how little this book is used in the common schools of the state.[98]

In the third letter, Packard attacks as if he had maneuvered Mann into an indefensible position. This letter is extremely unfair. It makes Mann out as an opponent of any kind of religious teaching or religiously based morality in the common schools, and by indirection as opposing the use of the Bible. Packard then describes in detail a radical system of morals which he suggests bears a striking resemblance to that he alleges Mann to be advocating. This new system was promulgated "by one [Richard] Carlile, a man of unenviable notoriety in Great Britain," and Packard quotes from an address by that worthy sent to "men of science" from his "Temple of Reason." Here is a sample:

I would banish from our school-books every word about God, or devil, or heaven, or hell, as hypocritical and unmeaning words, mere words of sound, and would confine the attention of children and youth to such subjects as an every-day's experience shall evince to them to have a foundation in nature.

Therefore I would say that the books of children had better be filled with scientific subjects than with moral precepts. I would most strenu-

---

[96] *Ibid.*, Letter 2, p. 9.   [97] *Ibid.*, p. 10.

[98] *Ibid.* This is not straight pool. Packard could easily have found the truth from reading Mann's report, which was on public record.

ously exhort the reader to abandon the idea, if he does hold it, that morality is dependent on religion.[99]

Now Packard asks rhetorically, "Do we not find here the germ of the theory of the honorable secretary, *a morality from which religion is entirely separated by law?*"

The final letter sums up Packard's indictment and ends by calling upon "the good people of our country, of all parties and denominations, and especially upon the clergy . . . to unite their counsels and efforts to put down this newfangled philosophy of education." [100]

✦

The Packard series of letters was widely commented upon in the press and precipitated a rash of letters, pro and con, in the correspondence columns of several newspapers and journals. The religious issue was an explosive one, and only the right political conditions were required to set it off. Horace Mann had assumed office under a Whig administration. It so happened that a number of prominent political figures were Whig and Unitarian—being the while members of the state school board. This would include Mann himself, Governor Edward Everett, Lieutenant-Governor George Hull, President Jared Sparks of Harvard, and three others. Members of the out-of-power Democratic party were predominantly members of the Trinitarian churches.[101]

The division of sides over the fate of the school board did not divide cleanly along religious lines nor even along lines of party affiliation. In other words, Mann and the board were not an issue between the conservative and liberal religious groups, even though most of his critics were from the ranks of the Orthodox. Nor was the school question per se a Whig-Democrat fight. One of Mann's great champions in the legislature was Robert Rantoul, a Unitarian and a Democrat, while no one fought more persistently to abolish the board than Rev. Allen W. Dodge, a Trinitarian and a Whig.

The Democrats were, first of all, the party out of power and would

[99] *Ibid.,* p. 16.

[100] *Ibid.,* Letter 4, p. 23. In this letter Packard argued for a settlement of the problem through a majority vote. Many church people agreed with him, failing to see here a resurrection of the disastrous principle, "Cujus regio, ejus religio."

[101] See the discussion in Darling, *Political Changes in Massachusetts.*

naturally be alert for any subject of dispute that might help them back
into office. The question of local control versus state-wide control of
education was primarily a political issue between the parties. Taxation
and economy in government were other occasions of political dispute
which indirectly involved the school board. The sectarian issue, however, seemed ready for exploiting when the Democratic state convention convened in Boston in the fall of 1839. The party nominated
their perennial candidate, Marcus Morton. The chairman of the reso-
lutions committee was Orestes A. Brownson, then editor of the influential *Boston Quarterly Review*. Morton defeated Governor Everett
by a single vote in a campaign which, surprisingly enough, did not see
the education issue exploited by either side. The storm, however, was
only delayed.

Mann was partly aware of what was coming. In his diary, on January 5, 1840, he writes: "I enter upon another year not without some
gloom and apprehension, for *political madmen* are raising voice and
arm against the Board; but I enter it with a determination, that, I trust,
will prove a match for *secondary* causes. If the First Cause has doomed
our overthrow, I give it up, but, if anything short of that, I hold on."

Three weeks later Mann wrote in his diary that the new governor
had forgotten the board in his inaugural address. As a matter of fact,
the governor had not ignored the existence of the board. He had hinted
in a portion of his speech that he favored a plan, first put forth by
Brownson in an issue of the *Boston Quarterly Review* the preceding
October, which would eliminate state control of education and return
the control of the common schools to the towns and district committees.[102]

The governor's suggestion ripened into a bill presented March 7.
It had been prepared by the House Committee on Education and was
designed to abolish the Board of Education and the normal schools it
had established. Four of the committee of six signed the proposed measure. The two-man minority with Mann's assistance prepared a favorable report, upon whose acceptance hung the life of the school board.
Both reports are characterized by irrelevant argument and emotional
pleading. The majority report argued that the existence of a state school
board subverted the legislature into a mere instrument for executing

---

[102] See Brownson's two articles on the topic. *Boston Quarterly Review,* II
(Oct., 1839), 402, and III (April, 1840), 232.

the board's plans. Then, too, the centralizing tendency of the board, said the report, threatened to create a system along the lines of Prussia or France, one that would place a monopoly of power in the hands of the few. The report also brought up the principle of parental rights, a principle which was passed over by the minority.

The right to mould the political, moral and religious opinions of his children is a right exclusively and jealously reserved by our laws to every parent; and for government to attempt, directly or indirectly as to these matters, to stand in the parent's place, cannot fail to excite a feeling of jealousy with respect to our public schools, the results of which could not but be disastrous.[103]

What validity this last argument may have had was weakened by its exaggerated statement. The parental right referred to has a primacy in law but is not, nor can it ever be, recognized as absolute and exclusive.[104] The first two arguments, the threatened subordination of the legislature to the board and the danger of monopoly, ring hollow.

The majority argument about the impossibility of any "nonsectarian" religion or "neutral" politics appears stronger in the words of the man who perhaps most influenced the group who prepared it: Orestes A. Brownson.[105] His article on "The School Library," in contrast to many other Brownson articles, was temperate and well argued. It deserves better treatment than it has so far received by historians of this controversy. Brownson argued:

If they exclude whatever is sectarian, they must exclude all that relates to religion, for we know no doctrine of religion which some portion of our fellow-citizens do not controvert, and we know no political doctrine which can be maintained that has not a bearing in favor or against one or the other of the great parties which now divide our political world.[106]

[103] *CSJ*, II, No. 15 (Aug. 1, 1840), 227. (The *Common School Journal* carried both reports in this number, pp. 225–34.)

[104] Most Western nations at least theoretically have come to recognize that three agencies—family, Church, and State—share the right to educate.

[105] Brownson was still a Unitarian in 1839. (Arthur E. Bestor, "Horace Mann, Elizabeth Peabody and Orestes A. Brownson: An Unpublished Letter with Commentary," reprinted from *Proceedings of the Middle States Association of History and Social Science Teachers, 1940–41.*) At different periods Orestes Augustus Brownson was an agnostic, Presbyterian, and Unitarian-Universalist before becoming a Catholic in 1844. He died in 1876 still a Catholic.

[106] Brownson, "The School Library," *Boston Quarterly Review,* III (April, 1840), 232.

Brownson then makes a practical suggestion that, when a book is introduced into the library giving one side of a religious or political question, "the best book that can be found treating the opposite side shall be procured and admitted." [107]

The Mann-directed minority report made quick work of the charges of subverting the legislature and of infringing the rights of town or district. To the charge that the library would be a worthless impossibility unless it contained partisan and sectarian books, the report offered a concrete refutation—Paley's *Natural Theology*—"one of the soundest treatises ever written, and yet it has been well said of it, that no one could tell whether its author were orthodox or heterodox, churchman or dissenter."

The strongest point made in the minority report was the simple question, one still waiting today for an answer, how *do* you teach piety without inculcating sectarianism? What *do* you do about reconciling the two injunctions of the law of 1827 which together said: teach piety but don't introduce sectarian tenets? In the conclusion the report quoted in favor of its position Calvin Stowe, whose educational work in Ohio was well known in the commonwealth.

I pity the poor bigot or the narrow-souled unbeliever, who can form no idea of religious principle, except as a sectarian thing; who is himself so unsusceptible of ennobling emotions, that he cannot conceive it possible that any man should have a principle of virtue or piety superior to all external forms, and untrammelled by metaphysical systems.[108]

At the end of the debate on the bill, March 18, 1840, the vote was taken. The bill to abolish the state board was defeated; 245 votes

[107] *Ibid.* This suggestion of Brownson's should have struck Mann favorably. Mann actually urged a scientific approach to religious questions, whereby all sides and all arguments would be equally weighed. "If there are two schools, we announce the prevalent doctrine, but never fail to qualify it by a full and fair statement of the dissenting authorities. So while we announce, as settled, all the great points in which the whole Christian world substantially agrees . . . yet when we encounter controverted points, we ought frankly to state the great names and fairly to present arguments adducible for each, conducting the case magnanimously towards absent antagonists." Baccalaureate Address of 1857, *Life and Works*, V, 494.

[108] *CSJ*, II, No. 15 (Aug. 1, 1840), 233. Packard had quoted Stowe on his side in the third letter to Humphrey. Actually Stowe's views were in complete harmony with Mann's and the minority.

against, 182 in its favor. The following November, Governor Morton was replaced by the Whig candidate, John Davis, a choice which also proved a disappointment to Mann and his friends. His inaugural address was, as Mann styled it, "non-committal,—unworthy of the man, —unworthy of the State." The new governor did not attack the board, but the lack of open support made possible the last attempts in the legislature to eliminate the board.

The pretext this time was economy. A minority of the Committee on Education reported out a bill to transfer the powers and duties of the Board of Education to the Governor and his Council, and those of the secretary of the board to the Secretary of State. Mann's bitterness in the following journal entry is entirely understandable:

Thus another blow is aimed at our existence, and by men who would prefer that good should not be done, rather than that it should be done by men whose views on religious subjects differ from their own. The validity of their claim to Christianity is in the inverse ratio to the claim itself; they claim the whole, but possess nothing.[109]

The debate came near the end of the legislative session, when almost one half of the membership was absent. The languid atmosphere was accurately reflected in the paucity of the ballots. The measure was once more defeated: 131 votes against, 114 favorable. At last the Massachusetts State Board of Education was accepted as a permanent institution. Its secretary, the Honorable Horace Mann, however, had weathered only the first series of storms over the religious education question.

[109] Journal, Feb. 21, 1841.

IV. FINAL CONTROVERSIES

The year 1844 found Horace Mann embroiled in two disputes which kept the school question before the public mind throughout the year. The first controversy involved him with Edward A. Newton and the *Christian Witness,* the church organ of the Episcopalians.
During this quarrel, many of the issues of the school-library question
were gleaned over. There is here, however, a more precise coming to
grips with a definition of the term "Christianity" and an enumeration
by both sides of the precise doctrinal points which they considered "sectarian" or "nonsectarian," and thereby fit or unfit for common schools.
The second controversy, and perhaps the most famous of them all, was
with a group of Boston schoolmasters who were incensed over Mann's
Seventh Annual Report. Though in this dispute other points were also in
question, the major attack of the schoolmen centered on the issue of discipline. The theories in conflict stemmed directly from contradictory
theological positions regarding the condition of human nature consequent upon Adam's transgression as narrated in the Bible. Finally,
there was the exasperating encounter in 1846 with the Reverend
Matthew Hale Smith. This controversy was, in most respects, anti-

climactic, although it did give Mann an opportunity to restate portions
of his philosophy of character formation.

✦

In the fall of 1843, Mann and his wife returned from six months'
travel in Europe. The secretary had devoted most of his time to in-
specting the school systems of the countries he visited. His observations about foreign education were made public soon after his return,
in the *Seventh Report* and in articles in the *Common School Journal*.
Mann had not been gentle in his censures of the sectarian aspects of
the systems about which he was reporting, and the church-controlled
British school system in particular came in for severe censure. Episcopalian resentment was not slow to express itself.

The organ of the American Episcopal Church, the *Christian Witness
and Church Advocate,* carried an unsigned letter whose author asked
the somewhat loaded question:

Can any one tell wherein the system of Mr. Girard, and the present system of our "Board of Education," or rather of its Secretary, differs; or
where the essential line of agreement varies? I abstain from pressing the
subject further at present, desiring only at this time to draw the attention
of Christians of all denominations, holding Orthodox creeds, to the grave
question, with the hope that they will examine for themselves. . . .[1]

The letter was timed to profit from the wide publicity surrounding
the Girard College case, then being argued before the United States
Supreme Court by Daniel Webster. The family of Stephen Girard were
attempting to break his will establishing a home for boys in Philadelphia
from which clergymen of all sects would be barred in order to keep
the institution free from all sectarian influence. Webster argued that
such a procedure would lay "the axe at the root of Christianity itself,"
importing something "based upon Paine's *Age of Reason*" and "Volney's *Views of Religion."*

The writer of the letter to the *Witness* did not long remain
anonymous. His identity was immediately conjectured, and all conjec-
ture was removed when in the second letter, three months later, he

[1] *Christian Witness and Church Advocate,* Feb. 23, 1844. A pamphlet published
the same year collected this correspondence and other pertinent articles: *The
Common School Controversy.*

appended the initials "E. A. N."[2] In the opening letter, Newton stated the issue about which the correspondence would swirl. Webster, according to Newton, had conclusively proved that Girard's plan, though professedly based upon principles of morality, was entirely separated from religion. But Webster had likewise shown that "it was not in the power of man to separate them, demonstrating them to be inseparable—as co-existing, or not at all; and that, without religion, there could be no such thing existing as genuine charity."[3]

The Reverend M. A. DeWolfe Howe, the editor, was in firm agreement with Newton; so that when Mann wrote to the *Witness* in order to present his answer to the Newton letter, the paper published, in Mann's words, "a very brief and imperfect synopsis of his communication incorporated into a full column and a half of the editor's comments," which were "a reiteration and justification of the most offensive of the original charges."[4] The next week the enterprising *Witness* editor printed an extract from the *Christian Reflector,* a Baptist journal, again introduced by his own editorial remarks. He ended up by agreeing with the opinion that "the present system of the Board of Education differs *none too much* to say the least, from the system of Mr. Girard." And he warned that "there is such a hue and cry kept up, at this day, by all the enemies of true religion about sectarianism, that good men need to be on their guard, lest there be an infringement on rights *more sacred* than those of *sect.*"[5]

On March 16 Mann had written to the *Witness* and in a hurt tone protested that he had never given provocation for this attack by the Episcopalians. His letter continues:

In none of my writings, in none of my lectures, has there ever been a syllable against American Episcopacy or Episcopalians. I have, it is true, in two or three instances spoken against the English National Church, of its relation to the state, and to the million and a half of uneducated, unschooled children of the state. But I have never spoken of the *faith* or *worship* even of English Episcopalians; and unless American Episcopalians choose to identify themselves with the English, in their relation to the state, and to

---

[2] Edward A. Newton had been a member of the original school board but resigned in 1838 because he opposed the library plan.

[3] *The Common School Controversy,* p. 1.

[4] *Ibid.,* p. 7.   [5] *Ibid.,* pp. 6–7.

education, I see not how my speaking of the English Episcopal Church could give cause of offence to the American.[6]

Mann gave free vent to his private feelings in a letter to George Combe:

The Episcopalians here have always borne me a grudge because I have condemned the spirit of the English Church in denying all education to the people, which they could not pervert to the purpose of proselytism.[7]

The suggested identity between the Massachusetts system and that of the Girard plan as depicted by Webster was deeply resented by Mann. In his reply he painstakingly details the differences, which he feels should be obvious to anyone in good faith. He asks: "Is the exclusion of sectarianism synonymous with the exclusion of Christianity?" Indeed, the board had attempted to follow out the law of the land by excluding sectarianism, but it had at the same time been responsible for a great increase in Christian Bible-reading in the schools. In fact, in the only schools where the board had immediate jurisdiction, the normal schools, the Bible had from their founding been read each day. "Is the New Testament, then, no part of Christianity?" As for the school library, several of the books approved by the board "breathe the purest sentiments of Christianity, and glow with the spirit of devotion; while not a single work of an opposite character or tendency has been admitted into the series." [8]

Mann paints a dark picture of what would come about if the common schools were allowed to become "nurseries of proselytism—battle grounds where each contending sect shall fight for the propagation of its own faith," and offers as the ultimate in horrors:

How long would it be, before we should have schools for the Come-outers, for the Millerites, and the Mormonites? How long, before one portion of the children would be sent to school in their "ascension robes," and before another portion, instead of the Bible, would carry a Catechism, whose first doctrine would be that "God is the Lord, and Joseph Smith is his prophet"? [9]

The Newton party had deplored the absence in the school system of "what Orthodox men hold to be the doctrines of grace." Mann

[6] *Ibid.*, p. 8.   [7] *Life and Works*, I, 225.
[8] *The Common School Controversy*, p. 11.   [9] *Ibid.*

scored a point in suggesting that what was really meant here was Newton's idea of the doctrine of grace, since Newton certainly wouldn't
want a return of the "dreaded Papists'" doctrine on grace. In the next
part of his letter Mann lists items of Christian truth which he feels can
be taught commonwealth children without infringing on the constitutional provisions to prevent sectarianism from developing in the
common schools. This enumeration is important because it provided
specific items of what Mann considered a Christianity freed from sectarianism. Children in the common schools, he said, can be taught:

1. To love the Lord their God with all their heart, and their neighbor as
   themselves;
2. To do to others as they would be done by;
3. To do justly, to love mercy and to walk humbly with God;
4. To visit the fatherless and widows in their affliction and to keep themselves unspotted from the world;
5. To honor father and mother;
6. To keep the Sabbath holy;
7. Not to steal;
8. Not to kill;
9. Not to bear false witness against neighbors;
10. Not to covet.[10]

After listing these points in a series of questions to the editor and
stoutly affirming his own conviction that these may be taught under
the provision of the constitution and the laws, Mann adds even more
approved doctrinal material: "Nay, sir, I refer you to that awe-inspiring
description of the judgment in the twenty-fifth chapter of Matthew,
and I say, that there is not a single *action* or *omission* there mentioned,
for which the righteous are to be rewarded and the wicked punished,
that may not be taught, inculcated, or warned against, in all our
schools." [11]

Mann states that such is likewise the board's opinion and inquires:

Are these things, and everything else of a kindred character, which the
Scriptures contain, *non-essentials* in Christianity? According to your language they are; for all these the Board would admit, and you aver that

[10] *Ibid.*, p. 12. Numbers 1 and 5–10 of the enumeration are among the Ten
Commandments. Number 2 is the Golden Rule (Matt. VII:12 and Luke VI:31);
3 and 4 are old Mann favorites from the prophecy of Micheas (VI:8) and the
epistle of James (I:27) respectively.

[11] *Ibid.*

"the agreement between the system of Mr. Girard and that which is in action here lies in their *both* excluding Christianity as an essential element of education." [12]

In the same number of the *Witness,* the editor also made a few points. He ridiculed Mann's justification for the exclusion of sectarian Christianity as something required by the law of the commonwealth. He dubbed the 1827 law "the great fortress from which this scheme of allowing nothing but the morality of the Bible to be taught in our schools is most manfully defended." In reply to Mann's list of specific truths of Christianity that could be taught in school, the editor admitted: "They are very well so far as they go; they are important to the social uprightness and welfare of man, but they leave untouched what we, and all Orthodox Christians esteem the essentials of Christianity,—the way of salvation by Jesus Christ." [13] To Mann's claim that the board was responsible for an increase in religious teaching, the editor had a retort. Even granted that there might be "more religious teaching of a certain cast" in the schools than formerly, this was a dubious gain. "More teachers impart something which *they call* religion. But some are silenced, or modified into moral lecturers, who once dispensed truths which *are* religion." [14]

If Mann could be specific when pressed and get down to details, so could the *Christian Witness.* What were "sectarian" doctrines, the divisive things the law was seeking to keep out of common school education? Here are some examples, says the *Witness:*

That every congregation of faithful men are competent to organize an independent church, and appoint and authorize all its officers; or that there is but one scriptural mode of baptism; or that an itinerant ministry and class-meetings are important features of a church economy; or that Episcopacy is essential to the perfect order of the church. [15]

That these were points of sectarian difference when the common school system of Massachusetts was instituted was the *Witness*'s contention. But things have changed. "Universalism, Millerism, Mormonism and other 'comeoutisms'" have sprung up since, and must the liberality of our fathers be interpreted, so as to give place "to heresies, which concern the very vitals of Christianity"? [16] The editor thinks that tolera-

[12] *Ibid.*   [13] *Ibid.,* p. 15.   [14] *Ibid.*   [15] *Ibid.*   [16] *Ibid.*

tion can be carried only to a certain point. We can't permit everyone
to define "sectarian" or make us accept his definition of it. The next
step will be to allow the Bible to be read in the schools only "provided
Catholics be not forced to read a sectarian version"—which, in fact,
was what some Papists were arguing even then in Philadelphia! He
concludes with a resounding rhetorical note: "No; readers—give not
to every individual schismatic, come-outer, and infidel, unlimited use
of the word 'sectarian.' They will employ it to rob you of the gospel
of Jesus Christ." [17]

Mann's further efforts to secure a hearing for his case for the nonsectarian character of the school system availed nothing with the reverend editor of the *Witness*. Howe simply refused Mann any more
space in his columns and sent back Mann's letter unaccepted. Mann sent
the rejected letter to the Boston *Courier,* with a note passionate in its
intensity. Mann explained that the importance of this subject transcended anything personal between himself and the editor, but because

the prevalence of his views, or of those which I advocate, involves the
question of *life* or *death* to our common school system, and as he refuses to
allow my second letter—though strictly confined to a reply to his comments on my first—to appear in his paper, I will thank you to publish it
in yours.[18]

This second letter of Mann's sheds further light on his understanding of "sectarianism." He meets the *Witness* attack squarely, correcting
false interpretations of points he had earlier made. His final point contains the key to what Horace Mann meant by "sectarian" as opposed to
"Christian."

[17] *Ibid.,* p. 16.
[18] *Ibid.,* p. 18. The *Witness* for Feb. 28, 1845, referred to the effort that "has
been made by the Romanists, and pertinaciously persevered in, to exclude the
word of God from the Common Schools in New York," and warned that the
same influence was at work at home. The local attempts to eliminate sectarianism will eventually result in shutting out the Bible "when challenged to it by
the Romanists, on the ground, that it is illiberal, and sectarian." The way is being prepared "negatively, by the policy which the Secretary of the Board of Education is pursuing, who is exerting his far-reaching influence to keep out of our
schools all positive religious instruction, or, at least to prevent anything from
being taught in them that wears the semblance of religion, except the code of
morals which constitutes the life and soul of Unitarian divinity."

Mann's enumeration of specific doctrines of "nonsectarian" truth eligible to be taught in the common schools had been dismissed lightly by the *Witness* editor with the remark that "they are very well so far as they go." Mann immediately spies an opening here and makes a thrust:

To this extent, then, you are committed. And if you acknowledge this—if all Christians acknowledge this—then I say, it is not "sectarian." Sectarianism is that which belongs to a part, and not to the *whole*. Far less is it, as you affirm, a "stinted type" of sectarianism. And here I leave this charge, against our system, of being "sectarian," having clinched its falseness by a blow from your own hands.[19]

This much is clear then. Mann considered any doctrine believed by all Christians as a truly Christian one; a doctrine believed only by a part of Christendom would consequently be "sectarian." To the *Witness*'s listing of what it considered essential doctrines of Christianity, Mann replied:

You insist that in our public schools—established for the whole, and supported by taxes levied upon the whole—certain scriptural doctrines shall be taught; such as that "God was in Christ, reconciling the world unto himself;" that "we are by nature children of wrath;" that "the blood of Jesus Christ cleanseth from all sin," and that "by grace are we saved through faith." [20]

Very well, says Mann. The Bible is now read in all our schools, and ordinarily by the scholars themselves. These doctrines or declarations being in the Bible, are they not in the schools also? And here Mann gets down to the issue of "true" religion as opposed to "man-made":

But perhaps you desire something more for the schools? Perhaps you desire, not only that these passages should be read, but that certain articles of faith, or formularies, more or less in number, embodying these passages in a manner more acceptable to you than as found in the original texts, should be taught with them.[21]

Though, Mann continues the argument, you are free to teach your own formularies of Christian truths out of school to any extent you wish, yet you insist that they should be taught in the school, too. But then surely you must have teachers in the schools whom you can trust

---

[19] *The Common School Controversy*, p. 20.   [20] *Ibid.*   [21] *Ibid.*

to teach them. Now look at the situation you've created. We have as many as five thousand different individuals, in a year, employed to teach our public schools. Can you trust so many to do so important a work, without a previous examination by "some committee, synod, presbytery, council, or conclave"?

It will then be necessary to appoint an examining body who will see that "none but teachers of the right faith get possession of the schools." But since you have no law authorizing such an examining body, you must go to the legislature and have it passed. And "when you have the law, and the teachers ready to carry out your purposes; then, will you be so good as to tell me wherein your system will differ from an established religion! If such a system will not be that union of church and state from which our fathers, as you call them, fled into the wilderness, will you or your correspondent tell me where the essential line of agreement varies?" [22] This argument has never been more cogently presented.

The *Christian Witness* for May 17, 1844, put Edward A. Newton back in the middle of the discussion, carrying a lengthy letter from him. Much of this communication is weak and evasive. Newton, for instance, protests that he has been misinterpreted. He really hadn't intended much by his earlier comparison of the systems of Girard and the Board of Education. He had not "the most distant idea of charging them or their Secretary with being disciples of D'Alembert, or Volney, or Paine, and their like, or of intimating that they were pursuing their system on the unhallowed principles of those enemies both to God and man." Nor did he mean "to compare the two systems as *altogether* in agreement," for at the time he had not read the "whole speech of Mr. Webster as since published." [23]

Mann's final letter, dated May 24, 1844, is a long one. Like his preceding letter this, too, appeared originally in the Boston *Courier*. The secretary is aroused now and gives no quarter to his opponents. He shatters Newton's flimsy explanation of the Girard reference and then attacks some of the assertions, presumably factual, upon which Newton had reared his conclusions. He challenges Newton's statement that the Orthodox denominations had "for near two centuries, at all times, then

[22] *Ibid.*, pp. 20–21.   [23] *Ibid.*

and now" constituted nine tenths of the population of the common-wealth. Mann says:

That population is now about 750,000. One tenth is 75,000. The Universal-ists alone are estimated at nearly or quite this number. The number of Unitarians may be somewhat, though not very much less. The Christ-ians have between twenty and thirty organized societies. While there are very few Orthodox people belonging to Unitarian congregations, it is well known that there is no inconsiderable number of Unitarians who wor-ship with the Orthodox. The opinion of some of the best informed men is, that at least one quarter of the people of Massachusetts are what is called, by way of distinction, Liberal Christians. Some estimate the number at one third. Then there are the Nothingarians and Deists, who, taken to-gether, are probably more numerous than either of the above. The Cath-olics of Boston and its vicinity have been estimated at thirty thousand; and theirs is an orthodoxy which only a portion of the Episcopalians favor. Yet Mr. Newton avers that the Orthodox have been, *and now are,* "nine tenths of the population of the Commonwealth." [24]

There was no official census to which either party could appeal for con-firmation. It is clear, however, that Mann's division—even if some-what exaggerated—was closer to the real situation than the sweeping statement of Newton's.[25]

Newton had raised the further question, "Does any one believe that the Puritan Fathers, of whom we so highly boast, would have sub-mitted to this?"—that is, to an exemption for nonbelievers from sec-tarian teaching in the schools, and to equal privileges for all.[26] Mann gives a fervent answer in the affirmative:

[24] *Ibid.*

[25] Dr. Clark (Joseph S. Clark, *A Historical Sketch of the Congregational Churches in Massachusetts, 1620–1858,* p. 282), lists the number of the churches in 1858 as follows:

Congregationalists (Or-thodox)	490	Roman Catholics	64	Wesleyan Methodists 13
		Christ-ians	37	Swedenborgians 11
Episcopal Methodists	277	Friends Meetings	24	Presbyterians 7
Baptists	266	Free-will Baptists	21	Shakers 4
Unitarians	170	Protestant or Independ-		Unclassified 12
Universalists	135	ent Methodists	20	
Episcopalians	65	Second Adventists	15	

At the close of the Revolution, Clark says the numbers were: "Roman Catholic, one; Universalists, three; Quakers, six; Episcopalians, eleven; Baptists, sixty-eight; Congregationalists, three hundred and thirty" (*ibid.,* p. 218).

[26] *The Common School Controversy,* p. 31.

Did they now live, with the more clearly-defined notions of religious
liberty and of human rights, which have been evolved by two centuries
of experience and investigation; did they live in our times, when certainly more than one third part of the people of this Commonwealth have
become dissenters from their faith, I should consider it the foulest of
all dishonors I could cast upon their name, to say they would not have
yielded the law of force and the rigors of compulsion to the demands of
justice and the spirit of the age.[27]

Mann closes his letter on an irenic note. He does not ask for a
return to the ancient laws, either political or religious, but that all
the citizenry should work, through the common schools, to do what
they can "for the improvement of the habits, for the enlightening of
the intellect, for the cultivation of the affections, for enkindling love
to God and man on the altar of every heart, and for a sacred adhesion
to that principle of Jesus,—now so openly disavowed and practically
denied,—to do to others as we would that they should do to us."[28]

The point of the controversy with Newton and the *Witness* was the
question: Can there be a nonsectarian Christianity? Newton and the
Episcopal journal held that there were certain essential doctrines which
united all true Christians: those who did not hold these were simply
not Christians. They further argued that Mann was corrupting the
Christian education of the school children by permitting in the schools
only the *morality* of the Bible and not these essential doctrines. Mann
vigorously denied their assumption. He insisted that there *was* a
common Christianity apart from any or all sectarian interpretations
or embellishments of it. He insisted that the so-called essential doctrines of the Orthodox, along with all other valid Christian doctrines,
were implicitly contained in the Bible, which he and the board for
years had promoted in the schools. Finally, Mann denied the Newton
assertion that the vast majority of commonwealth citizens were still
orthodox Christian believers and presumably willing to have the "essential" doctrines of Christianity taught to their children in the common
schools.

✦

Mann had only the summer of that year for peace and relative quiet.
When September came around, a pamphlet of 144 pages was published

27 *Ibid*.   28 *Ibid*., p. 32.

by an organization of the masters of the Boston grammar schools, to which 31 of the teachers affixed their signatures. It was entitled *Remarks on the Seventh Annual Report of the Hon. Horace Mann, Secretary of the Massachusetts Board of Education.* This was to launch a vigorous "battle of the books," the immediate cause of which was the 199-page *Seventh Annual Report* distributed the preceding winter. Mann shortly published a 176-page answer: *Reply to the "Remarks" of Thirty-one Boston Schoolmasters on the Seventh Annual Report.* Then came the schoolmasters' turn with *Rejoinder to the "Reply" of Hon. Horace Mann, Secretary of the Massachusetts Board of Education, to the "Remarks" of the Association of Boston Masters upon His Seventh Annual Report,* which went on for 215 pages. Mann's return was confined this time to 124 pages and was entitled *Answer to the "Rejoinder" of Twenty-nine Boston Schoolmasters, Part of the "Thirty-one" Who Published "Remarks" on the Seventh Annual Report of the Secretary of the Massachusetts School Board.*[29] The schoolmen, though, got the last word in print with their final shot, *Penitential Tears; or, A Cry from the Dust, by "The Thirty-one," Prostrated and Pulverized by the Hand of Horace Mann, Secretary,* an opus occupying a modest 59 pages.

Only the last of the four sections of the schoolmasters' *Remarks* directly concerns us here. This dealt with discipline in the schools. Since the psychological suppositions underlying any theory of discipline are ordinarily related to basic theological beliefs, this part of the schoolmasters' booklet, as could be expected, was the most acrimonious portion of the *Remarks* and was a repetition in part of earlier disputes.

The Boston masters strongly resented what they viewed as a caricature of their disciplinary methods. In his *Seventh Annual Report,* it is true, Mann had exalted the Prussian system of schooling where, he claimed, corporal punishment was conspicuously absent, and had gone out of his way to criticize the methods prevailing in the United States, making his contrast sharper by exaggerating certain abuses.[30] Mann,

[29] One of the original 31 signers publicly dissociated himself from the *Remarks,* claiming that he had given his signature with the stipulation that certain passages would be modified, a proviso, he charged, which had not been honored by the publisher. This signer was William J. Adams. Another of the group, Barnum Field, did not associate himself with the *Rejoinder* though reaffirming his participation in the *Remarks.*

[30] Writing fifty years later, Compayré says: "There is certainly some exaggera-

however, for many years prior to his European trip, had entertained
the same views on discipline and had widely published them. Though
corporal chastisement, at times even flogging, was still widely accepted,
there were many school people who agreed with him that the rod
should be used only in moderation and as a last resort. No doubt
many signers of the *Remarks* were in agreement at heart with the
secretary over the discipline issue. However, the heat of polemic precluded a calm discussion of immediate pedagogical differences, and
the main battle came to be fought over a distant article of theology.

In the *Remarks* the schoolmasters solemnly insisted that all obedience must recognize the existence of abstract authority which originates in God. They quoted St. Paul in their favor: "Let every soul
be subject unto the higher powers. For there is no power but of God;
the powers that be are ordained of God. Whosoever therefore resisteth
the power, resisteth the ordinance of God." [31] They then proceeded
with their exegesis and application of the text.

It is here plainly shown to be the bounden duty of all, to recognise and
obey rightful authority wherever it exists in the great chain, from the
highest to the lowest; and distinctly as authority; not waiting for the
dictates of inclination or feeling; not demanding to know the reason of
the command, as a necessary condition of obedience; but simply asking if
it be really the voice of rightful authority that speaks. On the other hand,
this duty on the part of the subject, clearly implies an equal obligation on
every one in whom authority is vested, firmly to maintain it, to insist
upon obedience, and to accept no substitute, unless he feels an honest necessity for doing so.[32]

Now Horace Mann would readily have agreed that obedience had
to be maintained, but he would have insisted that this could be obtained through kindness and understanding, rather than by the rod.
He had never advocated the entire elimination of corporal punishment.
This group of malcontents had, in his eyes, carefully selected certain

---

tion here; gentleness has never been claimed as the chief quality of German
schoolmasters." Compayré, *Horace Mann and the Public School,* pp. 44–45. It was
true that Mann went to Germany as an enthusiast and saw pretty well the things
he wanted to see there. Some of the readers of the *Seventh Report* nicknamed
him "the Prussian."

[31] *Remarks,* p. 129. The reference is to Romans XIII:1–2.

[32] *Ibid.* Our schools seem to have been thoroughly emancipated since 1844!

of his statements, twisted them out of context, and used them in an opposite sense than that intended. Mann was furious.[33] His hastily written *Reply to the "Remarks"* was more notable for its sarcasm and bombast than for logic and authority. Hubbell calls it "a poor piece of work" and says that "until now his writings had been dignified, worthy and strong; but this was written in a bitter and sarcastic spirit, and was hasty and ill-thought-out, and though done with a peculiar strength, he descended to levels in his defense and counterattack quite unworthy of a man of his quality and power." [34]

In the *Reply* Mann took up one by one the criticisms of the schoolmen, which had ranged over the entire field. He defends his policy of seeking uniformity of textbooks. A footnote here confirms one reason for some of the sectarian opposition to the school libraries. "The most persevering and unprincipled opposition I have ever encountered," he writes, "originated in my declining to recommend, for adoption in the Common Schools of Massachusetts, a highly sectarian library, prepared in another State." [35]

Mann had not, he reminds the teachers, sought the office of secretary, but the office had sought him. On his part, he had stayed in year after year to the detriment of his health and his fortune. "Some men, it is true, have tried to get me out, but nobody has tried to get in." He restates the Board of Education's avowed policy of not showing favor or disfavor to any one political or religious party. To the charge that the board was attempting to eliminate the Bible from the schools, he stated his belief:

The Bible should continue to be used in our schools; but still, that it shall be left with the local authorities,—where the law now leaves it,—to say, in what manner, in what classes, etc., it shall be used. I suppose it to be their belief, as it is mine, that the Bible makes known to us the rule of

[33] The schoolmasters had mixed vinegar with their ink. Sample: "Next came Phrenology with all its organs and propensities, rejecting all fear, emulation, and punishments; but in this country its great champions and advocates, who required brick without giving straw, proved to be unworthy disciples of Combe and Spurzheim. They had hardly told the fame and wonders of this new science before they all fell, as in one night, into a mesmeric sleep." (*Ibid.,* p. 8.) The point made is not clear but there's no mistaking the mockery of the secretary's penchant for phrenology. Spurzheim was one of the originators of phrenology.

[34] Hubbell, *Horace Mann,* p. 111.   [35] *Reply to the "Remarks,"* p. 168.

life and the means of salvation; and that, in the language of the apostle, it is a "faithful saying, and worthy of all acceptation, that Christ Jesus came into the world to save sinners." [36]

The secretary, however, would regard it as a flagrant transgression of duty to countenance any sectarian interpretation of the good book, that is, "to select any one of those innumerable guideboards,—whether pointing forward, right, left, or backward,—which fallible men have set up along the way, and to proclaim that the kingdom of heaven is only to be sought for in that particular direction." [37]

Yet, angry tone and all, the *Reply* did have an explosive force and silenced some of the criticism. The dignified *North American Review* spoke of it in a generally sympathetic article which pointed out:

If Mr. Mann has not written his "Reply" with equal prudence, the fault must be attributed to the ardor of his attachment to the cause, and to the magnitude of the provocation he had received. He has not only amply vindicated himself, but has retorted upon his assailants with terrible severity. Though he dislikes the use of the rod for children, he evidently has no objection to whipping schoolmasters, and in this case, he has certainly plied the birch with remarkable dexterity and strength of arm.[38]

A correspondent writing in the Boston *Atlas* who styled himself "Justice" held a different opinion of Mr. Mann's *Reply*. Because it does sum up the spirit which launched this particular attack on Mann and the *Seventh Report*, it is worthy of citing here. The letter begins:

The "Reply" is an appeal to morbid sensibility and popular prejudice. It depicts to timorous mothers the shocking evil of having their children governed in the fear of punishment on their disobedience. It panders to the spirit of insubordination which distinguishes our time. It proceeds upon the false philosophy or theology which assumes inherent goodness in children, to be educed—and not inborn refractoriness, to be restrained and quelled.[39]

This was, then, between Orthodox and Liberal—or better, between extreme Orthodox and the Liberals—the theological nub of the affair. Had original sin so vitiated human nature that the child could be trained in righteousness only by vigorous application of the rod, or could a child be led gently to his duties through kindness and love?

---

[36] *Ibid.*, p. 171.   [37] *Ibid.*
[38] *North American Review*, LX (Jan., 1845), 236–37.
[39] Boston *Atlas*, XIII (Dec. 5, 1844), 135.

But "Justice" finds another grave flaw in Mann's *Reply*. Its *maximum pessimum,* he writes,

> its pre-eminent fault, is its malversation of Holy Scripture. The Bible is quoted with a frequency which seems to betoken great respect, but with an almost uniform misapplication, which, at the hands of so shrewd a man and so ripe a scholar, can be attributed to nothing less than irreverence.[40]

After this thrust, which to Mann's sensitive nature would be intolerable, "Justice" proceeds to give an example.

> The expression "the whole creation groaneth and travaileth in pain until now," is actually applied to the hitherto continued severity of school discipline; and the distresses of the human race under the scourge of sin, and its longings for redemption are punned out of notice to introduce the moans of a transgressing schoolboy, sighing for deliverance from the fear of the ferule.[41]

Horace Mann was not famous for his sense of humor, but anyone who had read five pages of his writings would know his deep respect for the Bible. If Mann had a slight smile on his face at the aptness of this biblical verse as a description of the groans of the long-suffering schoolboy, his assailant had none. He warns Mann that this disparagement will recoil upon him. And he brings his pen around in one final humorless flourish: "But the rational, sober, just, religious, reflecting, conservative and respectable, will abide by old principles and tried servants with closer tenacity, until wit and malice are silent, and reason, temperance and charity have something to allege." [42]

As the sesquipedalian titles multiplied, so did the irrelevancies and confusions in the argument. The schoolmasters' *Rejoinder to the "Reply"* had four separate sections written by different individuals. The section which treated school discipline bore the signature of one Joseph Hale, an advocate of the "New Light" Calvinism. This extreme form of the old Orthodox Puritanism, it will be recalled, regarded any co-operation with God's grace as sinful self-love and urged an almost brute submission to the divine activity. This was logical, if one accepted the Calvinist interpretation of the fall of man from grace. In any event, Hale's section of the *Rejoinder* was based upon a principle in flat contradiction to everything that Mann believed in and had been striving

[40] *Ibid.*   [41] *Ibid.*   [42] *Ibid.*

for in the schools. Hale granted that moral persuasives might well be used to bring old and young to a sense of duty, but argued for "the naked doctrine, that physical coercion is, in certain cases, necessary, natural, and proper." He scoffed at the "pseudo-philanthropy" which had made sympathy an abnormal and "predominant feature of the age." [43]

Hale's next remarks have a modern ring. Their author attacks the tendency to "sink the individual in the community, or association, or corporation; merge self-love into philanthropy; convert *I* into *We;* and blend the race, en masse, into one grand brotherhood of mutual love and worship, which would seem to put paradise to the blush, and to make an immortality on earth, far preferable to the worship of God in heaven. . . . It is this vain desire to spiritualize and deify the natural man, that leads us to mistake a faith in the human, for a faith in the divine." [44]

What did this long, wordy battle with the schoolmasters decide? For one thing, the controversy exposed certain abuses in school discipline and rallied wide public opinion against them. Perhaps still more important, Mann and his supporters, who were a majority, showed how absurd was the arbitrary application of the theological principle to which the schoolmasters' document appealed in justification of the rod. The zealous use of the rod no doubt continued long after this altercation, but its justification in the name of religion had been to a great extent discredited. The best parts of the *Seventh Annual Report,* where Mann described many of the fine new techniques in foreign pedagogy, opened the eyes of many commonwealth teachers and had beneficent results in the schools in Massachusetts and elsewhere in the United States.

Despite its many other strong points, the report had exaggerated conditions in the local schools. Mann's black picture of backward pedagogy and sadistic disciplinary practices could not be found generally verifiable. Unfortunately, he had publicly slurred the teaching profession; so, at least, the schoolmasters felt. They gave back in kind.

Writing to Combe, Mann claimed that the forces behind the controversy were the religious fanatics "who think it is necessary first to

[43] *Rejoinder to the "Reply,"* 4th section, p. 52   [44] *Ibid.,* p. 53.

put me down, that they may afterwards carry out their plans of introducing doctrines into our schools." He was convinced, he wrote, on the best authority that "an extensive conspiracy is now formed to break down the Board of Education, as a preliminary measure to teaching sectarianism in the schools." [45] The sectarian point of view was no doubt a factor in the minds of some of the masters, especially in regard to the disciplinary section of the *Remarks,* but Mann's analysis left out other important factors.

William Torrey Harris, discussing the controversy, has called attention to the fact that "every new movement in education has run the gauntlet of fierce and bitter opposition before adoption." Harris, in fact, pays tribute to the conspicuous ability of the conservative party in this and other school struggles and states that their penetrating criticism of innovation is what purifies "the gold from the dross in a large measure already before the stage of practical experiment has begun." He finally cautions us that "we are apt to become impatient and blame too severely the conservative party in Massachusetts." [46]

✦

The last public controversy, that with the Reverend Matthew Hale Smith, opened up no new problems but was rather a repetition in a somewhat shriller key of preceding debates over Bible-reading, the use of the rod, and religion in the common schools.[47] In a sermon preached before the Church and Society of the Pilgrims, in Boston, October 10, 1846, this very Orthodox divine spoke upon the "Increase of Intemperance: Crime and Juvenile Depravity—Its Cause and Cure." [48] The

[45] *Life and Works,* I, 228.

[46] Payson Smith, Winship, and Harris, *Horace Mann and Our Schools,* p. 24.

[47] Matthew Hale Smith remains an enigma. Certain Mann apologists have loaded him with abuse and attributed to him venal motives. Yet Smith had a considerable following. He gave his sermons in the most respected churches, and they were commented upon favorably by many of the religious journals of the day.

[48] Matthew Hale Smith, *The Bible, the Rod, and Religion.* Here are some of Smith's particulars: "Even now, in our best schools in this city, insubordination and licentiousness abound. They are developed in the circulation of obscene French prints in school, and in the efforts of girls in school to corrupt their associates. The boys and girls, some of them, have a room in this city, furnished with all that panders to base and wicked passions, where youth of both sexes, belonging to public schools, assemble at night." (Excerpt from the sermon, p. 12.)

root of much of this evil, said Smith, is found in the absence of good
home training and in the attempt made by those who have influence
over the young to amend the legislation of God. "Men, wise above
that which is written, have made common schools the theatre of their
experiments and labors." Sinister forces have attempted, and with par-
tial success, to do three things with the schools:

1. To get out of them the Bible and all religious instruction. 2. To abolish
the use of the rod, and all correction, but a little talk. 3. To make common schools a counterpoise to religious instruction at home and in Sabbath
schools.[49]

The Board of Education had abetted this work in two ways, Smith's
charge continued:

1. By allowing an individual, under the sanction of its authority, to disseminate through the land crude and destructive principles believed to be
at war with the Bible and with the best interests of the young for time
and eternity.
2. By a library which excludes books as sectarian that inculcate truths,
which *nine-tenths of professed Christians of all names believe,* while it
accepts others that inculcate the most deadly heresy—even universal salvation.[50]

Mann must have felt frustrated when he read this sermon in the
Boston *Recorder,* where it appeared after being delivered on two occasions by Smith. Here were all the old arguments trotted out once more,
arguments which he had had to cope with every year since taking
office. His first letter to Smith was calm enough. He tried to show that
the primary responsibility for Bible or moral instruction rested with
the local school committees and that, although it had no authority over
the local school, the board had labored to get the Bible *into* the common schools rather than *out* of them. He denied the charge that the
board had tried to abolish the use of the rod and repeated the points
he had made with the Boston schoolmasters. He defended the nonsectarian character of the school library and asked Smith to cite chapter and verse to prove his charge of "deadly heresy." [51]

Smith now shifted the grounds of his attack. He charged Mann
with promoting a system which would elevate "the intellectual over

[49] *Ibid.,* p. 11.   [50] *Ibid.*   [51] *Ibid.,* p. 24.

the moral, and man above God" in the schools; with opposing the use of the *whole* Bible as a school book; with opposing religious instruction in that he had ruled out truths and sanctions which nine tenths of professing Christians believed essential. He asked Mann if he favored the use of the rod as a "principle" (*sic*) means of enforcing obedience and stated that the library exerted an evil influence in calling "that religious which I do not." [52]

Under date of November 9, 1846, Mann again replied in a long-suffering vein. "If you have read my writings, you know that I have said, without qualification, without exception, and in so many words, that it is my belief that the Bible makes known to us the rule of life, and the means of salvation, and that it is my wish (I have no authority in the matter) that it should continue in our schools." [53]

Mann wearily repeated that he was in favor of the rod, not as a principal means, but as an auxiliary or supplementary means when other motives had failed.[54] He again asks Smith to name the books in the school library which breathe these terrible heresies. To Smith's accusation that Mann is opposed to religious instruction, Mann replies bluntly: "You do not understand so on any competent authority; and if you had examined the proper sources of information, you would have 'understood' precisely the reverse." Mann finishes this point, avowing that

every one who has availed himself of the means of arriving at the truth, on this point, knows that I am in favor of religious instruction in our schools, to the extremest verge to which it can be carried without invading those rights of conscience which are established by the laws of God, and guaranteed to us by the Constitution of the State.[55]

The legal exactness and careful precision of Mann's argumentation were lost on Smith. In reply to the November 9 letter the enterprising divine did not send Mann a reply but had his own 25-page answer published in booklet form along with the original sermon and other related articles. In the reply he strikes a new note concerning the Bible in the schools. Yes, Mann wants the Bible in the school, but this is a

[52] *Ibid.*, p. 27.   [53] *Ibid.*, p. 32.
[54] *Ibid.* Smith wrote "principle" for "principal" and Mann would not let him get away with such an orthographical slip.
[55] *Ibid.*, p. 33.

fiendish move aiming really to get the Bible out of the school. How?
Here are Smith's words:

You may introduce the Bible into every school in the State, yet if it goes
in under any other light than the Inspired Word of God—the rule of faith
and duty—a Book, "able to make men wise unto salvation"—a Book full
of inspired maxims, sustained by sanctions given by its author—if its
binding force is thrown off or impaired, your influence is against the Book
—it ceases to be the Bible, as Christians cherish it—its moral power is
gone.[56]

This breath-taking indictment concludes with Smith's voiced conviction that the man who rejects a part of the Bible must reject the
whole. The reason? Because the Bible claims *"entire inspiration."*
And he quotes St. Paul's statement to Timothy: *"All* Scripture is given
by the inspiration of God, and is *profitable* for doctrine." [57]

Smith's reply contains some strange passages. He tells Mann that
"in your letter, you demand that I shall sustain what I have said, from
what you have written. It may be difficult for me to do so, for you
may hold certain opinions that you do not choose to print. But is this
proof that you do not hold them, or that they are not destructive?" [58]
Mann, or anyone else for that matter, would have found it difficult
to answer this or the next statement: "I must be allowed to prove my
position by calling to the stand such proof as I may think proper." [59]
Smith can think of no plan more effective to get the Bible ultimately
out of the schools than that which "rejects a part as not true, and
another part as not fit to be read. The bitterest enemy the Bible ever
had, could do no more—would ask no more—than this. You condemn
the Bible out of its own mouth. Those who believe and so teach, are
displacing the Bible for human codes of ethics." [60]

Was Horace Mann open to valid criticism here for his views on
selective Bible-reading in the schools? Four years earlier in his Fourth
of July Oration given in Boston, Mann had given voice to a favorite
theme of his that the "lives of great and good men should have been
held up for admiration and example; and especially the life and

---

[56] *Ibid.,* pp. 36–37.

[57] His reference: Second Epistle to Timothy, III:16. Smith here is taking the
Catholic position.

[58] *The Bible, the Rod, and Religion,* p. 38.   [59] *Ibid.*

[60] *Ibid.,* p. 39.

character of Jesus Christ, as the sublimest pattern of benevolence, of purity, of self-sacrifice, ever exhibited to mortals." He then laid down a principle to which Matthew Hale Smith and many more reasonable critics might have had legitimate objection:

In every course of studies, all the practical and preceptive parts of the Gospel should have been sacredly included; and all dogmatical theology and sectarianism sacredly excluded. In no school should the Bible have been opened to reveal the sword of the polemic, but to unloose the dove of peace.[61]

Once more we see that Mann viewed Christianity as almost exclusively an ethical religion—a practical and preceptive guide for moral conduct. Smith was more right than he knew in asserting that the secretary did not hold the Orthodox belief in the inspiration of the Bible. To his sister Lydia, Mann had once written:

What we learn from books, even what we think we are taught in the Bible, may be mistake or misapprehension; but the lessons we learn from our own consciousness are the very voice of the Being that created us; and about it can there be any mistake? [62]

Several years after the rancor of the Smith dispute had faded away Mann wrote to his wife from Washington: "I agree with you that history is bad reading for children. What, then, must be thought of a great part of the Old Testament, which records as terrible crimes as any to be found on record? It is too terrible a world to make children acquainted with." [63] Mann, then, did not subscribe to the rigid fundamentalist position on private interpretation of the Bible. At the dedication of Antioch College he amplified his position:

For the true interpretation of by far the greater and more essential part of this book, we need only a common degree of intelligence, a conscience void of offence, and that fear of the Lord which is the beginning of wisdom. But for the interpretation of some other parts, all forms of knowledge become needed auxiliaries—scientific, literary, historical, ethical—philology, philosophy, jurisprudence, government; in fine, a knowledge of all those departments of the universe, including our own bodies and minds, which illustrate and exemplify the power, wisdom, and goodness of God.[64]

[61] *Life and Works,* IV, 365–66.   [62] *Ibid.,* I, 51.
[63] *Letter to Mary Mann,* July 27, 1852, *ibid.,* I, 376.
[64] Reply to Bible Presentation at Antioch College, *ibid.,* V, 310–11.

Smith next objects to the theological character of the Mann theory
of school discipline and claims that Mann, in advocating his position,
is fully as sectarian as he charges Smith and the Orthodox are. The
shaft is not completely off target, despite the clumsy marksmanship.
More will be said on this later. With a stroke of your pen, says Smith,
you dispose of certain fundamental truths which are at the base of the
scheme of redemption. You assume the native purity of children, in
opposition to the Bible, which asserts that our race are "by nature,
children of wrath." On this *sectarian* assumption, you build your
theory to abolish the rod, but I advocate the use of the rod because
God sanctions it in the Bible. You also settle one of the gravest questions in theology when you affirm that punishment is simply for the
good of the punished.[65] It was an easy task for Mann to dispose of
this twisted piece of Calvinism by a *reductio ad absurdum*. Let all
children, then, without exception be flogged—hour by hour, day and
night, all through their lives.[66]

On the other hand, the charge that Mann himself was sectarian will
not easily down. The Reverend Mr. Smith recalls the constitutional
mandate that schoolmasters teach the principles of piety. But, asks
Smith, "who is to judge what those principles are? How they shall be
taught? By what sanctions they shall be enforced? Who shall decide
what sectarianism is?" Smith presses the issue:

Who, speaking by authority, shall proclaim what we may teach, what we
may not, of religion in schools? You have already done this, by authority,

[65] *The Bible, the Rod, and Religion*, p. 42. The Boston *Recorder* (Jan. 14,
1847) put Smith's argument more cogently: "As to the matter of religious instruction in common schools, the honorable Secretary notoriously occupies
ground, which meets the ardent approbation of all that class of religionists, who
'believe Christianity in general, but disbelieve it in particular.' Everything is
sectarianism with him, except what squares exactly with the notions of Universalists and those who have been absurdly called 'pious deists' and theophilanthro-
pists. Teach one jot of truth more, and you are sectarian, and shall lose your
school, or your school shall lose its proportion of the public fund for education.
What is this, but to establish by law, that Universalism and Deism, which are
much the same, only that Universalism pretends to have rather more respect for
the Bible than Deism does, shall be the State religion, taught by public authority,
to the exclusion of the views of evangelical dissenters of every name?"

[66] The first law of exegesis, as it is of historical criticism, is to present *all* the
pertinent texts that bear on the point. It is folly to attempt the erection of a
theory of education on a single text of the Bible.

or without it. Certain views that you entertain, you call religion, or "piety." These you allow to be taught in schools, you enforce them in your lectures, reports, and Journal. Those which clash with your peculiar views, you reject as "dogmatic theology," or "sectarianism." [67]

Smith cites specific instances to establish his general charge:

If I may not teach native depravity in schools, because the Constitution forbids it, may you teach native holiness? If I may not teach the doctrine of Election, as explained in Rom. ix., may you so pervert and misapply I John, iv, 18, as you have done, to sustain your view of no corporal punishment? If I may not teach the strict Divinity of Jesus Christ, from John i, 18, may you so teach his humanity as to contradict the Word of Inspiration that he was "God manifest in the flesh"? If I may not warn children of future punishment, as I read Matt. xxv, may you teach that there is no punishment after death?

It is proper to keep dogmatic theology out of school. Let it be kept out on both sides—the dogmatism of unbelief, as well as the dogmatism of belief.[68]

Matthew Hale Smith has suffered, perhaps deservedly, from historians of these controversies. It is hard to absolve him from charges of unfairness in some of his argumentation. But on this particular point of Mann's dogmatism and sectarianism he scores well. This is not to argue the validity of his plea for teaching "New Light" Calvinism in the *common* schools of Massachusetts. Such a course of action would have been highly undesirable, in fact impossible. Horace Mann rightly saw that in a pluralistic society religious freedom would be impaired if the theology of the dominant group were imposed upon all who would frequent the common school. And yet in his vigorous efforts to prevent sectarian control of the school systems he had to take a number of theological positions which, when summed up, come very close to a description of Unitarianism or the religious aspects of deistic phrenology.

Smith charged him with substituting "for the principles of piety allowed by the Constitution, nothing above, nothing more than Deism, bald and blank." [69] Mann, however, as far as the historical record re-

---

[67] *The Bible, the Rod, and Religion*, p. 44.   [68] *Ibid.*, pp. 48–49.
[69] The *Recorder* leaped in again with an editorial (Jan. 14, 1847): "It is time to ask, why the Commonwealth should continue to pay a man a bountiful salary, to enable him to revolutionize our excellent system of education; to remodel it

veals, remained throughout his life insensitive to accusations of this sort. Mann was so sincerely convinced of his religious philosophy— and of its Christian basis—that he could be impervious to charges of "deism" or "atheism." After all, the early Christian martyrs had been derided by the pagan mobs as "atheists" because they refused to worship *all* the gods.

✦

When pressed by Smith regarding his policy on the Bible, Mann fell back upon an argument to which he had appealed frequently during his career as secretary. His theory was simply that "the Bible shall go into our public schools enshielded from harm, by the great Protestant doctrine of the inviolability of conscience, the right and the sanctity of private judgment, without note or interpreter." When in his *Seventh Annual Report* he praised the Prussian system for its attention to the Bible, Mann explained that the sectarian tendency was absent there because the "teacher being amply possessed of a knowledge of the whole chain of events, and of all biographical incidents; and bringing to the exercise a heart glowing with the love to man, and with devotion to his duty as a former of character of children, has no necessity or occasion to fall back upon the formulas of a creed." [70] With this ideal, Mann contrasted the teacher who, because he lacks knowledge of the wonderful works of God and of Providence, is "constrained to recur again and again, to the few words or sentences of his form of faith, whatever that faith may be."

In the *Eleventh Annual Report* the secretary describes the universal use of the Bible in commonwealth schools. Then he again recites the argument, so plain in his own eyes, that whoever "believes in the

---

after the plans of transcendental dreamers and perfectibility men; to publish controversial pamphlets against 'Boston Masters,' and all others who shall dare to object to his sweeping innovations; and to carry out a subtle contrivance for supplanting the inculcation of the piety of the gospel, by means of a deistical scheme of morals, foisted in by the help of garblings of the Bible and the popular cry of 'no sectarianism.' Is there no danger in investing a man with the power of deciding officially, who is a sectary, and who is not—what is piety and what is not—what is catholic, and what is schismatical—how far the Bible shall be admitted, and how far it must be disallowed?"

[70] *Seventh Annual Report*, p. 125.

Sacred Scriptures, has his belief, in form and in spirit, in the schools; and his children read and hear the words themselves which contain it." By introducing the Bible, the local authorities "introduce what all its believers hold to be the rule of faith and practice; and although by excluding a peculiarity which one denomination believes to be true, they do but exclude what other denominations believe to be erroneous." [71]

In his valedictory report, the Twelfth, Mann most thoroughly treats of the Bible as the great means to mold character in the common schools.[72] This is his final official act and he is at pains in this report to vindicate himself and the board against the long series of charges and insinuations that the system they had been advocating was "an irreligious, or anti-Christian, or an un-Christian system." Everyone admits, says Mann, that since our public schools are not intended to be theological seminaries, the law debars them from inculcating the peculiar and distinctive doctrines of any one religious denomination. But "our system earnestly inculcates all Christian morals; it founds its morals on the basis of religion; it welcomes the religion of the Bible; and, in receiving the Bible, it allows it to do what it is allowed to do in no other system,—*to speak for itself.*" [73]

Mann's next statement is the classical Protestant position: "The Bible is the acknowledged expositor of Christianity. In strictness, Christianity has no other authoritative expounder." [74]

Hinsdale calls Mann's position "perfectly unassailable, save from two points of view." The first is the "Catholic doctrine that the Church is the foundation of all sound teaching in morals and in religion, and private judgment is a deadly error." The second is the "thesis put forward by those persons who contend that the Bible itself is a sectarian book standing on the same ground as the Koran or the Vedas." [75] This is a remarkable oversimplification. To say nothing at all of the Catholic

---

[71] *Life and Works,* IV, 177.

[72] Mann gives pp. 98–144 (*Twelfth Annual Report,* facsimile ed.) to a discussion of religious education. This is excellent reading. There is hardly an argument advanced today on either side of the question of religion in public education that is not anticipated in this report.

[73] *Ibid.,* pp. 116–17.   [74] *Ibid.,* p. 121.

[75] Hinsdale, *Horace Mann and the Common School Revival,* p. 225.

objection, which Hinsdale only imperfectly represents, his analysis seems to ignore the fact that the principle of private interpretation was the precise source of these many years of conflict between Mann and his Protestant critics.[76]

The question whether the Bible was itself a sectarian book did not arise, it is true, during Mann's tenure of office, but in the *Twelfth Report* Mann indicates that he is aware of the possible difficulty. This is part of his proof that his system is a truly Christian one. He says:

If the Bible is in the schools, we can see a reason why a Jew, who disbelieves in the mission of our Savior; or a Mahomedan who believes in that of the Prophet, should desire, by oral instruction, or catechism, or otherwise, to foist in his own views, and thereby smother all conflicting views; but even they would not dare to say that the schools where the Bible was found, were either anti-Christian or un-Christian. So far from this, if they were candid, they would acknowledge that the system of Christianity was in the schools, and that they wished to neutralize and discard it, by hostile means.[77]

Horace Mann seemingly could never understand how Christian critics of his system could interpret it as anti-Christian or un-Christian. In the same report he again patiently tries to explain:

If the Bible, then, is the exponent of Christianity; if the Bible contains the communications, precepts, and doctrines, which make up the religious system, called and known as Christianity; if the Bible makes known those truths, which, according to the faith of Christians, are able to make men wise unto salvation; and if this Bible is in the schools how can it be said that Christianity is excluded from the schools; or how can it be said that the school system, which adopts and uses the Bible, is an anti-Christian, or an un-Christian system? [78]

[76] Compulsory Bible-reading in the common schools was a major Catholic grievance in the school controversy of 1840 in New York. Fr. John Power, spokesman for Archbishop John Hughes, stated it this way: "The Holy Scriptures are read every day, with the restriction that no specific tenets are to be inculcated. Here we find the great demarcation principle between the Catholic Church and the Sectaries introduced silently. The Catholic Church tells her children they must be taught by *authority*. The Sectaries say, read the Bible, judge for yourselves. The Protestant principle is therefore acted upon, slyly inculcated, and the schools are Sectarian." The New York *Freeman's Journal*, July 11, 1840, cited in Connors, *Church-State Relationships*, p. 56.

[77] *Twelfth Annual Report*, p. 123.   [78] *Ibid.*, p. 122.

His personal interpretation of biblical fundamentalism, furthermore, seemed to Horace Mann the only one compatible with science. He insists that just as "science is the interpreter of Nature" inasmuch as "it reverently inquires: it listens to know; it seeks; it knocks to obtain communication; and then all that it does is reverently to record Nature's processes, and accept them as true"—so science demands that "religion shall proceed on similar exegetical principles." [79] Therefore when religion proclaims that she has a revelation from God recorded in a book called the Bible, and that that book is therefore the very speech and utterance of God, and when "God thus rises to speak from his own book, whether in the family, in the school, or the church," science declares that it is not only inconsistent, but "impious, for any man or any body of men to rush forward and push him—Jehovah,—aside, and then read some government-prepared or man-prepared articles, as containing a better announcement of God's will, a superior exposition of His attributes than He, the all-wise, was himself about to announce." [80] "How can science," asks Mann, "ever coalesce and cooperate with any such form of religion as that, which repudiates its own chosen and sovereign authority, vetoes its acknowledged law-giver, and forges a code of its own, which it attempts to pass off in the very presence, and to the very Being who, having issued the original, must know the counterfeit?" [81]

There are today still unresolved difficulties in this position and its assumption of Protestant Christian unity around the Bible. Under the conditions of those times, however, almost any other position but Mann's compromise would have meant the disintegration of the common school—at least as we know it today. He kept the Christian Bible in the schools but would not permit the sects to interpret it. A general Christian influence should permeate the schools but any specific sectarian influence was to be shut out. [82]

In summation it might be well to itemize here the central ideas which make up Horace Mann's philosophy of character education.

[79] "Demands of the Age on Colleges," *Life and Works,* V, 451.

[80] *Ibid.* Compare this same thought as expressed in the *Twelfth Annual Report,* p. 130.

[81] "Demands of the Age on Colleges," *Life and Works,* V, 451.

[82] See Hinsdale, *Horace Mann and the Common School Revival,* p. 232.

All of these "theses," as we might call them, appear over and over in the Annual Reports, in his speeches on education and religion, in his private journals, and in articles in the *Common School Journal*. At the age of forty-one, when Mann accepted the post of secretary of the Massachusetts board, these ideas were already fixed permanently in his philosophy of education. A study of his complete writings does not reveal any notable differences between, let us say, the thought in the first reports and in the talks on education he gave to teacher gatherings in Ohio during the last years of his life. His conviction of the validity of these ideas, however, did deepen with age and experience.

The Mann theses might be stated as follows:

1. The principal aim of education is the development of the child's moral and religious character. There should be no attempt to separate morality and religion, i.e., the "nonsectarian" or "natural" religion.

2. Character formation is the direct responsibility of the common school; in fact, the common school is the most perfect agency for such formation.

3. As much religious instruction must be given in the common school as is compatible with religious freedom. In teaching religion the school must not favor any one sect in the community but should inculcate the generally agreed upon moral and religious beliefs of Christianity. The sectarian spirit is by every means to be shunned.

4. Natural religion (i.e., the "religion of heaven" as opposed to man-made creedal religions) means obedience to all of God's laws—physical, moral, spiritual, religious. This is the true substance of Christianity, whose primary law is the Golden Rule.

5. The Bible, without note or interpreter, is the means par excellence of realizing this primary aim of education because it breathes God's laws and presents illustrious examples of conduct, above all that of Jesus Christ.

✦

Love for humanity, the Golden Rule, the social betterment of the race, were for Horace Mann the genuine coin of religion. This meant *doing* for one's fellows rather than preoccupying one's self with private prayer and worship. "Christ," he said, "never wrote a 'Tract' in his life, but he went about doing good. His professed followers write 'Tracts' but stay in their luxurious homes, while the hungry, the naked, the sick, and the prisoner are left as Lazarus was by Dives." [83]

This humanitarianism, of course, characterized many nineteenth-century movements. The deists, phrenologists, transcendentalists, universalists, the followers of Locke, Bentham, Swedenborg, and Comte, all tended, consciously or unconsciously, to replace supernatural religion by the service of humanity. The haunting memories of youth rather than any native lack of devotion inclined Mann further in this direction.

Religious contemplation, however, did have a definite place. So far as we can thence derive strength in the performance of our duties, Mann said, we have a duty to contemplate the perfect nature of God and the example of Jesus Christ. And "should we be translated to a world where our fellow-beings can no longer be benefited by our efforts, then, indeed, it would be our duty and our pleasure to regard the supreme perfection with supreme love." [84] He concludes the thought with these words: "But, while we are on earth, the burden of our duties is towards man"—this for Mann is the "entire texture of the New Testament." [85]

He distrusted all human authority in matters of religion. This was derogatory to reason and intelligence and resulted in substituting sectarianism for "the laws." Hence his statement that "the only religion, therefore, with which science will freely and rejoicingly consent to live and work, is an unsectarian religion. Any other union is forced and unnatural, involving discord, dishonest compliances, and a suspension of progress in the pursuit of truth." [86]

Horace Mann was intensely sincere in his personal belief and public dedication to ethical Christianity. In the final report he made of his stewardship of the Massachusetts schools he quotes once more the 1827

[83] "Demands of the Age on Colleges," *Life and Works,* V, 432.

[84] *Life and Works,* I, 50.

[85] *Ibid.* Mann's next sentence is fascinating: "Where else in the whole book is there such anxious repetition as in one of the last injunctions of Christ?—'lovest thou me? If thou lovest me, feed my lambs;' and again, 'If thou lovest me, feed my sheep;' and again, the third time, 'Feed my sheep.'" Catholics interpret this same text as a bestowal of the spiritual primacy in Christ's Church upon Simon Peter, the first Pope.

[86] "Demands of the Age on Colleges," *ibid.,* V, 450,

law enjoining all teachers to inculcate "the principles of piety, justice
and a sacred regard to truth, love to their country, humanity and universal benevolence, sobriety, industry, and frugality, chastity, moderation, and temperance, and those other virtues which are the ornament
of human society, and the basis upon which a republican constitution
is founded." [87] And then he inquires:

Are not these virtues and graces part and parcel of Christianity? In other
words, can there be Christianity without them? While these virtues and
these duties towards God and man, are inculcated in our schools, any
one who says that the schools are anti-Christian or un-Christian, expressly
affirms that his own system of Christianity does not embrace any one of
this radiant catalogue; that it rejects them all; that it embraces their opposites! [88]

Now there is a flaw in this logic. Mann's words could be turned back
upon him quite neatly:

Are not these same virtues and graces part and parcel of Confucianism?
In other words, can there be Confucianism without them? While these
virtues and these duties towards God and man, are inculcated in our
schools, any one who says that the schools are anti-Confucian or un-
Confucian, expressly affirms that his own system of Confucianism does not
embrace any one of this radiant catalogue; that it rejects them all; that it
embraces their opposites!

The point, of course, one that never seems to have entered Mann's
head, is that his system of a moralistic nature religion could as well
have been based upon the Koran, the Vedas, or the maxims of Con-
fucius. Perhaps this is one of its virtues. For there is an intrinsic contradiction in the Massachusetts law of 1827, and all similar laws, which
makes their strict enforcement an impossibility. The Massachusetts
law stated that nothing favorable to any sect or tenet could be taught
in the common schools. If this means anything, it means that there is
not a single religious belief or moral practice of one group in society
which could not be challenged in law by another group. If, for example, Sect A believes in a Triune God, the contradictory belief of
Sect B (which does not) cancels out belief in a Triune God. The
common school must remain silent here. Similarly with other religious

[87] *Twelfth Annual Report*, p. 123.   [88] *Ibid.*

propositions, such as the resurrection and miracles of Jesus Christ; the nature of the "church"; the eternity of God; the existence of divinely appointed sanctions. This holds also for any ethical pattern involving marriage, divorce, birth control, gambling, drinking, blood transfusions, vaccination, nudity, flag saluting, military service, etc., etc. An affirmation of any of these items would work in favor of a group which advocated the belief or ethical practice in question—which inexorably means that it would work against any group holding the contradictory position. Fortunately, there are always compromises quietly accepted by society which mitigate the rigors of legal logic and save us from our rationalized irrationalities.

The system of compromise on the religious issue of which Mann was the principal advocate incidentally did set in motion a process which has resulted in the legal secularization of most modern public school education. Today Mann would be severely criticized by some groups who have concerned themselves with the question of moral and spiritual values in the public schools for their children. These groups, more faithfully applying Mann's principle, would indict his system for not providing for the non-Protestant Christian, the non-Christian, or the nonbeliever. The assumption of general Protestant or Christian unity that Mann followed was of questionable validity even during his years as secretary.

Horace Mann fought to exclude anything distinctively sectarian from the Massachusetts schools, but in so doing he consciously and unconsciously promoted his own kind of "common-denominator" Christianity. Sectarian Christianity was to be excluded on the principle that in a divided Christian community the religious freedom of all could be safeguarded only by eliminating doctrines and practices offensive to any one group in the community. A second principle, however, was also operative in his policy. This was his lifelong conviction of the inherently evil nature of sectarianism. Yet Mann wanted neither atheism nor religious neutralism in the schools. In the *Twelfth Annual Report* he wrote:

Among the infinite errors and enormities, resulting from systems of religion devised by man, and enforced by the terrors of human government, have been those dreaded reactions, which have abjured all religion, spurned its obligations, and voted the Deity into non-existence. This extreme is, if possible, more fatal than that by which it was produced.[89]

Horace Mann helped to establish a principle which, granted the dilemma of inculcating a unifying value philosophy in institutions designed to serve a heterogeneous religious population, has kept our common school system in existence. He wrote:

Between these extremes, philanthropic and godly men have sought to find a medium which should avoid both the evils of ecclesiastical tyranny, and the greater evils of atheism. And this medium has at length been supposed to be found. It is promulgated in the great principle, *that government should do all that it can to facilitate the acquisition of religious truth; but shall leave the decision of the question, what religious truth is, to the arbitrament, without human appeal, of each man's reason and conscience.*[90]

The principle turned out to be only a compromise, for the "medium" between sectarianism and atheism became in practice a form of sectarianism which did not long satisfy even the more liberal religious groups. Nonetheless, Mann's intuition of the principle and his long fight to realize it are his great contribution to our modern philosophy of character education for "common" schools in a religiously pluralistic society. Whether the principle can ever be satisfactorily applied is a question that history, at least in the United States, has not yet answered.

[89] *Ibid.,* pp. 110–11.   [90] *Ibid.* Emphasis added.

PART THREE

WILLIAM TORREY HARRIS

1835–1908

V. NEW ENGLAND AND ST. LOUIS

The similarities in the lives of Horace Mann and William Torrey Harris are striking. In a score of ways the paths of these two educators followed the same patterns as they progressed toward similar goals. Both were Yankees of Congregationalist upbringing who revolted from traditional orthodoxy and yet remained deeply religious. Both showed interest in the scientific and pseudoscientific philosophies of the day, particularly phrenology. Both attracted the attention of the educational world through a series of masterly reports, prepared in discharge of high supervisory offices, which are still regarded as models. Both carried on their educational work on the Atlantic seaboard as well as in the newer West. Both wrote extensively and lectured widely on education and related topics. Both enjoyed the high esteem of their school contemporaries. The policies toward religion and character formation for the public schools that they advocated made them both the center of controversy. Both, finally, had a profound and lasting influence on the American philosophy of public education.

Nicholas Murray Butler has said that "the history of American education and of our American contributions to philosophical thought cannot be understood or estimated without knowledge of the life work of Dr. William Torrey Harris." [1] As early as 1888 Harris was called "the most potent influence upon the public school system and the teachers of America." [2]

This tribute is typical of many offered him by leaders in education:

As United States Commissioner of Education he was the most eminent philosophical, professional, educational official of the world. No other American public school official except Horace Mann has commanded respect in official circles throughout the world as did he. No other American has received anything approaching the almost idolatrous worship of America's public school men which he received during the years in which he was the official professional leader of the school people of the United States.[3]

Finally, James L. Hupp, while granting that "it may be unjust to name a period for one man when there were so many others who contributed to the progress of education during the same years," nevertheless insisted that one seemed justified in using Harris's name to represent the last quarter of the nineteenth-century period in American education.[4]

Along with the similarities in the careers of Mann and Harris there are at the same time notable differences, many of them the result of the changing patterns of American civilization which characterized the two periods. Harris saw a different type of public school taking shape out of the incorporation of millions of immigrants into American life, the rapid change-over to a predominantly urban civilization, the emergence of America as an industrial power, and the binding of the last great ties between the East and the West. Many of the problems that he had to meet were either different, or their context demanded different solutions, from those of Mann's day. This is part of the meaning of Merle Curti's statement that while it was Mann (along

---

[1] Nicholas Murray Butler, in foreword to Leidecker, *Yankee Teacher*.

[2] Kasson, "William Torrey Harris, LL.D.," *Education*, VIII (June, 1888), 619.

[3] Winship, "Friends and Acquaintances: William Torrey Harris," *Journal of Education*, CI (May 28, 1925), 603. In this article Winship, then state superintendent of Massachusetts schools, tells how he arranged to have President Harrison appoint Dr. Harris to the U.S. commissionership. Leidecker (*Yankee Teacher*, pp. 456–62) disputes this.

[4] "William Torrey Harris," in *Ten Famous American Educators*, ed. by John L. Clifton, p. 188. Harris spoke 145 times to NEA-sponsored national assemblies —a record total. See Wesley, *NEA: The First Hundred Years*, p. 48.

with Henry Barnard) "who laid the foundations of the American public school system, it was William T. Harris who presided over the rearing of the structure." [5]

Although the distinctive schemes of values advocated by the two men for the common school were conditioned in great part by a different *Zeitgeist*, the distinctions are even more attributable to personal philosophies. Both men were philosophers of social reform, though Harris dwelt more in the world of the mind than in the school world itself. Yet he was no ivory-tower contemplative. He was responsible in large measure for the inclusion today of art and music, scientific and manual studies in the curriculum. He fought for and established successful high schools when such institutions were still not universally accepted. He made the individual school library a normal tool in the school.[6] It was Harris who brought Susan E. Blow to the Des Peres School in St. Louis and made the kindergarten an integral part of the public school system.[7] It is as the philosopher of education, however, that he is best remembered. Harris was more broadly educated, was more enlightened, than Mann, and possessed what Butler has called "the one truly great philosophical mind which has yet appeared on the western continent." [8]

✦

William Torrey Harris was born in 1835 at North Killingly, Connecticut. Both sides of his family, the Torreys and the Harrises, were justly proud of their place in New England history. William was a pupil first in the town school and then, in 1844 when the family moved from their farm to Providence, in the city school system there. After he had reached thirteen he attended various New England academies —as he put it, "say, one term each at five different academies." He tells how, during this period, he became entranced with the sublime poetic form of Milton's *Paradise Lost,* and "eagerly studied its view

---

[5] Curti, *Social Ideas of American Educators,* p. 310.

[6] Cook, *William Torrey Harris in the Saint Louis Public Schools, passim.*

[7] Blow, "In Memoriam, Dr. William T. Harris," *Kindergarten Review,* XX, (Dec., 1909), 260. The lady records her great esteem in the Harris obituary.

[8] Letter to Charles M. Perry, Nov. 7, 1929. Quoted in Perry, ed., *The St. Louis Movement,* p. 51. Dr. Perry has here assembled some letters and testimonials from surviving members and spectators of the St. Louis Movement.

of the world, Calvinist as I was by family and church education." [9]

He must have been an extraordinarily gifted youngster, for he later wrote:

I taught school in the country for two winter sessions, after my third and fifth academical terms respectively. I used my winter evenings in study. During the first winter, at the age of sixteen years I mastered geometry and trigonometry. The second winter I devoted entirely to Locke's "Essay on the Human Understanding," having read somewhere that Franklin prided himself on reading that work at my age.[10]

Harris confessed that at first it was incomparably dull reading, but "bringing into requisition the discipline of mind that I had acquired at Andover, I soon became really interested in Locke's refutation of innate ideas."

He entered Yale in 1854, but before the end of his junior year he was to turn his back upon formal schooling and New England and head west to St. Louis. During the Yale years he underwent what he styled *Die Aufklärung*—"that clearing up which arrives when one breaks away from use and wont, throws off adherence to blind authority, and begins to think for himself." [11] He began to read with avidity a class of literature whose chief interest was its protest against some phase or other of authority. This class would include geological books offering a rationalist interpretation of Genesis and astronomical books hinting of some far-off nebular condition of the universe at variance with the scriptures.[12]

Phrenological books and magazines, too, he found fascinating, professing as they did "to find a natural basis for an inventory of the powers of the mind, and, consequently, an ideal standard of perfect development which would serve as a basis for criticism of all human views and actions." [13] During this period Harris was brimming with the "exhilaration of the reformer who sees the evils of the past and knows the true remedy." This *élan* propelled him successively into "mesmerism, spiritualism, water-cure, vegetarianism, socialism, and all manner of reform." But still it was to phrenology that he turned

[9] "How I Was Educated," *Forum*, I (Aug., 1886), 558.
[10] *Ibid.*, pp. 559–60.
[11] "Books That Have Helped Me," *Forum*, III (April, 1887), 142.
[12] *Ibid.*, p. 143.   [13] *Ibid.*

with the most eager expectation in what he called his "era of hobbies." He found Fowler's *Memory and Intellectual Improvement* a help in strengthening his memory.[14] In the winter of 1856–57, however, during his third year in college, he became acquainted with a man, Amos Bronson Alcott, who was to become a lifelong inspiration and friend, and who decisively changed the course of the young man's thought.[15]

In their first conversations Harris found that Alcott's "Pythagorean views of diet were attractive, and his doctrine of the light and dark temperaments seemed to be in conformity with the principles that phrenology taught." [16] The gentle mystic of Concord stirred something within the novice-philosopher with the "glad tidings" of transcendentalism. Harris was tired, he later wrote, of "commonplace and of the new 'isms' that I had taken up all related to external matters. They were reforms of the outward dress, new fashions of clothing, but not reforms that led to new mounts of vision. They did not unfold the possibility of infinite growth in insight or will-power." [17] He was developing a distaste for the "long-haired men and short-haired women"—the crowd of reformers who had originally so impressed him.

His youthful mind was soon aware of the materialistic limitations of phrenology, and he began to chide the phrenologists for their failure to see the consequences of their own definition of faculties. He wrote:

They are so engrossed with making out the map of protuberances on the cranium, that they give slight attention to a study of the intellectual relation of mental powers that are supposed to dwell in the convolutions underneath those protuberances.[18]

[14] *Ibid.* Orson Fowler was one of the most famous propagators of the flamboyant type of phrenology.

[15] Alcott came to look upon Harris as his spiritual heir. He wanted Harris to undertake "a biographical account of him when he should complete his earthly career" and dictated to him "an inventory of his spiritual real estate." (Sanborn and Harris, *A. Bronson Alcott, His Life and Philosophy,* II, 553.)

[16] *Ibid.,* p. 546.   [17] *Ibid.,* p. 549.

[18] *Ibid.,* p. 547. A study of the pages mentioned from this book by Sanborn and Harris will convince anyone of the falsity of the statement that Harris was a proponent of the "faculty" psychology of Christian Wolff (1679–1754) and Thomas Reid (1710–96).

The phrenologists cultivated the mental faculties "rather as muscles than as spiritual sources of power." Inasmuch as the founders of phrenology scarcely knew even the superficial features of the faculties of reflection, how could they tell their disciples, he asks, "what steps must be followed to gain the higher powers of insight?" He himself now set out on a new intellectual tack. "The doctrine of Transcendentalism," he says, "was just the most needed step in my culture. The obscure depths were illuminated, and I began my descent below the surfaces and illusions of common sensuous experience and tradition." [19]

Alcott's doctrine of preexistence and of the primordial creative power of the soul began "to work a revolution" within the young man. He was impressed by Alcott's deep conviction and concluded that idealism had much to recommend it and hence it was "worth my time to understand this strange doctrine, which turned topsy-turvy all our current views." [20]

As a consequence of his meeting with Alcott, Harris, on his return to Yale, avidly read Thoreau and Emerson. Having abandoned the simplicist view of the world of matter as ultimate reality, he began his lifelong dedication to philosophical idealism. He next sought out Alcott's *Orphic Sayings,* of which he made his own shorthand copy. The essays on "Calculus" and "Spirit and Matter" aroused "what there was in me of speculative power," and in pondering these mystical aphorisms his nascent idealism waxed strong. He considered these lines of Alcott written in gold:

The sensible world is Spirit in magnitude, outspread before the senses for their analysis, but whose synthesis is the soul herself, whose prothesis is God. Matter is but the confine of Spirit, limning her to sense. [21]

The stiff formalism of the Yale curriculum now palled upon his restless spirit. A farmer's son, he still hankered after the soil. [22] His

---

[19] *Ibid.,* p. 549. Later Harris in his idealism would veer away from the Platonism of Alcott and Emerson and swing closer to pure Hegelianism. There remained in him, however, a strong streak of New England transcendentalism. When U.S. Commissioner of Education he would preach it as one of the perennial values of liberal education, as in this excerpt from the Alcott memoir: "Transcendentalism means at bottom the emancipation of the soul from prosaic bondage to the present here and now. There shall be a perspective to our vision both in time and place. We inherit all ages and all countries; let us enter into our heritage." (*Ibid.,* pp. 596–97.)

[20] *Ibid.,* p. 550.   [21] Quoted in *ibid.,* p. 551.

[22] In the first "General Scrapbook" he kept during this period are articles on

brother John had already gone West, and Harris senior had been seeking a new homestead in the rich new farming lands of Illinois, Wisconsin, and Minnesota. William's health, never robust during his collegiate years, may also have influenced the decision to follow them. At any rate, he dropped out of school in the middle of his junior year, remarking that Yale had taught him all it could teach him. He settled down in St. Louis and provisionally supported himself by teaching the new Pitman shorthand method which he had acquired at Yale. In 1858 he took a position in the public school system of the city as an assistant teacher, and within ten years was superintendent of schools.

During his first days in St. Louis he wrote a description of himself back home to Sarah Bugbee, whom he was soon to make his wife. This intimate letter documents another phase in the twenty-two-year-old's philosophical development. To Sarah he writes: "I am a vegetarian and have been for three years and a half." He confesses, though, that several times he had experimented with meat "to test its effect on my system, which I find to be rather bad than otherwise." He avows himself a "freethinker and actor." He describes himself as "an eclectic in philosophy but with a leaning towards idealism." The letter contains more outpourings of his ebullient mind:

I am somewhat of a spiritualist. Nay, more, I am an entire believer in the spiritual nature of man and in the communication of man with the spirits who have put off the flesh. I totally disapprove of the sensual philosophy that ignores the intuitions of the soul. I love music, poetry and painting and sculpture. I love natural science, metaphysics, and above all theology. I am a phrenologist and moreover I write shorthand at the rate of about 100 words per minute. . . .

I am somewhat of an astronomer and moreover a geologist. I am no believer in the pretended powers of fortunetellers and yet I think that there are natural intuitions in the human soul called "premonitions." I think that the human soul is so great and its powers so mysterious that we scarcely know anything of it as yet.

I am not an atheist and yet I believe in no God as the popular mind does.[23]

---

farming in the West. Lectures and articles by Horace Mann and Theodore Parker were also pasted into the book.

[23] Letter cited in Leidecker, *Yankee Teacher*, pp. 83–84. The charge of atheism continually haunted Harris's circle. At his first meeting with the St. Louis philosophers, even Emerson jocosely called them his "German Atheists." *The Letters of Ralph Waldo Emerson,* ed. by Ralph L. Rusk, V, 514.

Through correspondence with his college friends Harris kept an ear open for any stirrings in the intellectual world back at Yale. To a classmate who had shown interest in Harris's conversion to idealism, he penned this note: "I want to make as many idealists as I can. It will be a splendid thing if I can open their eyes to the new life of the soul that appears. The pure reason has in store for them such rich treasures that they ought to come out of the poor understanding and arise into the regions of the truth of Plato and Emerson." [24]

✦

St. Louis, athwart the crossroads of America, was in 1857 the booming capital of America's frontier. Here was the beginning and end of the wagon-train routes to the West and Northwest over which crawled a thick traffic of men—homesteaders, gold diggers, missionaries, soldiers, colporteurs, and adventurers. Over the great water highway flowing past its doors the wealth of the North and South poured into St. Louis. Settlers, by the tens of thousands, streamed in from the older part of America and from Europe, to share in the city's "manifest destiny." St. Louis had a population in 1840 of 16,469; in 1850, 77,860; and in 1860, 160,773. For decades the name of this burgeoning city of the Mississippi Valley would be identified with that of William Torrey Harris. [25]

Denton J. Snider, with Harris one of the leaders of the cultural development known as the "St. Louis Movement," wistfully recalls their hopes in this passage from his memoirs:

This huge dreamy potentiality of civic grandeur we all believed to be quite on the point of pitching over into a colossal reality. Just that was the strongest, most pronounced trait of the town at this time: it clung to an unquestioning faith in its own indefeasible fortune. This was bound to come, and in a hurry; we did not even need to fight for our greatness, it would be forced upon us.

And we did not seriously fight for it, but with calm resignation awaited

[24] Letter of January 22, 1858, quoted in Leidecker, *Yankee Teacher*, p. 117.

[25] In his preface (*ibid.*, p. viii) Leidecker recounts the following anecdote: "A young man from Webster Groves, a soldier in the army, but interested in philosophy, met Henri Bergson not many years ago in Paris. In the course of conversation he mentioned that he came from St. Louis. 'Oh,' said Bergson, 'that is the city Dr. Harris made famous by his great insight into philosophy.' "

the resistless downpour of riches, population, and life's other blessings from the fascinated Gods. Such was the divine belief which became a kind of St. Louis religion, and entered deeply into the character of the city, of the individual citizens, not sparing the philosophers whose special claim was to pierce to the Pure Essences underneath all lying appearances.[26]

William Harris immediately fell in love with St. Louis and learned to love it more through one of his literary favorites, Goethe's *Wilhelm Meister*. He tells us that he "now left off reading books of mere protest" and began to realize that "the abstract independence of the spirit of protest is only a half-freedom, and in this respect not entitled to its assumption of airs of superiority over blind obedience to authority." [27] This for him was the lesson of *Wilhelm Meister*. He turned round from his attitude of carping criticism of the civilization in which he lived, and became "a sympathizing student of its means and purposes." He anticipated Frederick Jackson Turner's theme of the constructive spirit of the border:

Man finds raw nature before him, and is impelled to energetic activity to subdue the wilderness and transform it into a reflection of his will. Hence, on the frontier, man becomes a builder of civilization and has no leisure to criticize it. If he does not like his results he may easily change them, where all is so fluid; or he may accept them as the best he can realize under the circumstances. In the older communities there is a pressure from above that irritates the young man of much aspiration. Somebody else's will has already done what he would do. He does not find his place as a builder so easily as in the West. He uses his superfluous energies, therefore, in grumbling or even in active tearing down.[28]

The starting point of the St. Louis Movement, according to some historians, was the founding in January, 1866, of the St. Louis Philosophical Society.[29] But since this event, in turn, traced its origin back

[26] Snider, *The St. Louis Movement*, pp. 14–15.

[27] "Books That Have Helped Me," *Forum*, III (April, 1887), 145.

[28] *Ibid.* "There is perhaps no spot in America where during the last quarter of a century illustrations of the powers of the human mind over nature have been so numerous and so impressive as in St. Louis. In a city so young and so large, the geographical and commercial centre between west, east, and south, the inference that in a more than poetic sense thought is creative and man is the maker of the world, is not merely congenial, but to a certain degree spontaneous and irresistible." (G. Stanley Hall, "Philosophy in the United States," *Mind, IV* [Jan., 1879], 100.)

[29] There was a Kant Club and a Hegel Club as well as a Philosophical So-

eight years earlier to the meeting of William T. Harris with the many-sided genius Henry Conrad Brockmeyer, this juncture of talent can more truly be called the beginning.[30] Already through reading Theodore Parker, Harris had come under the influence of the "four great philosophic lights" that "had ascended into the sky to shine for ages." [31] These were, of course, Kant, Fichte, Schelling, and Hegel. Sharing Parker's own enthusiasm for German idealism, Harris had "resolved to devote so much of my life to the study of these writers as would suffice to enable me to think over their thoughts and see them as true, or else see their fallacies." His motive in this resolve? The awareness that he needed philosophy "in order to meet its attacks on my favorite 'ism,' phrenology." [32] Regardless of his earlier motive, the association with Brockmeyer was to animate and ennoble his resolve to devote himself to German philosophy.

Brockmeyer, unpolished and undisciplined though he was, had a rare brilliance. In the eyes of Harris he was a Plato reincarnate.[33] Harris, in fact, paid him the supreme compliment, calling him "a thinker of the same order of mind as Hegel." In the preface to his translation of Hegel's *Logic,* Harris writes that Brockmeyer

ciety. Pochmann seems to be right in saying that the Kant Club came first and out of it grew the Philosophical Society. The Hegel Club became defunct in 1866 when it was merged with the newly organized Philosophical Society. See Pochmann, *New England Transcendentalism and St. Louis Hegelianism,* p. 134.

[30] "Brockmeyer was a student of Kant, and an enthusiastic admirer of Hegel. Fresh from his studies, he became actuated with the spirit of modernism, of vocationalism, and determined to learn a trade. He selected that of a stovemolder; later, influenced by Thoreau, he lived as a hermit in the wood; then, reinvigorated, returned to St. Louis to enter the practice of law. He raised a regiment which served through the Civil War, and earned in later years the plaudits of all good citizens for his rugged honesty and his intellectual insight." (F. A. Fitzpatrick, in the *Educational Review* for January, 1910.) He also was elected Lieutenant-Governor of Missouri, wrote the state constitution, and was altogether a fabulous character.

[31] "Books That Have Helped Me," *Forum,* III (April, 1887), 144.

[32] *Ibid.,* pp. 144–45.

[33] Harris, too, was an object of veneration. "I met the other inspirer, I met the other man more intimately, who seemed to me to have walked out of the Paradise of Dante and who has been like the great St. John who, at the very last moment of the whole paradisiacal experience took Dante and showed him the illumination on the heavens above." (Louis J. Block, speaking in 1921 on the occasion of Denton Snider's eightieth birthday celebration, speech in D. H. Harris, *The Early St. Louis Movement,* p. 17.)

before reading Hegel, except the few pages in Hedge's *German Prose Writers,* had divined Hegel's chief ideas and the position of his system, and informed me on my first acquaintance with him in 1858 that Hegel was the great man among modern philosophers, and that his large logic was the work to get.[34]

Harris pays generous tribute also to Brockmeyer's "deep insights and his poetic power of setting them forth with symbols and imagery" which furnished him and his friends of those early years all of their outside stimulus in the study of German philosophy. Perhaps it was the practical side of Hegel and of Brockmeyer himself, or the happy combination of theoretical and practical, that best explains their appeal for the very alive young minds that made up the St. Louis Philosophical Society.

Harris records how impressed they all were with Brockmeyer's easy faculty of putting Hegel to work in everyday life. "Even the hunting of wild turkeys or squirrels was the occasion for the use of philosophy," and we used it, continues Harris, "to solve all problems connected with school-teaching and school management." [35] Politics and tactics, political parties, and the clash of armies gave them limitless raw material for the dialectic. Thus, according to the St. Louis Hegelians, Fort Sumter was the "thesis"; Camp Jackson, the "antithesis"; and Lincoln's declaration of war, the "synthesis." [36] Or in another triad, the illusory real-estate boom in St. Louis was the "thesis"; the founding of the St. Louis Philosophical Society, the "antithesis"; and the building of the great Eads Bridge across the Mississippi, the "synthesis." Even the keen rivalry with Chicago was squeezed into a triad, and many St. Louisans smugly viewed the disastrous Chicago fire of 1870 as initiating the phase of ultimate St. Louis triumph in the "synthesis." [37]

---

[34] *Hegel's Logic,* p. xii.   [35] *Ibid.,* p. xiii.

[36] Governor Jackson of Missouri, an ardent secessionist, set up Camp Jackson to train a state militia for the Confederacy. A hastily assembled little army of Unionists, almost all Germans, surprised and took Camp Jackson. This skirmish has been called the "first decisive fight for the Federal Union." In fact, the future course of the Civil War was partially determined here. Ulysses S. Grant and William Tecumseh Sherman were both in St. Louis at the time and were interested observers: one month later they asked for active duty and were wearing colonels' uniforms in the Union army. This explains why the Hegelians enshrined the Camp Jackson skirmish as "the first great St. Louis Deed."

[37] Snider (*The St. Louis Movement,* p. 75) tells how: "A searching test of our

Brockmeyer's room on St. Louis's east side was the first academe where the little band gathered for initiation into the gnosis of German idealism. Night after night under Brockmeyer's leadership they strove to unravel the skein. They pored over Kant's *Critique of Pure Reason* and then advanced to Hegel. For Brockmeyer had announced to his followers that they must go beyond New England transcendentalism. They must go beyond Kant to an even greater, to the culmination of the German philosophical movement—Hegel.[38]

The neophytes soon discovered that philosophy is a maiden who must be patiently wooed. Snider's roguish comment on this Hegelian phase could have been repeated by any of the group. He wrote that "my whole intellectual effort was concentrated upon acquiring the philosophy of the master and working it over into my own mentality, and even into my own vocabulary." And this went on for five or six years during which "I not only thought Hegel, but lived Hegel, was Hegel. All that I had ever known or done I Hegelized with a sort of desperation." [39]

---

hearts was offered by the great Chicago fire of 1870. Of course we with some public display sent money for the homeless and provisions for the hungry . . . but privately everywhere could be heard without unhappy tears the pious scriptural ejaculation: 'Again the fire of heaven has fallen upon Sodom and Gomorrah; may it complete its divinely appointed work!' " When the 1870 census was made public, and St. Louis's expected population was drastically below expectations, people wept with rage and charged that Chicago influence had corrupted the census-takers.

[38] Asked how that was to be accomplished, Brockmeyer already had the answer: "By following the precepts of Kant's criticism, Hegel's speculative logic, and Goethe's humanism as exemplified in *Faust,* which is the greatest literary embodiment of both and the greatest poem of all time." Snider, *A Writer of Books,* p. 391. Harris likewise admired the poem: "It is, if I am not mistaken, the most interesting event in literary history, that Goethe should conduct his hero from pantheistic agnosticism to Christian theism." In "Emerson's Relation to Goethe and Carlyle," in Sanborn, ed., *The Genius and Character of Emerson,* pp. 386–419.

[39] Snider, *The St. Louis Movement,* p. 119. The hunger for philosophy was widespread. D. H. Harris (*The Early St. Louis Movement,* p. 20) tells of one group in Illinois, "The Quincy School of Philosophy," under the guidance of Samuel Emery. They had gotten their hands on a copy of Brockmeyer's manuscript translation of Hegel's *Logic* and "they were studying, these men and women, business men leaving their business, women leaving their various avocations and coming together once a week in Quincy to study the logic of Hegel." This was an outgrowth of the St. Louis Movement.

In his turn, Harris writes that it took him a full year to break through the shell of Kant's *Critique* to the kernel. But the experience was a rewarding one, for he calls this a real epoch in his life and even states that "it seemed to me that I had just begun to find life worth living." He refers to this year as an intellectual step "as great as the whole step from birth up to the time I began to study Kant." [40] He found Fichte and Hegel, however, more difficult to comprehend than Kant.

Two works of Hegel impressed him more deeply than all other books: the *Logic* and the *Lectures on the Philosophy of History*. His feeling in reading the *Logic,* he wrote, was that of "being ushered into a sort of high court of reason, in which all ideas of the mind are summoned to the bar and put on trial." Harris speaks in the tones of a full-throated idealism in these lines:

The mental atmosphere of the book has a quieting and soothing effect on the student. All the collisions and petty details of terrestrial affairs seem to fall away, and one gazes, as it were, into their eternal archetypes, and sees the essence of the conflict, the problem reduced to its lowest terms. [41]

Platonic contemplation may have been powerfully alluring to Harris and his companions, but here at their feet unfolded a frontier that had to be spiritualized through the ministrations of Hegel. "For they had decided," Pochmann says, "that the future salvation of the nation lay in translating Hegel's *Logik,* for only Hegel could save the nation from itself." [42] Then there was the problem of recruits. The cultural life of St. Louis eddied and swirled about in certain recognizable patterns—the Catholic, the Southern, the New England, and the German. The last two contributed about equally to the membership of the movement.

The Catholics, numerically strong, were split along national lines and exerted small influence as a group, although there were many prominent Catholic leaders. Yet Snider is the authority for saying that

[40] "Books That Have Helped Me," *Forum,* III (April, 1887), 147.

[41] *Ibid.,* p. 149. "This work of Hegel's [*Logic*] comes nearer to being a genuine theodicy, a justification of Providence in human history, than any other work I know" (*ibid.*).

[42] Pochmann, *New England Transcendentalism and St. Louis Hegelianism,* p. 12.

there never was a pronounced Catholic in the Philosophical Society, "though Dr. Harris himself, in his later years, showed a tendency to Catholicize, as some of us thought, through his sympathetic study of Aquinas and the Scholastics, as well as on account of his self-surrendering love of the poet Dante." [43]

Much of the activity of the St. Louis Movement took place in and around the public schools and never became allied with either of the city's colleges. For this reason the relatively small group of New Englanders who staffed the schools were influential far beyond their number.[44] St. Louis continued to bear the stamp of a Southern city, not because of Southern leadership, which waned and died with the fortunes of the Confederacy, but because of the river and the climate.

The St. Louis Movement in philosophy has been called "the natural child of German romantic literature and American romantic politics." [45] Beginning with the two decades before the Civil War, when turbulence in the German states forced many leaders and thinkers to seek a haven on freer shores, the German element in the population grew in political and cultural importance. St. Louis welcomed them with opportunities only dreamed of in the Old World, and in a short time Teutonic vigor had impregnated Hegel's "city of the future."

The immediate post-bellum years were marked by an amazing proliferation of cultural organizations. St. Louis was blessed with clubs, classes, circles, and societies that defied count—dedicated to music, painting, science, literature, sculpture, law, linguistics, politics, and, above all, philosophy. The sun which lighted and warmed all lesser planets in the St. Louis cultural universe was the Philosophical Society. In addition to Brockmeyer, Harris, and Snider, other outstanding members were: Thomas Davidson, the Plato scholar; Adolph Ernst Kroeger, the American translator of Fichte; J. Gabriel Woerner, the novelist; and George H. Howison, the builder of the University of

---

[43] Snider, *The St. Louis Movement,* p. 19.

[44] The high school of those days was commonly the cultural hub of the community. Colleges were few in number, and a high school diploma was entree enough to cultured society.

[45] Harvey Gates Townsend, "The Political Philosophy of Hegel in a Frontier Society," in Schaub, ed., *William Torrey Harris, 1835–1935,* p. 69.

California's Department of Philosophy. Still others prominent in the
movement were: John Calvin Learned, James Kendall Hosmer, Susan
E. Blow, Anna Callender Brackett, Senator Carl Schurz, and Joseph
Pulitzer.[46]

Hegel had put a master key to the universe in the talented hands
of these people. A casual glance over the table of contents of a volume
of the *Journal of Speculative Philosophy,* for instance, reveals how
amazingly broad was the ambit of cultural and intellectual subjects
discussed by members of the group.[47] "Self-activity" found expression
in over one thousand books and learned articles that stemmed from
the St. Louis Movement—whose spiritual patron was Georg Wilhelm
Friedrich Hegel.[48]

Brockmeyer himself, the genius and president of the philosophical
club, did little writing. His few contributions to the *Journal of Speculative Philosophy* were rewritten by Harris.[49] The belabored *A Mechanic's Diary* was not written for publication. His son later put it

[46] One enthusiast demurred at the limitations in the title "St. Louis Movement." He thought that in all fairness the movement should have a national
title. Even more, he compared it with "the great thinking movement of the
Middle Ages that centered around St. Thomas Aquinas" or with the more modern philosophical movement that centered around Immanuel Kant. (Louis J.
Block in D. H. Harris, *The Early St. Louis Movement,* pp. 14–18.) John Dewey
must have been perplexed at the honor extended him by the same party, who
co-opted him for the movement: "Professor John Dewey, whatever his weight
and influence now is, got his inspiration, his start from the St. Louis Movement
and he belongs to the St. Louis Movement. He may not think that he does, and
possibly if you spoke to him about it, he might deny it, but nevertheless he does
organically belong to it." (*Ibid.,* p. 26.)

[47] In 1867 Harris launched the *Journal* and remained its editor for some
twenty-two years. The *Journal* is an American landmark. It not only had a critical impact upon American thought by providing the first translations of the
German philosophers, but provided a forum for a generation of American thinkers, among others: Peirce, Howison, Morris, Royce, James, and Dewey.

[48] Despite this mountain of paper and ink, the St. Louis Movement did not
produce a single classic. Snider (*The St. Louis Movement,* pp. 99–100) calls attention to the contrast with the New England Transcendentalist Movement,
which owed much of its success and permanent influence to the quality of its
literature, especially to the pen of Emerson.

[49] Snider (*The St. Louis Movement,* p. 208) said that "the cream of Brockmeyer's genius usually got quite skimmed off when he squeezed it through his
pen-point into ink."

together, as he explains, "in crude fashion" and had it printed "for
my own personal use and that of some of father's and my friends." [50]
Brockmeyer's claim to fame rests rather on the inspiration he summoned up in Denton Snider, William Harris, and a score of others in
the movement. What has survived in the movement is largely to be
found in the writings of Snider and Harris, who were equally pro-
lific.[51]

Harris was deeply in Brockmeyer's debt. The cardinal principle of
his philosophy of education, Hegelian "self-activity," was mediated
in large part by Brockmeyer. In *A Mechanic's Diary* Brockmeyer
wrote these lines whose thought will be found in a more literary
fashion in the writings of Harris: "With self-determination as the ultimate principle of the universe, thought has arrived at totality, and
therefore at true objective internality, and not merely the subjective
internality that predicates concerning an external." [52] The heavy ethical
emphasis in Harris is to be found also in his friend and teacher, who
wrote: "Vice is a determination, a negation"—and with a deft Hegelian twist of the wrist—"but to negate this negation through the process
of moral reformation, the result is an affirmative virtue." [53] Through
Brockmeyer's eyes Harris had seen the dialectic operating in his own
life. He could trace there the three "moments"—the phase of positiv-
ism; next, his conversion to transcendentalism; finally, his transcending
of transcendentalism.

✦

Among the philosophical group in St. Louis, Harris was looked upon
as one of the most articulate champions of orthodox Christianity, but
back in his home town members of his family viewed him as a "freethinker," even as an infidel. From his Yale days his mother and grand-

[50] Letter of E. C. Brokmeyer to Charles M. Perry, quoted in Perry, ed., *The
St. Louis Movement*, p. 50. Brockmeyer's family and friends followed different
spellings of the name, although the seer himself usually followed the "Brockmeyer" spelling.

[51] Snider's printed works run to over fifty volumes.

[52] Brokmeyer, *A Mechanic's Diary*, p. 24; quoted in "William Torrey Harris
and the St. Louis Movement in Philosophy," in Schaub, ed., *William Torrey
Harris, 1835–1935*, pp. 30–31.

[53] Brokmeyer, *A Mechanic's Diary*, p. 60.

mother had always feared the worst. Perhaps at their instigation the Putnam pastor, Rev. J. P. Watson, wrote to Harris in December, 1865, urging that he affiliate at once with the Congregational church in St. Louis. The alternative presented in the letter was dismissal from the church rolls. Papers of transfer were enclosed, as Leidecker records the incident, containing a statement of Harris's present relation to the church, but without an endorsement or voucher for his "late religious walk and piety." [54] Six months later the pastor wrote again to the prodigal. This time Harris replied with a full statement of his religious philosophy. His letter is dated from St. Louis, July 16, 1866. In the letter he patiently records the development of his religious thought. In 1856, after an extensive reading of what he says he had not dared to read before, he saw the imperfections in the popular theology and no longer felt that it bound him. "My protest," he says, "had been against all institutions and not religion alone. I challenge them all to make themselves valid to my intellect or else hold their peace."

This full-dress apologia seems a little out of proportion, unless Harris was using the occasion to reassure all the Orthodox in his family. In any event, his conclusions end up pretty much on the Orthodox side of the ledger, albeit written in a broad Hegelian script. He tells of his acceptance of the dogmas of personal immortality, a personal God, the Trinity, Adam's fall and Christ's redemption—qualified by a statement that must have seemed highly puzzling to his readers:

All the dogmas of Christianity are slightly symbolical statements of the inevitable philosophical results, [and] they follow a purification of the thinking from the stage of mere reflection or sensuous imagining. It is moreover evident that religion is a perennial form of the relation between the historical man and the absolute. The Christian religion has all the ideas in their speculative intent.[55]

He wags a finger at the "so-called liberal sects of Christians" which revolt at dogmas they misunderstand but restate them to suit themselves, thereby missing the speculative intent of dogma. The Unitarians are a prime example of this rebellion. They revolted, he says, at what "I now see to be the deepest and truest dogma, that of the Trinity, of 3 persons in one God, the class who with Beecher deny the

[54] Leidecker, *Yankee Teacher*, pp. 232–37.   [55] *Ibid.*, p. 236.

doctrine of the understanding, reflection, rightly called finite (or human), for the speculative one of the reason." This conviction about the Trinity, however, seems to have been a rather fresh one, for in the next sentence he says, "the Trinity is the last point I have got a glimpse into last winter." He concludes the missive by a description of his religious odyssey "as the coming out of negative scepticism through the piety of the intellect and arriving again at the stand point of unity and harmony with the dogmas I professed at first." In somewhat anticlimactic fashion, Harris affirms his present desire to remain affiliated with the Congregationalist Church and hopes "that the Presbyterian rules do not press so hard [as] you seem to think in your letter."[56]

Harris had every intention of remaining a Christian, even though the Christianity he professed had more Hegel in it than Christ.

✦

The St. Louis Movement in philosophy can be best understood against the backdrop of nineteenth-century America as a phase of the larger conflict between naturalism and idealism. Under the impact of Spencerian Naturalism and Darwinian Evolutionism many pillars of the old religious orthodoxy were teetering. There was a prevailing fear that the new science would sweep away everything of value, leaving behind only "the meaningless evolutions of matter determined by a mindless mechanism." Some looked upon Harris as another Noah sent to save his people from the flood of materialism and agnosticism which was inundating the believing world. They may have been looking for too much, but their hope rightly focused upon Harris's strategic place in the countermovement to preserve the traditional values. The leaders of the St. Louis Movement were molded in the Christian tradition. Accordingly, they sought for an interpretation which, without compromising their intellectual integrity, would enable them to accept the results of science and yet safeguard the spiritual heritage of Western civilization. The problem for the rank and file was "to adjust their thought and feeling to new actualities without losing the sense of identity with older values and conditions."[57]

[56] *Ibid.*, pp. 236–37.
[57] Curti, *Social Ideas of American Educators*, p. 310. A. C. McGiffert writes: "The religious crisis was acute. Either a medieval man and a Christian, or a

And so the eyes of many turned to William Torrey Harris, who loomed on the late nineteenth-century horizon as the great defender of philosophical and religious values in the schools. Many people applauded his fierce opposition to the deterministic philosophy of Spencer and the "unmoral" educational principles of Herbart.[58] Harris told them plainly the question they must answer to ease the social malaise:

Are right and wrong mere conventional distinctions, or do they rest on the nature of man and the structure of the universe? If we arrive at "free-thinking," what basis for morality have we then? [59]

Again, it was Hegel and idealism that would be the foundation for their solid faith in "God, freedom and immortality," and the strong wall to preserve the schools from the inroads of agnosticism and determinism.

His insistence, then, upon the complete divorce between religion and public education may appear at odds with this conviction. The explanation of this apparent discrepancy will be found mainly in his Hegelian philosophy of institutions, as well as in his acceptance of certain principles followed also by Horace Mann.

---

modern man and a skeptic—this seemed the sole alternative as viewed by many of the clearest-headed thinkers of the day." (*Protestant Thought before Kant*, p. 253.)

[58] In fact, the occasion for launching the *Journal of Speculative Philosophy* was the refusal by the *Atlantic Monthly* and the *North American Review* to publish his criticism of Herbert Spencer. Harris wrote in the introductory number of his new journal: "There is no need to speak of the immense religious movements now going on in this country and in England. The tendency to break with the traditional and to accept only what bears for the soul its own justification, is widely active and can end only in the demand that reason shall find and establish a philosophical basis for all those great ideas which are taught as religious dogmas. Thus it is that side by side with the naturalism of such men as Renan, a school of mystics is beginning to spring up who prefer to ignore utterly all historical wrappages and cling only to the speculative kernel itself. The vortex between the traditional faith and the intellectual conviction cannot be closed by renouncing the latter, but only by deepening it to speculative insight." (*Journal of Speculative Philosophy*, I [Jan., 1867], 1–2.)

[59] W. T. Harris, "Thoughts on the Basis of Agnosticism," *Journal of Speculative Philosophy*, xv (April, 1881), 114.

VI. THE DEFENSE OF HEGEL'S
INSTITUTIONAL MORALITY

One reason for the wide influence of William Torrey Harris was the prodigious output from his pen. To a young man, his secretary during several years of his term as U.S. Commissioner of Education, Harris gave this counsel:

If you have any thoughts to give to the world which you consider of value, get them printed; disseminate them. My own plan of doing this, when I was unknown to the reading world, was to get my essays published, no matter how obscure the journal in which they appeared. I asked no compensation for them, other than a few hundred reprints, which I scattered among those interested in education, art, and philosophy. Before long authors were sending me their own lucubrations. By such means I established associations and came in touch with the thinking men of the world over.[1]

---

[1] Schaub, ed., *William Torrey Harris, 1835–1935,* p. 3. There is a reprint copy of "Art Education, the True Industrial Education" in the Butler Library which has rubber-stamped on the frontispiece: PRIVATELY PRINTED AND DONATED TO THE BUREAU OF EDUCATION BY W. T. HARRIS. No one followed Harris's advice more loyally than he himself. *The 1907 Report of the Commissioner of Education,* the year after his retirement, gives 479 titles. Actually the number of distinct pieces from his pen is at least double, for many of

His editorship of the *Journal of Speculative Philosophy* has already been mentioned.[2] In collaboration with two other editors, Harris brought out the Appleton series of school readers and edited fifty-seven volumes of Appleton's International Educational Series, which involved on his part an introduction, analysis, and commentary. For years he served as editor of *Webster's International Dictionary of the English Language*. His own estimate that he had contributed some forty articles to Johnson's *Universal Cyclopaedia* has been revised upward by Leidecker, who claims to have counted about one hundred signed articles.[3] In addition, Harris's name was a fixture in the pages of the leading journals and reviews of the period.

This mass of material indicates the size of the problem that faces anyone who would attempt an analysis of Dr. Harris's thought in one or several areas. Aggravating the problem is the span of years covered by these writings. Quite conceivably the thought expressed by Harris in 1865 might differ greatly from that expressed in 1905. Fortunately, from the viewpoint of the Harris scholar there is no shift in basic educational philosophy over the years as there is in the life span of John Dewey. Harris mastered Hegel and German idealist thinking, applied it consistently, and found little to discard or add over the years. This is not to imply that Harris was intransigent in his basic attitudes, for he did try to adapt his educational principles to the exigencies of the New Education.

✦

these articles and speeches were printed in other magazines with only slight changes. The complete Harris papers were presented to the Library of Congress on September 15, 1953, by his daughter, Miss Edith Davidson Harris. The approximately 13,475 items occupy 19.8 feet of shelf space. (See *Library of Congress Quarterly Journal of Current Acquisitions*, XI, 3, for a description of the material.)

[2] Mueder and Sears credit Harris with the introduction of the phrase "speculative philosophy" into English philosophical usage (*The Development of American Philosophy*, p. 218). In his *La Philosophie en Amérique*, p. 106, L. van Becelaere writes: "Cette revue a eu pour oeuvre de vulgariser et d'accréditer les conceptions de l'Idéalisme allemand parmi la societé lettrée des Etats-Unis, et, à ce titre, on pourrait, avec quelque emphase, qualifier le Dr. Harris de patriarche de l'Idéalisme germanique en Amérique; car s'il n'en fut pas le premier introducteur, il en a été le plus efficace et le plus persévérant promoteur, dans ce pays."

[3] Leidecker, *Yankee Teacher*, p. 334.

The philosophy of education espoused by Harris is related to his understanding of the nature and function of institutions.[4] Harris and Hegel take as their starting point: Reason—supreme reality. Reason is "spontaneous, self-originating, free." Its loftiest attribute is transcendental freedom which is above physical law. Its highest motive is the moral one. Man is a *causa sui,* a self-determining being, intended precisely for infinite moral progress. But man by himself is unable to realize his great potential. Hence the need for institutions.

Harris adopts the Hegelian definition of education as the process through which the individual man becomes ethical.[5] He explains that for the German thinker the ethical expresses the true general nature of man—the forms in which he can live in society and become civilized. Each individual man is born without ethical principles or habits. He must acquire them, or else he cannot participate in the blessings of civilized life. "To make man ethical means, then, to fit him to live in the institutions of civilization—to cooperate with them, and to participate in their fruits." [6]

In an early article he writes:

By nature he [man] is totally depraved; that is, he is a mere animal, and governed by animal impulses and desires, without ever rising to the ideas of reason. . . . Out of the savage state man ascends by making himself new natures, one above the other; he realizes his ideas in institutions, and finds in these ideal worlds his real home and his true nature.[7]

Now this is good Hegelian doctrine except for what seems to be a Calvinistic phrase, "totally depraved." It is certain, despite the phrase, that Harris did not hold the condition of human depravity as the consequence of religious belief.[8] The phrase must be understood in an Hegelian context, that is, in the sense of human incompleteness or of

---

[4] One of the essays in the *Internationale Zeitschrift für Erziehung* gives a thoughtful analysis of Harris's philosophy of institutions.

[5] See "The Church, the State, and the School," *North American Review,* CXXXIII (Sept., 1881), 215-27.

[6] *Ibid.,* p. 215.

[7] "Nature vs. Human Nature, or the Spiritual," *American Journal of Education,* III (Jan., 1871), 4-5. This article does not carry Harris's name.

[8] This phrase has proved a trap for at least one writer. See Clare, *The Sociological Theories of William Torrey Harris,* p. 20 *et seq.*

imperfection which could be remedied only through the institutions of civilization. A study of Harris's works makes it clear that Calvinism had little influence upon his philosophy of education. The point regarding depravity may appear insignificant, but in some educational philosophies it is the starting point.

In a paper read before the National Prison Association at Cincinnati, Harris discusses "depravity." [9] Man has two natures, he says, one as animal, as individual, as passive product of heredity and of his physical environment. The other nature is realized in institutions like the family, civil society, the Church, the State. Now in the Harris lexicon the first nature may also be called the "natural" man and the latter, the "spiritual" man. Left to his own impulses (i.e., the desires springing from appetite), the individual man is selfish, but when he subordinates his spiritual existence to the social whole and its institutions, he is unselfish and altruistic. He calls life lived in institutions "a secondary and higher self of man"; but the individual life of appetite and desire is "a primary and degraded form of self."

Hegel had written that "education is the process through which the individual is led to attain his freedom." [10] So education set a man free, liberated him. Why is this true? Because as a mere individual, isolated from the community, man cannot ascend above savagery. It is only when man comes to avail himself of the aggregate observations of mankind that he is placed in a position to get a worth-while inventory of the world. As an individual, man is an insignificant affair; as a social whole he constitutes a living miracle. He reaps what others sow, he avails himself of the lives of others without having to pay the heavy price of first experience. He is saved the trouble of trying over again what has been found to be error, and hence is saved also the pain which comes from it.[11] Harris adds a remarkable religious application for this analysis of man's dual nature. "Human society," he says, "is founded on the deep mystery of vicarious atonement which

[9] *The Philosophy of Crime and Punishment*, p. 3.

[10] Quoted by Harris in the *Twentieth Annual Report of the Board of Directors of the Saint Louis Public Schools for the Year Ending August 1, 1874*, p. 41. This is the form for the full title of each report. An abbreviated form will be used henceforth for references to the twelve reports prepared by Harris.

[11] *The Philosophy of Crime and Punishment*, p. 4.

is announced in the creeds of Christendom. The social whole learns and suffers for the first cost of its experience, dividing up the pain among the myriads of human beings who contribute this experience."

But what provision has human life developed for the purposes of realizing the spiritual or rational nature that is implicit or potential in the race of man? In the article entitled "The Church, the State, and the School," he replies that there are four chief institutions in civilized life: family, civil society, the State, the Church.[12] But where is the school? Its absence in this enumeration is disconcerting until the school's unique role in Harris's thought is understood. He is not discounting the importance of the school but distinguishing its peculiar nature. For the school comes between the institutions of the family and civil society, partaking somewhat of the nature of the four enumerated, and forming a transition from the family to the other three.

Wherever civilization develops, there develops the school, as supplementary to the family, and propaedeutic to the State, the Church, and civil society. The more advanced a civilization, the greater the complexity of its forms and usages—the more extended its fabric of institutions; hence, too, the more important the school, as a special institution devoted wholly to the work of training the immature individual for taking part in those complex forms of life.[13]

The school, however, is not alone in the field. Each of the other institutions gives a kind of education peculiar to itself which none other can properly give. In fact, continues Harris, there is nothing which the school can give so valuable or so indispensable as the education furnished within the family, civil society, State, or Church. "Strange as this may seem," he writes, "to those prepossessed of the idea that all education is a monopoly of the school, it is a truth so

[12] *North American Review,* CXXXIII (Sept., 1881), 216. Here is the same thought expressed in a 1902 article, seven years prior to his death: "There are educative influences, first in the family, second in the industrial community, third in the political State, and fourth in the Church—taking the Church in a broad sense as the collective instrumentalities that teach the accepted view of the world which is expressed in the prevailing civilization." ("How the School Strengthens the Individuality of the Pupil," *Educational Review,* XXIV [Oct., 1902], 229.)

[13] "The Church, the State, and the School," *North American Review,* CXXXIII (Sept., 1881), 216.

fundamental that no correct view can be formed in regard to the school without considering it." [14]

In the light of this explanation, his conclusion seems reasonable enough: it is impossible for the school alone to give the education which the five institutions together should give. It is an error then— a frequent one, he says—"to demand of the school all kinds of education: education for trades and business, education in religion, education in politics and statesmanship, education in habits which the nurture of the family should supply." [15]

The Church in Harris's hierarchy of institutions is the highest educational institution, because it reveals the highest principle to man, that of the Creator of the world. In revealing this principle, the Church reveals the origin and destiny of the world, of nature, and of the world of man. Elsewhere he writes that the Church initiates into the mysteries of the origin and destiny of man and of his relation to God.

It is no finite or temporary ideal of man that is furnished by religion, nor is it an ideal of character that should have national boundaries. It relates to the essential nature of man *as* man, and concerns life here and hereafter. As religion has furnished the ultimate ground of all obligation, and founded morals (or the code of ideal conduct between man and man)— in short, all education of the will—so, too, it has instituted and preserved *intellectual* education; in all early civilizations the priestly caste alone has access to knowledge.[16]

Writing in the 1880s Harris presupposes universal acceptance of his supposition that America is a Christian nation. For he says that if "our religion were Buddhism or Brahminism, for instance, instead of Christianity, we should believe in a God without any form whatever, not even the form of consciousness or personality." [17]

But a world could not be, he argues, in the image of a formless God. If God is not personal, an infinite idea, an absolute form, then man cannot be immortal, but must be destroyed, and lost when he

[14] *Ibid.*, p. 217
[15] "The Education of the Family, and the Education of the School," *Journal of the American Social Science Association,* XV (Feb., 1882), 1.
[16] "The Church, the State, and the School," *North American Review,* CXXXIII (Sept., 1881), 222.
[17] "The Education of the Family, and the Education of the School," *Journal of the American Social Science Association,* XV (Feb., 1882), 1.

returns to the first principle. Under such an education as a pantheistic religion teaches, "there can be only despotism in the State, slavery in the social community, and patriarchal rule in the family." On the other hand, with the Christian ideal of a divine-human God there is all hope for the individual man, for Christian civilization progresses toward the preservation and education of each individual. For "each human being is an immortal soul infinitely precious to God, and institutions shall be established to reach out and bring within the fluence of civilization all and each."

The education of the State comes next in importance. Again, this ranking is thoroughly consistent with Hegelian philosophy. The State's distinctive contribution to education is the building up of self-respect and strong individuality "under a free government, where each citizen is permitted to assist in making the laws." As to the social community, it educates the individual by preparing him for his business vocation, which will humanize or dehumanize him, according as it girds him for a "rational employment or a brutish one."

Next comes the education of the family. This furnishes the human being with

his bundle of habits, his forms of behavior toward his superiors and equals; his habits of personal cleanliness, of proper dress, of proper eating and drinking, and, in short of the general conduct of life. It gives the knowledge of his native tongue, ideas of right and wrong. All other institutions presuppose in the child that he has learned these great fundamental lessons from family nurture. If he has been so unfortunate as to have missed the priceless blessing of family nurture, the other institutions can make very little of him.[18]

All these forces in the growth of a Christian civilization for two thousand years have increased the power of each individual to enjoy more fully the produce of mankind's labors and the wisdom of mankind's thought. Harris seems never to tire of repeating that no person completes his education at school, because the nature of spiritual life is to be a perpetual education unfolding eternally, and "man's ideal is the divine-human Exemplar—all-knowing, all-powerful to do, and all-benevolent. The most the school can do therefore is teach the indi-

[18] *Ibid.,* p. 2.

vidual how to carry on his education by the aid of the printed page and the proper use of his social opportunities." [19]

The free being has the power of cooperating with his race in such a way as to avail himself by intercommunication of the experience of all: "Each lives for the benefit of all, and all for each so infinite growth in knowledge and holiness becomes possible." Harris sums up the ideal of human life in this

infinite combination of humanity extending through an infinite future of immortal life; growth in the image of the Personal God through membership in the infinite invisible Church. The principle of grace is realized in human institutions. By social combination each gives his individual mite to the whole and receives in turn the aggregate gift of the social whole, thus making him rich by an infinite return.[20]

In the light of the preceding, the next statement of Dr. Harris's comes as no surprise. "Religion," he says, "is the primary foundation, not only of morality, but also of the school and even of the state itself." [21] Why? In another article he explains that as civilization develops, "one institution after another borrows from religion the form of its divine principle, and is allowed to organize itself independently when this is accomplished." He indicates the development:

First, there is the emancipation of the State from the Church; then the emancipation of civil society and the family; with them the school is emancipated. But emancipation here does not mean the casting off of religion. On the contrary, there is no freedom or independence in these

[19] "Our Educational System: What It Is; Why It Is; What It Accomplishes," *Chautauquan*, XV (April, 1892), 16.

[20] "Philosophy Made Simple," *Chautauquan*, VI (May, 1886), 439-40.

[21] "The Present Need of Moral Training in the Public Schools," *Journal of Education*, XXVII (March, 1888), 131. Clare thinks that Dr. Harris is dogmatic in his claim here that the State cannot exist without religion, and denies that Harris is here faithful to Hegel. Clare's first point is in the area of opinion. Given Harris's understanding of idealism, his position can be argued. That he doesn't reflect Hegel is not made any clearer by the two quotations Clare brings forward to prove that Hegel "ridicules" the very idea that the State cannot exist without religion. Neither citation is *ad rem*. In any event, those familiar with the frequently murky depths of Hegelian thought will not be astonished that contradictory interpretations of his thought are pulled out by fishermen angling for different fish.

institutions unless they borrow a divine principle revealed in religion for their organic form.[22]

For example, the State borrows the divine attribute of justice, and hence, "not only may but *must* be separated from the Church as an institution." But he at once adds that "it will nevertheless be in a deep fundamental harmony with the Church." The divine principles revealed in religion have, states Harris further on in the article, penetrated all institutions of civilization and "still form their life and substance, although they have become independent of the Church." [23]

Harris contends here that "the Church remains the most powerful instrumentality of education in the world." An observation in this paragraph is important. In it Harris says:

Religion demands the exclusive devotion of one day in seven, as well as a varying proportion of each day, to religious ceremonies, and it demands this of all. The Church demands the recognition of its doctrines by all the other institutions, and it is only by this concession, tacitly or explicitly, that they have become emancipated from the temporal control of the Church. It still claims almost immediate supervision over the family.[24]

In the conclusion of the article "The Church, the State, and the School," Harris reaffirms his conviction that relative to the other four institutions the school is not the most important institution in education. "In fact," he says, "as we look upon each of the others, we are inclined to call them, in turn, each the more important." This is required in order to justify Harris's approach to the problem of moral training in the school, as we shall see in the next chapter.[25]

[22] "The Church, the State, and the School," *North American Review,* CXXXIII (Sept., 1881), 222.

[23] *Ibid.,* p. 225.   [24] *Ibid.*

[25] Harris was still fully committed to the value of universal free public education. He firmly believed that "only a people with universal education can sustain a republican form of government" ("Our Educational System: What It Is; Why It Is; What It Accomplishes," *Chautauquan,* XV [April, 1892], 17). He repeats the philosophy of Horace Mann that "where the people are to obey the laws made for them by an hereditary ruling class, it may be necessary that the people shall be taught in the schools so much as will enable them to read and understand those laws. But where the people are to make the laws as well as obey them, what limit can there be to the school education required except the full preparation of the individual citizen to carry on his education for himself?"

All social institutions, but especially the school, had an ethical responsibility in Harris's scheme of things. In a series on "The History and Philosophy of Education," he writes that education must make the individual obedient to the requirements of the social institutions under which he lives and must develop "some degree of independence and self-activity in him." [26]

The basis of all true education must be moral. How do we educate the heart? How do we educate for character? By the two disciplines, says Harris, "by that of the will in correct habit, and by that of the intellect in a correct view of the world." [27] When practical habit and intellectual view coincide, "then it becomes a matter of the heart, and character is the result." He cites approvingly here Novalis's description of character as "a completely developed will," but adds that it is also a completely developed intellect "because in God intellect and will are one; so in man the highest aim is to unite insight with moral will. Self-activity becomes intellect, self-activity becomes will. At first self-activity is mere spontaneity without reflection. The highest character is infinitely reflected self-activity." [28]

Dr. Harris gave this advice to teachers:

Educate toward a knowledge of truth, a love of the beautiful, a habit of doing good, because only through these forms can the self-activity continue to develop progressively in this universe. These forms—the true, the beautiful, and the good—will bring the individual into union with his fellow-men through all eternity, and make him a participator in the divine-human work of civilization and culture and the perfection of man in the image of God.[29]

The moral imperative is to operate on all levels of formal education, but in particular on the collegiate and postgraduate level. Why? Because even though the world-view is one of the first things given to the child by the family, it is given on simple authority in the guise of religion. Higher education, on the contrary, has for its chief object the intellectual vision of the unity that makes the world an image of the divine Reason: blind faith becomes intellectual and moral insight.

[26] "The History and Philosophy of Education," *Chautauquan*, III (Oct., 1882), 28.
[27] "Psychological Inquiry," *Education*, VI (Nov., 1885), 157.
[28] *Ibid.*, p. 158.   [29] *Ibid.*, pp. 157–58.

✦

William Torrey Harris has been called the "Conservator." In the sense that he fought to preserve what he considered the hard-won heritage of humanity this is preeminently true. His supply of opponents, far from thinning with the years, increased as the decades rolled by. At one or another interval Harris challenged the tenets, in whole or in part, of Rousseau, Pestalozzi, Spencer, Herbart, Froebel, Darwin, Parker, Stearns, the McMurrys, DeGarmo, James, and Dewey. One could conclude that Harris was the sole defender of a very lonesome island. One might more understandingly conclude that he was rigorously discriminating and slow to accept the new and the untried in education. Yet in every encounter Harris gave a good account of himself.

As a rule he had little patience with the agnostic school. First principles were to him the stuff out of which any reasonable approach to life must be fashioned. A man knew these and held them through solid conviction. One of the few sarcastic twists to his polemic occurs in this passage:

A sacred college of agnostics that should undertake to place on its Index Prohibitory any or all questions relating to God, Freedom, or Immortality, must base its action either on the fact that its limited investigation has hitherto been unsuccessful in finding a solution, or on the fact that its investigation has discovered necessary limits in the nature of human knowledge. The mere fact of such a want of success on the part of the agnostic does not justify him in pronouncing anything either unknown or unknowable. It warrants only the modest attitude of the skeptic who affirms his own present ignorance. What man has a right to affirm besides his own ignorance the ignorance of all men? [30]

As the intellectual leaders of America turned more and more toward science and its methods in their quest for truth, some groups predicted dire consequences for the schools. Harris, though, did not share these fears. He faced the question: "Is pantheism the legitimate outcome of modern science?" in an article bearing that title, which appeared in the *Journal of Speculative Philosophy* in October, 1885,

[30] "Immortality of the Individual," *Journal of Speculative Philosophy*, XIX (April, 1885), 193.

and which had been prepared the preceding summer for a symposium at the Concord School of Philosophy.[31] "The question is," he wrote,

whether modern science leads toward a belief in a personal God or toward a belief in a blind unconscious power, or, finally, whether science finds only things and forces in the universe without unity in a first principle. For there are three hypotheses instead of two—atheism, pantheism, and theism.[32]

His classification, even with heavy Hegelian overtones, is not without validity:

To him who finds no necessity for an ultimate unity of all things there is only *atheism*. To him who sees the necessity of unity, but finds it a mere essence or substance from which things in their multiplicity arise, and into which they return, there is *pantheism*. Finally, the *theist* sees the necessity of unity, but, more than this, sees the necessity of the form of personality as the form of any ultimate unity or totality.[33]

In the body of the article, he distinguishes three stages of scientific thought. In the initial stage, which tends to atheism, "the First Principle is seen only as an atom, or rather a universe of atoms." To the holder of this view there is not one supreme being but "many coordinate personalities existing in accidental relation to each other." The second stage of scientific perception takes place when the essential dependence of one thing upon another is clearly perceived, and this by itself leads to pantheism. But in the third stage, which is marked by reflection, the totality of relation in the universe is seen—"relation traced out and necessarily returning to the being from whence it started." Accordingly, Harris decides that science, in the best sense, i.e., the Hegelian, is theistic—that is, when it studies all things "in the light of the history of their evolution progressing toward perfect form or conscious being."

Again, the ultraconservatives feared the impact of the "new psychology" upon education. For his part, Harris, as early as 1895, went on

---

[31] The Concord School of Philosophy was a summer course of lectures and discussions upon philosophical and aesthetical subjects under the guidance of A. Bronson Alcott and Harris. It lasted from 1879 until 1887.

[32] "Is Pantheism the Legitimate Outcome of Modern Science?" *Journal of Speculative Philosophy*, XIX (Oct., 1885), 407.

[33] *Ibid.*, pp. 407–8.

record affirming that it would prove a boon. He was of the further opinion that much could be expected from the direct physiological study of brain and nerves as well as from the observation of child development.[34]

By 1904 Harris, serene in his conviction that there was no basic incompatibility between religion and science, was bestowing his blessing upon science: "It is the insight into the transcendent first cause that provides through theism for an enlightened natural science." [35]

Like any convinced idealist Harris bristled at talk of a "return to nature." Like many before and after him, he incorrectly ascribes this doctrine to Rousseau and bluntly labels it "the greatest heresy in educational doctrine." [36] He has only scorn for Basedow, whom he considers the extreme disciple of Rousseau and one who "tends always to the grossest naturalism." He is gentler toward Pestalozzi, who "is moderated ever by his deep instincts and religious culture." [37]

Harris's critical eye turned toward the course of study at the Cook County Normal School in Illinois, to which educational enthusiasts were flocking from all over the country to learn about "object lessons" and "child-centered curriculum." Harris complained that Colonel Francis W. Parker did not give his students a sound appreciation of inorganic nature, i.e., the world of spirit, because of the stress upon organic nature. More serious was Parker's effort to unify all knowledge around nature à la Froebel. "My difficulty with his theory relates to the fact that he does not seem to draw a sharp and fast line between

[34] "The Old Psychology vs. the New," *Journal of Education*, XLI (May 2, 1895), 295–96.

[35] "Primary and Secondary Phases of Causality: Natural Science Founded on the Latter and Theology on the Former," paper read before the American Philosophical Association at Philadelphia, Dec. 29, 1904.

[36] W. T. Harris in Lang, ed., *Educational Creeds of the 19th Century*, p. 37. Rousseau in the *Emile* did urge that education should *follow* nature, i.e., the natural stages of child development; that until he was roughly fourteen, the child should discover knowledge in nature and be kept from books.

[37] "The Theory of American Education," *American Journal of Education*, IV (Jan., 1871), 4. Harris found much to esteem in Herbart and Spencer. In fact, he took over Herbart's doctrine of aperception, believing it the complement of Pestalozzi's sense-perception. See W. T. Harris, "Herbart and Pestalozzi Compared," *Educational Review*, V (May, 1893), 417–23; "The Best Works on Pedagogy for Young Teachers," *Journal of Education*, XXXIII (Feb. 26, 1891), 131.

the products of spiritual being and the products of nature by them-selves." [38] Good idealist that he was, Harris could never agree that the spiritual studies of mankind—religion, history, jurisprudence, literature, and the arts—could derive from purely natural studies.

In the midst of the unsettling excitement over evolution, Harris kept his feet on the ground. He saw good in the principles advanced by Darwin and Huxley and decided that schools could profit thereby. True, Harris may have been seeing Hegel where there was only Darwin but, again, his remarks are not without their validity.

He includes in his 1872 report to the St. Louis school board a chapter on "Course of Study." He informs the board that

the great influence of Darwin upon scientific thought seems to be in this direction: all living beings shall be studied in their histories. . . . What-ever may be said about "natural selection," (or as Hegel called it, "the struggle of ideas and the victory of the deepest one"), is only preliminary and not exhaustive. The study of the totality of its history will reveal to us the purpose—the final cause—the teleology—of the struggle for exist-ence in a living process. All struggles imply two opposing forces—in this instance the living animal struggling to attain his ideal type against the obstinate resistance of surrounding circumstances. What that ideal type is, will be manifest if we study the tendency of his struggles in his history.

In this sense Darwin's labors are not hostile to those who claim the purest spiritual views. If idealism has any truth—if there is any basis for a spiritual theory of the universe—it will become manifest to us in a study of a history of the world and of mankind. Educational thinkers, above all others, must be active in this field, and see to it that no merely preliminary and half-views be forced upon them.[39]

The superintendent, consequently, does not foresee the need for any radical revision of the present curriculum. He suggests a policy of "wait and see." After all, wasn't it reliable old Plato "who first showed us the natural transition between idea and idea—that one idea involves another through which it is limited and defined—that, accordingly, in arriving at the clear comprehension of one idea we are obliged to pass over to other ideas and return to the first"? This necessity is really just "the famous Platonic *dialectic.*"

[38] "The Necessity of Five Co-ordinate Groups in a Complete Course of Study," *Education*, XVI (Nov., 1895), 129.
[39] *Eighteenth Annual Report*, pp. 141–42.

Seventeen years later, apropos of evolution, Harris says that science has only substituted an immanent teleology for the old doctrine of external teleology. "By rejecting the old mechanical teleology which makes nature a machine in the hand of God, evolution has come to see the teleology which God has breathed into nature—to see, in short, that nature is through and through teleological."[40] And it is the idealist who, through introspection, sees how every particle of nature is governed by ideals.

One of Harris's perennial antagonists was Herbert Spencer. It will be recalled that the rejection of his manuscript on Spencer led to the founding of the *Journal of Speculative Philosophy*. The rejected article found place, quite naturally, in the first issue of the *Journal*.[41] One point of disagreement between the two educators concerned the origin of human consciousness and volition. Spencer argued that such mental phenomena were produced by nature or were links in a larger chain of natural causality. Harris argued, on the contrary, that will and consciousness are forms of self-activity.[42] He rejected Spencer's idea that each child should be brought to school to learn the art of complete living. The Harris criticism continues:

With him education is something useful for showing how to take care of the body and how to perform the lower social functions—the preparation of food, clothing, and shelter. The first education, according to him, is not that which relates to man's spiritual life and to the preparation of man to understand the view of the world entertained by his civilization; that would be the religious ideal and the social ideal.[43]

The Spencerian dictum that "the first knowledge which man should seek is the knowledge which goes to direct self-preservation" would be anathema to anyone who shared Harris's ideals. Spencer had urged that in selecting subjects for study the principle of a "return to nature" should be followed. Hence the natural sciences should be the principal burden of the curriculum. Harris fails to see the validity

[40] *Thoughts on Educational Psychology* (Reprints from articles in the *Illinois School Journal*, 1890), p. 6.

[41] "Herbert Spencer," *Journal of Speculative Philosophy*, I (1867), 6–22.

[42] "Herbert Spencer and His Influence on Education," *Journal of Proceedings and Addresses of the NEA, 1904*, pp. 47–48.

[43] "Herbert Spencer and What to Study," *Educational Review*, XXIV (Sept., 1902), 136.

of a method which "passes from body to mind, or from the events of the animal kingdom to those of spiritual life, interpreting the latter through the former." No; this for Harris is an inversion of the proper order.[44]

On the other hand, Harris agrees with Spencer that education should *conduce* to "complete living." But whereas Spencer had defined this in individualistic terms, Harris defines complete living in social terms. The one logically placed self-preservation, natural sciences, in first place in his course of studies; the other, just as logically, put the humanities in first place.[45]

The function of the will in education was likewise a point of disagreement between Harris and the followers of the German philosopher Johann Herbart. Herbart denied the transcendental will. Further, he taught that the will grows out of desire: desire and strong motives are the sole determinants of will.[46] Harris hastens to reassure his readers that "these gentlemen [Gilbert, the McMurrys, and DeGarmo] who attempt to support Herbart's heresy in regard to the will are all of them earnest men in moral education." He commended them for their regard in creating moral desire in the pupil. But he still insisted

[44] See "The Danger of Using Biological Analogies in Reasoning on Educational Subjects," *Journal of Education* (March 13, 1902). Reprinted.

[45] "Herbert Spencer and What To Study," *Educational Review*, XXIV (Sept., 1902), 149. Clare (*The Sociological Theories of William Torrey Harris*, p. 127) makes this interesting observation: "Spencer's criticisms of education have served to sharpen the controversy between the supporters of 'classical' and 'practical' courses of study." Harris urged college educators to investigate the merits of both courses so that necessary adjustments of the secondary school curriculum could be made. See "On the Relation of the College to the Common School," *American Institute of Instruction Lectures, 1883*, pp. 144–45.

[46] W. T. Harris, "Herbart's Unmoral Education," *Education*, XVI (Nov., 1895), 180. In this article Harris explains that "the word 'transcendental,' as applied to the will by Kant, means simply to describe the power of the will to originate independent action and to modify its environment or the chain of forces connected with its body and give to them new directions—perform with them deeds which realize motives and ideals it may have." The common understanding of Kant's system during this period, says Beard, was the declaration that "the great ideas of God, soul, freedom, right, duty, and immortality cannot be tested at all by our contacts with the world of material things but 'transcend' the experiences of our senses; they are intuitively inexorable and are discovered to be absolutely true by introspection, or the internal examination of our mental structure." (Charles A. and Mary R. Beard, *The Rise of American Civilization*, I, 730–31.)

that the personal conviction of responsibility lies at the basis of all truly moral action. In deciding between two motives, a moral and an immoral one, the individual must not feel that whatever he does is merely a link in the chain of causation and that he is an irresponsible agent in the hands of motives or forces; he must feel that he is responsible; that is to say, he must feel that he originates a new chain of action and that it is his chain of actions, and that the deed and its consequences belong to him.[47]

This Harris calls moral consciousness or transcendental freedom, and says that everything below this is not moral nor immoral, but *unmoral.* In other words, for Harris, the awareness of responsibility is what makes a creature moral. His fight is for free will. The next words in this article have a slightly plaintive note:

It is all well enough to declaim against metaphysics and to postpone to the hereafter subtle discussions which require a lifetime of careful and precise thinking. But one must draw a line before the doctrine of free will.[48]

For if a person is not conscious of his free will, the essential characteristics of moral action will be lacking.

The practical consequences of the Herbart doctrine were what Harris mainly feared. He explicitly states that his only objection to the doctrine of interest is its attempt to substitute for original self-activity.[49] This, in turn, would lead to weakened discipline. For the disciplinary side of the school appeals directly to the will of the pupil, reminding him constantly of responsibility, training him to inhibit his natural impulses, and helping him to form habits of self-control. Harris's opinion was that even if a school could govern by interest in such a way as to make no appeal to the responsibility of the pupil, such a school would really be inferior as a means of moral training and of will development. It would lead everything by the intellect instead of by the will. In conclusion, he gives his opinion that will training has been overdone in some cases and that the awareness of responsibility has been made precocious in some schools. He grants that a greater stress on interest would improve the schools, but he likewise thinks that "it will not be a good move for American schools to make interest a

[47] "Herbart's Unmoral Education," *Education,* XVI (Nov., 1895), 180.
[48] *Ibid.,* p. 179.
[49] "In What Does Spiritual Evolution Consist?" *Education,* XVII (March, 1896), 420–21.

substitute for immediate will training as it exists among us in the form of school discipline." [50]

The National Herbart Society Year Book for 1895 carried a 38-page article by John Dewey setting forth a critical analysis of the idea of interest and of its relation to will. Dr. Harris praised this article, calling it "the most valuable discussion of all that have appeared on this important subject." [51] Dewey, says Harris, "thinks profoundly and writes luminously. His views nearly always provoke dissent, but a fruitful dissent." Harris thought he saw a hint in Dewey of his own thought on will and self-interest. The Dewey phrase that he likes is "self-expression." This is a modification of the orthodox doctrine on will through which he thinks Dewey has made original self-determination more palatable to the Herbartians. He cites Dewey's own words:

An interest is primarily a form of self-expressive activity. If we examine this activity on the side of the content of expression of what is done, we get its objective features, the ideas, objects, etc., to which the interest is attached, about which it clusters. If we take into account that it is self-expression, that self finds itself, is reflected back to itself, in this content, we get its emotional or feeling side. [52]

Harris takes this to mean that Dewey considers the will self-expressive activity in so far as it has the power of modifying the external stream of causality. Why does the self seek expression? In order to realize a consciousness of self. Therefore, self-expression postulates interests. This, for Harris, rescues the doctrine of interest from the crass determinism of the materialists. Self-expression furnished a ready-made definition for the fundamental interest of all interests. The self desires to express itself in order that it may thereby become conscious. The self builds in the world of time and space an expression, a revelation of itself; it in fact duplicates itself, makes itself an object for itself. And this grounds the doctrine of interest on the most fundamental basis, the most spiritual that can be named. So, concludes Harris, Dewey does appeal to a higher principle than mere interest.

[50] *Ibid.*, p. 421.
[51] "Professor John Dewey's Doctrine of Interest as Related to Will," *Educational Review*, XI (May, 1896), 486.
[52] *Ibid.*, p. 487.

This position, in fact, puts Harris in mind of Hegel's *Philosophie des Rechts;* it treats the will as a transcendental originator of new determinations in space and time and as a continual act of self-revelation. *Ecco!* What finer praise! Again Hegel has saved the day and reconciled what many people then, and most people today, regard as contradictories.

✦

In the Harris theory of institutions, it is clear that ethical and spiritual values played a dominant role. Did he, though, identify these values with religious values? Did he separate the moral and religious side of education? The next chapter will take this question up in detail, but no treatment of Harris's theory of the values in social institutions would be complete without an understanding of his theory of religions.

The conception of the Trinity embodied in the Church was for Harris the archetype of all institutions. The Church had the perfect institutional inspiration and form, and all secular institutions were to be modeled upon it. Religion in this sense was, for Harris, a natural thing. That is, the religious process was "the search for the first cause, the originating source, which derivative or imperfect beings demand as the logical condition of their existence." [53]

Harris follows Hegel's division of religions into three genera.[54] (1) There is the process of *nature-religion* which situates the divine in heavenly bodies, in plants, and in animals. This embraces all primitive cults of history up to that of the Egyptians. Since they reverentially built "eternal dwellings for the soul's material encasing, the body," architecture is nature-religion's chief form of worship. (2) *Art-religion* comes next historically. Here, as among the Greeks, the beautiful is worshipped as divine. Hence the preoccupation with developing the body beautiful. Sculptors fix these graceful forms in stone and poets externalize beautiful activity in epic, lyric, and dramatic poetry. These media in some way depict the internal struggles of the subjective and individual against the objective and universal. Elsewhere Harris calls

[53] Harmon, *The Social Philosophy of the St. Louis Hegelians,* p. 77.
[54] W. T. Harris, *Hegel's Logic,* preface. This book was published in Griggs's Philosophical Classics, the editor of which was George Sylvester Morris.

this kind of artistic activity "an act of worship of the beautiful." [55]
(3) *Revealed religion* for Hegel is the religion that "reveals rather
than is revealed, the religion of a self-revealing God." Through the
religion of art—and here he quotes Hegel directly—"Spirit ascends
from the form of substance (or of the conscious being, man) and
represents it as performing self-conscious deeds; in the religions of
the feared and dreaded substance (pantheistic religions of the Orient)
self-consciousness is not preserved, and in its blind faith, it does not
yet recognize itself." [56]

From substance to subject—this, Harris says, is the "great word"
with Hegel, and characterized the difference between oriental and
occidental religions. Asia clings to despotic forms, because its highest
principle is conceived as substance and not as subject. It conceives the
absolute as a pure empty infinite devoid of all properties, qualities, and
attributes. For it cannot discern any other alternative than finitude on
the one hand, or an empty infinite on the other. Europe, however, conceives its idea of the highest principle as perfect form, rather than
perfect formlessness; as perfect fullness of being, rather than perfect
emptiness.

Hegel's great discovery, in Harris's judgment, is that pure "subject"
or self-determination—the self-active, *causa sui,* that which is its own
object—is perfect being. That "self-activity" receives so much emphasis
in the Harris philosophy of education is then quite understandable.
Perfect being eternally knows itself and thus eternally makes itself an
object; but recognizing itself therein, it elevates the object into self-
activity and independence. Thus it forever "returns to itself from its
other." Now this constitutes absolute subject: that which knows itself
as object and recognizes only itself in its object. This is God. If man,
however, as consciousness, is in the image of absolute subject, his
development will be an ascent toward the divine. In knowing himself,
man will know with some degree the adequacy of the divine.

God, it follows, is a revealed God, for revelation must follow
consciousness. His works reveal Him. His creation is a manifestation
of His will, and in the creation of intelligent beings He reveals His

[55] See the unusual treatment of the point in *Art Education.*
[56] *Hegel's Logic,* p. 104. The entire chapter in which this quotation appears
discusses religion, which is the fifth general topic of Hegel's *Phenomenology.*

own intelligence. Harris agrees with Hegel that Christianity is the absolute religion. However, Harris parts from Hegel in his method of relating nature to the absolute idea, insisting that Hegel himself has not deduced here the logical consequences of his system. And yet:

The wrong explanation of the use of Nature, strange to say, does not vitiate Hegel's theory of human life and of the Christian church. His doctrine of the Trinity makes the Second Person, or Logos, to be Nature, whereas it should make the Logos to be eternally a Person like the First, and Nature should be the *Processio* of the Holy Spirit. But he rightly interprets the doctrine of the invisible Church as the body whose spirit is the Holy Spirit.[57]

This faulty interpretation of the *Logic* gives rise, Harris continues, to a species of pantheism which claims "that the Absolute is real only in the process of Nature, and his personality actual only in historical persons." This is not Hegel's precise doctrine, says Harris, but it may be inferred from that part of it which makes Nature to be the Second Person of the Trinity. Harris puts this criticism of Hegel's system forward as a new one, and one in whose truth he is confident.[58]

The pivotal idea of self-activity is found in religion, too. This is of course a long day's journey beyond the deterministic pessimism of Harris's Calvinist forebears. The world of finitude is a product of grace, for it is a free gift of independent existence where none was deserved. The imperfection attached to finitude does not forfeit this gift of grace. Self-activity increases it, i.e., the gift of grace progresses by self-activity toward the perfect form and becomes more independent. At the same time it grows more in the likeness of the absolute and hence more in unity with it.

Like John Dewey later, Harris is impressed by the intimate relation between religion and art. Harris defines as art "all realizations of the beautiful, all the diverse forms under which nations or peoples have endeavored to body forth in matter a *manifestation* of the Highest in their consciousness."[59] He likes the definition of art which describes it as "a means of manifesting the Divine in material form for the apprehension of the senses and the reason." This definition makes art

---

[57] *Ibid.,* pp. xiv–xv.   [58] *Ibid.,* p. xv.
[59] "The Relation of Religion to Art," *Journal of Speculative Philosophy,* X (April, 1876), 204.

one of the three highest products of the soul which deal with the beautiful, the good, and the true.[60]

Religion, on the other hand, has a more sublime function. Religion offers more than some aesthetic feeling of the divine presence or intimations of the great ultimate fact of the world. It realizes the divine for us in the depths of our minds and hearts: religion must feel devotion rather than aesthetic enjoyment.[61] Religion portrays the divine far more adequately than art. In the external form presented by art we can have only the *"effects* of spirit—its *manifestation*. But in religion we have *revelation,* and revelation is essential to all religion."

The latter part of the same article gives a striking example of how thoroughly Harris had "Hegelized" his Christianity. This paragraph illuminates the dialectic of the divine activity:

In Religion the Divine appears as creator and destroyer of natural things, as the dominant ruler elevated above nature, now manifesting Himself in the material as the Beautiful or Sublime, now manifesting Himself as the negative might that destroys the material form and reduces it to higher uses. These two phases combined make revelation, and hence it will be seen that revelation contains manifestation and its opposite, or annulment. In the annulment of the beautiful the ugly reveals itself, and hence Religion essentially contains the element (or moment) of the ugly. The phase of formation is followed by the phase of deformation, and this precedes the genesis of higher forms.[62]

Harris sums up the relations of art, philosophy, and religion: art may be defined as the piety of the senses; religion as the piety of the heart; and philosophy as the piety of the intellect.[63]

---

[60] "Beauty in Art vs. Beauty in Nature," in *Report of the U.S. Commissioner of Education, 1898–1899,* I, 692.

[61] "The Relation of Religion to Art," *Journal of Speculative Philosophy,* X (April, 1876), 208–9.

[62] *Ibid.,* p. 207.

[63] *Ibid.* Did Harris believe in art for art's sake? In a tribute to his literary friend Brother Azarias (Patrick Mullany) of the Brothers of the Christian Schools, Harris praised him for having repudiated the "spurious aesthetic doctrine set forth by modern literary editors . . . that art has no other aim than to construct the form for the form's sake" with no care for the moral result. ("In Memoriam: Brother Azarias," Document #320 in Harris Collection of Library of Congress, p. 4.) This was 1893. Four years later, though, he wrote:

Harris has already said that the first social culture is religion and that religion is the foundation of social life. The ideas of religion are not the thoughts of individual scholars but the aggregate results of a "social activity of intellect." Individual thought is modified by the thought of the community so that it comes to the individual with the substantial impress of authority.

This leads to the Harris idea of the "Church." His own Congregationalist associations, no doubt, had colored his views on this matter, but he still presents them within a Hegelian frame. Each modification in religious doctrine comes about through individual innovation but "at the expense of disaster to the innovator's life." For he has to sacrifice his life to effect this assimilation of the popular faith. Thus both Church Fathers and heresiarchs contribute to the evolution of doctrine. There is room for everybody in Harris's Church and place for every idea:

Members include not only the Saint Bernards, but also the Voltaires. The Church receives the new views, but does not by any means adopt them until it has submitted them to the negative process of criticism and elimination, and finally to the transforming process that selects the available portions for assimilation and nutriment. This is certainly the slowest and most conservative spiritual process that goes on in civilization.[64]

Despite this broadmindedness, Harris was definitely committed to his own concept of Christianity—which was, it is clear by now, thoroughly Hegelian. For both men Christianity was the absolute or fully perfected religion. Harris lauded Hegel's chapter on the intro-

---

"Art has an end of its own, and to be art of a very high character it must show that the beautiful object exists for itself, and does not exist for the sake of other objects—not even for morals or religion. But of course the highest art will be found in harmony with both morals and religion." (*The Aesthetic Element in Education,* address read before the National Council of Education at Milwaukee, 1897, p. 9.)

[64] "Philosophy in Outline," *Journal of Speculative Philosophy,* XVII (Oct., 1883), 354. This excerpt is from the same article: "Man makes his environment into the image of his true self when he puts on the form of the divine Second Person, as the One who gives Himself freely to lift up imperfect beings. As that form is the elevation of the finite into participation with Himself, so man's spiritual function is the realization of higher selves through institutions—the invisible Church, which is formed of all the intelligent beings collected from all worlds in the universe. The social combination of man with man is thus the means of realizing the divine."

duction of Christianity as "one of his profoundest (and obscurest) analyses," and called no passage more worthy of study than Hegel's discussion of the elements of Christianity. For

Hegel sees in the doctrine of the incarnation, crucifixion, resurrection, and ascension of Christ, the adequate religious statement of this final doctrine of the creation of the individual for immortality and reconciliation with God.[65]

✦

Natural religion retains its more usual meaning for Harris, as witness his statement that "a mere natural religion does not admit of science, of free thought, and the investigation of matter and force. For these are the elements that the savage worships or dreads with a mortal fear, as evil demons, and spends his whole life in trying to propitiate them with ceremonies and sacrifices." [66] As long as backward peoples are under modes of life which have grown out of a natural religion, they cannot fully realize the meaning of the Christian doctrine as taught by the missionary. For everything must be transformed by the light of Christianity before it is fully understood. The missionary teaches God's message to man and impresses on the minds of the heathen people to whom he is sent

the doctrine of the true God who loved man and sent his divine Son to die for him in order that he might be saved. This doctrine of the divine-human nature of the true God, contains in it, as in a germ, all of Christian civilization. All of the good things which form the power and the glory of the most advanced nations of the world form as a result from this doctrine.[67]

The poor heathen cannot be taught science, the useful arts, literature, history, and philosophy without emancipating them from their heathen

[65] "George William Frederick Hegel," in Warner, ed., *A Library of the World's Best Literature,* XII, 7177–78.

[66] "The Educative Work at Missions," paper read at the Ecumenical Conference on Foreign Missions, April 25, 1900. Document #711 in Harris Collection, Library of Congress.

[67] *Ibid.* Harris also believed that God had designed America as the saving force of Europe and the West against the Orient. "Through God's Providence America is destined to alleviate the tensions and stave off revolutions in Europe by allowing the discontented republican and internationalist spirits to come to her shore." ("Church and State," *The Western,* IV [March, 1874], 113–36.)

creed, because all of these have "a particular cast given them by the religious doctrine of Christianity."

Any discussion of a man's religious philosophy must inevitably touch upon his notion of sanctions. Harris frequently referred to "sin," "hell," "purgatory," and "punishment." These were much more to him than literary tags from his favorite poem with its phases of the *Paradiso, Purgatorio,* and *Inferno.* An article entitled "Is God the Author of Sin?" in which many of the orthodox Christian concepts of retribution are presented stands out. Harris's emphasis upon human freedom has been mentioned. In this article he argues for freedom as the sole basis upon which Christianity in its true essence can be grounded. God is not, he says, the author of sin but of its possibility as a contingence of freedom, for human freedom is the gift of grace. Hell properly so called is the creation of the sinner:

Sin, being an act that is directed against the universe—that is, against God and one's fellow men—is such to create an environment that is hostile to one, an environment that pains and punishes one. A finite being cannot flee from his environment and if this is made to be hostile he is in Hell or Purgatory.[68]

A final question here is the relation in Harris's mind between philosophy and theology. Traditionally the two have been considered distinct disciplines, and care has usually been taken to distinguish one from the other. Harris has left several definitions of philosophy. He speaks of it as the "highest speculative activity"; as the discipline that leads man "to the threshold of religion, and puts him into that frame of mind in which he can receive doctrine into his heart";[69] as the discovery of the "necessary *a priori* elements or factors in experience"; and as the investigation of "the theological conditions of existence and experience."[70]

This is quite clear, until he defines religion as "an insight into the final and deepest order of being—the truth which is under all seeming

---

[68] Document #424 in Harris Papers in Library of Congress. Much of this same matter is treated in "Dante's Doctrine of Sin," in the *Year-book of the American Dante Society, 1890–91,* pp. 69–81.

[69] "Philosophy in Outline," *Journal of Speculative Philosophy,* XVII (July, 1883), 311–12.

[70] *Ibid.,* pp. 296–97. See the entire article.

or imperfect being, whether inorganic, or plant, or animal, or human." [71] This smacks of Horace Mann's "religion of heaven." Now we are somewhat confused, despite Harris's words that

philosophy is not religion, nor a substitute for religion, any more than it is art or a substitute for art. There is a distinction, also, betweeen philosophy and theology, although philosophy is a necessary constituent of theology. While theology must necessarily contain a historical and biographical element, and endeavor to find in that element the manifestation of necessary and universal principles, philosophy, on the other hand, devotes itself exclusively to the consideration of those universal and necessary conditions of existence which are found to exist in experience, not as furnished by experience, but as logical, *a priori* conditions of experience itself.[72]

In any event, the fact remains that Harris was not a conventional follower of Christianity, Catholic or Protestant. Like Horace Mann, William Torrey Harris invested many traditional phrases, such as "divine-human," "Trinity," "Christianity," "faith, hope, and charity," and "Church" with meanings that were strange to those not initiated into his own peculiar religious philosophy. Harris held with Hegel that *"revealed religion* is the religion of a *revealed* God, and not specially the religion which is communicated by any divinely inspired revelation." [73]

Here is an amazing rupture with all Christian tradition, for this simply undercuts the support of the Christian religion, which is based upon scriptural revelation. In other words, revelation as the act of God Himself inspiring men to make a written record which in turn has inspirational value for its readers becomes a sheer accident to Christianity. There could then be, according to these words of Harris, a Christianity without a single verse of the Bible or any kind of oral tradition.

Some of his friends said of Harris that his deity was the goddess of reason. That his system of ultimate values is more complicated than this has been indicated in this chapter. Yet, if a single aspect of his religious philosophy—upon which his ideas concerning character edu-

[71] "The Danger of Using Biological Analogies," *Journal of Education* (March 13, 1902), p. 14.
[72] "Philosophy in Outline," *Journal of Speculative Philosophy,* XVII (July, 1883), 310.
[73] *Ibid.* "Not specially," i.e., not specifically.

cation and the place of religion in the schools will hinge—can be taken
as characteristic, it is indeed the rational. But here, paradoxically
enough, Harris can serenely write that all morals are summed up in
the idea of the creation of the will in its attempts to will will. For he
makes his own the Hegelian dictum put forth to explain the whole
of human nature and the material universe:

The Will wills Will! [74]

[74] "Professor John Dewey's Doctrine of Interest as Related to Will," *Educational Review*, XI (May, 1896), 487–88.

VII.   THE SEPARATION OF RELIGION
FROM THE SCHOOL

In 1867 William Torrey Harris was appointed assistant superintendent of the St. Louis public school system. The thirty-two-year-old New Englander was the personal choice of Superintendent Ira Divoll, then badly failing in health. The next spring Divoll resigned and Harris was elected superintendent by the school board. During his twelve years in the office, Harris made the St. Louis school system a model for the nation. Emerson considered Harris's system superior to that of Boston.

The bitter controversies over religion in public education which had agitated New England and the Middle Atlantic States were likewise felt along the Mississippi. The problem of inculcating religious values in the Massachusetts public schools without at the same time promoting sectarian interests, we saw to have been treated by Horace Mann in two ways. He promoted what he considered basic religious principles common to all creeds, i.e., religious beliefs whose character was presumably not distinctive of any single sect. Secondly, he strove to promote in the common schools a knowledge and love of the great ethical principles which govern man's ideal relation to his fellows.

Moreover, Mann insisted that the public school assume a large responsibility for moral and religious training, and regarded Bible-reading in the schools as an important means to this end. From the preceding chapters where Harris's philosophy of education was examined one might expect that he should be equally active in promoting religion in the public schools. He was not. However, Harris did not originate a policy here: he inherited one.

During his first year as school superintendent, he came face to face with the problem. The public schools were under fire from several directions. Articles in the St. Louis newspapers charged that "children were educated to be radicals in politics and infidels in religion and trained for the brothel or the jail, as well as to become enemies of the social order and good government."[1] A member of the state legislature published articles in the *Missouri Republican* charging that the public schools were immoral and dangerous pesthouses. He hinted darkly at widespread immorality and claimed that "infanticide, demoralization, divorce, despair, and prison were the consequences of girls visiting the schools."[2]

The Methodists were unhappy because the Bible was not being taught in the schools. The Presbyterians complained that Harris was propagating irreligion and creating infidels. The Catholics clamored for a share in the public funds for their own schools and discussed the alternative of sending all parochial school students to public schools.[3] These criticisms, whatever factual basis they may have had, were misdirected to the extent that they were aimed at the new superintendent. Harris not only did not have a Massachusetts law of 1827 to guide his policies prescribing that piety be promoted in the schools, but he had a contrary directive to obey. Before 1840, on the occasion of the dedication of the first public school in St. Louis, a mass meeting

[1] Quoted in Leidecker, *Yankee Teacher*, p. 290.

[2] *Ibid.*, p. 291. Some of Harris's scrapbooks from this period are on deposit with the Missouri Historical Society, St. Louis, but Harris hadn't the historian in mind when he prepared them. Newspaper clippings, for instance, are put down in the book pasted closely together without any indication of their date or source.

[3] In fact, Catholic authorities announced in 1878 that the 15,000 children in the parochial schools would be sent to the public schools. This threat, however, was not carried out.

of the citizens had taken place at the North Presbyterian Church to decide a policy for religious instruction in the school. Without a dissent, says Henry Barnard, the group voted against the introduction of religious exercises in the school.[4]

✦

In his 1869 report to the school board, the young superintendent discussed the controversy. His remarks are a corollary of his position that the responsibility for education must be divided among all the institutions in society. He calls it a mistake on the part of some people that they wish to thrust upon the public schools the responsibility for the complete education of the child. When told that the State declines to take charge of religious education, these same critics argue for its inseparableness from secular education and demand that "the State shall proceed to surrender to them the secular part of the education, in order that they may unite with it the religious part in such proportion as they approve."[5]

The great lesson of history, in Harris's judgment, was that the separation of Church and State is the safeguard of individual liberty. Freedom for all to follow the dictates of conscience is the cornerstone of republican institutions, and these can never flourish except upon the conviction that the secular itself is of vital importance. Every instance in history of union between Church and State has tended, he says, to the "corruption of the former and the weakening of the latter." Consequently, we in America have separated secular and religious instruction far more than in Europe, even to such an extent as "almost to secularize our parochial schools."[6] The question of the separation of Church and State, says Harris, is the deepest political question in modern history, and "the study of the philosophy of history alone can give us the solution of these problems."[7] The public school system has

---

[4] *American Journal of Education*, XXX (Sept., 1880), 637. Harris himself said: "I cannot find that our schools have ever since their foundation in 1838 permitted so much as the reading of the Bible in them. I believe that this perfect secularity has done much to bring about the perfect intermingling of all denominations in our schools which has existed for so long." (*Seventeenth Annual Report*, 1871, p. 17.)

[5] *Fifteenth Annual Report*, p. 21.   [6] *Ibid.*, pp. 21–22.

[7] "Moral Education," *American Journal of Education*, IX (Jan., 1876), 4.

been regulated with a sincere desire to respect the feelings and wishes of all. Let the community see to it that our public schools are free from sectarian bias of whatever kind, and then the Church, by its appropriate instrumentalities, will best perform its mission.[8]

In his 1871 report Harris devoted many pages to a more thorough discussion of the problem. Whether special religious instruction should be given in public schools, he writes, depends on whether the teaching of morality can have place apart from special religious instruction. He insists that religion and the State should be separate in order to secure the highest perfection of each, but "this doctrine is not based on the denial of the supreme importance of religion, but on the principle that the modern state exists for the realization of one of the principles unfolded by religion." [9] This moral function can be performed only when the two exist independently.

On the other hand, Harris is clear in his insistence that morality is indispensable to the system of education. "Whatever separation may be made of religion," he says, "morality must be provided for." He acknowledges that religion contains the ultimate ground of obligation, and so must necessarily furnish the ground for the system of ethics that grows up under it. But since the Church and the State have become independent, why may not the school and the Church also sunder to mutual advantage? There follows one of his favorite arguments:

Whatever the Church has nurtured to such a maturity that it can live and thrive on its own inherent value, should be no longer supported by mere ecclesiastical authority. If the code of moral duties is supported and recognized fully by the State as necessary to the well-being of society, morality will not lose, but religion will gain by letting the State have charge of moral education.[10]

If youth in the schools are trained to habits of ready obedience to the command of duty, irrespective of appeals to self-interest or to religious obligation, character must needs be formed whose basis is "self-control, self-denial, or preference of what is right for mere inclination." Religion then becomes the gainer, for it will find its

[8] *Fifteenth Annual Report*, p. 22.   [9] *Seventeenth Annual Report*, p. 26.
[10] *Ibid.*, p. 27.

presuppositions already developed in the mind of youth, just as it now finds a ready entrance into a community where the State has organized justice. This is seen in the contrary situation in a country where the State is not developed: violence reigns, and religion finds superstition and fear where there should be reverence and love. If the Church has the whole care of education, it inculcates duties on the ground of religious obligation, and the morality thus formed gives it no reciprocal support.

According to Harris, all public schools do lay a great deal of stress on discipline, which includes behavior as its chief item. The most effective moral training is that which forms habits of doing and acting in such a way as to aid others—one's fellow pupils and the teacher— in doing reasonable deeds. However, this ability demands that the pupil be regular and punctual at school, industrious in learning his lessons, and careful not to interfere with others so as to prevent them from study. "The discipline of the school requires a strict adherence to the forms of action that resemble those of a well-drilled company of soldiers." [11]

Another aim of discipline in the school is to prepare pupils for later responsibility in the community:

We believe that a child can easily learn the lesson of willing obedience to lawful authority. We would therefore, place him upon the basis upon which he must stand when he leaves our care; under such circumstances alone we can predict that those whose school record is good will make useful citizens.[12]

Harris desired not merely order but *discipline* in the school. Order can be secured by "the terrors of the law," but he wanted the pupils to identify themselves with the right and the true. Until discipline should affect the character, instead of temporarily modifying the conduct, there may be order, he said, but not a very high or valuable discipline.[13] The "discipline" theory, in its classic form a casualty to the New Education, required that "the pupil must be silent and refrain from whispering or talking; he must repress his tendency to

[11] W. T. Harris, *Public Schools in the District of Columbia,* Senate Executive Document #12, 52d Congress, 2d Session, 1892.
[12] *Seventeenth Annual Report,* p. 65.   [13] *Ibid.*

prate or chatter; he must learn to hold back the fierce impulse to utter himself and wait for reflection to come to his mind."[14]

Although Harris's ideas on discipline today seem excessively rigid, they were normal for the time. As a matter of fact, his view was quite balanced, as these next lines indicate:

The school that is strictly disciplined by harsh methods, corporal punishment and the like, may become poisonous to the higher virtues. But the school that is governed by laxity, neglecting industry, silence, and punctuality, is far more deadly in its effects on the character. The martinet system of discipline is moral in so far as it gives those habits of prompt combination with one's fellows, but it is better adapted to galley slaves and prison convicts than to children of the public schools.[15]

He was in fact strongly opposed to the use of corporal punishment, except as a final resort, and made a practice of faithfully listing in his official reports the rare cases that occurred in the schools.

The charges bandied about that the public schools were responsible for the increase in crime and delinquency annoyed him but provided an occasion for a calm answer in which he emphasized pertinent data on the relative incidence of crime among the literate and the illiterate. Harris felt that those who hurled charges of immorality and infidelity against the public schools were ignorant of their high moral tone. To anyone familiar with the methods of the schools, it seemed obvious that the school had a salutary effect upon the morals of the pupil. Good discipline, which did prevail in the Harris schools, was solid and effective moral training. No wonder then, he concludes, that those citizens who have attended school, even for the short period required to learn reading and writing, are found to be seven times less likely to reach the jail or the prison than those who are entirely illiterate.[16]

---

[14] *Public Schools in the District of Columbia*, p. 1. Harris seized on Darwin for a buttressing argument: "If it is true, as scientific men tell us, that man has descended from the anthropoid apes, we can see more clearly the significance of this moral training which suppresses the tendency to prate and chatter. The mere instinct for expression of the half-cultured child is to utter what comes first to his mind." ("Relation of School Discipline to Moral Education," in National Herbart Society, *Third Yearbook, 1897,* p. 62.)

[15] "On the Normal School Course of Study," *Report of the Alumnae Association,* State Normal School, Framingham, Mass., 1889, p. 30.

[16] "The Church, the State, and the School," *North American Review,* CXXXIII (Sept., 1881), 226–27.

But neither school nor Church should be considered totally account-able for blame or praise in these matters. "It is not the education of the school alone, nor of the Church nor of the family alone, that can produce the happy results required. Each has its special province—all are necessary to the result." On occasion, Harris also rose to the defense of the education given by the Church. A valuable function of this education, he pointed out, is its conterbalance to the secularizing tendency of the school. The materialistic trend in modern education diminishes respect for authority and increases disdain for religion. And yet stability in society is contingent upon the principle of obedi-ence to authority.[17] The Church can greatly smooth this transition from blind obedience to reasoned autonomy. "The work of religious teachers is chiefly that of educating the people into an abiding respect for authority." For religion itself is nothing without faith in authority. "Hence the clergy are the most conservative portion of society, and woe betide society were this otherwise."[18]

✦

In the 1872 report wherein he discusses moral training, Harris itemizes the duties of "(1) punctuality, (2) regularity, (3) silence, (4) truth, (5) industry, (6) respect for the rights of others."[19] The first place invariably accorded to punctuality in all such lists is de-liberate on Harris's part. He esteemed it as "one of the moral virtues which underlie social life." The ghosts of his thrifty New England forebears would have approved, as would the orderly Hegel, his mak-ing punctuality a virtue almost worthy of cultivation for its own sake, and decidedly worth cultivating for the community's sake. "Lack of punctuality," writes Harris, "causes the many to suffer for the one" in joint undertakings. Strict observance of punctuality is every year becoming more essential to success as "we approach an era in which steam and machinery have to play a large part in the industrial life of every man."[20]

[17] "Isolation in the School—How It Hinders and How It Helps," *Journal of Proceedings and Addresses of the NEA, 1901*, p. 360.

[18] "Vocation Versus Culture; or the Two Aspects of Education," *American Institute of Instruction Lectures, 1891*, p. 2.

[19] *Eighteenth Annual Report*, p. 16.

[20] *Twenty-fifth Annual Report, 1879*, p. 34.

The superintendent was in deadly earnest. Each report laboriously listed statistics on tardiness and absences for the entire school system. The names of the high school graduates who had never, or seldom, been tardy or absent were given a place of honor in his printed reports. In 1872 he wrote that "the best feature of our statistics is this item of punctuality. Nearly two-thirds of our pupils were not tardy at all, and the remaining one-third were tardy on an average only three times during the year."[21]

His pride is only lightly veiled in the report for the year 1876 where he writes:

The number of cases of tardiness has reached the ratio of 52 to the 100 pupils enrolled during the year, a number unprecedented in the history of the schools of St. Louis, or, it may be affirmed, in the history of the school system in any other large city in this country. It confirms my remarks of last year, to the effect that the efforts of our teachers in securing punctual habits are gradually but surely working a reform in the habits of the community.[22]

The Harris philosophy of character formation demanded that "sleep, business, play, indisposition, all must give way to the duty of obedience to this external requirement to observe the particular moment of time and conform to it." But punctuality only begins when the pupil has arrived at the school. "He must have his lesson ready at the appointed time, and must rise from his seat at the tap of the bell, move to line, return: in short he must go through all the evolutions with observance of rhythm."[23]

Regularity is a close second to punctuality in the Harris hierarchy of virtues, for in essence it is punctuality reduced to a system. Conformity to the requirements of time in a particular instance is punctuality; made general, it becomes regularity. Combination in school rests on these two virtues. "They are," he says, "the most elementary of the moral code—its alphabet, in short."[24]

Out of this comes the possibility of training to general habits of proper position for sitting and standing, proper modes of speaking

---

[21] *Eighteenth Annual Report*, p. 16.

[22] *Twenty-second Annual Report*, p. 17.

[23] "Moral Education in Schools," *Education*, III (Sept., 1883), 5.

[24] *Ibid*. By "combination" he means the ability to associate with others for a mutual objective.

and of addressing others, and in general the formalities of polite intercourse. Music plays an important role here. Rhythm presupposes in the highest degree the training in punctual and regular habits, and "a conscious participation in the result is reached by the pupil through his enjoyment of the harmony he assists in producing." [25] From this also arises the disposition to interior silence and reflection out of which thought can originate.

✦

There is a pattern in these different observations cut from the cloth of Kant, Goethe, and Hegel. In the *Journal of Speculative Philosophy* Harris gives an Hegelian definition of ethics: "Whatever lifts man above immediate existence, the wants and impulses of the present moment, and gives him self-control, is called ethical." In explaining this definition Harris says that the ethical is grounded in man's existence in the species and in the possibility of the realization of the species in the individual. This forms part of his proof for personal immortality, the complement or sanction of the ethical idea. Ethics rests on the idea of a social whole representing the totality of mankind and on the idea of an immortal life as the condition of realizing in each man the life of the whole. And so ethics lays stress on the attitude of renunciation by the individual:

The special man must deny himself, sacrifice the present moment in order to attain the higher form of eternity. To act indifferently toward the present moment is to "act disinterestedly," as it is called. It is the preference of reflected good for immediate good—my good reflected from all humanity, my good after their good and through their good, and not my good before their good and instead of their good.[26]

This ideal (the individual must realize in himself the species and receive only such good as comes to him from all humanity) presupposes and necessitates the social union of the world of intelligences: "Each shall help all—a finite act; all shall help each—an infinite act. Each one thus participating in the infinite, invisible communion of souls shall thus be made infinite and divine. Hence the Invisible

[25] *Seventeenth Annual Report,* p. 32.
[26] "Immortality of the Individual," *Journal of Speculative Philosophy,* XIX (April, 1885), 214.

Church of all immortal spirits becomes the Institution whose eternity
is as divine as the Creator's." [27]

Hence, too, the primacy of obedience in education. In fact, the
general form of all school work is obedience. This means that

the will of the pupil comes into relation with the will of the teacher and
yields to its sway. The will of the pupil inhibits its own wayward impulses,
suppresses them, and supplants them by a higher rational will. In the act
of obedience to a higher will the pupil becomes conscious of responsibility.[28]

Yet this responsibility implies an awareness of freedom: to use the
phrase of the founder of "the great system of ethics in modern times,
Immanuel Kant," the child learns in the school to have a sense of
"transcendental freedom." [29] A child becomes conscious of its ability
to accept or refuse, to obey or disobey. It becomes aware of its power
to originate actions and to give a new form to the chain of causation
in which it finds itself. Harris calls the pupil's accountability at each
and every moment for all that he does "the great fact in the school-
room."

✦

Harris set about a classification of moral virtues, which he embodied
in several journal articles and in the "Report of the Committee on
Moral Education" to the National Council of Education.[30] Although
Harris was only one of five men who signed the report—the others
being William A. Mowrey, J. H. Hoose, H. S. Tarbell, and G. Stanley
Hall—the report is his work.[31] He (and the committee) divided
moral duties or habits into three classes: mechanical, social, and
religious.

[27] *Ibid.,* p. 218.
[28] National Herbart Society, *Third Yearbook, 1897,* p. 65.
[29] *Ibid.,* p. 66.
[30] "Moral Education in Schools," *Education,* III (Sept., 1883), 1–14. The same
matter is treated in the article "Relation of School Discipline to Moral Education," in National Herbart Society, *Third Yearbook.* Large sections are identical
in phrasing.
[31] Another article entitled "Moral Education in the Common Schools," read
by Harris at the 1883 Saratoga meeting of the American Social Science Association, is substantially identical with this report. This address was reprinted in
the *Journal of Social Science,* XVIII (May, 1884), 122–34. The name of G.
Stanley Hall among the signatories sets up some interesting conjectures: see
Chapter VIII.

Mechanical virtues are those in which the youth exercises a minimum of moral choice and obeys an external rule prescribed for him. Harris calls this the lowest species of moral discipline: "Youth learns self-denial and self-control, and not much besides."[32] Social duties are those which govern the relation of man to man, and which are properly called "moral" duties. In this form of moral discipline, the youth learns to obey principle rather than the immediate will of another or a mechanical prescription. Thirdly, there are religious duties, or those based on the relation to God as revealed in religion. In these, according to Harris, the youth learns the ultimate grounds of obligation and gains both a "practical principle for the conduct of life and a theoretic principle on which to base his view of the world." In Harris's religious doctrine man formulates his theory of the origin and destiny of nature and the human race, and at the same time defines "his eternal vocation, his fundamental duties."[33]

Harris speaks of the discipline of obedience in its strict form, such as found in the classroom, as having four other applications which remain valid under all conditions of society. The first three deal with obedience toward parents, employers, civil and military authority. The fourth is "towards the Divine Will, howsoever revealed," whose meaning is that

the individual comes more and more to a personal insight into the necessity of the divine law as revealed in Scripture, in nature, and especially in human life, and he becomes through this emancipated relatively from the direct personal control of men, even of the wisest and best, and becomes rather a law unto himself. He outgrows mere mechanical obedience, and arrives at a truly moral will in which the law is written on the heart.[34]

Since mechanical duties are elementary and basic, moral education must begin in merely mechanical obedience and develop gradually out of this stage toward individual responsibility. The strictly moral duties fall into two classes, those relating to the individual himself

[32] This thought is repeated over and over: "These very simple duties seem mechanical, and are often despised; but *they underlie all higher ethics and make possible all great combinations*" (Harris's emphasis). "Our Public Schools: Can Morality Be Taught without Sectarianism?" *Journal of Education*, XXIX (Feb. 14, 1889), 1.

[33] "Moral Education in the Common Schools," *Journal of Social Science*, XVIII (May, 1884), 134.

[34] "Moral Education in Schools," *Education*, III (Sept., 1883), 4.

and those relating to his fellows. The basis of duties to self is "the consciousness of a higher nature in the individual and of the duty of bringing out and realizing this higher nature. Duties to others recognize this higher ideal nature as something general, and hence as also the true inward self of our fellow-men." [35]

Harris offers broad definitions of the social virtues. For instance, he says courtesy includes "all forms of politeness, good-breeding, urbanity, decorum, modesty, respect for public opinion, liberality, magnanimity, etc." He likewise attributes several forms or species to justice, "as, for example, (a) honesty, the fairdealing with others respecting their rights of person, property, and reputation; (b) truth-telling or honesty in speech—honesty itself being truth-acting. Such names as integrity, uprightness, righteousness, express further distinctions that belong to this staunch virtue." [36]

The school is more effective in teaching the forms of justice than those of courtesy. Truthtelling notably receives the full emphasis of all the power of school discipline. "Every lesson is an exercise in digging out and closely defining the truth—in extending the realm of clearness and certainty further, and in limiting the region of ignorance and guesswork." [37]

For Harris, morals included a wide range of virtues which border on the province of religion and even overlap it in the case of faith, hope, and charity—"which the Church calls celestial virtues to distinguish them from the secular virtues of prudence, fortitude, temperance and justice." [38] Probably the most extraordinary feature of Harris's treatment of moral virtue is the extension of the theological virtues of faith, hope, and charity to the secular order. Traditional Catholic and Protestant teaching has reserved these names for those distinctive human acts and habits whose principle and object is something strictly supernatural.

Harris begins his lengthy treatment by remarking that what are called "celestial" virtues by the theologians—faith, hope, and charity—are higher than the secular or "cardinal" virtues. The question then arises, he says, whether any instruction in these duties can be given

[35] *Ibid.*, p. 7.   [36] *Ibid.*   [37] *Ibid.*, p. 8.
[38] "School Statistics and Morals," *Journal of Proceedings and Addresses of the NEA, 1893*, p. 1.

which is not at the same time sectarian? An affirmative answer will have to show only that "each of these virtues has a *secular meaning more fundamental than the so-called cardinal virtues*." [39]

He then proceeds to define faith as the "true knowledge of the first principle of the universe." Everybody assumes, he says, some theory of the origin and destiny of the world. Christendom begins with "a personal Creator of divine-human nature, who admits man to Grace in such a way that he is not destroyed by the results of his essential imperfection, but is redeemed in some special way." In Christian countries prevailing institutions and confessions of faith recognize this belief in a divine-human God. In fact, natural science itself may be said to presuppose this doctrine, "inasmuch as it is based on the deeply-lying assumption that the world is a manifestation of Reason." He continues:

This view of the world is very properly called Faith, inasmuch as it is not pieced together from the experience of the senses nor a product of individual reflection unaided by the deep intuitions of the spiritual seers of the race.

Faith is a secular virtue as well as a theological virtue, and whoever teaches another view of the world—that is to say, he who teaches that man is not immortal and that Nature does not reveal the Divine Reason—teaches a doctrine subversive of faith in this peculiar sense, and also subversive of man's life in all that makes it worth living.[40]

There is an unfortunate lack of precision here. Harris has not distinguished knowledge through faith (i.e., knowledge received on the word of another) from knowledge directly experienced, nor has he really distinguished natural (secular) faith from supernatural (theological) faith.

Hope, for Harris, is the practical side of faith. Since faith is not properly the belief in some theory of the world but in *the* particular theory of the world that Christianity teaches, so hope is not a mere anticipation of *some* future event but the firm expectation that the destiny of the world is in accord with the scheme of faith, no matter how much any present appearances may be against it. Accordingly

[39] "Moral Education in Schools," *Education,* III (Sept., 1883), 9. Emphasis added.
[40] *Ibid.*

the individual acts upon his conviction. This is the basis of the highest practical doing in the world. And what happens in the classroom?

A teacher may teach faith and hope in the views of the world which he expresses and in his dealings with his school, in his teaching of history, in his comments on the reading-lessons, in his treatment of the aspirations of his pupil. Although none of these things may be consciously traced to their source by the pupils, yet their instinct will discover genuine faith and hope whenever it exists. Nothing is so difficult to conceal as one's conviction in regard to the origin and destiny of the world and of man.[41]

Harris's understanding of "charity" also would appear to many as a curious mélange of the natural and supernatural. He calls charity the "concrete embodiment and application of that view of the world which Faith and Hope establish." The next words are striking when it is kept in mind that he is speaking of a *secular* motivation, entirely appropriate for character building in the public school:

The world is made and governed by Divine Grace, and that grace will triumph in the world. Hence, says the individual, "Let me be filled with this principle and hold within myself this divine feeling of grace toward all fellow creatures." Charity is, therefore, not almsgiving, but a devotion to others: "Sell all thou hast . . . and follow me." Faith perceives the principle; Hope acts upon it where it is not yet visible; Charity sets it up in the soul and lives it.[42]

Charity is the highest of the virtues and has, according to Harris, the largest family of synonyms: "humility, considerateness, heroism, gratitude, friendliness, and various shades of love in the family (parental, filial, fraternal, and conjugal), sympathy, pity, benevolence, kindness, toleration, patriotism, generosity, public-spirit, philanthropy, beneficence, concord, harmony, peaceableness, tenderness, forgiveness, mercy, grace, long-suffering, etc." [43]

The typical form of charity that may be cultivated in the school is kindness. If this pervades the school, it can prove a fountain of virtues. The celestial virtues themselves "must be taught by example rather than by precept, and by the general demeanor of the teacher, and by the atmosphere of the school." [44] The lack of these celestial virtues

---

[41] *Ibid.,* p. 10.   [42] *Ibid.*   [43] *Ibid.,* pp. 10–11.

[44] "On the Normal School Course of Study," *Report of the Alumnae Association,* State Normal School, Framingham, Mass., 1889, p. 30.

produces crime, i.e., it sets intellect, will, and heart against one's fellow men. "Very justly, then, do theologians claim that religious education in this broad sense is the foundation of the institutions of civilization."[45] There ensues the immediate qualification that it does not necessarily follow that the school should be an appanage of the Church, or that anything but secular education should be attempted in it. Harris's statement that the classroom should be exclusively devoted to secular education comes less reassuringly in the wake of his words on the teaching of the celestial virtues. Despite his protests to the contrary, hasn't Harris here proposed a shadowy "nonsectarian" Christian religion, somewhat like Horace Mann's proposal for the Massachusetts schools?

Harris is perhaps aware of an inconsistency here. In a State which has no established Church, he asks, and in a system of public schools that is not controlled by denominations, what shall be the fate of dogmatic instruction in morals, "especially in that part of morals which rests upon the celestial virtues"? Though the problem seems a simple one in parochial schools and denominational schools, he sees a complication. For the stricter the control, the less likely the spirit of tolerance and charity toward others. *"Were the community homogeneous in its profession of faith, dogmatic religious instruction could still properly remain in the school."* [46]

This seems an extraordinary admission in view of his position, to be explained later, that religious and secular instruction in the same school are essentially incompatible. However, in the practical order there is slight possibility that such religious homogeneity will come about, for "the progress of American society is not, however, in that direction." As a matter of fact, "it is not impossible that the Church may yet see formal religious instruction, even to the ceremony of reading the Bible, leave the common schools altogether."[47]

In the parallel article written for the *Journal of Social Science*, Harris adds several thoughts which do not appear in the committee report.

[45] "School Statistics and Morals," *Journal of Proceedings and Addresses of the NEA, 1893*, p. 1.

[46] *Ibid.*, p. 11. Emphasis added. See the concluding chapter.

[47] *Ibid.*

A formal reading of the Bible "without note or comment," or a formal prayer on opening school, is surely not religious or moral instruction in any such efficient sense as to warrant any Christian man or woman in sitting down in content, and claiming a religious hold on the popular education. Such a delusive content is indeed too prevalent.[48]

In an earlier article he strikes a blow for the moral autonomy of the school:

Frequently it has been admitted by its friends that education without special religious instruction—at least, without reading of the Bible—is pernicious and immoral. I think it is sufficiently evident that such is not the case, but rather the opposite. But in this exposition I wish to be explicitly understood as claiming only that Public School education is moral and completely so, on its own basis; that it lays the basis for religion, *but is not a substitute for religion*. It is not a substitute for the State because it teaches justice—it only prepares an indispensable culture for the citizen of the State. The State must exist; Religion must exist and complement the structure of human culture begun in moral education.[49]

Although Bible-reading and prayer were common practices in most school systems during the period in question, they did not have a place in the St. Louis schools. Harris agreed fully with the policy that the schools should be completely secular. He also agreed that there was a very great need for a widespread evangelical movement to begin, "that shall make real once more the faith that is well-nigh become a mere formula." This, however, was not the task of the schools. His active support of an evangelical crusade by the churches does not imply, he insists, any support for "the undoing of the separation of Church and State, even in the common schools, nor for the struggle to maintain a frigid and bloodless 'non-sectarian,' so-called, religion in our schools." The total responsibility belongs to the churches. Let them be alert to the danger, and "proselyte by new means and appliances as well adapted to the present day as the Sunday-school movement was seventy years ago." [50]

No, let Church and State be kept separate. The clearer the separation, the more general the movement toward the adoption of religion

---

[48] "Moral Education in the Common Schools," *Journal of Social Science,* XVIII (May, 1884), 132.

[49] "Moral Education," *American Journal of Education,* VIII (Nov., 1875), 5.

[50] "Moral Education in the Common Schools," *Journal of Social Science,* XVIII (May, 1884), 133.

as the foundation of all institutions. The wider the separation, the more their organic unity will be seen: "For science is, in the best analysis, the perception of holiness as the law of nature—a perfect self-consistency of creative reason; justice and the State, with approximating exactness, define the holy as the law of the will of the State; morality is the ideal of right reason seeing what is holy in the nature of Being itself." [51]

But separation of religion from the school did not mean that moral instruction ought not to be given. "I think," he wrote in the *Journal of Education,* "that morality can be taught, and that it is taught in our public schools, and in all good private schools, without sectarianism, and even apart from religious instruction, although I believe that religion is the ultimate ground of morality." [52]

Harris spent a good fifty years trying to make others see what he saw so clearly, that there was

an important discrimination between instruction in the theory of morals and an inculcation of moral habits. . . . To study the physiology of digestion does not satisfy the appetite for food. One may know the theory of morality, but he is not moral unless he acquires and practices moral habits. Moral education relates strictly to the will, and is a training in habits of action. [53]

Accordingly, the school was discharging its full responsibility by maintaining "discipline." To those who advanced the argument that if you omit religion from the school, you omit it altogether from life, because the school furnishes the only education that the child receives, Harris pointed out that this was to ignore the education of the family, the Church, the community, as well as other influences. His line of argument has a modern ring. The school cannot take the place of these other educative agencies, "no matter how important that work is, nor how sadly it is neglected by them." Responsibility should be laid at the proper doors:

If there is irreligion, practical atheism in the community, the Church is evidently not as efficient as it ought to be, and the family is also derelict. If the

[51] "The Present Need of Moral Training in the Public Schools," *Journal of Education,* XXVII (March, 1888), 131–32.

[52] "Our Public Schools: Can Morality Be Taught without Sectarianism?" *Journal of Education,* XXIX (Feb. 14, 1889), 1.

[53] *Morality in the Schools,* pp. 1–2.

school secures good behavior and a knowledge of letters and science, it has contributed its share. The Church can then confine its labors to the work of teaching its holy doctrines instead of wasting much energy in doing the secular work of teaching reading, arithmetic, and geography, as a foundation of its religious instruction.[54]

The chief source of difficulty in harmonizing conflicting views on the weighty problem of religion in public education, according to Harris, is this failure to discriminate between religion and morality. Several times he has stated that religion is the ultimate ground of morality. This meant that "the idea which man forms of the First Principle determines all his ideas of the origin and destiny of man and nature," and these ideas determine ultimately his conduct of life. The ethical code of Christianity, however, differs from all others for the reason "that it lays more stress on the condescending grace of God than they do." Nevertheless, morality is still not religion. Why? His answer:

Simply because religion involves acts of devotion and sacrifice of a ceremonial character. Morality involves behavior toward others and toward one's self and a ceremonial entirely different from that of religion; namely, the conventional ceremonial which we call the code of politeness, manners, and behavior toward others. The whole of this behavior can be taught, and is taught best, without bringing it into the same place and time with religious instruction. Moral behavior relates to details which appear unessential when placed side by side with the doctrine of man's relation to God. The strictly moral duties concern the relation of man to man, and for this reason are all finite when compared with the subject-matter of religion. The religious duty of the salvation of the soul is so all-engrossing that it obscures the relations of man to society.[55]

One consequence he draws from this is puzzling. Harris remarks that the direct mediation of man with God tends to displace the finite mediation of man with his fellow men. In the primitive Christian era, converts to Christianity fled to the wilderness in order to live the "holy life of hermits and realize a more direct communion with God, apart from the distractions incident to civil life." In fact, Harris calls the beggar hermit, "who is the symbol of the utter annulment of the secular world," the nearest approach to the divine life and instances

[54] *Ibid.*, p. 3.
[55] *Ibid.*, pp. 5–6. See also "The Division of School Funds for Religious Purposes," *Atlantic Monthly*, XXXVIII (Aug., 1876), 180.

Calderon's representation of him thus in his *World Theatre.* "Productive industry and beggary are antitheses." [56] Is Harris saying here that religion is antisocial? Must the religious man invariably renounce society?

✦

The most detailed presentation of his thought on the general subject of religion in the schools was given by Harris in a 1903 address before the National Council of Education at Boston entitled "The Separation of the Church from the Tax-supported School." [57] Substantially the same material is to be found in an 1889 symposium: "Our Public Schools: Can Morality Be Taught without Sectarianism?" [58] as well as in an 1876 article, "The Division of School Funds for Religious Purposes." [59] The 1903 Boston talk, in some form, was reprinted in several journals, including the *Independent,* the *Educational Review,* and the *Literary Digest.*

There was considerable opposition, even resentment, toward some of the views expressed in the talk. The Boston *Pilot,* a Catholic journal, reported that Dr. Harris's conclusions were pronounced by several of the delegates present "twenty-five years behind the times." [60] The Boston *Congregationalist* commented critically upon the complete divorce urged by Harris between religious instruction and the public schools.[61] Among his more articulate critics was a Jesuit priest, Rev. Timothy Brosnahan, who published his animadversions in a booklet, *Dr. Harris and the Agnostic School House.* These will be taken up in the concluding section of this chapter.

Harris opened the address with his usual premise, that the question of religious education in the schools supported by public taxes was not the question of the importance of religion. The precise question was of "the most fitting occasion for efficient instruction in religion on the one hand, and on the other hand the question of guarding the rights of private conscience and the separation of Church and State."

[56] *Morality in the Schools,* p. 6.
[57] *Educational Review,* XXVI (Oct., 1903), 222–35.
[58] *Journal of Education,* XXIX (Feb. 14, 1889), 1.
[59] *Atlantic Monthly,* XXXVIII (Aug., 1876), 171–84.
[60] Cited in the *Literary Digest* (editorial), XXVII, No. 9 (Aug. 29, 1903), 261.
[61] *Ibid.*

He asks, on what grounds is the claim made that the Church and
the State are each more efficient when completely separated in their
functions? Why do proponents of absolute separation argue that religion without an established Church is more spiritual, more devoted
to the highest interests of the soul? Upon what do they base their
claims that the State which does not permit itself to interfere in
religious matters administers justice in a more efficient manner, and
"that the school supported by the State teaches the secular branches of
instruction with greater success"? [62]

When one realizes the parallel between the emancipation of the
State from the tutelage of the Church and the need of the school to
free itself from the Church, the reasoning of the proponents of separation becomes plain. Justice is the leading virtue of the secular order
and of its highest institution, the State. This means that each man
shall have his deed returned to him. A deed that injures the State is
punished in proportion to the harm inflicted upon society. On the
other hand, religion does not consider the external act so much as the
inward state of the soul. The opposing methods of dealing with sin
and crime would be confounded unless religion and the State were
separate, for repentance and forgiveness have no place in a secular
order governed strictly by justice, nor condemnation and punishment
in a divine order tempered by grace and mercy.[63] Harris now applies
his analogy (on which, he says, the separation of the Church and
State is based) to education and the school.

The principle of religious instruction is authority; that of secular instruction
is demonstration and verification. It is obvious that these two principles
should not be brought into the same school, but separated as widely as
possible. Religious truth is revealed in allegoric and symbolic form, and is to
be apprehended not merely by the intellect, but also by the imagination and
the heart. The analytic understanding is necessarily hostile and skeptical in
its attitude towards religious truth.[64]

For example, the pupil is taught in mathematics to love demonstration
and logical proof, and he is taught in history to verify its sources and

[62] "The Separation of the Church from the Tax-supported School," *Educational Review*, XXVI (Oct., 1903), 222–23.

[63] *Ibid.*, p. 223. See also *Morality in the Schools, #5.*

[64] "The Separation of the Church from the Tax-supported School," *Educational Review*, XXVI (Oct., 1903), 224.

to submit all tradition to probabilities of common experience. The habit of thinking, even the attitude of mind, cultivated in secular instruction is out of place applied to the elevated themes dealt with in religious faith. Why is this true?

Because religious instruction should be surrounded with solemnity. It should be approached with ceremonial preparation, so as to lift up the mind to the dignity of the lesson received. Christianity is indeed the religion of the revealed God, but there is no revelation possible to the mind immersed in trivialities and self-conceit. In religious lessons wherein the divine is taught as revealed to the human race, it is right that the raw, immature intellect of youth shall not be called upon to exercise a critical judgment, for the youth at his best cannot grasp the rationality of the dogmas which contain the deepest insights of the religious consciousness of the race.[65]

In the secular branches, continues Harris, the mind is to be trained to keep all its powers awake. Thought is to be alert and critical; faith is to be dormant. In religion, faith in authority is to be the chief organ, and the critical faculty of the intellect is to be kept subordinate.[66] The conclusion is obvious: the mind must not be changed too abruptly from secular studies to religious contemplation. The spirit of authority loves dogmatic assertion and the memorizing of the exact words of the textbook. It represses the investigating spirit and stifles independent thinking. Arithmetic, algebra, and geometry cannot be learned by authority. Geography and history can be learned properly only by the mind that carefully observes facts and verifies the statements of others. Grammar requires severe application of definitions and logical distinctions.[67]

The Church, on the other hand,

has thru long ages learned the proper method of religious instruction. It elevates sense-perception thru solemn music addressed to the ear, and works of art which represent to the eye the divine self-sacrifice for the salvation of man. It clothes its doctrine in the language of the Bible, a book sacredly kept apart from other literature, and held in such exceptional reverence that it is taken entirely out of the natural order of experience. The symbolic language of the Psalms, the Prophets, and the Gospels, has come to possess a maximum power of suggestiveness, a mighty influence to induce what is

[65] *Ibid.*, p. 225.   [66] *Morality in the Schools,* #6.
[67] "The Separation of the Church from the Tax-supported School," *Educational Review,* XXVI (Oct., 1903), 225.

called the religious frame of mind. The highest wisdom of the race is expounded before the people of the congregation in such language and such significant acts of worship as to touch the hearts of young and old with like effect.[68]

It is a practical fact, according to Harris, that the mingling of religious and secular instruction "cultivates habits of flippant and shallow reasoning on sacred themes, thus sapping the foundations of piety." For corroboration he appeals to the examples of Germany, Austria, and other states that place religious lessons on the regular school program so many hours a week. The pupils in these countries are well taught in secular studies but learn to hold in contempt the contents of religious lessons. They bring their critical intellects to bear on dogmas and become skeptical of all religious truth: "Is not the Germany of today the most skeptical of all peoples? Is not its educated class famous for its free thinking so-called?" France is another example. There until recently the Church has had its own way with religious instruction, and where can you find another class of people in the world so abounding in atheism as the French educated class? [69]

In view of these differences in method and in spirit, it is clear, concludes Harris, that the school cannot successfully undertake religious instruction. He does make an exception for the boarding school, whether of elementary or of college grade, because the school thereupon assumes the principle of familial authority. The religion taught, however, "can not be of the kind known as unsectarian religion; it must be the religion of a particular denomination." [70]

On the point of "unsectarian" or "nonsectarian" religion, Harris holds a different view from Mann's. He dismisses the notion as something not only unsatisfactory but says that "it is impossible to have any such unsectarian religion that is not regarded as sectarian by the more earnest religious denominations." He has more to say:

The reading of the Bible, the offering of prayers, the teaching of some simple catechism, are devices borrowed from some particular forms of Protestantism—namely, from those forms which do not use the ceremonial of the

[68] *Ibid.*, p. 226.   [69] *Morality in the Schools,* #6.
[70] "The Separation of the Church from the Tax-supported School," *Educational Review,* XXVI (Oct., 1903), 226.

Church in the most impressive manner to create a spiritual sense in the pupils who are receiving religious instruction.[71]

Some advocates of the "unsectarian" approach to religious instruction in the public schools are influenced by their fear of the intolerance that results from cultivating religious differences. They argue, says Harris, that there are certain essential things in religion, such as "the being of God, His revelation of His will in the Bible, which they think all people in modern civilization should desire to have made a part of school instruction." Harris sees no validity in this position, because

it amounts only to the setting up of a new religious sect, and adding one more to the many denominations of religious belief. It is impossible to make a generalization of Christianity without depriving it of something that is necessary to the form of religion, namely, an appeal to the senses and the imagination.[72]

This is a profound insight into the nature of religious commitment, but one that Horace Mann never could see.[73] It is entirely true that religion is more than an abstract theological theory addressed to the educated intellect. Religion takes on the flesh of symbols directed partly to the imagination, partly to the understanding, for religion is received and exercised both exteriorly and interiorly by man.

Harris's appreciation of the practical impossibility of "nonsectarianism" is solidly based. He points out that even the bare enumeration of Christian doctrines in language partly secular was impossible in the common school curriculum. His argument merits attention. The necessary condition of the rights of conscience of all citizens alike in the State schools makes it impossible to bring in religious ceremonial or teach doctrines distinctively religious. There is no such thing as an undenominational religion. The next point is extremely well made:

Even the doctrine of the existence of God implies a specific conception of Him, and the conception of the divine varies from that of the finite deities of animism to the infinite deity of East Indian pantheism and the Holy Bible. It varies from the pantheistic Brahma, whose concept is that of negation of all attributes, to the Jehovah of the Bible, who is self-determined and personal, but elevated entirely above nature.

[71] *Ibid.*, p. 227.   [72] *Ibid.*, p. 228.   [73] See Chapter IV.

Mere deism is opposed to all the creeds of Christendom. When we come to teaching a live religion in the schools we see that it must take a denominational form, and, moreover, it must take on the form of authority, and address itself to the religious sense and not to the mere intellect.[74]

But since all the studies of the school are addressed to the intellect, they are in opposition to the "healthful action of the religious sense." There is a single conclusion: "The proper place for instruction in religion is the Church—only as propounded from the sacred desk and clothed in the consecrated text of the Bible can the dogmas of Christianity be made to edify the people of the congregation, young and old alike."

William Torrey Harris did not agree with Horace Mann on the place of the Bible in the common schools. He is consistent in his opposition to the Bible as an instrument of religious training in the public school. The Bible must be kept isolated from all other books because its effectiveness for religious instruction is due to its "consecration as a divine book coming direct from God and not thru the authorship of man." Private interpretation, moreover, presents difficulties, for it is in the nature of things "that what is symbolic has two meanings, the one literal and the other symbolic," and

it requires, therefore, the authoritative interpretation of the Church to settle the orthodox meaning. The spiritual sense is other-worldly and when its insights are translated into what is secular it may be made to contravene the moral world order, and this has happened in a myriad cases.[75]

Again, inexorably, Harris draws a conclusion from which even Bible-reading is not exempt, that in the nature of things religious instruction cannot be farmed out to the secular school "without degenerating into mere deism bereft of a living Providence, or else changing the school into a parochial school and destroying the efficiency of secular instruction." Hence the complete secularization of the school, for Harris, was the only feasible way of settling the question of religious instruction.[76] He points for corroboration to the very

[74] "The Separation of the Church from the Tax-supported School," *Educational Review*, XXVI (Oct., 1903), 231–32.
[75] *Ibid.*, p. 234.
[76] *Morality in the Schools*, #8. These lines are not without relevance today: "The public school should be careful to exclude not only the sectarian religious instruction of Protestantism, but also the sectarian interpretation of history, and

general adoption of the public school by Catholic parents. Where the greatest pains are taken to avoid proselyting Catholic children by Protestant influence, says Harris, the Catholic is most ready to patronize it. The Catholic hierarchy will recognize the purely secular public school soon after it recognizes the principle of the separation of Church and State—a principle now pretty generally recognized, he thinks, by the Catholic laity. The spirit of the times calls for a wider and wider separation of the Church from secular institutions but, repeats Harris, "such separation does not make them godless nor the Church less powerful, but quite the contrary."

On the other hand Harris saw no solution to the problem of religious education in the establishment of school systems under the control of the different religious denominations. He was not only unalterably opposed to any division of tax-derived school funds for this purpose but objected on principle to the existence of religious school systems. He feared that these would foment divisiveness and result in intolerance.[77] Harris was thoroughly convinced that the principle of growth into independence, i.e., through maturation one part of an organism achieves its freedom, was the highest principle in the uni-

---

in general make the public school a place where the Catholic may feel safe to leave his children. In St. Louis, the superintendent gave (and gives) permits to all children whose parents requested it, allowing them to be absent two hours in each week for religious instruction under the supervision of priest or pastor. This is one device which does not conflict with the principle of the separation of Church and State, and yet treats conscientious scruples with respect. The other plan of permitting the pastor to enter the school and teach religion conflicts with the constitutional provisions of the majority of the States of the Union. It is not a settlement possible with our present temper or with the conviction toward which we see all nations approaching." (*Ibid.*) Harris, of course, wrote these clairvoyant lines long before the U.S. Supreme Court decisions in the *McCollum* or *Zorach* cases.

[77] Harris, though, enjoyed the best of personal relations with individual leaders in parochial school education. In 1899 he was invited to a celebration at the Catholic University of America and asked to make the formal introduction of Bishop John Lancaster Spalding, who was the occasional speaker. The commissioner called Spalding "the most beloved of American educational leaders." He further said: "All serious and earnest-minded thinkers engaged in solving the problems of education, whether in the north, the south, the east or the west of this country, have received help from the personal counsels or from the educational writings of the Bishop of Peoria." (Document #620 in the Harris Collection of the Library of Congress. The introduction is written in longhand.)

verse, and could now be invoked to justify the school's autonomy and its right to give moral training apart from the Church's religious education. He appeals to the great thinkers of the ages for support, urging that this principle

is found suggested in Leibnitz's system of monads, in Plato's system of ideas, in Aristotle's first and second entelechies, in Hegel's absolute idea, and throughout the profound speculations of the great churchmen, such as St. Augustine, Thomas Aquinas, and St. Anselm, as well as in the writings of the German mystics, Meister Eckhart, Tauler, Jacob Boehme, and others.[78]

Ever since the thirteenth century, "the age in which Thomas Aquinas, perhaps the greatest thinker of all Christendom," unfolded the nature of justice and saw in it the divine foundation of the State and the importance of state supremacy in civil affairs, the conviction has gathered strength that the secular must develop independently of the ecclesiastical. In finding its own necessary conditions of development, the State will come to reflect the divine ideal of the Christian Church. "These institutions organized separately on their own principles will best subserve the cause of religion and further the interests of God's kingdom." The principle of maturity was all very fine; but here, as on many other occasions, the scholarly Dr. Harris strode over the hill-tops alone while leaving most of his auditors and readers to struggle in the valleys below.

Enough has been set forth in this study concerning his religious philosophy to make the charges of atheism and infidelity seem preposterous. Nevertheless, throughout his career Harris was intermittently charged by opponents with being a German rationalist, atheist, deist, freethinker, agnostic, and skeptic.[79] It is understandable that many people would find in his remarks about religion and public

[78] "The Division of School Funds for Religious Purposes," *Atlantic Monthly*, XXXVIII (Aug., 1876), 184. Harris here seems to have fallen into a double *petitio principii*. The point at issue concerns the schools and not the State: (1) Is formal education the exclusive responsibility of the secular State? (2) If so, must it be governed by the same secular principles which control the State?

[79] The name of Harris was several times proposed for the superintendency of the Boston schools, but "religionists," according to Leidecker (*Yankee Teacher*, pp. 379-80), successfully opposed him. He quotes a letter signed by a "Christian parent" which appeared during the 1876 election for superintendent, whose final sentence read: "Give us an educated Catholic, an educated Hebrew—anyone but an infidel!"

education grounds for doubting his orthodoxy; even his mother and grandmother, remember, did not understand him. He was *not* an orthodox believer, and he did use unconventional phrases to give flesh to his profoundly cerebral insights into the world of spirit. After all, if it takes an Hegelian to understand Hegel, by the same token it takes a Hegel to understand an Hegelian.

✦

Not all Harris critics were like the gentlemanly Father Brosnahan, who prefaced his criticism of the passages in the Boston address on the incompatibility of religious and secular learning with a personal tribute to Dr. Harris: "In advancing his doctrine of godless education, he has spoken of religion with a reverence, and with a devotion even, that clearly indicate his sincerity." But however admirable the commissioner's personal qualities and honorable his intentions, the Jesuit was firmly convinced that his educational principles deserved reprobation.

He finds that Harris's paper is equivalently pleading for the exclusion of religion from all schools in which instruction in secular knowledge is given, "whether supported by public taxes, by church revenues, by private contributions, or by any other means whatsoever." This was also the criticism of the Boston *Congregationalist,* where it was said that if Dr. Harris's contention is admitted, religious instruction has no place "either in private schools, colleges, or any institutions for the mental discipline and development of students." [80] Harris's strictures, it should be kept in mind, were all the more serious because of his position as the U.S. Commissioner of Education.

The spirit of the school and the spirit of the Church are not inconsistent and irreconcilable, writes Brosnahan. When Harris speaks of the necessity of pomp and ritual for the communication of religious truth, he is simply ignorant of the methods used in parochial schools, to say nothing of their use "by Christ, His apostles and the missionaries of the Church." Harris would create a Dr. Jekyll–Mr. Hyde mentality in the child who is caught between a religious atmosphere at home and one hostile to religion at school. Brosnahan concedes

[80] Quoted in "Religious Instruction in Public Schools," *Literary Digest,* XXVII (Aug. 29, 1903), 261.

that "secular knowledge may be so communicated as to produce infidelity and atheism"; but he emphatically denies that secular instruction necessarily produces a habit of mind that is hostile and skeptical in its attitude toward religious truth.[81]

Moreover, the principle of authority, fundamental in religious education, enters also into secular education. For authority means either a moral power by which one has jurisdiction over others with a correlative duty of obedience; or the intellectual worth of a witness to a fact, founded on his competence and veracity, by which his testimony merits acceptance and belief by those under his authority. A superior's authority is exercised over the will, a witness's authority over the intellect. Now in both senses, says Brosnahan, the principle of authority is operative in the classroom, as almost any lesson in history or geography makes plain.

Brosnahan smiles at Harris's claim that pupils in public elementary schools are really "taught in history to verify the sources and to submit all tradition to the probabilities of common experience." Asks the clerical critic: Do little boys and girls dig into ancient tomes, original records, and documents from archives, collate passages from various languages, to verify the sources of history? But even when authority in teaching history has been shifted from the classroom teacher back to the original sources, he argues, authority is still not banished from the school, for tradition and authority are precisely what establish the sources of history.[82]

Brosnahan closes his critique on a pensive note:

Could Horace Mann have revisited the scenes of his earthly labors . . . and heard the amazingly frank avowal of Dr. Harris that the thinking cultivated in the class-rooms of the public schools is, and must necessarily be, "hostile and sceptical in its attitude towards religious truth," those of us who are acquainted with his life may fancy with what a torrent of consuming wrath he would have repudiated such an issue of his principles and labors.

Nevertheless, it would not be difficult to show that the present school policy regarding morality and religion is the natural outcome of the character he impressed on the public school system in the fourth decade of the last century. Had the present conditions of our schools been foreseen, I

[81] Brosnahan, *Dr. Harris and the Agnostic School House*, p. 10.
[82] *Ibid.*, p. 13.

do not hesitate to assert, considering the religious character of the New Englanders of two generations ago, that the Horace Mann movement would have died at its inception.[83]

Brosnahan's last comment is open to question for at least two reasons. Local practice many times blissfully ignores the logic of theory, doing what it happily wants rather than what it logically ought. Given the conditions of nineteenth-century America, the public school movement would inevitably have come about—though possibly in a modified form. If Horace Mann had presented the religious education issue in the same clear-cut fashion as did William Torrey Harris, the "nonsectarian" compromise would probably not have been attempted in public education, but some more realistic approach made to the problem along the lines of a "released-time" or "dismissed-time" program in cooperation with the churches. In any event, the Jesuit's comment does dramatize the differences in the educational philosophies of the two educators, Mann and Harris.

By way of summary, we can here list the chief principles of Harris's philosophy of character education:

1. All institutions in society are responsible for character education, but each in its own way.

2. The school is the most effective agent for moral training through its atmosphere of discipline.

3. The development of moral habits in the school lays the groundwork for religious education in the Church.

4. The "celestial" or theological virtues of faith, hope, and charity are a part of the school's moral formation because these possess a secular base.

5. The Church alone because of its authoritarian methods and its sacred surroundings can teach religious truth.

6. Bible-reading has no proper place in the school because this is a religious exercise demanding authority and ceremonial.

7. Any general "nonsectarian" approach to religion in the common schools is only establishing one more sect.

8. The school must by the nature of things attend exclusively to secular learning; accordingly, the school must be *completely* secularized.

[83] *Ibid.*

✦

A number of suggestions have been advanced to explain the obscurity into which the name of William Torrey Harris fell almost immediately after his death in 1908. Part of the eclipse is explained by the fact that Harris never held a chair at a college or university, where he might have built up a following of young scholars to spread his doctrine throughout the academic world. It is true that he was intimately associated with the Concord School of Philosophy during its eight summers of existence, but this was never more than an opportunity for mutual aesthetic and philosophical inspiration among a coterie, despite its founders' ambitions.[84]

Nicholas Murray Butler, one of the young men deeply influenced by Harris, suggested that "unhappily, Dr. Harris is never likely to receive the recognition which is his just due because of the fact that he never cast his philosophy into any single ordered exposition." [85] Butler's further remark that Harris "served so well that his service is already almost forgotten" has been interpreted by one scholar as meaning that

the American public school system is so much the development of Harris' principles and the result of his labors that the product, especially in its fundamental organizational aspects, is indistinguishable from the principles that motivated and shaped it.[86]

Kurt Leidecker has advanced the most plausible explanation of Harris's relative oblivion.[87] For many years Harris had talked about

[84] Winship, who was editor of the *Journal of Education* (New England and National), liked Harris but disliked the Concord School. He wrote: "Alcott, Harris and Company built a small, plain board shack on the side of the hill in the Alcott yard and announced 'The Concord School of Philosophy.' A few, very few persons tried to listen to the mystical lectures in that plain building on the hillside. Almost everybody made fun of the whole affair. I went out there and it was literally too funny for words. The whole thing was short-lived, and for many years no one could say 'Concord School of Philosophy' with a sober face." (*Journal of Education*, CI [May 28, 1925], 603.) This is rather crude. For an historical presentation see Pochmann or Schaub.

[85] Letter to Charles M. Perry, in Perry, ed., *The St. Louis Movement*, pp. 51–52.

[86] Pochmann, *New England Transcendentalism and St. Louis Hegelianism*, p. 114.

[87] Leidecker, *Yankee Teacher*, p. 533.

publishing a book to systematize the articles and addresses he had prepared on educational psychology. The book, *Psychologic Foundations of Education: An Attempt to Show the Genesis of the Higher Faculties of the Mind,* finally appeared in 1898. Twenty or thirty years earlier the book would perhaps have modified the course of American thought, but in 1898 its appearance identified the author with a philosophy and psychology of education which were well on the way out. Harris and his kind of Hegelian idealism were being displaced by something newer. His theories of formal discipline and ethical psychology were giving way before the "New Education." A new prophet had arisen whose message was more appealing to the ears of twentieth-century America. He was young John Dewey, admirer and friend but hardly a disciple of William Torrey Harris.

Dewey knew Harris, having lectured with him at Concord. In 1881 he had sent an article on the "Metaphysical Assumptions of Materialism" to Editor Harris for consideration for the *Journal of Speculative Philosophy.* The youthful author was anxious to know if Dr. Harris considered him fitted to continue the professional study of philosophy. Harris gave Dewey warm encouragement, which Jane Dewey says "decided the new author to continue his studies and led him to write two other articles which were published by Dr. Harris." [88] In 1886 when Dewey published his first book, *Psychology,* he wrote to Harris to acknowledge the effect on him of Harris's kind judgment. Dewey reminded Harris that when he sent his first article to the *Journal of Speculative Philosophy* he was a schoolteacher with little time for philosophic work. It was Harris's encouragement that decided him on the course he had been doubtfully considering—the study and teaching of philosophy. So it was that, in a sense, Harris was a progenitor of this first book. [89]

[88] *The Philosophy of John Dewey,* ed. by Paul A. Schilpp, p. 14. See footnote 2 in Chapter VIII. There is a charming diffidence in young Dewey's letter to Harris. (Letter of May 1, 1881. The original letter is in the School of Philosophy Library at the University of Southern California.)

[89] Letter of Dec. 17, 1886. Dewey continues: "I may perhaps, add also that when I was first studying the German philosophers I read something of yours on them of which one sentence has always remained with me—you spoke of the 'Great *psychological* movement from Kant to Hegel.' The remark was rather a mystery to me at the time, but it has gradually become clearer and one thing I have attempted to [do] is to translate a part at least of the significance of that

However, the idealism of Hegel, the soul of Harris's educational philosophy, was in Dewey's hands undergoing a metamorphosis whose new Darwinian lineaments Harris would recognize with difficulty and probably disown. But to be true to the inflexible inner dynamism of the Hegelian dialectic, Harris's philosophy had to pass into an antithetical stage. Did the grand old man find solace in this thought as he felt the mantle slipping from his shoulders?

---

movement into our present psychological language. I hope that you may find that it hasn't lost too much in the process of translation." (The original letter is in the School of Philosophy Library, University of Southern California.)

PART FOUR

JOHN DEWEY

1859–1952

VIII. FROM HEGEL AND DARWIN
TO JOHN DEWEY

John Dewey, who attempted to fuse the imperatives of
science and nature, democracy and humanity, has in some measure
touched every stone in the modern American educational structure.
The development of Dewey's thought was mirrored in the vast
changes that took place in modern education during his life span. His
unique place has been described by his closest disciple, William Heard
Kilpatrick:

Pestalozzi had prepared the ground. Froebel and Herbart had helped.
Horace Mann, Henry Barnard, William T. Harris, Stanley Hall, Francis
W. Parker, and others had carried America further along the Pestalozzi
road. But one thing was lacking. No one of these men, nor all combined,
had given an adequate theory for a thoroughgoing democratic, science-
respecting education. This Professor Dewey has done.[1]

[1] "Apprentice Citizens," *Saturday Review* (Oct. 22, 1949), p. 12. Kilpatrick
says that work under Dewey "remade my philosophy of life and education," and
rates him the third greatest philosopher of all time, "next after Plato and Aristotle and above Kant and Hegel." After achieving fame for his own contribution
to education, Kilpatrick noted in his diary: "Sometimes I am vexed with myself
that I find so little to object to in John Dewey's position" (Diary, April 17, 1930).
As a young instructor he consecrated himself to advance Dewey's teachings: "I

The philosopher of democratic education was born in 1859, the same year that Horace Mann died and Darwin's *Origin of Species* appeared. The confluence of the three events is striking, for the ideas of these men were to meet and mingle at the crossroads of twentieth-century civilization. Darwin's evolutionary hypothesis was to give a decided cast to Dewey's instrumentalist philosophy, and Mann's dream of an America educated for democracy was to become Dewey's own.

A Yankee, like the other two subjects of this study, John Dewey was born at Burlington, Vermont, the third of the four sons of Lucina Rich and Archibald Sprague Dewey.[2] Vermonters in those days were educated as much by the industrial and agricultural chores of the small-town household as they were by the local school. Old and young shared the activities and responsibilities of family and community life to a greater degree than is done today. Dewey's own reflections upon this point are contained in the authoritative biography written by his daughters:

The realization that the most important parts of his own education until he entered college were obtained outside the school-room played a large role in his educational work, in which such importance is attached, both in theory and in practice, to occupational activities as the most effective approaches to genuine learning and to personal intellectual discipline.[3]

John was fifteen when he graduated from high school, then not an unusual feat for a boy. In the fall of 1875 he entered the University of Vermont, a friendly little institution where the few hundred students all knew one another, sat together in pretty much the same classes, and were personally acquainted with the eight members of the college faculty. All students followed a prescribed curriculum including the traditional courses in Latin, Greek, and mathematics. One course in

---

feel in some measure that I am best qualified of those about here to interpret Dewey. His own lectures are frequently impenetrable to even intelligent students." Tenenbaum, *William Heard Kilpatrick*, p. 75.

[2] Jane M. Dewey, in collaboration with two of her sisters, edited a short biography of her father from material which he furnished. A prefatory note states that "in the emphasis on varied influences and in the philosophical portions it may be regarded as an autobiography." The biography appears in Schilpp, ed., *The Philosophy of John Dewey*, 2d ed.

[3] *Ibid.*, p. 9.

the junior year stood out for Dewey. This was a course in physiology taught from a text of Thomas Huxley. Dewey recalled that "there was derived from that study a sense of interdependence and inter-related unity that gave form to intellectual stirrings that had been previously inchoate, and created a kind of type or model of a view of things to which material in any field ought to conform." [4] This course led him "to desire a world and a life that would have the same properties as had the human organism in the picture of it derived from study of Huxley's treatment." [5] Student curiosity would explain much of this interest in evolution, for what undergraduate can remain indifferent to the allurement of a radically new idea, espe-cially when it is regarded by most of the community elders as for-bidden fruit? However, evolution drew Dewey's attention to the larger topic of the relation between the natural sciences and traditional beliefs. British periodicals like the *Fortnightly,* the *Contemporary Review,* and the *Nineteenth Century* which reflected the excitement of this conflict were, he says, his "chief intellectual stimulus" at this period and affected him "more deeply than his regular courses in philosophy." [6]

There was a proud tradition in philosophy at the university. Ver-mont's President James Marsh had edited in 1829 an American edition of Coleridge's *Aids to Reflection* which became one of the main channels through which flowed the thought of Kant, Schelling, and Hegel to American shores. The philosophy courses given by Professor H. A. P. Torrey during Dewey's college days were built on in-tuitionalism as systematized by the Scottish school of realism. The dry bones of Scotch philosophy were somewhat enlivened by ideas and

[4] John Dewey, "From Absolutism to Experimentalism," in *Contemporary American Philosophy,* ed. by Adams and Montague, II, 13.

[5] *Ibid.,* p. 11. During the decade immediately before Darwin published his *Origin of Species,* there were already several American scientists, e.g., Benjamin Silliman, Samuel Haldeman, Asa Gray, who were moving in the direction of Darwin's interpretation of life and preparing the American learned public for Darwin's findings. Emerson's 1854 lecture on "Poetry and Imagination" is an astonishing example of prescience. Darwin himself stated that "the two most striking reviews of the *Origin* were those in the *North American Review* and *The New York Times.*" See Charles A. and Mary R. Beard, *The Rise of American Civilization,* II, 742 *et seq.*

[6] Schilpp, ed., *The Philosophy of John Dewey,* p. 11.

topics still stemming from Marsh, who had also taught philosophy with great success. This philosophical school, prior to the spread of German idealism, was hailed in America as the "chief intellectual bulwark of moral and religious beliefs against the dissolving effect of English empiricism." Young Dewey discovered in the library Harriet Martineau's condensation of Auguste Comte's *Positive Philosophy,* and this, he says, awakened his lifelong interest in the interaction of social conditions with the development of thought in science and in philosophy.[7]

During the three years following his graduation from college, Dewey taught school and continued his philosophical studies privately. The reception accorded his first philosophical essay submitted to William Torrey Harris for the *Journal of Speculative Philosophy* [8] and the encouragement of Professor Torrey decided the young man on philosophy as his lifework. Accordingly in the fall of 1882 John Dewey entered the Johns Hopkins University to begin graduate studies.

The choice of philosophy as an occupation was hardly a promising one for a layman, the field long having been considered a clerical preserve. In surveying the state of philosophy in the colleges of the United States in 1879, G. Stanley Hall gloomily wrote "that there is

[7] *Ibid.,* p. 12. Of this period Dewey states: "I do not mention this theological and intuitional phase because it had any lasting influence upon my own development, except negatively. I learned the terminology of an intuitional philosophy, but it did not go deep, and in no way did it satisfy what I was dimly reaching for. I was brought up in a conventionally evangelical atmosphere of the more 'liberal' sort; and the struggles that later arose between acceptance of that faith and the discarding of traditional and institutional creeds came from personal experiences and not from the effects of philosophical teaching." (Adams and Montague, eds., *Contemporary American Philosophy,* II, 15–16.)

[8] The eagerness with which Dewey awaited publication of his first article is known to every young author. He wrote Harris to inquire if he had had time to look over a second article he had submitted, on Spinoza, and asked when there might be a probability of the first article being published. Since Harris must be terribly busy with the Concord Summer School, young Dewey offered to help move things along, "as I have considerable leisure time." He even offered to read proofs and told Harris to call on him for help at any time. He asked if Harris wished any translations for the *Journal.* A memo by Harris on this letter reads: "Expecting to print your article on Materialism in the Apr. no. J.S.P. and we'd like to put the Spinoza article in Notes and Discussions, July." (Letter of July 1, 1882; original letter in the School of Philosophy Library at the University of Southern California.)

very small chance that a well-equipped student of philosophy in any of its departments will secure a position as a teacher of the subject. Such a one could find a career as a writer, editor, or instructor in other branches, or he may bring his mind into some sort of platonising conformity with the milder forms of orthodoxy and teach a philosophy with reservations." [9] Hall further claimed that there were less than half a dozen colleges where metaphysical thought was entirely freed from reference to theological formulae.

The founding of the Johns Hopkins University in 1876, with Daniel Coit Gilman as its first president, marked the real beginning of the graduate school in the United States. The Baltimore institution was soon enrolling a good share of the American graduate student talent that heretofore had prepared for the life of scholarship at distant places like Edinburgh, Berlin, Heidelberg, and Jena.

The three men who staffed the Hopkins philosophy department were Charles Sanders Peirce, George Sylvester Morris, and G. Stanley Hall. Strangely enough, during his two years of graduate study Dewey was not attracted into the orbit of Peirce and pragmatism. Dewey complained to Harris that Johns Hopkins gave no direct instruction in philosophic logic, and added: "Mr. Peirce lectures on Logic, but the lectures appeal more strongly to the mathematical students than to the philosophical." [10] The young man had imbibed the idealist's dislike for formal logic, and this undoubtedly kept him from discovering Peirce, whom he seems to have set down as a mere logician. The

[9] G. Stanley Hall, "Philosophy in the United States," *Mind*, IV (Jan., 1879), 91.

[10] Letter of Jan. 17, 1884. In this same letter Dewey gave Harris some account of his work in philosophy at the university. He said that he was working with Professor Morris in two courses—one, lectures on German philosophy with the emphasis upon Kant; the other, a course upon Spinoza's *Ethics*. He announced that the subject for his doctoral thesis was Kant's psychology. This meant Kant's "philosophy of spirit (so far as he has any) or the subjective side of his theory of knowledge." In addition to giving a general account of Kant's theory of sense, imagination, etc., "I hope to be able to point out that he had the conception of Reason or Spirit as the centre and organic unity of the entire sphere of man's experience." Dewey maintained that in so far as Kant was true to this conception, he established the modern philosophic method. Dewey hoped to bring out, too, that "so far as he was false to it he fell into his own defects, contradictions, etc." It was this question of *method,* Dewey concluded, "which interests me most just at present." (The original letter is in the School of Philosophy Library, University of Southern California.)

discovery came twenty years later after Dewey had shed his Hegelianism and had arrived at a basic position in philosophy quite similar to that of Peirce.

Hall and more especially Morris had much to do with the intellectual formation of Dewey. Dewey described Morris as a man of intense intellectual enthusiasms, as one who put emotional loyalty along with intellectual understanding into all his teaching. George S. Morris had reacted against the narrow orthodoxy of his puritan upbringing but had never slackened in his basic religious convictions. He had found in German idealism a life synthesis which welded together his religious and philosophical ideals. Of this unity Dewey later recorded: "We do him wrong to speak of his religious faith and his philosophic knowledge as if they were two separate things capable of reacting upon each other." [11] Morris, with the optimism of a convinced idealist, never took the attack of materialistic naturalism upon Christianity too seriously. After all, history was on the side of religion, and from the nature of things the cause of religion was identical with the cause of philosophy; moreover, "philosophy is, among other things, and first of all, the demonstrative, experimental refutation of Agnosticism." [12]

The professor and the graduate student became fast friends. Dewey said that he had never known a more single-hearted and whole-souled man, a man of a single piece all the way through, and "while he had long since deviated from Morris' philosophic faith, he should be happy to believe that the influence of the spirit of his teaching had been an enduring one." It was perfectly natural that Dewey, like any young and impressionable student unacquainted with any system of thought, should have been deeply affected, "to the point of at least temporary conversion," by the enthusiastic and scholarly young professor. Dewey calls attention, however, to the fact that Morris was not the only source of his early Hegelianism. This was also the time of new ferment in English thought, part of the reaction against "atomic individualism and sensationalistic empiricism." Thomas Hill Green

[11] *The Palladium,* XXI (1889), 115.

[12] Quoted in Marc E. Jones, *George Sylvester Morris,* p. 288. Dewey himself could never see any validity in the agnostic position and so dismissed it as a meaningless compromise between supernaturalism and scientific naturalism.

and other English neo-Hegelians, Lord Haldane and his group who wrote the *Essays in Philosophical Criticism,* were part of a movement in England which Dewey says was at the time the vital and constructive one in philosophy. This was the influence that fell in with and reinforced that of Professor Morris.

Hegel's thought, however, had also for Dewey what he calls a "subjective" appeal. It fulfilled during this youthful phase an intense emotional craving for life-unity which only "intellectualized subject-matter could satisfy." Writing nearly a half-century later, Dewey speaks of his emancipation through Hegel:

The sense of divisions and separations that were, I suppose, borne in upon me as a consequence of a heritage of New England culture, divisions by way of isolation of self from the world, of soul from body, of nature from God, brought a painful oppression—or rather, they were an inward laceration. My earlier philosophic study had been an intellectual formula; it operated as an immense release, a liberation. Hegel's treatment of human culture, of institutions and the arts, involved the same dissolution of hard-and-fast dividing walls, and had a special attraction for me.[13]

The conflict of traditional religious beliefs with the new opinions of science was somehow the source of what Dewey calls "a trying personal crisis," yet it never constituted for him a major problem in philosophy.

This might look as if the two things were kept apart; in reality it was due to a feeling that any genuinely sound religious experience could and should adapt itself to whatever beliefs one found oneself intellectually entitled to hold—a half unconscious sense at first, but one which ensuing years have deepened into a fundamental conviction. . . . I have not been able to attach much importance to religion as a philosophic problem; for the effect of that attachment seems to be in the end a subornation of candid philosophic thinking to the alleged but factitious needs of some special set of convictions.[14]

This idea is thoroughly consistent with Dewey's antidualism, and in the next chapter we shall see its full import. He had enough faith in the depth of the religious tendencies of men, he writes, "to believe that they will adapt themselves to any required intellectual change, and that it is futile (and likely to be dishonest) to forecast prematurely

[13] Adams and Montague, eds., *Contemporary American Philosophy,* II, 18–19.
[14] *Ibid.,* pp. 19–20.

just what forms the religious interest will take as a final consequence of the great intellectual transformation that is going on." [15]

On the other hand Dewey did find in social problems the "intellectual sustenance" he felt others derived from religion. In a long letter to Harris, written while he was at Johns Hopkins, Dewey gave his opinion on the role the universities should play in fostering an interest in social problems. In this letter he poured out his soul. While he realized the great benefits of the university courses, he presumed that the professors were fully aware of "their inadequacy in extent to cover the ground which a University ought to cover." Dewey expressed his concern as to how America would ever be able to establish a foundation in philosophical matters unless there was thorough university instruction in philosophy. Despite the seeming constant progress, "so far as I can see very little is doing yet." The prime needs lay in the fields of ethics and social philosophy; this latter Dewey labeled "the philosophy of social relations generally—family, economic and political." He paid tribute to the calibre of both the faculty and the students in the history department of the university, where he was taking a minor. But even here no provision was made to instruct the students in the philosophical side of their subjects. There was no attempt to cover the philosophy of history and social ethics in the broad sense, and "as long as it remains so," Dewey felt, "they don't get more than half the good of their own courses." [16]

He welcomed and made his own Auguste Comte's idea that the disorganized character of Western modern culture is due to a disintegrative individualism, and that a synthesis of science should be a regulative method of an organized social life.[17] He thought he had

[15] *Ibid.*, p. 20. This follows: "As I have been frequently criticized for undue reticence about the problem of religion, I insert this explanation: it seems to me that the great solicitude of many persons, professing belief in the universality of the need for religion, about the present and future of religion proves that in fact they are moved more by partisan interest in a particular religion than by interest in religious experience."

[16] Letter of Jan. 17, 1884. Dewey concludes this letter with a strong plea for the role of philosophy in university education, hoping that after the public appetite for sciences in education had been satisfied, there would be "a humble agitation in favor of smuggling philosophy in somewhere." (The original letter is in the School of Philosophy Library, University of Southern California.)

[17] However, Dewey says: "Neither the idea of three stages of the evolution of society nor Comte's construction of a new religion interested him especially." (Adams and Montague, eds., *Contemporary American Philosophy*, II, 20.)

found in Hegel these same criticisms of society combined with "a deeper and more far-reaching integration."

Though Hegelianism faded out of Dewey's life during the next fifteen years, it left a permanent deposit in his mind.[18] The rigid structuration in Hegel, the formal schematism which Dewey came to find artificial, eventually turned him away from the system. Dewey is quick to own, nonetheless, that in Hegel's ideas there is often extraordinary depth. "Were it possible for me to be a devotee of any system, I still should believe that there is greater richness and greater variety of insight in Hegel than in any other single systematic philosopher—though when I say this I exclude Plato, who still provides my favourite philosophic reading." [19]

John Dewey's other philosophy mentor at Hopkins was G. Stanley Hall, whose philosophical position was poles apart from that of Morris. Hall was a disciple of Wundt and in his discursive lectures on psychological topics, both experimental and theoretical, emphasized the intimate relation between psychology and philosophy which waited to be worked out on the basis of the new experimental psychology. Writing to Harris, Dewey told him that he would soon start work in psychology with Professor Hall. The two courses anticipated dealt with physiological-psychology and speculative psychology, which, said Dewey, would be concerned especially with the psychological basis of ethics. He was also eagerly looking forward to Hall's seminar on pedagogy, which was to be treated from the ethical side. "This last statement," he added, "is however rather superfluous to one who knows Dr. Hall, as ethics and education are pretty much identical in his broad and suggestive treatment of them." [20]

The Dewey biography tells of Hall's influence, how experiment was overthrowing the older "rational" psychology traditionally associated

[18] *Ibid.,* p. 21. Hegelianism is a rather generic term. For Dewey and Morris it was a type of Neo-Kantianism—a complementing and purification of Kant by Hegel—with overlays of Platonic idealism and Aristotelian realism. The emphasis is more on psychological epistemology than on ontology.

[19] Of Plato he adds that "I am unable to find in him that all-comprehensive and overriding system which later interpretation has, as it seems to me, conferred upon him as a dubious boon." Dewey thought that the ancient skeptics, who also claimed Plato as a father, were nearer to the truth than "those who force him into the frame of a rigidly systematized doctrine." (*Ibid.,* p. 21.)

[20] Letter of Jan. 17, 1884. The original is in the School of Philosophy Library, University of Southern California.

with philosophy, "and probably an ambition to help bring about an alliance of the new psychology with philosophy was directing Dewey's intellectual activity to a greater extent than he realized."

In his first book, *Psychology,* published in 1887, Dewey strives to serve both masters: his debt to Hall is clear but Morris also has picked up counters. Morton White characterizes the *Psychology* as "a valiant attempt to retain as much of Hegel and neo-Hegelianism as could be retained by one who extolled the 'new psychology.'"[21] Hall turned around and attacked Dewey in a review of the book precisely for trying to impose Hegelian dogma upon what Hall took to be the facts of experimental psychology.[22]

Dewey inherited from Morris strong convictions on the vital aspect of the knowing process and on the organic integrity of experience. These proved for Dewey time-tested weapons in the long warfare against the many-headed dragon of philosophical dualism. Morris had embodied his own thought on the nature of knowledge and experience in two critical books: *British Thought and Thinkers* and *Kant's Critique of Pure Reason.* The two central theses of what was to become Dewey's instrumentalist philosophy, activism and antidualism, can be seen in embryo in these works of Morris.[23] In the book on Kant, Morris assails the separation of the noumenal from the phenomenal order and other characteristic dualisms of Kantian idealistic philosophy. The work on the British philosophers criticizes bitterly the passive theory of mind held by the empiricists. Their notion of the abstractive process, according to Morris's criticism, "mutilates man, tearing the organic whole of his living experience into miserable shreds."[24] Morris argued that experience is an organic, living whole, which becomes lifeless once it is dissected by analytic empiricism. The British empiricists were guilty, too, in his book, of isolating the two

[21] White, *The Origin of Dewey's Instrumentalism,* p. 9. This study is the most penetrating analysis yet made of the topic. As a Columbia doctoral thesis it deservedly won the Woodbridge Prize.

[22] *American Journal of Psychology,* I (Nov., 1887), 146–64.

[23] See White, *The Origin of Dewey's Instrumentalism,* pp. 3–63.

[24] Morris, "Philosophy and Its Specific Problems," *Princeton Review,* n.s. IX (1882), 215. Morris's strong feeling is partially explained by the fact that briefly he was himself a devotee of British empiricism. Dewey's own antiempiricist attitude is partially inherited.

factors in the knowledge-situation: the object to be known and the subject fitted to know. Once isolated in empirical fashion, subject and object could only be mechanically related.

Morris himself taught that there were two types of relations: mechanical and organic. Object A is mechanically related to object B when there is no third living thing of which they both form part. (The collision between two billiard balls is a mechanical one.) A and B are organically related, however, if there is a third living thing, a kind of container, within which both A and B function as parts. Now man's empirical consciousness, according to Morris, is the "container" of the objects of knowledge and so stands in an organic relation to them. *Universal* consciousness is that third thing—and this is elementary Hegelianism—which embraces empirical conscious-ness and the objects of knowledge. Accordingly empirical conscious-ness and the objects of knowledge participate in the common spirit or life of this larger living whole: *universal* consciousness. This last is the living unity Morris continually appeals to in his writings. White calls this somewhat involved idea the most influential concept upon Dewey's early writings and makes this penetrating observation:

Here we have not only an epistemological device for unifying the subject and object of knowledge, but a unity which is alleged to exist throughout the world. In social theory this is a particularly important notion, since it stresses the unity of all social action. It is the basis upon which almost any dualism is attacked. And here, perhaps, we have the means for making clear what dualism meant for the early Dewey. It was any doctrine which maintained that two things are mechanically related, when as a matter of fact they are organically related. This stimulated Dewey to hunt for these organic relations throughout his life. First in epistemology; then in bi-ology; then in sociology.[25]

It is important to remember that until 1890 Dewey based his attacks on dualism, discontinuity, and passivity upon this Morris-Hegelian theory of universal consciousness. These were the years before Dewey had undertaken his extensive studies in psychology, or in Darwinian biology, or in modern sociology. This was still the Hegelian period. During this period the continuity Dewey defended between man and nature was not built on the biological concept of Darwin but upon

[25] White, *The Origin of Dewey's Instrumentalism*, p. 32.

universal consciousness. The activity Dewey opposed to passivist theories of knowledge was not manual and bodily but, as White says, "a vague, sometimes even mentalistic (in Dewey's sense today) 'energy of intelligence.'" [26]

To explain his own intellectual development for the Adams-Montague volume John Dewey singles out four special points. The first is the importance of education. He says that interest in the theory and practice of education "fused with and brought together what might otherwise have been separate interests—that in psychology and that in social institutions and social life." His philosophizing centered in education "as the supreme human interest in which, moreover, other problems, cosmological, moral, logical come to a head." [27]

As Dewey's thought progressed he became more and more troubled, he says, by a second point, the intellectual scandal involved in the current (and traditional) dualism in logical standpoint and method between something called "science" on the one hand and something called "morals" on the other.

I have long felt that the construction of a logic, that is, a method of effective inquiry, which would apply without abrupt breach of continuity to the fields designated by both of these words, is at once our needed theoretical solvent and the supply of our greatest practical want. This belief has had much more to do with the development of what I termed, for lack of a better word, "instrumentalism," than have most of the reasons that have been assigned.[28]

The third point listed by Dewey is the influence of William James, in particular through his idea of vitalism as developed in *Principles of Psychology*. Though he objected to James's understanding of consciousness as something apart by itself, Dewey praised what he called the enormous advance in substituting the "stream of consciousness" concept for discrete elementary states of the mind. He further singles out for praise the objective strain in James "having its roots in a return to the earlier biological conception of the *psyche*, but a return possessed of a new force and value due to the immense progress made by biology since the time of Aristotle." Even though other philosophers

[26] *Ibid.*, p. 33.
[27] Adams and Montague, eds., *Contemporary American Philosophy*, II, 22.
[28] *Ibid.*, p. 23.

had written at length about the idea of organism, in Dewey's judgment they had taken the idea of life structurally and hence statically.
"It was reserved for James to think of life in terms of life in action."
James thereby cleared the philosophical channels of a heavy charge of
bad psychology silted up by tradition, and allowed the close connection
between philosophy and psychology to be seen. Now men can link
philosophy to the significant issues of actual experience by constant
interaction with the methods and conclusions of psychology.[29]

Growing out of this new Jamesian emphasis on the human biological
approach to human philosophy, a fourth influence came to bear upon
Dewey's thought, "the perception of the importance of distinctive social
categories, especially communication and participation." Dewey concludes his intellectual biography by voicing his conviction that much
of our philosophizing needs to be redone from this point of view, so
that ultimately there will result an "integrated synthesis in a philosophy
congruous with modern science and related to actual needs in education, morals, and religion." [30]

Through the good offices of Professor Morris, who had terminated
his connection with Johns Hopkins, Dewey was invited in 1884 to
assume an instructorship in philosophy at the University of Michigan.
Morris had recently been advanced to the headship of the department.
That Dewey fitted in well and was highly regarded can be gathered
both from his rapid advance in academic rank as well as from the
tributes of his students. One of them wrote:

As nearly as I could judge, before the time of Dr. Morris and his able
assistant, Dr. Dewey, the Department of Philosophy occupied a vague and
dusty corner, set apart for those isolated metaphysical discussions that seem
out of relation to everything. But it gradually began to dawn upon us as

[29] *Ibid.*, pp. 23–24. Dewey wrote to James: "So far as I am concerned I have
simply been rendering back in logical vocabulary what was already your own."
One of Dewey's prominent disciples demurs: "Of course Dewey was too modest.
He was not rendering back, he was selecting, varying and transforming. The
more fully he assimilated James' ideas, the more they became different and new.
He was aware of divergencies and more reticent than James about how far they
agreed. He preferred to denote that which he rendered back by the word *Instrumentalism*, rather than *Pragmatism*, or *Humanism*." Horace Kallen, "Dewey and
Pragmatism," in *John Dewey, Philosopher of Science and Freedom*, ed. by Sidney
Hook, pp. 34–35.
[30] Adams and Montague, eds., *Contemporary American Philosophy*, II, 25–26.

we listened to the lectures that what we called philosophy was really an explanation of life itself in all its relations and import.[31]

During the summer of 1886 Dewey married Alice Chipman, a student his own age at the university, who had taught school for several years to put herself through college.

After four pleasant years at Michigan, Dewey accepted a full professorship at the University of Minnesota. During the ensuing year Morris died and Dewey was invited to return to Ann Arbor to assume charge of the Michigan department. His assistant was James H. Tufts, who was to become a close friend and his collaborator in the *Ethics*. Tufts left Michigan in 1891 to take a chair at the newly opened University of Chicago, where Dewey himself was drawn in 1894.

After Tufts's departure the Michigan department added two teachers of philosophy, one of whom was George H. Mead. Dewey has generously acknowledged his debt to Mead in the Jane Dewey biography. Mead's principal interest was the bearing of biological theories upon scientific psychology. Up to then the psychologists and philosophers who had recognized any relation between psychological phenomena and the human body had situated the physical basis of mind in the brain alone or in an isolated nervous system, which meant isolation from the relations of the organism to its environment.[32] In his contrary approach, Mead began "from the idea of the organism acting and reacting in an environment." For him the nervous system, brain included, was an organ which regulated the relations of the organism as a whole with the objective conditions of life. The description of all psychological phenomena must then be patterned on this point of view.

Dewey gives credit to Mead also for another central idea in the instrumentalist philosophy. Mead had developed an original theory of the psychical "as the state occurring when previously established relations of organism and environment break down and new relations have not yet been built up." A parallel theory of the origin and nature of the self grows out of this same interaction but the relations are of human beings with one another. Dewey says he took these ideas over from Mead and made them a part of his subsequent philosophy, "so

[31] Quoted in Wenley, *The Life and Work of George Sylvester Morris*, p. 304.
[32] Schilpp, ed., *The Philosophy of John Dewey*, pp. 25–26.

that, from the nineties on, the influence of Mead ranked with that of James."

His brief teaching experience before he enrolled at Johns Hopkins can be considered the start of John Dewey's interest in the public schools. While at Michigan he had ample opportunity to learn more about public education. The university formed a part of the state school system, and the high schools of the state were regularly visited by members of the university faculty. Dewey's interest in general education was stimulated by these visits as well as by his membership in the Schoolmasters Club of Michigan, formed in order to bring secondary and college education closer through conferences and committees. He lectured frequently at teachers' institutes and various conventions on his studies of the learning process. A growing conviction of the social importance of philosophy and an uneasiness over the stress upon pure theorizing set Dewey thinking about an experimental school. He was convinced that the current educational methods, especially in the primary schools, were at odds with the principles of child psychology and development.

This was one of the reasons, he says, for his acceptance of the offer from the University of Chicago in 1894. The university had agreed to include pedagogy with philosophy and psychology in the new department he was to head. Within a few years there had been established an elementary school, "the Laboratory School," later known as "the Dewey School," which bore the same general relation to the department of pedagogy that laboratories in the physical sciences bear to these subjects. Dewey's most popular book, *The School and Society,* consists of lectures given to raise money for this experimental school. The ten years at Chicago mark one of Dewey's most productive literary periods.

Dewey mentions in the Adams-Montague volume that after his movement from idealism to his naturalistic and pragmatic experimentalism, personal contacts had, on the whole, more influence in directing his thought than the books he read. In the Jane Dewey biography there are many names mentioned, among them: Francis W. Parker, the DeGarmos and the McMurrys, and William T. Harris. Dewey speaks of "the friendly conflict of different schools of educational thought of these years," which marked the beginnings of the progressive movement. His long friendship and collaboration with Ella Flagg Young

led him to regard Mrs. Young as "the wisest person in school matters
with whom he has come in contact in any way." To her and his wife
John Dewey attributed the greatest practical educational influence of
those years.[33]

An unfortunate tension between Dewey and the president of the
university, William Rainey Harper, over the relations of the experimental school to the university was resolved by Dewey's resignation in
1904. In a letter of April 25, 1904, to his old friend Harris, Dewey explained that he had submitted his resignation because he "could not
work harmoniously under the conditions which the President's methods . . . created and imposed." Since his resignation had not as yet
been presented to the university trustees, the information given to
Harris was still confidential, but in view of their past relationship
Dewey felt he should inform Harris of the step he was taking. In a
postscript he asked Harris's advice and asserted his own continuing
belief in "education of democracy." [34]

When an old friend of Hopkins days, J. McKeen Cattell of the
department of philosophy and psychology at Columbia University,
learned that Dewey was available, he was instrumental in getting him
for the philosophy faculty of Columbia. Three days after sending Harris
the news of his break with Chicago, Dewey wrote to inform him of his
acceptance of the professorship at Columbia, which had been offered by
President Nicholas Murray Butler himself. He said that he had written
Cattell previously, after having written to Harris, "but did not expect
things to move along at this rate and in this way." He concluded by
saying that he was still in doubt as to whether to devote himself to philosophical or to administrative work.

Here is Harris's reply, dated April 30:

Your letter of April 25th and your still more recent letter are before me.
I am of course very much astonished. I do not think it possible that the
President of Chicago University can be persuaded to accept your resignation, but if you force it on him by accepting another call he can not help
himself. When I read your first letter, the combination was exactly what

[33] *Ibid.*, pp. 28–29. Mrs. Young, who became superintendent of the Chicago
school system, was the first woman superintendent of a large city system. She was
also the first woman president of the NEA.

[34] The original of this letter and of the following two letters referred to are in
the School of Philosophy Library, University of Southern California.

occurred to me as most desirable, and I am glad, very glad, to know of the outcome. It is a tremendous opportunity both for Columbia and for you. I do not know its equal in either point.

I have been thinking about the importance of your taking a position with a great deal more administrative responsibility. I shall be glad at any time to assist your purposes to my utmost ability.

Thus began John Dewey's nearly half a century of association with Columbia University and its Teachers College.

✦

The generic title of the philosophy espoused by John Dewey is "pragmatism." Although his "instrumentalism" shows marked differences from the pragmatism of William James, Charles Sanders Peirce, or Henri Bergson, it does share their fundamental starting point. All species of pragmatism are at one in their insistence upon practicality or usefulness as the criterion of truth. Pragmatism objects to the traditional philosophy which holds that concepts, judgments, and reasoning are representative of reality, or anything more than symbols and hypotheses to facilitate man's use of experience in the practical order. Dewey wrote that philosophy's chief function was "not to find out what difference ready-made formulae make, if true, but to arrive at and to clarify their meaning as programs of behavior for modifying the existent world." [35]

Evolution had conclusively demonstrated that an hypothesis, provided it explains the facts in question, fulfills the function of what is traditionally called an established law. If evolution, put forward as an *hypothesis,* was able satisfactorily to explain the facts observed in plant and animal life, there was little need to speculate further over the truth of the hypothesis itself. If the hypothesis functioned, nothing further was needed. Since hypothesis and provisional explanation worked as well as general law, there arose the tendency among the pragmatists to equate postulates with axioms and to regard as valid any principle that operates satisfactorily.

The type of pragmatism espoused by John Dewey is called *instrumentalism* because it makes use of thought or idea as an instrument for action. Ideas are the tools by which man transforms problematic

[35] *Essays in Experimental Logic,* p. 312.

situations in his experience so that the original difficulties, discontinuities, and incoherences disappear.[36] This philosophy has sometimes been called *humanism* because of its emphasis on the continuity of values in the stream of human experience, and sometimes *experimentalism* because it is built upon the scientific method of controlled and verifiable observation.

To someone formed in one of the traditional schools of philosophy, Dewey, like Nietzsche, appears to be philosophizing with a hammer in his hand. Dewey's instrumentalism is not just another method of organizing speculative thought or systematizing ultimate truths. In his philosophy there is no place for speculative thought in the traditional sense, nor are there such things as ultimate truths. Instrumentalism is a revolutionary departure from all traditional philosophies—realist, idealist, sensist, or empiricist—and yet it has inherited from all of these. Though John Dewey by the middle of the 1890s had abandoned Hegelian absolutism, he retained the Hegelian method. For Hegel, be it remembered, the method of philosophy was the reconciliation of opposites—static thesis from which rises a dynamic antithesis resulting in an organic synthesis. Dewey, as we shall see, made extensive use of this approach to the problems of society.

But the Deweyan notion of philosophy itself is a radical departure from the tradition which understood philosophy to be the science of ultimate causes or the study of all things according to the first principles of being. Dewey does not include metaphysics, at least in the traditional sense, in his philosophy, and so he by-passes most of the questions that philosophers have traditionally raised.[37] As his friend and collaborator Sidney Hook has said: "Whoever then looks to Dewey to find out whether God or chance is the cause of the universe, whether the soul of man is immortal, whether life is good, bad, or has an absolute meaning, is doomed to disappointment."[38]

[36] See Hook, *John Dewey*, p. 193 *et seq.*

[37] Of course, it always takes a metaphysics to reject another metaphysics. That is, it requires one theory of reality to replace another. Some of Dewey's most trenchant critics have pressed him on this point. He seems to have dismissed the philosophy of Thomas Aquinas as something "already dim, faded and remote." Yet to millions of intelligent men, it is the *philosophia perennis*. Morris R. Cohen's remark may have relevance here: "Neglect is not a philosophic refutation." ("Some Difficulties with John Dewey's Anthropocentric Naturalism," in *Studies in Philosophy and Science*, p. 157.)

[38] Hook, *John Dewey*, p. 212.

During his early years Dewey was troubled in working out the relation between the new empirical psychology and philosophy. He seems to have looked upon the effort to distinguish them as self-defeating. At times the two appear to be practically synonymous. Since psychology was strictly a genetic study of man in his environment, its purpose was social. Dewey did not admit a philosophical method as opposed to a scientific method; he used the scientific method in philosophy and assigned philosophy a social function. Philosophy and psychology no longer had to do with speculations (i.e., in the Scholastic-Lockian sense) not immediately verifiable in experience, but rather with the conflicts immanent in man's daily experience. In other words, philosophy became the application of the scientific method to the *problems of society,* rather than a quest for absolute knowledge about principles of reality. From this point of view, instrumentalism can be considered the culmination of the positivist movement in philosophy which began with Saint-Simon and Comte at the start of the nineteenth century.

John Dewey made no apologies for ignoring metaphysics: to him it was simply the pursuit of the chimerical. Let him here explain his notion of the nature of philosophic inquiry:

Philosophy is itself a mode of knowing, and of knowing wherein reflective thinking is much in play. It is hence self-contradictory for an instrumental pragmatism to set up claims to supplying a metaphysics or ontology. As a mode of knowledge, it arises, like any intellectual undertaking, out of certain typical perplexities and conflicts of behavior and its purpose is to help straighten these out.[39]

Philosophy may render things more intelligible or give greater insight into existence, but these considerations are subject to the final criterion of what it means to acquire insight and to make things intelligible, "namely, service of special purposes in behavior, and limit by the *special* problems in which the need of insight arises." But this is not to say, Dewey continues, that instrumentalism is merely a methodology

[39] "Some Implications of Anti-Intellectualism," *Journal of Philosophy,* VII (Sept. 1, 1910), 479. A recent study of Deweyan philosophy makes this statement: "By the end of the second decade of this century, Dewey's antipathy to metaphysics had noticeably weakened; in *Experience and Nature* his earlier position is definitely repudiated, and he admits unequivocally the validity of ontological speculation." Feldman, *The Philosophy of John Dewey,* p. 9. This is only partially correct.

or an epistemology preliminary to more ultimate philosophic or metaphysical inquiries, "for it involves the doctrine that the origin, structure, and purpose of knowing are such as to render nugatory any wholesale inquiries into the nature of Being." [40]

Central to the instrumentalist philosophy is the idea that man is part of the perfect continuum of nature. We shall explore this continuity more in detail when we take up Dewey's moral theory in the next chapter. Here it is sufficient to point out that Dewey emphasizes the fact that "man with his habits, institutions, desires, thoughts, aspirations, ideals and struggles, is within nature, an integral part of it," and that this perfect continuity is "the philosophical basis and practical inspiration for effort to employ nature as an ally of human ideals and goods such as no dualism can possibly provide." [41] In *Experience and Nature* Dewey argues that "if man is within nature, not a little god outside, and is within as a mode of energy inseparably connected with other modes, interaction is the one unescapable trait of every human concern; thinking, even philosophic thinking, is not exempt." [42]

Does his denial of duality put Dewey in the camp of the monists? Not if he can help it. Dewey avowed that he had "not a chemical trace of interest" in epistemological monism. Nor would he accept the classification of his theory of knowing as an epistemological dualism, which

[40] "Some Implications of Anti-Intellectualism," *Journal of Philosophy,* VII (Sept. 1, 1910), 479. In 1938 Dewey did extend an olive branch to the speculative world. He wrote that "empirical and experimental philosophy has no quarrel with science": the fact that science provides the only means we have for learning about man and the world in which he lives doesn't make philosophy unnecessary. However, "the elimination does rule out *one* kind of philosophy, namely, that which held that philosophy is a higher form of knowledge than the scientific kind, one which furnishes knowledge of ultimate higher reality. But it does not follow from the elimination of this particular type of philosophy that philosophy itself must go." ("The Relation of Science and Philosophy as the Basis of Education," *School and Society,* XLVII [April 9, 1938], 470.) Many philosophers would not be quick to clasp the proffered hand. It is only fair, however, to keep in mind that experimentalism deals with more than facts. Writes Dewey: "There exist, in other words, values as well as known facts and principles and philosophy is concerned primarily with values—with the ends for the sake of which man acts. Given the most extensive and accurate system of knowledge, and man is still faced with the question of what he is going to do about it and what he is going to do with the knowledge in his possession." (*Ibid.*)

[41] *Individualism, Old and New,* p. 153.

[42] *Experience and Nature,* p. 434.

he scoffs at as "two monisms stuck loosely together, so that all the difficulties in monism are in it multiplied by two." If his position is to be labeled, says Dewey, "I should prefer to call it empirical pluralism, for it is actuated by respect for the plurality of observable facts." [43]

Continuity in the processes of nature is a corollary of the evolutionary thesis. John Dewey speaks of this relation frequently. In 1892 he wrote in an article, "Green's Theory of Moral Motive," that "in the theory of evolution this unity of process has ceased to be either a supernatural datum or a merely philosophic speculation. It has assumed the proportions of fact." [44]

Six years later, in an article entitled "Evolution and Ethics," he said:

In the present environment, flexibility of function, the enlargement of the range of uses to which one and the same organ, grossly considered, may be put, is a great, almost the supreme, condition of success. As such, any change in that direction is a favorable variation which must be selected. In a word, the difference between man and animal is not that selection has ceased, but that selection along the line of variations which enlarge and intensify the environment is active as never before. [45]

And in 1909 in the essay which gave its title to the collection of writings called *The Influence of Darwin on Philosophy*, he writes that this influence "resides in his having conquered the phenomena of life for the principle of transition, and thereby freed the new logic for application to mind and morals and life." [46]

After Darwin, he continues, interest has shifted from "the wholesale essence back of special changes to the question of how special changes serve and defeat concrete purposes." The shift is from an intelligence that shaped things once for all to the particular intelligences which things are even now shaping, from an ultimate goal of good to the direct increments of justice and happiness that intelligent administration of existent conditions may beget and that present carelessness or stupidity will destroy or forgo. [47]

[43] "Duality and Dualism," *Journal of Philosophy*, XIV (Aug. 30, 1917), 491.
[44] *Philosophic Review*, I (Nov., 1892), 611.
[45] *Monist*, VIII (April, 1898), 340.
[46] *The Influence of Darwin on Philosophy*, pp. 8–9. The original lecture was given at Columbia in 1909.
[47] *Ibid.*

✦

While a complete presentation of Dewey's theory of knowledge is outside the limits of the present study, certain elements of that theory must be understood before his moral ideas can be thoroughly grasped.[48] Instrumentalism teaches that knowledge is a *doing* and the satisfactory outcome of this doing is called *knowledge*. Both empiricist and rationalistic traditions have erred, according to this theory, inasmuch as they maintained that knowledge was merely declarative of what antecedently existed in reality. Knowledge is not a grasp of antecedent reality nor the contemplation of eternal essences which are supposedly a stable element underlying the flux of our kaleidoscopic world of experience. We have already mentioned Dewey's disdain for the "spectator theory of knowledge"—a legacy from George Morris. Since Dewey has rejected all dualism and has argued for a strict genetic continuity in all of nature, he can not suffer any division in the knowing experience between the faculty and the human organism, nor between the knower and the environment. The systems of the past, from Plato through Locke to the present, have all laid hold, agrees Dewey, of "*some* actual constituent of knowing, but have failed to place it in the context in which it actually functions."[49] Dewey feels that he has remedied this failure by restoring the knowing activity from the mental to the phenomenal or true experiential order.

When he comes to defining truth, Dewey refers to two definitions of Peirce:

The best definition of *truth* from the logical standpoint which is known to me is that of Peirce: "The opinion which is fated to be ultimately agreed to by all who investigate is what we mean by the truth, and the object represented by this opinion is the real." A more complicated (and more suggestive) statement is the following: "Truth is that concordance of an abstract statement with the ideal limit towards which endless investigation

[48] For a comparison of the Dewey position with a traditional theory of knowledge and reality see Fleckenstein, *A Critique of John Dewey's Theory of the Nature and the Knowledge of Reality in the Light of the Principles of Thomism.*

[49] "Experience, Knowledge and Value: A Rejoinder," in Schilpp, ed., *The Philosophy of John Dewey*, p. 561. Dewey resented his critics' charge that he had dismissed all other theories of knowing as of *no* value. He did, however, furnish his critics with some handle for this charge. See Arthur E. Murphy, "Dewey's Epistemology and Metaphysics," *ibid.*, pp. 193–227.

would tend to bring scientific belief, which concordance the abstract statement may possess by virtue of the confession of its inaccuracy and one-sided-
ness, and this confession is an essential ingredient of truth." [50]

Truth, like inquiry itself, will be something that continually progresses.
"The moment philosophy supposes it can find a final and comprehensive solution, it ceases to be inquiry and becomes either apologetics or
propaganda." [51] To the point likewise is the familiar Dewey maxim:
"If it is better to travel than to arrive, it is because traveling is a constant arriving, while arrival that precludes further traveling is most
easily attained by going to sleep or dying." [52]

Sensation, in Dewey's book, is a process of stimulus-response whereby the organism is made aware of a problematic situation and read-
justs itself to its environment, thus insuring continuity with nature.
Proof? Why,

only the peculiar hypnotic effect exercised by exclusive preoccupation with
knowledge could have led thinkers to identify experience with reception of
sensations, when five minutes' observation of a child would have disclosed
that sensations count only as stimuli and registers of motor activity ex-
pended in doing things. [53]

Sensation, then, is not a type of knowledge nor is it productive of
knowledge.

The view that the *idea* is some sort of mental "re-presentation" or
reduplication of the world of the nonego borne by the senses to the
mind, along with the perennial concern of epistemology to show the
conformity between the mental idea and the reality represented, is
lightly dismissed by Dewey:

The problem of how a mind can know an external world, or even know
that there is such a thing, is like the problem of how an animal eats things
external to itself; it is the kind of problem that arises only if one assumes
that a hibernating bear living off its own stored substance defines the normal
procedure, ignoring moreover the question where the bear got its stored
material. [54]

For ideas, according to instrumentalism, are not mental representations
of an already existent reality. Since reality is already there to begin

[50] Footnote, p. 345, in *Logic*. The two quotations are from Peirce, *Collected
Papers*, V, 268 and 394.
[51] *Logic*, p. 35.   [52] *Human Nature and Conduct*, p. 282.
[53] *Quest for Certainty*, p. 156.   [54] *Experience and Nature*, p. 278.

with, why this pointless reduplication? The elements of hesitation and
doubt in a learning situation give rise to ideas as to possible solutions vis-à-vis an actual problem. Dewey insists upon the fact that an
idea, intellectually, cannot be defined by its structure, but only by its
function and use.[55] Ideas originate, then, in problem-situations. There
is nothing "intellectual" about their occurrence: the intellectual element consists in *what we do with them* and how we use them. This
helps to clarify the following enigmatic statement:

So far as thoughts in this particular meaning are concerned, it is true to
say "it thinks" (as when we say "it rains"), rather than "I think." Only
when a person tries to get control of the *conditions* that determine the
occurrence of a suggestion, and only when he accepts responsibility for using
the suggestion to see what follows from it, is it significant to introduce the
"I" as the agent and source of thought.[56]

In *Human Nature and Conduct* he propounds the same thought,
which has been construed by some of his critics as a denial of man's
intellectual nature. "Intelligence becomes ours in the degree in which
we use it and accept responsibility for consequences. It is not ours
originally or by production. 'It thinks' is a truer psychological statement than 'I think.' "[57] Granted the premises underlying instrumentalism, these admittedly startling statements take on meaning and are
coherent with the whole system. The same can be said of these statements:

"Thought" is not a property of something termed intellect or reason apart
from nature. It is a mode of directed overt action. Ideas are anticipatory
plans and designs which take effect in concrete reconstruction of antecedent
conditions of existence.[58]

Apart from conversation, from discourse and communication, there is no
thought and no meaning, only just events, dumb, preposterous, destructive.[59]

[55] *How We Think*, p. 136.   [56] *Ibid.*, p. 42.
[57] *Human Nature and Conduct*, p. 314.   [58] *Quest for Certainty*, pp. 166–67.
[59] "Events and Meanings," in *Characters and Events*, I, 129. Compare these
statements with the following: "The intellectual (as distinct from the moral) end
of education is entirely and only the logical in this sense; namely, the formation
of careful, alert and thorough habits of thinking." (*How We Think*, pp. 57–58.)

✦

In the foregoing sketch of John Dewey's intellectual formation and short analysis of his theory of knowledge, it was inevitable that the stress be speculative. It would be far from accurate, however, to conclude that Dewey's philosophy was spun in an ivory tower. His philosophy of instrumentalism is intended above all as a philosophy to be lived, a design for living. Dewey was a keen student of the history of philosophy and had a firsthand acquaintance with the great classics, despite what has appeared to some of his critics as a biased presentation of some traditional ideas.[60] But far more than books or ideas, social forces were the fire that forged Deweyan instrumentalism. John Dewey was too much the Jeffersonian democrat not to be uneasy with the socially conservative philosophy of the American neo-Hegelians, especially that symbolized by William T. Harris. Dewey saw bold new challenges in America's transformation from an agrarian democracy, still tied to Old World tradition, to an urbanized industrial society that was creating a truly New World. He fought for a reevaluation of the shifting social scene according to new principles, so that all men could freely share in the life of democracy.[61] Political democracy would be meaningless unless it were based upon a social and cultural democracy, and ultimately an industrial and economic democracy—and to these ends he devoted his considerable talents.

The overcrowded foreign-language neighborhoods of Detroit and Chicago, the unhealthy slums and the ostentatious wealth of New York and Boston, the struggle of the labor unions and the teaching profession for independence, religious bigotry in politics, international

[60] For example, Dewey assumes that the dualism of Descartes, i.e., a non-extended spiritual substance (soul) placed in conjunction with an extended material substance (body) in a union called man, was shared by the entire scholastic tradition. Or that psycho-physico parallelism or Malebranchian occasionalism was widely taught by scholastic philosophers. Dewey could hardly have been so hard on Aristotle for dividing the knowing situation if he had really understood the dictum: "Sensible in actu est sensus in actu, et intelligible in actu est intellectus in actu."

[61] Dewey collaborated closely with Jane Addams in the work of the settlement houses. His daughter writes: "Dewey's faith in democracy as a guiding force in education took on both a sharper and a deeper meaning because of Hull House and Jane Addams." (Schilpp, ed., *The Philosophy of John Dewey*, p. 30.)

tensions—all these were grist for his philosophical mill. Instrumentalism was baked in the oven of a dynamic American environment. Traditions had little meaning or force, argued Dewey, in a nation still
coming to birth. Such a land needed a philosophy calling for experiment—"intelligently directed trial and error, rather than one based
upon a priori principles." And the primary subject matter of this
philosophy was the behavior of the human animal. We turn now to
examine in detail Dewey's thoughts regarding the ethical and moral
patterns of man's life.

IX. FAITH AND MORALS

FOR A DEMOCRACY

To anyone familiar with the ethical and religious theory in
John Dewey's *A Common Faith,* published in 1934, it comes as a
curiosity that the same man once wrote:

We believe that the cause of theology and morals is one, and that whatever
banishes God from the heart of things, with the same edict excludes the
ideal, the ethical, from the life of man. Whatever exiles theology makes
ethics an expatriate.[1]

These lines written in 1887, before his twenty-eighth birthday, represent a point of view that Dewey was not only shortly to abandon but
which he was to criticize for the remainder of his long life. The above
quotation is from one of his earliest journalistic sorties into the field
of ethics wherein the young author criticized Spencerian "scientific"
ethics. His opposition, he makes it plain, does not arise from any religious viewpoint but from his reasoned conviction that "the physical
interpretation of the universe is one which necessarily shuts out those
ideas and principles which are fundamental to ethics."

[1] "Ethics and Physical Science," *Andover Review,* VII (June, 1887), 576.

Before setting about his refutation Dewey in brilliant fashion presents a strong case for the other side. Since in less than a decade his own view will swing about to parallel what is here the object of his attack, there is warrant for consideration of this scientific or evolution-based ethics. The law of evolution, writes Dewey explaining the adversary point of view, shows man to be the most complete product of the same forces and principles that are at work everywhere in the world.

Now, this fact has two ethical bearings: it shows that man is not generically different from nature, and that consequently ethical science is not distinct in its methods and conceptions from physical science; and that, to determine the fundamental law of man's conduct, we have only to ascertain the fundamental law of the world. In short, ethics is freed from theological or metaphysical connections.[2]

The second bearing is that in the law of evolution itself is found the fundamental law of both the world and man. Evolution demonstrates the goal whither the universe is tending and also shows the means, the processes, by which it is reaching this goal. Continuing, the young critic says:

The law of evolution shows that we must give up the purely individualistic conception of man, and must regard him as one differentiation of a type of life which, in working itself out, has developed the individual. . . . This generic animal life, this type, is the social organism. Individual man has not an independent law for his own being; but, since he is a derivative product, an outgrowth of the social tissue, the law of his being is that of society as a connected whole.[3]

Dewey states his opponents' arguments well but for purposes of refutation. It was only a matter of a few years, however, before he became convinced of the truth of "scientific" ethics and gave up his "idealist" ethics.

The year 1894 is a chapter division in John Dewey's life. This date closed the Michigan years and opened the Chicago period. More important, Dewey's ethical writings up to 1894 show the strain of his striving to keep Hegel and Darwin in the same harness, but from that year can be dated the sharp ascendancy of Darwin and evolutionism

[2] *Ibid.*   [3] *Ibid.*

over Hegel and idealism.[4] The conversion was a gradual process and had been under way for several years.[5] It was in 1889 that Dewey's great friend and patron George Morris died, and Dewey returned to the University of Michigan to replace him. Now, though barely thirty, Dewey was a full professor and head of the philosophy department. Perhaps the assurance of his new position and the absence of Morris helped him achieve a greater philosophical independence and begin the break with his youthful idealism.

In the *Psychology* (1886) Dewey was still teaching that "the feeling that an act is right is the feeling that in that act the ideal—that is, the perfectly objective and universal—personality is realized," and that "the essence of social feeling is that in it man feels himself identified with a self more comprehensive, more permanent than his own private and particular being." [6]

In 1891 appeared *Outlines of a Critical Theory of Ethics* which, though idealist in tone, gives unmistakable signs of the shift from idealist organicism to an evolutionist instrumentalism. The same indications appear in briefer form in an article for the *International Journal of Ethics* published in January of that year. Here are some of Dewey's distinctive ideas in their earliest formulation:

Moral theory . . . is the analytic perception of the conditions and relations in hand in a given act—it is the action *in idea*. It is the construction of the act in thought against its outward construction. *It is, therefore, the doing—the act itself, in its emerging*. So far are we from a divorce of moral theory and practice that theory is the ideal act, and conduct is the executed insight. This is our thesis.[7]

It is a piece of scholasticism to suppose that a moral rule has its own self-defining and self-applying content. What truth-telling, what honesty, what

[4] Dewey selects 1903, the year of his *Studies in Logical Theory*, as the year that marks the "final and complete break with his early Hegelian idealism and launches his instrumental theory of reflective thought." In a letter written to William James that same year, however, Dewey says that the roots of his new theory go back about a dozen years. (See Schilpp, ed., *The Philosophy of John Dewey*, p. 33; and White, *The Origin of Dewey's Instrumentalism*, p. 99.)

[5] See the White study for a step-by-step analysis of the development of instrumentalism.

[6] *Psychology*, pp. 335–36.

[7] "Moral Theory and Practice," *International Journal of Ethics*, I (Jan., 1891), 188.

patience, what self-respect are change with every change of intelligence, with every added insight into the relations of men and things. It is only the breath of intelligence blowing through such rules that keeps them from the putrefaction which awaits all barren idealities.[8]

A man's duty is never to obey certain rules; his duty is always to respond to the nature of the actual demands which he finds made upon him— demands which do not proceed from abstract rules, nor from ideals, however awe-inspiring and exalted, but from the concrete relations to men and things in which he finds himself.[9]

In a letter to Harris dated May 30, 1893, Dewey sends him a quotation from Hegel and a note explaining a recent insight he has gained into the relativity of Hegel's absolute:

HEGEL, Werke, 7nter Bd., 2t Abth, page 14

Dem Geist geht aber in dieser Entwickelung nicht nur die logische Idee, sondern auch die auessere Natur vorher. Denn das schon in der einfachen *logischen* Idee enthaltene *Erkennen* ist nur der *von uns gedachte Begriff des Erkennens,* nicht das fuer sich selbst vorhandene Erkennen, nicht der wirkliche Geist, sondern bloss dessen Moeglichkeit.

My dear Dr. Harris:—

The above quotation from Hegel's Phil. of Spirit will serve as a text for some of the remarks I made last summer about the relation of the phil of spirit to that of nature and to the Logic—the effect of which was that the Idee, as found at the end of the Logic, is anything but the complete Absolute, being rather the (relatively empty) *form of the Absolute in thought,* and requiring therefore both nature and spirit as content to give it actuality.[10]

Few traces of idealism and transcendentalism remained in Dewey's thought when in 1894 he brought out *The Study of Ethics: A Syllabus.* In a prefatory note Dewey explains that the edition of his *Outlines of a Critical Theory of Ethics,* prepared for his Michigan students, is exhausted, and this demand seems "to justify the belief that, amid the prevalence of pathological and moralistic ethics, there is room for a theory which conceived of conduct as the normal and free living of life as it is." There is a new and confident tone to the voice that now asserts:

[8] *Ibid.,* p. 196.   [9] *Ibid.,* p. 200.
[10] Letter of May 30, 1893. The original is in the School of Philosophy Library, University of Southern California.

Moral conduct cannot be adequately conceived as the property or perform-ance of the agent alone. The agent corresponds to the organ biologically, and is thus, in itself, simply an instrument for exercising certain functions. Its structure, its aims, its interests, are controlled by the ends to be reached, and these ends include the *conditions* of action as well as the instrument.[11]

The *Syllabus* draws upon evolution to support the Deweyan denial of immediate moral truths. The evolutionary position, Dewey writes, "leaves no room for the belief in any faculty of moral knowledge separate from the whole process of experience, and cuts the ground out from any store of information given directly and immediately." [12]

Now scientific ethics is thoroughly his own. Between 1894 and 1934 Dewey will incorporate new laboratory findings in psychology, par-ticularly those of his Columbia colleague Thorndike, into his moral philosophy. He will increasingly enlarge the place of national and international problems in its application. But by 1894 the metal had been poured and hardened and henceforth, no matter what its surface configurations, will be easily recognizable as the distinctive ethics of instrumentalism.[13]

✦

It is in the area of moral and ethical theory—Dewey does not distinguish the two—that the most far-reaching consequences of his instrumentalist philosophy are to be found. What then for Dewey is the nature of morals and ethical conduct? Morals, in its broad sense, is a function of "the interaction between intrinsic human nature on the one hand and social customs and institutions on the other." [14] Moral science is not something with a separate province. It is physical,

[11] *The Study of Ethics*, p. 11.   [12] *Ibid.*, p. 90.

[13] That once it was fixed, John Dewey's philosophy of values did not undergo substantial modification is made clear by the publishing history of some of his most important early writings. Many of his early articles were later reprinted without modification in collections of essays that were introduced by Dewey's own preface. *Characters and Events* (1929) contains both articles on Renan (1892) and the important "Religion and Our Schools" (1908). *Moral Principles in Education* (1909) is an elaboration of "Ethical Principles Underlying Educa-tion" (1897). *My Pedagogic Creed* (1897) was reprinted several times, the latest by the NEA in 1939. In 1948 Dewey brought out an enlarged edition of *Recon-struction in Philosophy* (1920) with a new introduction.

[14] *Human Nature and Conduct*, pp. viii–ix.

biological, and historical knowledge placed in a human context where it will illuminate and guide the activities of man.[15] Hence, "there is no separate body of moral rules; no separate system of motive powers; no separate subject-matter of moral knowledge, and hence no such thing as an isolated ethical science." [16]

A moral principle in Dewey's lexicon is not a command to act or forbear acting in a given way, but *"it is a tool for analyzing a special situation,* the right or wrong being determined by the situation in its entirety, and not by the rule as such." Principles in the moral and ethical order are never norms of conduct but experimental methods of action. Or, as Dewey puts it: "The principle is not what justifies an activity, for the principle is but another name for the continuity of the activity." [17] Continuity is the key word. A morals based upon human nature (instead of upon a disregard for it) would find, he says, "the facts of man continuous with those of the rest of nature and would thereby ally ethics with physics and biology." [18] Moreover, it would find the nature and activities of one person "coterminous with those of other human beings, and therefore link ethics with the study of history, sociology, law and economics." [19]

Prior to the emergence of man from the evolutionary process and the formation of a human society, there may have been profound differences between the ethical and the cosmic. Now, however, all such differences are summed up in the fact that "the process and the forces bound up with the cosmic have come to consciousness in man." [20] That which was instinct in the animal is conscious impulse in man. That which was unconscious adaptation and survival in the animal is, with man, conscious deliberation and experimentation. This transfer from unconsciousness to consciousness is the "whole distinction of the moral from the unmoral."

Dewey will no longer allow the distinction between moral goods, like the virtues, and natural goods like health, economic security, art, science, and so forth.[21] His reasoning? Experimental logic, when carried into morals, makes every quality good inasmuch as it con-

---

[15] *Ibid.,* p. 296.   [16] *The Influence of Darwin on Philosophy,* p. 69.
[17] *Democracy and Education,* p. 410.   [18] *Human Nature and Conduct,* p. 12.
[19] *Ibid.*   [20] "Evolution and Ethics," *Monist,* VIII (April, 1898), 340.
[21] *Reconstruction in Philosophy,* p. 172.

tributes to the amelioration of existing ills. In so doing experimental logic enforces the moral meaning of the natural and social sciences. He even wonders whether the root difficulty of present social deficiencies does not lie in the traditional separation of natural and moral science. He affirms that

> when physics, chemistry, biology, medicine contribute to the detection of concrete human woes and to the development of plans for remedying them and relieving the human estate, they become moral; they become part of the apparatus of moral inquiry or science.[22]

At any moment conceptions which once seemed to belong exclusively to the biological or physical realms may assume moral import. This will happen whenever they are discovered to have a bearing on the common good.[23]

Dewey distinguishes three levels of human conduct: (1) where man's behavior is motivated by nonmoral impulses or needs; (2) where man with little reflection follows the standards of his group; (3) where man judges the situation for himself. Only the third is, strictly speaking, moral. The first level is not moral at all, and the second is a form of incipient morality. The entire process is one "in which man becomes more *rational,* more *social,* and finally more *moral.*"[24] This stage of finality, however, is only relative to man's moral growth, for moral science must be prepared to grow along with a progressing morality. As one critic has pointed out, "Relativity in moral standards is to take the place of the cult of fixed principles which is for Dewey another manifestation of man's longing for certainty in a world where he must learn to be content with hypotheses."[25]

Precisely what does Dewey mean by his "scientific approach" to morals? The clearest explanation is found in the chapter on "Moral Reconstruction" in *Reconstruction in Philosophy.* In sum, he says that in a scientific, as opposed to a traditional-type morality, inquiry is exacted. There is observation of the detailed make-up of the situation and analysis of its diverse factors. There is a clarification of what is

[22] *Ibid.,* p. 173.

[23] Dewey and Tufts, *Ethics* (1908; rev. ed., 1932), p. 312. The 1932 edition, at least the chapters prepared by Dewey, was substantially rewritten.

[24] *Ibid.,* p. 10 (1908 ed.).

[25] Martin Smith, *John Dewey and Moral Education,* Ch. IV, p. 4.

obscure in which the more insistent and vivid traits are discounted and the consequences of the various modes of action that suggest themselves are traced. The decision reached is regarded as something only hypothetical and tentative until the anticipated consequences that led to adoption are squared with actual consequences. And, concludes Dewey, "this inquiry is intelligence." [26]

The control of experience through intelligence is the only truly human way of coping with the moral. For moral goods and ends exist only when something has to be done. This very requirement for action —the fact that something has to be done—is proof that there are deficiencies or evils in the existent situation. Each deficiency or evil is unique: "The ill is just the specific ill that it is." As a consequence man must discover the good of the situation on the basis of the exact defect and trouble to be rectified. This good cannot be injected from without. It is true that "health, wealth, industry, temperance, amiability, courtesy, learning, esthetic capacity, initiative, courage, patience, enterprise, thoroughness and a multitude of other generalized ends are acknowledged as good," but these classifications should not be pursued as preexisting absolutes. They are rather suggested tools of insight whose value lies in promoting an individualized response in the individual situation.[27] The correctness of the exact definitions in moral theory, says Dewey, is a matter of no importance. The point is that all definitions must be given in the same terms, "not of mere 'oughts,' but of concrete ways of acting in reference to a situation, not unearthly, but of facts." [28]

It is out of the concrete problem-situation that moral theory arises. "Moral theory cannot emerge when there is positive belief as to what is right and what is wrong, for then there is no occasion for reflection." Only the "conflict of good ends and of standards and rules of right and wrong calls forth personal inquiry into the bases of morals." [29] Even if there were *in abstracto* some antecedent set of moral principles, asks Dewey of the transcendentalist, has anyone ever indicated even in the roughest way how these principles are to be applied? The

[26] *Reconstruction in Philosophy*, p. 164.   [27] *Ibid.*, p. 169.
[28] "Moral Theory and Practice," *International Journal of Ethics*, I (Jan., 1891), 187.
[29] *Ethics* (rev. ed.), p. 173.

opposition is clear: rigid dogmas backed by force as opposed to intelligent observation of a concrete situation "guided by the best wisdom already in our possession, which is the heart of the scientific method." [30]

But what then explains our moral failures? Replies Dewey: failure to apply the scientific method. Moral faults are due to some weakness of disposition, some absence of sympathy, some one-sided bias that makes us perform the judgment of the concrete case carelessly or perversely. Dewey puts little stress upon personal evil, for in instrumentalism evil is no longer a theological nor a metaphysical problem but rather "the practical problem of reducing, alleviating, as far as may be removing, the evils of life." That is, social life.[31] On the other hand, the virtues are those of the careful scientist approaching a problem:

Wide sympathy, keen sensitiveness, persistence in the face of the disagreeable, balance of interests enabling us to undertake the work of analysis and decision intelligently are the distinctively moral traits—the virtues or moral excellencies.[32]

John Dewey had been schooled in the liberal tradition, and he considered himself dedicated to the values of the human spirit. Consequently he was chagrined over the repeated failure of his critics to understand that its identification with science did not make instrumentalism a materialist philosophy. Dewey argues that instrumentalist ethics is no more akin to that espoused by materialism than to that of the transcendentalist school of metaphysics.[33] As a matter of fact, both schools deny the instrumentalist postulate for moral science, i.e., the continuity of scientific judgment, and this denial brings upon them both the back of Dewey's hand. Materialism denies the principle of

[30] "Challenge to Liberal Thought," in *Problems of Men*, p. 156.
[31] *Reconstruction in Philosophy*, p. 177.   [32] *Ibid.*, p. 164.
[33] As late as 1945 Dewey wrote in the preface of a Columbia University symposium: "The organized attack now being made against science and against technology as inherently materialistic and as usurping the place properly held by the abstract moral precepts—abstract because divorcing ends from the means by which they must be realized—defines the issue we now have to face. Shall we go backwards or shall we go ahead to discover and put into practice the means by which science and technology shall be made fundamental in the promotion of human welfare?" "The Democratic Faith and Education," in *The Authoritarian Attempt to Capture Education*, p. 1.

continuity of judgment and confuses continuity of method, i.e., the possibility of using a general statement regarding one object as a tool in the determination of some other, with immediate identity of subject matter. The materialist doesn't see that ethical experience is continuous with all other forms of experience. He incorrectly assimilates it to the physical *form* of objects defined in judgment.[34]

If it is once recognized that all scientific judgments, physical as well as ethical, are ultimately concerned with getting experience stated in objective (that is, universal) terms for the sake of the direction of further experience, . . . there will be no thought of trying to explain away the distinctive traits of any type of experience.[35]

Since conscious life is continuous, the possibility of using any one mode of experience to assist in the formation of any other is the ultimate postulate of *all* science—nonethical and ethical alike. Let the materialist note that this instrumental service makes it both possible and necessary to employ materialistic science in the construction of ethical theory.

On one occasion, stung by an article in which the author equated pragmatism with the materialist philosophy held and practiced by those in control of the Soviet Union, Dewey drew his broadsword and retorted that the Bolshevist philosophy

is as absolutistic as the philosophy with which M. Benda has allied himself, although the absolutism is that of "dialectical materialism" instead of what is presumably in the case of M. Benda a "spiritualist," possibly supernatural variety. In any case the conflict of the two philosophies with one another is that of rival absolutisms.[36]

Dewey reserves his heaviest gunfire, however, for the "transcendentalist" theories of ethics. Ethical theory, he claims, has been singularly hypnotized by the notion that its business was to discover

---

[34] *Reconstruction in Philosophy*, p. 164.

[35] *Logical Conditions of a Scientific Treatment of Morality*, p. 136.

[36] "William James' Morals and Julien Benda's," *Commentary*, V (Jan., 1948), 49. Paul Blanshard has written a full-length book drawing out the comparison between the absolutism of the Catholic Church and that of Communist Russia, *Communism, Democracy and Catholic Power*. John Dewey wrote a jacket endorsement for Mr. Blanshard's earlier book, *American Freedom and Catholic Power*, a work busied with the same theme. Paul Blanshard had done graduate seminar work under Dewey at Columbia University.

some final end or good or some ultimate and supreme law outside of actual experience. But those who approach ethics this way must face the question:

Is not the belief in the single, final and ultimate (whether conceived as good or as authoritative law) an intellectual product of that feudal organization which is disappearing historically and of that belief in a bounded, ordered cosmos, wherein rest is higher than motion, which has disappeared from natural science? [37]

Moreover, is not this notion that a moral judgment merely apprehends and enunciates some predetermined end-in-itself but a way of "denying the need for and existence of genuine moral judgment"? Yes, answers Dewey, because for anyone following this notion there is no truly problematic situation. There is only a person who is in a state of subjective ignorance or uncertainty. His business then is not to judge the objective situation in order to determine what course of action is morally satisfactory and right but "simply to come into intellectual possession of a predetermined end-in-itself." [38]

Human conceit is partially the source of this false morality. It has demanded that the whole universe be judged from the standpoint of the desire and disposition of the good man. The effect of religion, according to Dewey, has been to cherish this very conceit by making men think the universe invariably conspires to support the good and bring the evil to naught. By a subtle logic, the effect has been to render morals unreal and transcendental. For

since the world of actual experience does not guarantee this identity of character and outcome, it is inferred that there must be some ulterior truer reality which enforces the equation that is violated in this life. Hence the common notion of another world in which vice and virtue of character produce their exact moral need.[39]

Dewey will explain the origin of transcendental religion in a somewhat similar fashion, as we shall see.

His lash does not spare the utilitarians and their theory of morals. The equation of acts with consequences, he says, "is as much a fiction

[37] *Reconstruction in Philosophy*, pp. 161–62. These lines betray a strange ignorance of the Aristotelian teaching of act and potency.

[38] *Logic*, p. 168.   [39] *Human Nature and Conduct*, pp. 49–50.

of self-conceit as is the assumption of a fixed transcendental world wherein moral ideals are eternally and immutably real." Both utilitarians and transcendentalists deny in effect "the relevancy of time, of change, to morals, while time is of the essence in the moral struggle." [40]

✦

That men should continue to follow the traditional moralities and turn their backs upon the broad new road opened up by science, Dewey found puzzling. The crisis men face in having to choose between their traditional morality and the values of science need never have arisen. If men had associated their ideas about value with practical activity instead of with cognition of antecedent being, "they would *not* have been troubled by the findings of science" but would have welcomed them. He elaborates his thought:

But according to the religious and philosophic tradition of Europe, the valid status of all the highest values, the good, true and beautiful, was bound up with their being properties of ultimate and supreme Being, namely, God. All went well as long as what passed for natural science ceased to disclose in the objects of knowledge the possession of any such properties. Then some roundabout method had to be devised for substantiating them.[41]

For two thousand years, continues the indictment, the weight of the most influential and authoritatively orthodox tradition of thought has been devoted to the problem of a purely cognitive certification (perhaps by revelation, perhaps by intuition, perhaps by reason) of the antecedent immutable reality of truth, beauty, and goodness. As against such a doctrine, the conclusions of natural science constitute the materials of a serious problem. The appeal has been made to the Court of Knowledge and the verdict has been adverse.

All movements urging a return to the "ancient foundation of morals and social institutions" seemed to John Dewey a long step backwards in human progress. These advocates of a return to "supernaturalism"

[40] *Ibid.,* p. 51. Dewey, however, praises utilitarianism on other points. It insisted upon getting away from vague generalities and down to specifics. It subordinated law to human achievement. It taught that institutions are made for men and not vice versa. It made moral good natural, human, in touch with the natural goods of life. It opposed unearthly and otherworldly morality. (See *Reconstruction in Philosophy,* p. 180.)

[41] *Quest for Certainty,* pp. 42–43.

or "transcendentalism" would not dream of urging the abolition of all modern inventions and appliances that are the fruit of experimental extension of science. Yet logically, such is the direction in which they are moving. Are we compelled, asks Dewey, "to hold that one method obtains in natural science and another, radically different, in moral question"? Unless we accept the scientific method in morals, trouble lies in the offing.

Scientific method is now finding its way into the psychological field; it is already at home in anthropological study. As the conclusions reached in these studies find their way into general acceptance, is a conflict between science and moral beliefs to replace the old conflict between science and what was taken to be religion? And the question is the more pertinent because the religion in question was also the expression of a prescientific stage of culture.[42]

His own belief, which he would were more prevalent, he puts in the mouth of one of his speakers in "Nature's Good: A Conversation":

I do not believe for a moment in some different Reality beyond and behind Nature. I do not believe that a manipulation of the logical implications of science can give results which are to be put in the place of those which Science herself yields in her direct application. I accept Nature as something which is, not seems, and Science as her faithful transcript. Yet because I believe these things, not in spite of them, I believe in the existence of purpose and good.[43]

A corollary of the evolutionist principle is that continuous reconstruction of experience or growth is the sole end of the life process. Since all growth occurs in the total organism of society, the virtues of social growth take first place in the scheme of morality. Several times Dewey deplores the selfish, even antisocial, emphasis that tra-

[42] "Challenge to Liberal Thought," in *Problems of Men,* p. 155. Dewey looked upon the opposition to the birth-control movement as "an expression of an ever-recurring struggle between darkness and knowledge." Just as expanding knowledge of electricity brought with it so many benefits to mankind, "so scientific knowledge of the transmission of life enables mankind to bring that process under human direction. Because knowledge always means increased control, there can be no doubt of where ultimate victory will lie in this particular conflict. . . . How can anyone who believes in education fail to be opposed to this restriction on the flow of intelligence?" ("Education and Birth Control," *Nation,* CXXXIV [Jan. 27, 1932], 112.)

[43] *The Influence of Darwin on Philosophy,* p. 31.

ditional religion has put upon the salvation of the personal soul. This, he claims, has tended to restrict the ultimate scope of morals to the reflex effect of conduct on one's self.[44] This priority of the collectivity in society rather than of the individual is still another corollary which derives from the theory of evolutionary continuity, the starting point of Deweyan instrumentalism. "Society," says Dewey, "is a society of individuals and the individual is always a social individual. He has no existence by himself. He lives in, for, and by society."[45] The subject will recur in the next chapter.

In the practical order morals will be "customs, folkways, established collective habits." Dewey points out that this is a commonplace with the anthropologist, "even if the moral theorist generally suffers from an illusion that his own place and day is, or ought to be, an exception." But whether the moralist likes the idea or not, "always and everywhere" customs supply the standards for personal activities and they are the patterns into which individual activity must weave itself.[46] Nevertheless, man can "intelligently adapt customs to conditions, and thereby remake them. Customs in any case constitute moral standards. For they are active demands for certain ways of acting."[47]

The original edition of the *Ethics* carries this Hegelian-tinged thought concerning the place of the self in the moral life, "that the problem of morality is the formation, out of the body of original instinctive impulses which compose the natural self, of a voluntary self in which socialized desires and affections are dominant, and in which the last and controlling principle of deliberation is the love of the objects which will make this transformation possible."[48] Social interaction makes the character, for the principle of the continuum is absolute. Not only through habit does a given psychical attitude expand into a particular case, but every habit in its operation may directly or indirectly call up any other habit in a social situation. The

[44] *Quest for Certainty*, p. 31.

[45] "Ethical Principles Underlying Education," in National Herbart Society, *Third Yearbook, 1897*, p. 8.

[46] *Human Nature and Conduct*, p. 75.

[47] *Ibid*. Some social scientists have applied this principle to Dr. Kinsey's findings about sexual behavior.

[48] *Ethics*, p. 397 (1908 ed.). This section was completely rewritten for the 1932 revised edition.

term *character,* says Dewey, "denotes this complex continuum of interactions in its office of influencing final judgment." [49]

✦

The ethical system John Dewey presents, whatever its merits, is an innovation or a reconstruction. The question has been asked, whether the label "ethics" really fits. Dewey's system can hardly be classified as a personal ethics, but is there such a thing as a "cosmic" ethics? No one took more vigorous exception to the use of the term "cosmic" ethics than the John Dewey of the Hegelian years:

> Unless the term "ethics" is to be extended so as to lose all specific meaning, it cannot mean the behavior, the conduct, of the universe at large: it must mean the conduct of man. It implies that man has a certain end which he is to fulfill, to whose realization he is to devote his life.[50]

These words of the younger Dewey pose the issue clearly: Does man have an end to fulfill that is independent of society? Is his first responsibility to develop himself as a person and *thereby* serve society as a citizen? Has man a destiny that transcends the order of empirical time and space? The mature John Dewey's *point de départ* is precisely a negative reply to these questions.

Here in summary review are some leading points of Dewey's instrumentalist ethics or moral theory:

1. Ethics originates in the interaction between human nature and social customs and institutions.

2. Ethics as a positive science is continuous with the physical sciences, and as an essentially social science is continuous with the social sciences. Accordingly, there is no real distinction between moral and natural good, nor between moral and nonmoral knowledge.

3. The scientific method of intelligently controlling the problem-situation must be applied to ethical science.

4. A moral principle is a tool for analyzing a special situation, but the right or wrong is determined by the situation in its entirety, not by any rule as such.

[49] *Logical Conditions of a Scientific Treatment of Morality,* p. 126.
[50] "Ethics and Physical Science," *Andover Review,* VII (June, 1887), 585.

5. The ancient struggle between religion and science is now a conflict between transcendental ethics and a scientific ethics.

6. The defining and cataloguing of moral qualities or virtues is questionable because usually based upon the false assumption that there exists some antecedent fixed moral reality.

7. Growth is the moral aim of all life and education.

8. The customs of society are the source of all moral standards, but through intelligence man can adapt these.

✦

In drawing the intellectual portrait of John Dewey, Sidney Hook explains why one color is missing from the canvas. The fact that religions and religious philosophies, he writes, "find something lacking in the philosophy of John Dewey" should not cause surprise. And why?

Instead of the attempt to find a first cause or a final goal in existence, Dewey offers us an analysis of why all such questions make assumptions that render them self-defeating. They are self-defeating because in principle no observation can ever verify a statement whose subject is *the* whole universe, *the* totality, the scheme of things entire. Genuine problems and questions are always specific. They are always such that we can tell what would constitute evidence one way or another to make the answers to them more or less probable.[51]

The frequently astute Mr. Hook is perhaps not aware that to those who uphold "religions and religious philosophies" Dewey himself is offering a final and absolute goal for men's strivings, a goal to be gained by following a final and absolute method. To these people the above statements concerning the dimensions of total reality, the criterion for the genuineness of a problem, and the narrowing of verification to a process of empirical observation seem as dogmatic and arbitrary as any of the religious creeds or supernatural formulae that Dewey and Professor Hook himself find so distasteful. Those who accept "religions and religious philosophies" would moreover claim that Dewey has created a religious philosophy replete with virtues of faith, hope, and charity which he puts forward as a substitute for traditional religions. John Dewey's religious philosophy, at least from

[51] Hook, *John Dewey*, p. 211.

this other viewpoint, begins with an act of faith in the process of evolution. Having rejected the notion of the *super*-natural world with a transcendent deity and personal immortality, it wrests its values and ideals from concrete social experience. Its hope lies in the unlimited individual and social perfectibility of the race through the medium of science, and its charity is found in the bonds uniting it to the fecund nature from which mankind is continually evolving.

John Dewey was not an atheist: he was rather an "anti-theist." Still less was he an agnostic. In fact, he scoffed at agnosticism as an unscientific compromise or false neutrality, stating:

It is a continual marvel that so many men of science who have abandoned and even attacked all dogmatic authority, should take refuge for themselves in agnosticism—that they should not see that any lasting denial of dogmatic authority is impossible save as science itself advances to that comprehensive synthesis which will allow it to become a guide of conduct, a social motor.[52]

And in another work he says:

"Agnosticism" is a shadow cast by the eclipse of the supernatural. Of course, acknowledgment that we do not know what we do not know is a necessity of all intellectual integrity. But generalized agnosticism is only a halfway elimination of the supernatural. Its meaning departs when the intellectual outlook is directed wholly to the natural world.[53]

Dewey was thoroughly dedicated to a reconstruction of society through what many would call his "religion," although the word itself was anathema to him.[54] He makes much of the distinction between "religion" and "religious." The first he defines as a body of beliefs and practices organized upon an institutional basis; but "religious" is simply an attitude toward an object or ideal in experience. The Terry Lectures at Yale, printed as *A Common Faith* in 1934, are the most important statement of Dewey's mature views on ultimate values. This is his carefully worked out "scientific" religion for a democratic age. With this invitation to speak from one of the

[52] "Renan's Loss of Faith in Science," *Open Court*, VII (Jan. 5, 1893), 3515.
[53] *A Common Faith*, p. 86.
[54] *Ibid.*, 1st Lecture: "Religion versus the Religious," *passim*. In his *Intelligible Religion* Philip H. Phenix has treated at length the problem of definition and meaning of religion. See pp. 9–15. His own suggestion, as a working definition of religion: "Faith in some ultimate scheme of values."

very distinguished platforms in the American academic world, the
seventy-five-year-old Dewey was perhaps at the peak of his influence
and recognition. However, many of the ideas in *A Common Faith*
go back forty years earlier to two of his little-known essays on Ernest
Renan which we shall briefly consider here.[55]

In the first article Dewey warmly praises Renan's *Future of Science*
and joins himself to the author in his insistence that the ideal behind
the hunger for religion is embodied in the universe "and is to be
found and drawn thence by science." Yet there need be no fear that
science will destroy religion, for "whatever science takes away, it is
only because it presents us with deeper truth." This conception, says
Dewey, animates the book, and he offers a few selected quotations
from it to illustrate:

The man of science is the real "custodian of the sacred deposit"; "real religion is the culmination of the discipline and cultivation of the intelligence";
social and religious reform will assuredly come . . . . "but it will come from
enlarged science common to all, and operating in the unrestricted midst of
human intelligence"; "hence, science is a religion, it alone will henceforth
make the creeds, for science alone can solve for men the eternal problems,
the solution of which his nature imperatively demands." [56]

The substitution of a faith based on science for the "illusions and
superstitions" of Christianity was an idea common to many nineteenth-
century rationalist and positivist philosophers, but the parallels in
the thought of Renan and Dewey on the religion of science are particularly striking.[57] Dewey makes explicit in the articles what he says

[55] "Two Phases of Renan's Life: The Faith of 1850 and the Doubt of 1890,"
Open Court, VI (Dec. 29, 1892), 3505–6; "Renan's Loss of Faith in Science,"
ibid., VII (Jan. 5, 1893), 3512–15. The first six volumes of the journal carried
this heading in the masthead: "Devoted to the Work of Conciliating Religion
with Science," but with the issue of January 5, 1893, the dedicatory motto was
changed to: "Devoted to the Religion of Science." That issue featured a lengthy
statement of objectives. Some excerpts: "The religion of science is that religion
wherein man aspires to find the truth, scientifically proved, as ultimate. It does
not rely on human authority, even though that authority pretends to have special
revelations from some supernatural source. . . . [It] has no creed or dogma,
yet it has a clearly defined faith." (*Open Court*, VII [Jan. 5, 1893], 3635.)

[56] "Renan's Loss of Faith in Science," *Open Court*, VII (Jan. 5, 1893), 3514.

[57] The influence of Renan mingles here with Comte's. Some points of agreement between Deweyan instrumentalism and Comtian sociologism: unity of
method for science and philosophy; scientific method for moral science; relativity

is only suggested by Renan, namely, "that this religious outflowering
of science is to be expected when, on one hand, its scope has been
extended to take in humanity, and when, on the other, its practical
outcome, if not its abstruse results, has been made the possession of
all men." He continues, quoting from the ex-Sulpician:

It is not enough for the progress of human intelligence that a few isolated
thinkers should reach very advanced posts, and that a few heads shoot up
like wild oats above the common level. . . . It is a matter of great urgency
to enlarge the whirl of humanity; otherwise a few individuals might reach
heaven, while the mass is still dragging along the earth. . . . The moment
intellectual culture becomes a religion, from that moment it becomes bar-
barous to deprive a single soul of it.[58]

The new religion of science then was not to become a monopoly of
some leisured intellectual aristocracy. All men were entitled to the
benefits to be found in religion and in any other cultural activity.
This point will remain cardinal for Dewey. Ten years later he lauds
Emerson for this same insight, calling him "the first and as yet almost
the only Christian of the Intellect," because "against creed and system,
convention and institution, Emerson stands for restoring to the common man that which in the name of religion, of philosophy, of art and
of morality, has been embezzled from the common store and ap-
propriated to sectarian and class use." [59]

In the 1930s Dewey was still urging modern man to come to terms
with the advances in secular knowledge:

For science has forced a movement from the idea of a tight confined universe of which the world is the center and crown to belief in indefinite
multitudes not merely of solar systems but of universes. The exclusive and
self-centered history of man on this planet with the unique importance of
the drama of sin and redemption has been broadened to include an endless
sweep of developments among which the story of man on this planet is but

of moral truth; sociology the supreme science; humanity the focus of scientific,
religious, and social thought; the growth of proper relations between man and
humanity the aim of moral education. For some interesting speculations regarding
Renan's influence on Dewey, see Chadbourne, "Two Organizers of Divinity:
Ernest Renan and John Dewey," *Thought*, XXIV (Sept., 1949), 430–48.

[58] "Renan's Loss of Faith in Science," *Open Court*, VII (Jan. 5, 1893), 3514.

[59] "Emerson—the Philosopher of Democracy," *International Journal of Ethics*,
XIII (July, 1903), 411.

an inconsiderable incident, not the culmination of the meaning of the whole.[60]

Dewey recognizes that there are millions of devoted believers in whom both conceptions still exist side by side, but nonetheless,

anyone who has faced the full intellectual scope and depth of the change in the idea of the universe and of man's history, has no alternative but sur- render of the older conception of God or else a broadening out of it to meet the change in the conception of the universe and history to which the God believed in is related. History and anthropology have moreover made clear the tribal origin and status of the exclusive God.[61]

New methods of inquiry and reflection have become for the educated man today the final arbiter of all questions of fact, existence, and in- tellectual assent.[62] This is the revolution in "the seat of authority" which science has brought about. Scientific method, which is the method of intelligence in experimental action, can provide the au- thority that earlier centuries sought in fixed dogmas.[63] But let the religiously inclined take heart: this new faith "in the continued dis- closing of truth through directed cooperative human endeavor is more religious in quality than is any faith in a completed revelation." [64]

✦

The allegedly scientific basis of Dewey's moral and religious theories is better appreciated through his account of the origin of supernatural religion. He advances several explanations, all of which he calls anti- scientific. There is first of all the ancient inference from ignorance to the postulate of a "supernatural":

We lack, for example, knowledge of the relation of life to inanimate matter. Therefore supernatural intervention is assumed to have effected the transi-

[60] "A God or THE God?" review of *Is There a God? A Conversation,* by Henry N. Wieman, Douglas C. Macintosh, and Max Carl Otto, *Christian Cen- tury,* L (Feb. 8 and March 22, 1933), 193–96 and 394–95.

[61] *Ibid.* The reference is to THE God of the Old and the New Testament, of the Koran, or of any other monotheistic religion in which the group's deity is proclaimed as the uniquely true.

[62] "The Liberation of Modern Religion," *Yale Review,* n.s. XXIII (June, 1934), 753.

[63] "Religion, Science and Philosophy," *Southern Review,* 2d Series, I (Sum- mer, 1936), 53–54.

[64] *A Common Faith,* p. 26.

tion from brute to man. We do not know the relation of the organism—the brain and nervous system—to the occurrence of thought. Therefore, it is argued, there is a supernatural link. We do not know the relation of causes to results in social matters, and consequently we lack means of control. Therefore, it is inferred, we must resort to supernatural control.[65]

Admittedly, continues Dewey, it is difficult to avoid using the word "supernatural," but we must avoid the traditional meaning of the word. Anthropologists have pointed out that the distinction between natural and supernatural was between ordinary and extraordinary, between the prosaic and the unexpected. "As long as there was no defined area of the *natural,* that which is over and beyond the natural can have no significance." [66]

The introduction of the supernatural into belief is much more an affair of the psychology that generates works of art than of effort at scientific and philosophic explanation. It intensifies, writes Dewey, "emotional thrill and punctuates the interest that belongs to all break in familiar routine." Were the grip of the supernatural upon human thought exclusively, or even mainly, an intellectual thing, its hold would be slight. But theologies and cosmogonies have laid hold of imagination. "Most religions have identified their sacraments with the highest reaches of art, and the most authoritative beliefs have been clothed in a garb of pomp and pageantry that gives immediate delight to eye and ear and that evokes massive emotions of suspense, wonder, and awe." [67]

Apropos of an article by H. G. Wells, Dewey suggests another explanation of supernaturalism. In purporting to set forth the religion of the twentieth century the British writer had "transferred the statements of 'science' into religious terminology, rejected obsolescent definitions and reco-ordinated propositions that had drifted into

---

[65] *Ibid.,* p. 76. Reviewing John L. Childs's *Education and Morals,* Peter A. Bertocci had this criticism of a Deweyan principle: "In the name of science and empiricism, we are asked to adopt a scientific account of evolution, a view which presumably eventuates in a non-dualistic view of mind and a social view of personality. Why? *Because any other view is deemed unscientific and therefore false!* [Bertocci's emphasis.] But the whole issue between the supernaturalist, other non-naturalistic philosophers, and the experimentalist hinges on whether empiricism, in the restricted sense employed by science, is the only or adequate approach to truth." (*Harvard Educational Review,* XXI [Fall, 1951], 214–15.)

[66] *Quest for Certainty,* p. 11.   [67] *Art as Experience,* p. 30.

opposition," about which Dewey acridly comments: "So simple a matter is it to set forth modern religion, not just *a* modern religion!"

Dewey says he could make no sense out of Wells's thought until he came across the following passage, which he introduces with a paraphrase:

Between benevolent atheists and those "who have found God" there is, Mr. Wells says, this difference: "The benevolent atheist stands alone upon his own good will, without a reference, without a standard, trusting to his own impulse to goodness, relying upon his own moral strength . . . he has not really given himself or got away from himself. He has no one to whom he can give himself. His exaltation is self-centered, is priggishness. . . . His devotion is only the good will in himself, etc., etc." [68]

The American philosopher is aroused over Wells's dogmatism and suggests that "the only escape for Mr. Wells from an unrelieved egoism is recourse to a big *Alter Ego* upon whom is bestowed the name of God." There then came to mind, says Dewey, that psychological mechanism to which has been given the name "projection":

When an individual finds a conflict in himself which is offensive and with which he cannot successfully cope directly, he "projects" it into or upon another personality, and then finds rest. Uneasy and tortured egoism, finding no rest for itself in itself, creates a huge Ego which although finite and although not a creator of world, is still huge enough to be our King, Leader and Helper.[69]

In contrast Dewey turns from this type to "the humbleminded of all ages and places who live in the sense of the infinite ties, a few perceived but most of them obscure, which bind them to their fellows,

---

[68] "H. G. Wells, Theological Assembler," *Seven Arts Magazine,* II (July, 1917), 338.

[69] *Ibid.,* pp. 338–39. Nietzsche is the classical source of the "projection" explanation. He conceived religion as the result of psychological duplication. God is in reality the mirror of man. While man is in some kind of ecstatic state he becomes aware of an exalting power and love within. Not daring to ascribe these powerful feelings to himself, man makes them attributes of a *"super*human" being. Man accordingly divides the two aspects of his human nature between two spheres: an ordinary limited one which he calls man, and a rare, strong, and unlimited aspect which he calls *God.* "Religion is a matter of adulteration of the personality," says Nietzsche; and the human problem is to remount that fatal slope so as "gradually to regain possession of those lofty and proud states of the soul" of which we have wrongfully despoiled ourselves. (See Lubac, *The Drama of Atheist Humanism,* pp. 18–19.)

to the soil, to the air and to the light of day, and whose strength to suffer and to enjoy is renewed daily by contact and by intercourse." [70]

Dewey gives still another account for the origin of human belief in the supernatural, perhaps the most consistent with other tenets of instrumentalism: the incorrect assumption of an "antecedent inherent identity of actual and ideal which is also a kind of projection." Man quickly discovers that the actual is not the ideal, but since he needs an ideal he projects his dream to another and higher plane. Then, forgetting that the ideal is only the projection of his imagination, he hypostatizes this ideal world and henceforth regards it as a *reality*. Man's attempt to come to terms with the nonideal in life gives rise to the idea, for example, of "the fall of man." [71]

✦

Writing in the *Yale Review* in 1934, the same year that he delivered the Terry Lectures, John Dewey insists that his central criticism of the supernaturalist philosophy is the *identification* of the ideal with a particular Being, especially when that identification makes necessary the conclusion that this Being is outside of nature. "What I have tried to show," he says, "is that the ideal itself has its roots in natural conditions; it emerges when the imagination idealizes existence by laying hold of the possibilities offered to thought and action." [72]

What the moral effect upon mankind of belief in this God of tradition has been Dewey does not leave secret. Writing in the *Christian Century,* he agrees with Max Otto "that its beneficent effects have been, to put it mildly, much exaggerated." [73] And in *A Common Faith* he bluntly charges that "the connecting of religion with the supernatural has brought doubt upon present day religions and is sapping the religious life itself." [74] Dewey here gives credit to the Protestant denominations for having largely abandoned the idea of institutionalized ecclesiastical authority in religious affairs, and

[70] "H. G. Wells, Theological Assembler," *Seven Arts Magazine,* II (July, 1917), 339.

[71] *Quest for Certainty,* p. 301.

[72] "The Liberation of Modern Religion," *Yale Review,* n.s. XXIII (June, 1934), 764.

[73] "A God or THE God?" *Christian Century,* L (Feb. 8, 1933), 193.

[74] *A Common Faith,* pp. 29–30.

praises the more liberal Protestant groups for having mitigated the Calvinist doctrine of human depravity. Yet these denominations, even the more liberal, he says,

have retained a certain indispensable minimum of intellectual content. They ascribe peculiar religious force to certain literary documents and certain historical personages. Even when they have greatly reduced the bulk of intellectual content to be accepted, they have insisted at least upon this and immortality of the individual.[75]

Dewey pays tribute to the devotion of religious-minded people of the past and remarks that if men and women were actuated today with the same faith and ardor that have at times marked historic religions, the social consequences would be incalculable. To stir up such a faith and *élan* is no easy task, but we should be encouraged by the thought that "religions have attempted something similar, directed moreover toward a less promising object—the supernatural." [76] Dewey's conclusion is that "unless one gives up the whole struggle as hopeless, one has to choose between alternatives. One alternative is dependence upon the supernatural; the other the use of natural agencies." Advance in the religious thought of mankind has been retarded by a diversion of human energy into futile attempts to rationalize the doctrines entertained by historic religions.

Dewey, it is clear, is not suggesting doctrinal modifications in religion. He would abandon religion, at least in its general traditional understanding, because

the set that has thus been given the general mind is much more harmful, to my mind, than are the consequences of any one particular item of belief, serious as have been those flowing from acceptance of some of them.[77]

[75] *Ibid.,* pp. 30–31. Dewey himself had no illusions on this score: "I have no beliefs on the subject of personal immortality. It seems to be a subject, being one of continued existence, for science rather than philosophy, or a matter of physical evidence. If it can be proved, it would have to be along the lines of the psychical researchers, and so far I haven't been much impressed with their results." ("Personal Immortality: What I Believe," New York *Times* Easter Symposium, April 8, 1928.)

[76] *A Common Faith,* p. 81. Dewey expressed grave fears over the future of Protestantism confronted with this challenge. (See "Bishop Brown: A Fundamental Modernist," *New Republic,* XLVIII [Nov. 17, 1926], 371–72.)

[77] *A Common Faith,* p. 33.

The modern mind deludes itself thinking that the modern liberal version of the intellectual content of Christianity is more rational than some older doctrines against which it protested. Says Dewey:

Such is not the case. The theological philosophers of the Middle Ages had no greater difficulty in giving rational form to all the doctrines of the Roman church than has the liberal theologian of today in formulating and justifying intellectually the doctrines he entertains. This statement is as applicable to the doctrine of continuing miracles, penance, indulgences, saints and angels, etc., as to the trinity, incarnation, atonement, and the sacraments.[78]

The indictment by John Dewey of all historic religion—Protestant and Catholic, Orthodox and Liberal, Traditional and Modern, Eastern and Western—is as sweeping as it is necessary, on instrumentalist premises, to achieve Dewey's ideal of "the emancipation of the religious from religion." [79]

In *The Quest for Certainty* Dewey argues the humanist principle that "the demand of righteousness for reverence does not depend upon ability to prove the existence of an antecedent Being who is righteousness." [80] Dewey's idea of divinity is that of an impersonal force or relation coexisting in human experience whose only domicile is in an ideal order:

We are in the presence neither of ideals completely embodied in existence nor yet of ideals that are mere rootless ideals, fantasies, utopias. There are forces in nature and society that generate and support the ideals. They are further unified by the action that gives them coherence and solidity. It is this *active* relation between ideal and actual to which I would give the name God.[81]

[78] *Ibid.*, pp. 33–34.

[79] *Ibid.*, p. 27. It is hardly surprising that Dewey maintained a cool attitude toward the vicissitudes of traditional religions, certain of which he viewed as dangerous absolutisms. The personal observation, both in Russia and in Mexico, of governmental measures taken to root out the ancient religions evoked from him hardly more than the bland generality that such conflicts were "a belated chapter in the secular struggle of church and state for superior political authority." (See "Church and State in Mexico," *New Republic*, XLVIII [Aug. 25, 1926, 9–10]; and "Religion in the Soviet Union," *Current History*, XXXII [April, 1930], 31–36.)

[80] *Quest for Certainty*, p. 304.

[81] "The Liberation of Modern Religion," *Yale Review*, n.s. XXIII (June,

In contrast to the atheists Dewey would salvage the word "God" to denote such a union of the ideal and the actual. He makes the shrewd observation that aggressive atheism seems to have something in common with traditional supernaturalism. Both are exclusively preoccupied with man in isolation. For despite supernaturalism's reference to something beyond nature, it still makes the earth the moral center of the universe and man the apex of the whole scheme of things. Supernaturalism "regards the drama of sin and redemption enacted within the isolated and lonely soul of man as the one thing of ultimate importance. Apart from man, nature is held either accursed or negligible." [82]

On the other hand, Dewey indicts militant atheism for failing in natural piety. It looks upon man as a creature living in a hostile world issuing blasts of defiance, whereas a religious attitude needs "the sense of a connection of man, in the way of both dependence and support, with the enveloping world that the imagination feels is a universe." Hence the use of the word "God," or "divine," to convey the union of actual with ideal "may protect man from a sense of isolation and from consequent despair or defiance." Dewey at once denies that this involves pantheism, or what he dubs the "miscellaneous worship of everything in general." For he would select only those factors in existence that generate and support our idea of good as an end to be striven for.

The "divine" is thus a term of human choice and aspiration. A humanistic religion, if it excludes our relation to nature, is pale and thin, as it is presumptuous when it takes humanity as an object of worship. [83]

1934), 766. Also: "I would not insist that the name *must* be given. There are those who hold that the associations of the term with the supernatural are so numerous and close that any use of the word God is sure to give rise to misconception and be taken as a concession to traditional ideas." *A Common Faith*, p. 51.

[82] "The Liberation of Modern Religion," *Yale Review*, n.s. XXIII (June, 1934), 767. See also *A Common Faith*, pp. 53–54.

[83] "The Liberation of Modern Religion," *Yale Review*, n.s. XXIII (June, 1934), 768. "Dewey believes that it is possible to have a sense of dependence upon, and humility before, the cosmic forces on which we must rely even when we build shelters against them, without surrendering to supernaturalism or to the simple negativism of village *atheism*. Supernaturalism as a creed is hard to accept for a person of intelligence and courage; atheism as a doctrine isolates man from those relations of the physical world which support human achieve-

The real meaning of growth for a secularized humanism lies not in the growth of new beliefs based on scientific inquiry but in "the expansion and distribution of valid meanings and goods through large ranges of experiences." [84] It is no longer possible to confine religious values to the exclusive organs, channels, and objects established by theists and religionists. Yet the change that he advocates, however adverse its impact may be upon historic religions, is not fatal, repeats Dewey, to the religious values in our common experience.[85] In fact this transfer of idealizing imagination, thought, and emotion to natural human relations would not signify the destruction of churches that now exist, but rather offers the means for a recovery of vitality.

The fund of human values that are prized and that need to be cherished, values that are satisfied and rectified by *all* human concerns and arrangements, could be celebrated and reinforced, in different ways and with differing symbols, by the churches. In that way the churches would indeed become catholic.[86]

A sign of the times, as interpreted by Dewey, is the wider demand that the churches show a more active interest in social affairs, that "they stimulate action for a divine kingdom on earth." Yet he is pessimistic that as long as social values are related to the supernatural —a relation fostered by ecclesiastical cabals to shore up institutional religion—there will be an inherent inconsistency between this demand and the churches' efforts to execute it. And how does Dewey propose to cope with the problem? Let the churches accept a humbler place as only one of the human institutions concerned with the problems of humanity: "The surrender of claims to an exclusive and authoritative position," he says, "is a *sine qua non* for doing away with the dilemma in which churches now find themselves in respect to their sphere of social action." [87]

---

ment. *Natural piety recognizes the continuity between man and nature.* It acknowledges man's kinship of origin, but not of interest or aim, with other living things." Hook, *John Dewey,* pp. 213–14.

[84] "A God or THE God?" *Christian Century,* L (Feb. 8, 1933), 196.

[85] "The Liberation of Modern Religion," *Yale Review,* n.s. XXIII (June, 1934), 770.

[86] *A Common Faith,* pp. 82–83.

[87] *Ibid.* One third of *A Common Faith,* estimates Dewey, is "expressly devoted to the social implications of what I would put in the place of religions." (See Letter in *New Republic,* March 13, 1935.)

Let there be no misunderstanding, Dewey warns; his continual employment of the adjective *religious* here and elsewhere should in no wise be construed as "a disguised apology for what have passed as religions." He is proffering something in place of religion. Let any harshness in his statements be excused, he asks, because of his "firm belief that the claim on the part of religions to possess a monopoly of ideals and of the supernatural means by which alone, it is alleged, they can be furthered, stands in the way of the realization of distinctively religious values inherent in natural experience." To anyone who is still deceived into thinking that any kind of a compromise between the traditional understanding of religion and Dewey's instrumentalist philosophy is possible, these warning words are addressed:

The opposition between religious values as I conceive them and religions is not to be bridged. Just because the release of these values is so important, their identification with the creeds and cults of religions must be dissolved.[88]

✦

Traditional religions have built their aims, ideals, goods, and values upon the existence of a personal God who transcends empirical experience. Dewey would substitute a "vitalized appreciation of the cosmic evolutionary process that can be projected as an aim to be realized." Although the aims and ideals that move us are generated through imagination, they are not unreal: they are made of the hard stuff of the world of physical and social experience. This process of creation of ideals is experimental and continuous. For example, the artist, scientific man, or good citizen depends upon what others have already done and are presently doing around him. The sense of new values that become ends to be realized arises first in dim and uncertain form. As these values are dwelt upon and carried forward in action, they become definite and coherent. Interaction between aim and existent conditions improves and tests the ideal and simultaneously modifies conditions. Most important, ideals change as they are applied to existent situations. This process can be purified through the "elimi-

---

[88] *A Common Faith*, pp. 27–28. Claims to monopoly annoyed Dewey. He would not accept an argument based on the supposition that there was but a *single* "tradition" in religious values. (See "One Current Religious Problem," *Journal of Philosophy*, XXXIII [June 4, 1936], 326.)

nation of that irrelevant element that culminates in the idea of the supernatural." [89]

Dewey recognizes a functional identity between supernaturalism and what he advocates as a substitute. He explains that there are in existence, concretely and experimentally, goods like the values of "art in all its forms, of knowledge, of effort and of rest after striving, of education and fellowship and love, of growth in mind and body" —which are relatively embryonic. Many persons are shut out from generous participation in them. But "a clear and intense conception of a union of ideal ends with actual conditions is capable of arousing steady emotion," and in a distracted age the universal need for such an idea is urgent.

Whether one gives the name "God" to this union, operative in thought and action, is a matter for individual decision. But the *function* of such a working union of the ideal and actual seems to me to be identical with the force that has in fact been attached to the conception of God in all the religions that have a spiritual content.[90]

This force or function which is the essence of religious faith is to be found in "the unification of the self through allegiance to inclusive ideal ends, which imagination presents to us and to which the human will responds as worthy of controlling our desires and choices." [91] Such a faith is as broad as experience. Dewey tells us further that "any activity pursued in behalf of an ideal end against obstacles and in spite of threats of personal loss because of conviction of its general and enduring value is religious in quality." [92] It is our bond to society that will guarantee the reality of religious experience, for this experience is real "in so far as in the midst of effort to foresee and regulate future objects we are sustained and expanded in feebleness and failure by the sense of an enveloping whole." [93]

[89] *A Common Faith*, pp. 49–50.   [90] *Ibid.*, p. 52.
[91] "The Liberation of Modern Religion," *Yale Review*, n.s. XXIII (June, 1934), 754.
[92] *A Common Faith*, p. 27.   [93] *Human Nature and Conduct*, p. 264.

✦

In 1930 John Dewey summed up his thoughts on religion in the form of a "Credo" from which we append some statements as a summary and compact review of his value philosophy:

1) Faith in its newer sense signifies that experience itself is the sole ultimate authority.

2) Such a faith has in it all the elements of a philosophy. For it implies that the course and material of experience give support and stay to life, and that its possibilities provide all the ends and ideals that are to regulate conduct.

3) Religions have been saturated with the supernatural—and the supernatural signifies precisely that which lies beyond experience. Moral codes have been allied to this religious supernaturalism and have sought their foundation and sanction in it.

4) Contrast with such ideas, deeply imbedded in all Western culture, gives the philosophy of faith in experience a definite and profound meaning.

5) The outstanding fact in all branches of natural science is that to exist is to be in process, in change.

6) Although the idea of movement and change has made itself at home in the physical sciences, it has had comparatively little influence on the popular mind as the latter looks at religion, morals, economics, and politics.

7) In these fields it is still supposed that our choice is between confusion, anarchy, and something fixed and immutable.

8) It is assumed that Christianity is the final religion; Jesus the complete and unchanging embodiment of the divine and the human.

9) Faith in the divine author and authority in which Western civilization confided, inherited ideas of the soul and its destiny, of fixed revelation, of completely stable institutions, of automatic progress, have been made impossible for the cultivated mind of the Western world.

10) Does renunciation of the extra-empirical compel also an abandonment of all religion? It certainly exacts a surrender of that supernaturalism and fixed dogma and rigid institutionalism with which Christianity has been historically associated.[94]

[94] "Credo," *Forum*, LXXXIII (March, 1930), 176–82. This was reprinted in *Living Philosophies*, by Albert Einstein and others (New York: Simon and Schuster, 1931), pp. 21–35. A revision of "Credo" was published in 1939 as part of a larger work, *I Believe*, ed. by Clifton Fadiman (New York: Simon and Schuster), pp. 347–54.

X. FAITH AND MORALS
FOR DEMOCRACY'S SCHOOLS

In the preceding general treatment of the instrumentalist or experimentalist philosophy of moral and spiritual values, the words "social," "religious," "ethical," and "moral" were used by Dewey almost interchangeably. In the present treatment of the Deweyan philosophy of character education for the public schools, these same words are also interchanged, ordinarily, without perceptible difference in meaning. Repeating the pattern of the preceding chapter, we shall first take up Dewey's thought on the teaching of ethics or morality in the public schools and then discuss his ideas regarding religious faith in the schools.

✦

Between 1893, when Dewey wrote his first full article on moral and religious training in public education, and the last years of his life, his ideas remain basically the same. He will consistently reject any approach to ethics that proceeds from an a priori determination of morality. Dualistic practices, like the teaching of moral precepts or the predetermination of ethical applications in classroom matter, will come under his censure. He will insist that ethics be considered a complex of social relationships whose meaning is to be determined in actual experience. The intelligent control of these experiences is what he will call a reflective or scientific ethics.

The 1893 article begins with Dewey's stated opposition to that type of ethics which consists of "the conning over and drumming in of ethical precepts." [1] The most efficient moral teaching, he writes, is that "afforded by the constant bearing in upon the individual of the life-process of the school," the natural kind of instruction that "grows directly out of occurrences in the school itself." He protests against the kind of moral textbook built on the assumption that "if you can only teach a child moral rules and distinctions enough, you have somehow furthered his moral being." This is the antithesis of the scientific method of ethics and the destruction of its scientific aim. Dewey approves of the general discontent over this kind of classroom instruction but fears that to eliminate it from the classroom is only to scotch the snake: "The danger is that we are likely to interpret it as meaning that the ethical theory in question may be all right in itself, but is out of place in the schools."

With this said, he presents his own theory:

At all events, I wish to submit a certain conception of ethical theory upon which that theory seems to me thoroughly teachable in the schoolroom; not only teachable, indeed, but necessary to any well-adjusted curriculum.[2]

Since ethics, he explains, "is the statement of human relationships in action," in any proper study of ethics the pupil does not study hard-and-fast rules for conduct, but rather the ways in which men are

[1] "Teaching Ethics in the High School," *Educational Review*, VI (Nov., 1893), 313–21.

[2] *Ibid.*, p. 314. Dewey was not in complete sympathy with Felix Adler and his ethical culturists. He wrote: "An influential movement of the present time (I refer to the ethical culture movement) holds, as I understand it, that it is possible to separate the whole matter of the moral education of children and adults from theoretical considerations. With their contention that education can be (must be, I should say) separated from dogmatic theories I am heartily at one; but as, after all, a dogmatic theory is a contradiction in terms, the question is, whether such an emancipation can be effected without a positive theory of the moral life." ("The Chaos in Moral Training," *Popular Science Monthly*, XLV [Aug., 1894], 442.)

bound together in the complex relations of their interactions. Ethics is not introspective: the pupil does not study his own sentiments and moral attitudes but studies facts as objective as those of hydrostatics or dynamos. But these facts are also subjective "in the sense that since the pupil himself is one who is bound up in the complex of action, the ethical relations have an interest and concern for him which no action of fluid or of dynamo can possibly have."

Here is an example to illustrate the social and scientific character of the ethical teaching he approves.

Let the teacher, at the outset, ask the pupils how they would decide, if a case of seeming misery were presented to them, *whether* to relieve it and, if so, *how* to relieve. This should be done without any preliminary dwelling upon the question as a "moral" one; rather, it should be pointed out that the question is simply a practical one, and that ready-made moral considerations are to be put to one side. Above all, however, it should be made clear that the question is not what to do, *but how to decide what to do.*[3]

The object is not to get the children to argue about the moral rules which should control the giving of charity. "That," insists Dewey, "is a relapse into the method of precepts against which I have protested." The object is to habituate children mentally to construct actual scenes of human interaction and to consult them for practical instruction, the idea being that the children will begin to realize for themselves and in themselves the nature of the practical situations in which they will find themselves placed. He says: "The end of the method, then, is *the formation of a sympathetic imagination for human relations in action;* this is the ideal which is substituted for training in moral rules, or for analysis of one's sentiments and attitude in conduct."

Dewey anticipates an objection. If someone were to bring up the already overcrowded state of the curriculum and were to ask him to show the interrelations of this study to others, he says his reply would be: "If other studies do not correlate well with this one, so much the worse for them—they are the ones to give way, not it. For it is not the study of ethics I am urging; it is the study of *ethical relationships,*

[3] "Teaching Ethics in the High School," *Educational Review,* VII (Nov., 1893), 315.

the study, that is, of this complex world of which we are members." [4]

Four years later, in 1897, Dewey wrote "Ethical Principles Underlying Education," for the Herbart Society's yearbook.[5] Here he sets forth his conviction that there cannot be two sets of ethical principles or two forms of ethical theory, one for life in the school and the other for life outside the school. He distinguishes the social and the psychological aspect of ethical theory, each of which in the interplay covers the *entire* sphere of conduct. The individual, as such, does not make the final demand for moral action, nor establish the final end, nor furnish the ultimate standard of worth. These things are settled by the "constitution and development of the larger life into which he enters." But the individual, as agent, is required to face the moral demands of how he is to realize the values within himself—and this answer must be in psychological terms.[6]

All ethical and moral values, Dewey has already stated, originate in society. The moral responsibility of the school and of those who conduct it is then to society. Moreover, "apart from the thought of participation in social life the school has no end nor aim." [7] Dewey concludes the argument of the yearbook article:

There is nothing in the make-up of the human being, taken in an isolated way, which furnishes controlling ends and serves to mark out powers. If we leave out the aim supplied from social life we have nothing but the old "faculty psychology" to fall back upon to tell what is meant by power in general or what the specific powers are.[8]

This is so true that "we get no moral ideas, no moral standards for school life excepting as we so interpret in social terms."

The oft-printed *My Pedagogic Creed* repeats this pivotal point in the Dewey philosophy regarding the essentially social nature of morality. From its opening sentence—"I believe that all education proceeds by the participation of the individual in the social con-

<hr>

[4] *Ibid.*, pp. 319-20.

[5] National Herbart Society, *Third Yearbook, 1897*, p. 7.

[6] *Ibid.*, p. 10.

[7] *Ibid.*, pp. 10 and 12. See also *Democracy and Education*, "Theories of Morals," *passim* and conclusion, p. 418.

[8] "Ethical Principles Underlying Education," in National Herbart Society, *Third Yearbook, 1897*, p. 12. He is referring to the traditional notion of a "soul" and its powers, but displays a surprising ignorance of what this means.

sciousness of the race"—to its concluding statement, seventeen pages later—"In this way the teacher always is the prophet of the true God and the usherer in of the true kingdom of God"—Dewey proclaims his belief that society itself encompasses all of mankind's values.

Another principle central to John Dewey's philosophy of character education is the idea of the school as a mode of social life. Hence his statement that "the best and deepest moral training is precisely that which one gets through having to enter into proper relations with others in a unity of work and thought." [9] Present educational systems then, he says, so far as they destroy or neglect this unity, render it difficult or impossible to get any genuine, regular moral training.

Moral training, Dewey admonishes in a later article, "is frequently taken in too limited and rigid a way." The social work of the school is often restricted to training for citizenship, meaning the capacity to vote intelligently and to obey the law. He pleads for a broader conception, since it is futile to contract and cramp the ethical responsibility of the school in such a manner: the child must either live his social life as an integral unified being or suffer loss and create friction. [10] Furthermore, this larger field of indirect and vital moral education in which character is developed through all the agencies, instrumentalities, and materials of school life is far more influential than formalized instruction. He argues in *The School and Society* for the renewal of the school through various forms of active occupation. In this way the school "has a chance to affiliate itself with life, to become the child's habitat, where he learns through directed living, instead of being only a place to learn lessons having an abstract and remote reference to some possible living to be done in the future. It gets a chance to be a miniature community, an embryonic society." [11]

✦

The public schools of 1909 also had their critics whose chief complaint was the perennial one: the want of moral and spiritual training in the classroom. Dewey took up the schools' defense. He repeats Harris's argument that such criticism arises from confusion between *moral ideas* and *ideas about morality*. The critics look through the

[9] *My Pedagogic Creed*, p. 8.   [10] *Moral Principles in Education*, p. 8.
[11] *The School and Society*, p. 18. This was originally published in 1900.

school programs of study and find no place set apart for instruction in ethics or moral teaching. They assert that the public schools are doing nothing, or next to nothing, for character training. The teachers rightly resent such criticisms as an injustice, says Dewey, and "hold not only that they do 'teach morals,' but that they teach them every moment of the day, five days in the week." [12] Dewey praises the teachers for standing on a sound principle. All attempts to separate intellectual from moral training, or acquisition of information from growth in character, simply express "the failure to conceive and construct the school as a social institution, having social life and value within itself. Except so far as the school is an embryonic typical community life, moral training must be partly pathological and partly formal."

What is the meaning of Dewey's term "pathological"? Training is pathological, he explains, when stress is laid upon correcting wrong-doing instead of upon forming habits of positive service.

Our conceptions of moral education have been too narrow, too formal, and too pathological. We have associated the term ethical with certain special acts which are labeled virtues and are set off from the mass of other acts, and are still more divorced from the habitual images and motives of the children performing them. Moral instruction is thus associated with teaching about the particular virtues, or with instilling certain sentiments in regard to them. The moral has been conceived in too goody-goody a way.[13]

This narrow, formal, "pathological" concept is in marked contrast to his own idea that ultimate moral motives and forces are "nothing more or less than social intelligence—the power of observing and comprehending social situations, and social power—trained capacities of control—at work in the service of social interest and aims." In this conception "there is no fact which throws light upon the constitution of society, there is no power whose training adds to social resourcefulness that is not moral."

Another method of communicating moral and religious values in the classroom comes in for Dewey's rebuke. Nothing is more absurd in theory or harmful in practice, he tells a Midwest teachers' assembly, than the custom of first insisting upon the intrinsic ethical value of literature and then impressing by suggestion, question, and discourse

[12] *Ibid.*, pp. 3-4.   [13] *Ibid.*, pp. 42-43.

the moral point or lesson to be derived from the piece of literature.[14] This implies the teacher's lack of faith in the moral force of the ideas presented and an overweening faith in his own conversation and personal influence. While he talks about the moral import of a poem or story, he is in fact only using it as an occasion for his own moralizings. Of course, a teacher, like any skilled critic, may heighten another's appreciation of a work of art by indicating how it has subjectively affected him. But when "he decides in advance that the moral truth of a given poem or literary transcript *is* just thus and so, and then enforces this upon a class, he fixes in their differently formed minds a conventional, superficial interpretation which kills their natural organic response."

On the positive side, Dewey finds history the most effective conscious tool among the stock subjects of the curriculum for growth of desirable personal attitudes. Why is this so? History affords the materials for apprehending society's typical problems, the chief obstructions to development and the chief methods of progress, and above all the processes of history. In studying the history of science we learn reverence for the natural physical conditions of human well-being— "perhaps its chief moral accomplishment." The beginning of social studies, accordingly, must be social geography, "the frank recognition of the earth as the home of men acting in relation to one another." The essence of any geographical fact, in Dewey's explanation, is the consciousness of two persons, or two groups of persons, who are at once separated and connected by their physical environment. The interest is in seeing how these people are at once kept apart and brought together in their actions by the instrumentality of the physical environment: "The ultimate significance of lake, river, mountain, and plain is not physical but social—the part played in modifying and directing human relationships."

Dewey's peroration is a reminder to the teachers. Moral value accrues to "studies" to the degree that they give a sympathetic and imaginative appreciation of the social scene of which the student partakes. This involves a realization of his indebtedness to the great stream of human activity flowing through and about him, an awareness of the community of purpose in the large world of nature and society, his obligation of loyalty to his inheritance, and sincere devotion to the interests which have made him what he is.

If such moral training seems slow and roundabout, we may yet encourage ourselves with the reflection that virtue is not a miracle but a conquest, and character not an accident but the efficacious growth of organic powers.[15]

Repeatedly in talks over the years Dewey held the narrow "moralistic" view responsible for the failure to recognize that all the aims and values which are desirable in education are themselves moral. Discipline, natural development, culture, social efficiency, and personal refinement are true moral traits—"marks of a person who is a worthy member of that society which it is the business of education to further." This thought comes to full bloom in the 1916 *Democracy and Education,* wherein he calls these traits "phases of the growth of capacity nobly to share such a balanced experience." Education, he makes it plain, is not a mere means to such a life: "Education is such a life. To maintain capacity for such education is the essence of morals. For conscious life is a continual beginning afresh." [16]

✦

The scientific method is the inspiration of experimentalist philosophy. Dewey's insistence then upon the scientific attitude as indispensable for any teacher who would be true to the moral mandate laid upon the school is quite understandable. He affirms that the problem of the common schools in a democracy has reached only its first stage when they are provided for everybody—"until what shall be taught and how it is taught is settled upon the basis of formation of the scientific attitude, the so-called educational work of schools is a dangerously hit-or-miss affair as far as democracy is concerned." [17]

Dewey cannot insist too much that this is a moral and religious problem. Unhappily, though, the historic influence of religions has often been to magnify doctrines that are not subject to critical inquiry and test, thereby nullifying, in effect, the work of the schools. The cumulative result of such doctrines, he says,

[15] *Ibid.,* p. 27.   [16] *Democracy and Education,* p. 417.
[17] *Freedom and Culture,* p. 150.

in producing habits of mind at odds with the attitudes required for maintenance of democracy is probably much greater than is usually recognized.
Shrewd observers have said that one factor in the relatively easy victory
of totalitarianism in Germany was the void left by decay of former theological beliefs. Those who had lost one external authority upon which they
had depended were ready to turn to another one which was closer and more
tangible.[18]

As long as intellectual docility is the chief aim of the classroom, as
long "as it is esteemed more important for the young to acquire
correct beliefs than to be alert about the methods by which beliefs are
formed, the influence of science will be confined to those departments
in which it has won its victories in the past." [19]
Dewey points a sharp finger at the obstacle impeding the scientific
approach to the proper teaching of morals—"a philosophy that glorifies
the gulf between the 'material' and the 'spiritual,' between immutable
principles and social conditions in a state of rapid change." And it is
here, he says, that the school becomes a vital antidote, for "as far as
school education is a part of the required practical means, educational
theory or philosophy has the task and the opportunity of helping to
break down the philosophy of fixation that bolsters external authority
in opposition to free cooperation." [20] Furthermore,

it [the school] must contest the notion that morals are something wholly
separate from and above science and scientific method. It must help banish
the conception that the daily work and vocation of man are negligible in

[18] *Ibid.*, pp. 150–51. This same superficial argument has been heard with
reference to certain Iron Curtain countries steamrollered by Russian might.

[19] *Education Today,* p. 286. This work is a collection of 45 of Dewey's essays.
See also "The Primary Education Fetich," *ibid.*, pp. 28–29. The 1929 *Characters
and Events,* 2 vols., contains 113 Dewey essays.

[20] "Challenge to Liberal Thought," in *Problems of Men,* p. 159. This article
was printed first in *Fortune* (XXX [Aug., 1944], 154; XXXI [March, 1945],
10). *Education Digest* carried it in September, 1944; it is in the 1946 *Problems
of Men.* Few things made the soul of John Dewey writhe like the spectre of
dualism. Earlier he wrote: "Separation surrenders the concrete world of affairs
to the domain of mechanism fatalistically understood; it encourages mechanical
authority and mechanical obedience and discipline; while it sheds over a life
built out of mechanical subordinations the aureole of a superworldly ideal,
sentimental at best, fanatical and deadly at worst." ("Kant after Two Hundred
Years," *New Republic,* XXXVIII [April 30, 1924], 255.)

comparison with literary pursuits, and that human destiny here and now is of slight importance in comparison with some supernatural destiny. It must accept wholeheartedly the scientific way, not merely of technology, but of life in order to achieve the promise of modern democratic ideals.[21]

Twenty-five years later, *A Common Faith* repeats Dewey's solemn warning that there is only one way to this promised land:

I cannot understand how any realization of the democratic ideal as a vital moral and spiritual ideal in human affairs is possible without surrender of the conception of the basic division to which supernatural Christianity is committed.[22]

Statements like these invariably brought down upon Dewey's head the wrath of those who did not fully share his instrumentalist premises. He was attacked and denounced in classrooms and pulpits on all sides. Yet the storms of controversy that swirled about him did flush a bevy of questions: What kind of a democracy did people want America to be? What did they expect of the churches? What did they expect of the schools? John Dewey, in boldly challenging almost every tenet of traditional philosophy and religion, was forcing a great many people to take a deeper look at their own first principles.

✦

In view of the foregoing it could be anticipated that Dewey would not view with enthusiasm any attempt to draw up a list or catalogue of virtues and vices. He once wrote: "It is remarkable that men are so blind to the futility of a morality which merely blazons ideals, erects standards, asserts laws without finding in them any organic provision for their own realization." [23] For him a virtue reflects some definite existing custom, a vice some deviation from or violation of custom. The acts approved and disapproved have, therefore, "the same definiteness and fixity as belong to the customs to which they refer." This holds in what Dewey labels customary morality. In his own "reflective" morality, a list of virtues or vices would have a much more tentative status:

[21] "Challenge to Liberal Thought," in *Problems of Men*, p. 159.
[22] *A Common Faith*, p. 84.
[23] "Psychology and Social Practice," in *Educational Essays*, p. 162.

Chastity, kindness, honesty, patriotism, modesty, toleration, bravery, etc., cannot be given a fixed meaning, because each expresses an interest in objects and institutions which are changing.[24]

As interests, however, they may be permanent, since no community could last without such things as, "say, fair dealing, public spirit, regard for life, faithfulness to others." Because no two communities conceive the objects to which these qualities attach in the same ways, however, virtues can be defined "only on the basis of *qualities characteristic of interest,* not on the basis of permanent and uniform objects in which interest is taken." Accordingly, in the *Ethics* Dewey undertakes to discuss virtue through itemizing "the traits which must belong to an attitude if it is to be genuinely an interest, not by an enumeration of virtues as if they were separate entities." [25]

Dewey is not only cool toward the efforts to catalogue the moral virtues but opposes on principle the usual adult approach to moral education. He addressed the founding convention of the Religious Education Association in 1903 on the relation of modern psychology to religious education. Dewey cautioned his auditors to bring the child to appreciate "the truly religious aspects of his own growing life" and not to inoculate him externally "with beliefs and emotions which adults happen to have found serviceable to themselves." It is a serious disorder, the warning continued,

that the spiritual and emotional experiences of the adult are the proper measures of all religious life; so that, if the child is to have any religious life at all, he must have it in terms of the same consciousness of sin, repentance, redemption, etc., which are familiar to an adult.[26]

Such attempts to force prematurely upon the child either the mature ideas or the spiritual emotions of the adult run the risk of forestalling

[24] *Ethics,* pp. 280–81.

[25] Some of these traits: *"An interest must be wholehearted.* Virtue is integrity, vice is duplicity. Sincerity is another name for the same quality, for it signifies that devotion to an object is unmixed and undiluted." (*Ibid.,* p. 281.)

[26] Religious Education Association, *Proceedings of the First Annual Convention,* 1903, p. 62. A group of biblical teachers in leading educational institutions around the country laid the groundwork for the Religious Education Association back in 1895 with the founding of the Council of Seventy. Although Dewey did not take an active part in the foundation of the REA, he was a pioneer member.

future deeper experiences which might otherwise in their season become personal realities to him. Dewey urged a careful study of individual child growth, pointing out that "if a convention like this were to take steps to initiate and organize a movement for this sort of study, it would mark the dawn of a new day in religious education."

In his conclusion John Dewey called attention to the significance of the title of his address, "Religious Education as Conditioned by Modern Psychology and Pedagogy," which indicates, he said,

that it is possible to approach the subject of religious instruction in the reverent spirit of science, making the same sort of study of this problem that is made of any other educational problem. If methods of teaching, principles of selecting and using subject-matter, in all supposedly secular branches of education are being subjected to careful and systematic scientific study, how can those interested in religion—and who is not?—justify neglect of the most fundamental of all educational questions, the moral and religious? [27]

Twenty years later his complaint is the same. Adults distrust the intelligence of the child but make demands upon him calling for "a kind of conduct that requires a high order of intelligence, if it is to be intelligent at all." [28] This inconsistency is reconciled by "instilling in the child moral habits (based upon the philosophy of fixation)" which have "a maximum of emotional empressment and adamantine hold with a minimum of understanding." These habits are "usually deepest and most unget-at-able just where critical thought is most needed—in morals, religion and politics." But here Dewey's indictment would strike many as being on the harsh side:

These "infantilisms" account for the mass of irrationalities that prevail among men of otherwise rational tastes. These personal "hangovers" are the cause of what the student of culture calls survivals. But unfortunately these survivals are much more numerous and pervasive than the anthropologist and historian are wont to admit. To list them would perhaps oust one from "respectable" society.[29]

[27] *Ibid.*, p. 66.   [28] *Human Nature and Conduct*, p. 98.

[29] *Ibid.*, pp. 98–99. Here is Dewey's classic example: "Much of the current belief in immortality is not primary, but is the product of inculcation, from infancy throughout life, of the idea that persons are rewarded in heaven and punished in hell. If this is so, the waning of belief in the old theory of reward and punishment, together with increasing vagueness and dimness about both heaven and hell, is sure to lead to diminution of the importance of belief in future life. . . . Of belief in immortality more than of any other element of

Instrumentalism purported to slash away all such cultural tendrils by adhering to the principle that "life is development, and that developing, growing, is life." Translating this into its educational components, Dewey says: "This means (i) that the educational process has no end beyond itself; it is its own end, and that (ii) the educational process is one of continual reorganizing, reconstructing, transforming." [30] This last note harmonizes with the factors emphasized in the description of education Dewey gives in another work:

Education is by its nature an endless circle or spiral. It is an activity which *includes* science within itself. In its very process it sets more problems to be further studied, which then react into the educative process to change it still further, and thus demand more thought, more science, and so on, in everlasting sequence.[31]

The above lines make clearer Dewey's stress upon the need for continual revision of objectives in education: "There is no such thing as a fixed and final set of objectives, even for the time being or temporarily. Each day of teaching ought to enable a teacher to revise and better in some respect the objectives aimed at in previous work." [32] This principle is equally applicable to the moral bases of education. Rather than forcing the day-by-day experiences of the pupils to conform to certain rigidly preestablished patterns, let the moral values that arise in the classroom flow naturally in meaningful directions. For it must be kept in mind that

honesty, industry, temperance, justice, like health, wealth and learning, are not goods to be possessed as they would be if they expressed fixed ends to be attained. They are directions of change in the quality of experience. Growth itself is the only moral "end." [33]

It can be assumed that John Dewey would not cast a favorable eye upon the blackboards of the old-fashioned schoolhouse bordered with maxims celebrating these "virtues" and relevant verses from the

historic religions it holds good, I believe, that 'religion is the opium of peoples.' "
"Intimations of Mortality," review of Corliss Lamont, *The Illusion of Immortality*, in *New Republic*, LXXXII (April 24, 1935), 318.

[30] *Democracy and Education*, p. 59.
[31] *The Sources of a Science of Education*, p. 77.
[32] *Ibid.*, p. 75.   [33] *Reconstruction in Philosophy*, p. 177.

Bible.[34] What would he have thought of modern formulations of moral and spiritual values for our public schools?

✦

The most extended treatment of the problem of religion in education from Dewey's pen is an essay first published in 1908 in the *Hibbert Journal* and later reprinted both in *Characters and Events* (1929) and in *Intelligence in the Modern World* (1939).[35] Dewey sets himself the task of examining the dilemma of the generation whose great advance in scientific learning has made it uneasy because, "solitary among the ages, it is not a religious generation." Here is the anomaly: "The self-same learning which has made it aware that other times have had their life permeated with religious faith is part of the conditions which have rendered the religions of those periods impossible." But if we have discovered a lack here, exclaimed Dewey, let us set the machinery in motion to supply it.[36] Having aroused ourselves to search for the proper machinery, we should find the next step a short one. Education is the modern universal purveyor, and upon the schools shall rest the responsibility for seeing to it that we safeguard our religious heritage.

Dewey concedes that those who are now especially concerned with the maintenance and the spread of conscious and explicit religious

[34] Here is a typical supply house ad of the 1880s in one of the Bardeen series of *Papers on School Issues of the Day. XV: 9. Mottoes for the School-Room. By A. W. Edson, State Agent of Massachusetts. Per set of 12 on heavy colored card-board 7 x 4 inches, printed on both sides, $1.00, post-paid, $1.10. These mottoes are "Never Too Late," "Above All, Be Useful," "Dare to Say No," "God Bless Our School," "Avoid Anger," "Be Good, Do Good," "Think, Speak, Act the Truth," "Fear to Do Wrong," "Misspent Time Is Lost Forever," "Speak the Truth," "Act Well Your Part," "Strive to Excel," "Try, Try Again," "Be Diligent, Prompt and Useful," "Think Good Thoughts," "Learn to Study," "Before Pleasure Comes Duty," "Think First of Others," "Dare to Do Right," "Order Is Heaven's First Law," "A Will Makes a Way," "Study to Learn," "Hold Fast to Honor," "God Sees Me."

[35] "Religion and Our Schools," *Hibbert Journal*, VI (July, 1908), 796–809; *Characters and Events*, II, 504–16; *Intelligence in the Modern World*, pp. 702–15. Not only are the principles set forth in the 1908 article to be found unchanged in the later reprints which were published with Dewey's collaboration, but many of them are repeated in *A Common Faith* (1934); in "Religion, Science and Philosophy," *Southern Review*, 2d Series, I (Summer, 1936), 53–62; in the reprints of *Credo* (1939) and *My Pedagogic Creed* (1944).

[36] "Religion and Our Schools," *Hibbert Journal*, VI (July, 1908), 797.

instruction will hardly agree with his remarks. Nor will those who are already committed to special dogmas of religion "which are the monopoly of special ecclesiastic institutions."

With respect to them, the fight for special agencies and peculiar materials and methods of education in religion is a natural part of their business: just as, however, it is the business of those who do not believe that religion is a monopoly or a protected industry to contend, in the interest both of education and of religion, for keeping the schools free from what they must regard as a false bias.[37]

The strenuous efforts of adherents of traditional religion to keep up their monopolistic control over what flows into the minds of men is fully intelligible to Dewey, for these religionists believe themselves custodians of the channels through which divine assistance comes to mankind. This is to be expected. But when the arguments for special means proceed from *philosophic sources,* then, says Dewey, "a sense of unreality comes over me." Such people, apparently sympathetic to some type of released time or other religious instruction program for the schools, are castigated for ignoring in the practical social order the consequences of their denial of the supernatural. Dewey finds it hard "to account for the attitude of those who are convinced of the final departure of the supernatural interpretation of the world and of man, and who yet think that agencies like the church and the school must not be thoroughly reconstructed before they can be fit organs for nurturing types of religious feeling and thought which are consistent with modern democracy and modern science."

He confesses his displeasure with those who hold

that science has the same spiritual import as supernaturalism; that democracy translates into the same religious attitude as did feudalism; that it is only a matter of slight changes of phraseology, a development of old symbolism into new shades of meaning—such beliefs testify to that torpor of imagination which is the uniform effect of dogmatic belief.[38]

[37] *Ibid.* See also Dewey's preface to the 2d Conference on the Scientific Spirit and Democratic Faith. The proceedings were published as *The Authoritarian Attempt to Capture Education.*

[38] "Religion and Our Schools," *Hibbert Journal,* VI (July, 1908), 798. See "A God or THE God?" *Christian Century,* L (Feb. 8, and March 22, 1933), 193–96 and 394–95.

The reconstruction of the Church along scientific lines, writes Dewey, is a matter which concerns the whole community so far as its outcome is concerned, though the responsibility for its initiation belongs primarily to those within the churches. On the other hand, the whole community is charged with the primary responsibility for conducting the development and the reconstruction of other educational agencies, the public school in particular. However, those who "having become conscious in some degree of the modern ideas of nature, of man and society," and who are best able, consequently, "to forecast the direction which social changes are taking," have the prerogative of controlling the *philosophy* of public education.[39] The momentum of tradition cannot presently be resisted. A delaying tactic is called for. As Dewey cautions:

It is lucidity, sincerity, and the sense of reality which demand that, until the non-supernatural view is more completely elaborated in all its implications and is more completely in possession of the machinery of education, the schools shall keep hands off and shall do as little as possible. This is indeed a *laissez-faire* policy. It is frankly, avowedly so.[40]

Yet all must accept the responsibilities of living in an age marked by the "greatest intellectual readjustment history records." Nothing is to be gained by deliberate efforts "to return to religious ideas which have become incredible and to symbols which have been emptied of their content of obvious meaning." His plea rises in pitch:

Bearing the losses and inconveniences of our time as best we may, it is the part of men to labour persistently and patiently for the clarification and development of the positive creed of life implicit in democracy and in science, and to work for the transformation of all practical instrumentalities of education till they are in harmony with these ideas.[41]

Dewey repeats that until these ends are further along, "it is better that our schools should do nothing than that they should do wrong things." Yes, better is it for the schools to confine themselves to their obviously urgent tasks than that they should, "under the name of spiritual culture, form habits of mind which are at war with the habits of mind congruous with democracy and with science." This is not laziness nor cynicism; "it is honesty, courage, sobriety, and faith."

[39] "Religion and Our Schools," *Hibbert Journal,* VI (July, 1908), 799.
[40] *Ibid.*   [41] *Ibid.*

In this matter, why is there so strong a tradition, inquires John Dewey, against any connection of State and Church, so that there is dread even of the rudiments of religious teaching in state-maintained schools? His answer is that this tradition sprang up, not because of religious indifference or hostility to Christianity, despite the role played by eighteenth-century deism, but largely because of denominational rivalry. There was, however, an even deeper influence at work. The United States became a nation under historical conditions which "enabled it to share in and to appropriate the idea that the state life, the vitality of the social whole, is of more importance than the flourishing of any segment or class." The lesson of the two and a half centuries lying between the Protestant revolt and the formation of the nation was well learned: "The necessity of maintaining the integrity of the state as against all divisive ecclesiastical divisions." With a candor which should be more often imitated, Dewey gives his interpretation of what separation of Church and State really means:

Doubtless many of our ancestors would have been somewhat shocked to realise the full logic of their own attitude with respect to the subordination of churches to the state (falsely termed the *separation* of church and state); but the state idea was inherently of such vitality and constructive force as to carry the practical result, with or without conscious perception of its philosophy.[42]

Dewey counted the wide demands for religious instruction in the schools as a black mark against American democracy. For this general agitation means that, "from economic segregation and unassimilated immigration, the state-consciousness of the country had been sapped by the growth of social factions." This is strong meat and not for queasy stomachs. Does John Dewey hold then for the subordination of the churches to the State? Does he intend religion to be one more department of the State? Some of his critics have taken his words at their face value.

✦

Advancing to the question of what the possible content of a course in religion should be, Dewey says that we certainly cannot teach

[42] *Ibid.*, p. 801.

religion as some abstract essence: "We have got to teach *something* as religion, and that means practically *some* religion." Which? We cannot even give Christianity in general in the common schools, he says, for this would work a hardship on our Jewish fellow citizens who pay taxes, vote, and serve on school boards. "Even if we could teach Christianity," he puts the question, *"which* Christianity? Oriental in its origin, it has been since Latinised and Germanised, and there are even those who have dreamed of humanising it."

Dewey finds a further difficulty. We are fast becoming aware of the absurdity implied in calling things that happen to be studied and learned in the classroom "knowledge," when they have been acquired by methods frequently at odds with the methods which result in scientific knowledge. Here is the dilemma:

Can those who take the philosophic and historic view of religion as a flower and fruition of the human spirit in a congenial atmosphere tolerate the incongruity involved in "teaching" such an intimate and originally vital matter by external and formal methods? And can those who hold that true religion is something externally imported tolerate any other methods? Is it not confusion to seek a reconciliation of two such disparate ideas? [43]

Since the spirit of our schooling is permeated with the feeling that every subject, every topic, every fact, every professed truth, must submit to a certain impartiality and publicity, all learning must go to the same assay-room and be subjected to common tests. Yet it is the essence of dogmatic faiths to hold that any such "showdown" is sacrilegious and perverse. Religionists hold that the characteristic of religion is that it be "intellectually secret, not public; peculiarly revealed, not generally known; authoritatively declared, not communicated and tested in ordinary ways."

What is to be done about this growing antagonism, inquires Dewey, between the standard for coming to know in other subjects of the school and coming to know in religious matters? He will not say "that the antinomy is an inherent one, or that the day may not come when religion will be so thoroughly naturalised in the hearts and minds of men that it can be considered publicly, openly, and by common tests, even among religious people." It is pertinent, however, to point out that,

[43] *Ibid.,* p. 804.

as long as religion is conceived as it now is conceived by the great majority of professed religionists, there is something self-contradictory in speaking of education in religion in the same sense in which we speak of education in topics where the method of free inquiry has made its way. The "religious" would be the last to be willing that either the history or the content of religion should be taught in this spirit; while those to whom the scientific standpoint is not a merely technical device, but is the embodiment of integrity of mind, must protest against its being taught in any other spirit.[44]

But granted for the sake of argument that religion should be taught in the public schools, who would do the teaching? This brings us to the crux of the whole matter. Here Dewey asks if religion is a thing so specialized, so technical, so "informational," that, like geography or history or grammar, it may be taught at special hours, times, and places by those who have properly "got it up," and who have been approved as persons of fit character and adequate professional training. Our national temper and tradition do not find it feasible or desirable to put upon the regular teachers the burden of teaching a subject which has the nature of religion. On the other hand, the alternative plan of parceling out pupils among religious teachers drawn from their respective denominations brings us up against the precise factor which has done most to discredit the churches and the cause, not perhaps of religion, but of organized and institutional religion—"the multiplication of rival and competing religious bodies, each with its private inspiration and outlook."

Dewey's eloquence here is an echo of Horace Mann's as he recalls how our common schools, in bringing together children of different nationalities, languages, traditions, and creeds, and in assimilating them together upon the basis of what is common and public in American endeavor and achievement, are performing an infinitely significant religious work. "They are," he says,

promoting the social unity out of which in the end genuine religious unity must grow. Shall we interfere with this work? Shall we run the risk of undoing it to be introducing into education a subject which can be taught only by segregating pupils and turning them over at special hours to separate representatives of rival faiths? This would be deliberately to adopt a scheme which is predicated upon the maintenance of social divisions in just

[44] *Ibid.*, pp. 804–5. See *A Common Faith*, pp. 59–87.

the matter, religion, which is empty and futile save as it expresses the basic unities of life.[45]

He cites a British critic who, he says, calls us with some truth a "nation of villagers," but in the matter of education at least we have no intention or desire of letting go our hard-won *state-consciousness* in order to relapse into divisive provinciality. We are far, indeed, from the attainment of "an explicit and articulated consciousness of the religious significance of democracy in education, and of education in democracy." Nonetheless, Dewey is assured that in some dim but effective way the American public is already conscious that "its schools serve best the cause of religion in serving the cause of social unification; and that under certain conditions schools are more religious in substance and in promise without any of the conventional badges and machinery of religious instruction than they could be in cultivating these forms at the expense of a state-consciousness."

Dewey draws his essay to a close by returning to the opening question: Are Americans more or less religious? This consciousness of irreligion may only be an illusion, he answers, because even those who have nominally surrendered supernatural dogma still remain largely under the dominion of the ideas of those who have succeeded in identifying religion with the rites, symbols, and emotions associated with these dogmatic beliefs. As we watch the latter disappearing, we think we are growing irreligious, but "for all we know, the integrity of mind which is loosening the hold of these things is potentially much more religious than all that it is displacing."

If we measured the modern change from the standpoint, not of the supranatural, but of natural piety, i.e., "the sense of the permanent and inevitable implication of nature and man in a common career and destiny," it would appear as the growth of religion. When we note the decay of cohesion and influence among institutionalized religious groups of the familiar historic type, we conventionally judge that religion is on the decline. It well may be, however, that "their decadence is the fruit of a broader and more catholic principle of human intercourse and association which is too religious to tolerate these pretensions to monopolise truth and to make private possessions of spiritual insight and aspiration." This decadence of the historic form

[45] "Religion and Our Schools," *Hibbert Journal,* VI (July, 1908), 806–7.

of religion may well be symptomatic of the coming of "a fuller and deeper religion." Dewey declines the role of prophet. But he does claim to know that

so far as education is concerned, those who believe in religion as a natural expression of human experience must devote themselves to the development of the ideas of life which lie implicit in our still new science and our still newer democracy. They must interest themselves in the transformation of those institutions which still bear the dogmatic and the feudal stamp (and which do not?) till they are in accord with these ideas. In performing this service, it is their business to do what they can to prevent all public educational agencies from being employed in ways which inevitably impede the recognition of the spiritual import of science and of democracy, and hence of that type of religion which will be the fine flower of the modern spirit's achievement.[46]

John Dewey's faith in education was his faith in humanity itself as evolving dynamically in American democratic society. He did not seem embarrassed by charges that his attitude toward education in some respects transcended the scientific and verged upon the mystical. He once wrote that "if we have any ground to be religious about anything, we may take education religiously." [47] He elaborated the point:

I see no ground for criticizing those who regard education religiously. There have been many worse objects of faith and hope than the ideal possibilities of the development of human nature, and more harmful rites and cults than those which constitute a school system. Only if all faith that outruns sight is contemptible can education as an object of religious faith be condemned. This particular form of faith testifies to a generous conception of human nature and to the deep belief in the possibilities of human achievement in spite of all its past failures and errors.[48]

At least the religion of education, according to Dewey, had one advantage over other religions. However much or little *they* might conflict with science, here was a religion that could realize itself only through science: "Only, that is, through ways of understanding human nature in its concrete actuality and of discovering how its various factors are modified by interaction with the variety of conditions under which they operate." [49]

[46] *Ibid.*, pp. 808–9. See *A Common Faith*, pp. 1–29.
[47] "Education as a Religion," *New Republic*, XXXII (Sept. 13, 1922), 63.
[48] *Ibid.*, p. 64.
[49] *Ibid.*, p. 65. Compare this with Mann's thought on p. 93.

✦

It should be obvious beyond cavil that the differences separating
Dewey's philosophy of character education from Christian or traditional church-related philosophies do not lie in the accidental order.
They are basic and, as Dewey himself has stated, irreconcilable.[50]
John Dewey has presented a new *summum bonum,* the scientific
living of social democracy in an industrial age, which can not allow
place for values superior to those of the shared experience of democratic living. In his system traditional moral and spiritual values are
replaced by civic and social values.[51] The virtues held aloft for emulation are civic and social. These are discovered already woven into the
rich fabric of nature but, like the unremitting labor of Penelope, require constant reweaving. The energies of religious devotion are no
longer dissipated in flight to another world but are centripetal, en-
riching society itself. Belief in a transcendent personal deity gives way
to belief in the God *Demos* evolving from and continuous with those
mysterious forces of rationality, beauty, and goodness that are nature's
own, and continually in process of discovery by science. Sociality
toward man and piety toward nature adequately cover man's religious
experience. As one of his brother philosophers, remarking on the
absence of God from experimentalism, said: "John Dewey knows what
he is omitting, for it once was his own." [52]

John Dewey tolerated no faint facing of the implications of his
doctrine. He stated unequivocally:

The task of those who retain belief in democracy is to revive and maintain
in full vigor the original conviction of the intrinsic moral nature of democ-

[50] Yet several heroic attempts have been made to gainsay Dewey here. One
recent thesis undertook "to demonstrate that inasmuch as experimental philosophy
is grounded in the processes of nature, it can be utilized without alteration or
discount in the understanding of the processes of Christian education." The
author says that "the basic ideas appear obvious: Christians are men; men are
in nature; and experimental philosophy is performed in the field of education,
oriented particularly in the practical problems of American public school education." (Gutzke, *John Dewey's Thought and Its Implication for Christian Education,* pp. 5-6.)

[51] "To possess virtue . . . means to be fully and adequately what one is
capable of becoming through association with others in all the offices of life."
(*Democracy and Education,* p. 415.)

[52] Horne, *The Democratic Philosophy of Education,* pp. 529-30.

racy, now stated in ways congruous with present conditions of culture. We have advanced far enough to say that democracy is a way of life. We have yet to realize that it is a way of personal life and one which provides a moral standard for personal conduct.[53]

As would be expected from his attitude toward the churches, Dewey affords them little or no place in the educational picture. The slight emphasis upon the family and home as forces in education, however, is surprising. It is strange, for instance, that there is no entry under "home" or "family" in the comprehensive sixteen-page index to *Democracy and Education,* certainly the most complete exposition of the Deweyan philosophy of education.

Dewey's statement that "the moral and social quality of conduct are, in the last analysis, identical with each other" is not easy to understand.[54] One critic has called this concept "as confusing as to identify oneself with others," and elaborates his criticism:

After all, there are the personal and the social aspects of experience. They may not be separable in fact; they are so in thought. The moral side of life is the personal, how one thinks and feels and purposes. These may have their physiological accompaniments. When these personal ideas, feelings, and purposes express themselves overtly in acts affecting others, they become social. Man's social relations are reciprocally related to his moral life.[55]

The individual, in the Deweyan scheme of things, seems to be absorbed by society in some sort of mystical union by means of which "we put off mortality and live in the universal." [56] The traditional psychology with its doctrine of the original separate soul, mind, or consciousness is in truth, he charges, "a reflex of conditions which cut human nature off from its natural objective relations."

It implies first the severance of man from nature and then of each man from his fellows. The isolation of man from nature is duly manifested in the

[53] *Freedom and Culture,* p. 130. In a recent statement, Sidney Hook said: "Education for democracy, as John Dewey conceived it, is not an education based on the unchallengeable axioms of democratic faith but a consequence of inquiry, of finding out, of exploring imaginatively and historically the alternatives of policy and action open to men in deciding how to arrange human affairs." *New Leader* (July 8, 1957), pp. 9–10.

[54] *Democracy and Education,* p. 415. See also "The Forward View," in *The Teacher and Society,* the John Dewey Society Yearbook, I (1937), 334.

[55] Horne, *The Democratic Philosophy of Education,* p. 527.

[56] *Human Nature and Conduct,* p. 331.

split between mind and body—since body is clearly a connected part of nature.[57]

Dewey says, moroever, that any moral theory seriously influenced by popular psychological theory is bound "to emphasize states of consciousness, an inner private life, at the expense of acts which have public meaning and which incorporate and exact social relationships." [58] What Dewey calls "the humanist view of democracy" demands a reexamination of all forms of culture—education, science and art, morals and religion, industry and politics—to ascertain what effects they have "in release, maturing and fruition of the potentialities of human nature." [59] But the ultimate moral motives and forces are to be found in social intelligence at work in the service of social interests and aims.[60] Faith in these social capacities of human nature is Dewey's foundation of democracy.[61] Dewey looked down upon self-culture as something vicious.

The idea of perfecting any "inner" personality is a sure sign of social divisions. What is called inner is simply that which does not connect with others—which is not capable of free and full communication. What is termed spiritual culture has usually been futile, with something rotten about it, just because it has been conceived as a thing which a man might have internally —and therefore exclusively. What one is as a person is what one is as associated with others, in a free give and take of intercourse.[62]

Repeatedly we have heard Dewey state that the goal of life and education is growth. But the norm for growth is always the social one: "growth in shared experiences," "growth in associated living," "growth in the good society," etc. Dewey says that "an individual apart from social relations is a myth or a monstrosity." The increased interdependence of men in our civilization calls for a new type of individuality, one in which "the balance of the individual and the social will be organic." [63] It is hard to see how Dewey has left the scales balanced. It is harder to escape the conclusion that, despite the lip

---

[57] *Ibid.*, p. 85.   [58] *Ibid.*, p. 86.   [59] *Freedom and Culture*, p. 125.
[60] "Ethical Principles Underlying Education," in National Herbart Society, *Third Yearbook, 1897*, p. 26.
[61] "The Challenge of Democracy to Education," in *Problems of Men*, p. 59.
[62] *Democracy and Education*, p. 143.
[63] *Individualism, Old and New*, p. 50.

service he pays to individuality, Dewey has somehow lost the person in the towering shadow of society.

A final remark here might make for a more sympathetic understanding of Dewey's intransigent opposition toward moral and religious values as traditionally conceived. During his long life John Dewey was in the forefront of the struggle for social justice. He fought for a wider diffusion of the material and spiritual goods created by the economic progress and increased education of mankind. He was impatient with the churches which he regarded as reactionary pockets resisting the advance of humanity toward democracy's millennium. In his mind they were obscurantist in social matters and generally antidemocratic in structure. They stood for the very forces of privilege and power that had so long impeded science and perpetuated social stratification. They pointed to the mirage of otherworldly success, and men went running after idealized "moral and spiritual" values instead of working to release the rich human values in society itself.

Dewey feared that aesthetic and spiritual values were perched on a precarious base because they were reared upon a social and economic inequality—as at times they truly have been. Dewey puts bitter words on the lips of one of his conversationalists in the essay "Nature and Its Good: A Conversation":

Of course well-fed and well-read persons—with their possessions of wealth and of knowledge both gained at the expense of others—finally get bored; then they wax sentimental over their boredom and are worried about "Nature" and its relation to life. . . . [They] seek a new sensation in speculating why that brute old world out there will not stand for what you call spiritual and ideal values—for short, your egotisms.[64]

The speaker dismisses all such philosophizing as a symptom of the leisure class disease: "If you had to work to the limit and beyond, to keep soul and body together, and, more than that, to keep alive the soul of your family in its body, you would know the difference between your artificial problems and the genuine problems of life." [65]

And then follow these terribly sad words which could only have been born in a heart deeply in love with humanity and as deeply agonized over the selfishness of man to man:

[64] *The Influence of Darwin on Philosophy*, pp. 20–21.   [65] *Ibid.*, p. 21.

Your philosophic problems about the relation of "the universe to moral and spiritual good" exist only in the sentimentalism that generates them.

Granted the truth of the evolutionist premise, as understood by John Dewey, his humanistic faith possesses its own nobility. It was in the spirit of this very human humanism that Dewey wrote toward the end of his life:

Fidelity to the nature to which we belong, as parts however weak, demands that we cherish our desires and ideals till we have concerted them into intelligence, revised them in terms of the ways and means which nature makes possible. When we have used our thought to its utmost and have thrown into the moving unbalanced balance of things our puny strength, we know that though the universe slay us still we may trust, for our lot is one with whatever is good in existence. We know that such thought and effort is one condition of the coming into existence of the better.[66]

Those who accept the Judaeo-Christian philosophy of life can only regret that Dewey did not better understand and respect the free and intelligent human choice involved in a supernaturalist commitment. His antagonism toward religion, however misdirected they may think it, was motivated by a sincere desire for what he thought the best interests of humanity. Those who accept a traditional philosophy of humanism can regret that Dewey's dedication to the immediate ills of human society caused him to understimate the "unpractical" world of saint and stargazer, wherein an immortal soul might seek union with a Spirit that transcends the moil and pettiness of earth.

[66] Quoted in *John Dewey, Philosopher of Science and Freedom,* ed. by Sidney Hook, p. 37.

PART FIVE

CONCLUSION

XI. SOME MEANINGS FOR TODAY

The American experience with the common school is well into its second century and time has sharply etched the darks and lights in the problem area surveyed by this book. The study undertook to set forth the treatment of the common school philosophy of values by Horace Mann, William Torrey Harris, and John Dewey, the three leading philosophers of public school education. The extent of their influence, direct and indirect, upon the formulations of policy in the 1951 report of the NEA Educational Policies Commission, *Moral and Spiritual Values in the Public Schools,* becomes strikingly evident when this study and the report are read together. The principal affirmations that are common to the value philosophies examined and to the 1951 report can be briefly assembled.

The American people have insisted, and will continue to insist, upon a common school system as the most practical means of transmitting our public philosophy to the great majority of American children. The right of the State to establish a tax-supported school system and the duty of the citizenry, at least in their capacity as citizens (leaving aside their obligation as parents), to support it are no longer subjects of controversy.[1]

---

[1] Between 1891 and 1893 a famous controversy took place over the nature of

The American people have insisted no less constantly that the common school assume a proper responsibility for character formation, or, as it is more commonly designated today, "the inculcation of moral and spiritual values." These affirmations have been unmistakably clear in the writings of the three principals. The 1951 statement only continues this tradition when it says:

The American people have rightly expected the schools of this country to teach moral and spiritual values.[2]

And:

The public schools have a highly significant function in teaching moral and spiritual values.[3]

Each of the three subjects of this study stressed the basic moral nature of education. This is simply a reflection of the universal desire of a people who have repeatedly registered their conviction that education in the common public school should be something more than teaching children to read, write, and cipher. Today the consensus is as clear as ever that the school must play an important part in fitting the individual child for his destiny, in equipping him with "a sense of values which will lend dignity and direction to whatever else he may learn."[4] This is the contemporary witness of the 1951 document, which calls the development of moral and spiritual values "basic to all other educational objectives" and speaks of education uninspired by them as "directionless."[5] The statement urges "an unremitting concern for moral and spiritual values" as "a top priority for education."[6]

However, the history of the common school, as seen through the work of Mann, Harris, and Dewey, has also made it painfully apparent that the American people have been caught in an unresolved ambiguity. They have charged the common school with a responsi-

---

the State's right to educate. It was precipitated by a pamphlet, *Education, to Whom Does It Belong?* in which the author, Rev. Thomas Bouquillon, argued that the State had a special and proper right to teach human knowledge. His opponents held that the State's right was only a substitutional one. See Reilly, *The School Controversy.*

[2] *Moral and Spiritual Values in the Public Schools,* p. 3.
[3] *Ibid.,* p. 4.   [4] *Ibid.,* p. 13.   [5] *Ibid.,* pp. 6–7.
[6] *Ibid.,* p. 12.

bility for character education but they do not have a common view
as to what this entails. In fact, there is lessening agreement as to
the precise destiny or direction or end to be aimed at in a common
moral and spiritual values program. How then can a common school
discharge a moral mandate whose nature is the subject of dispute
among the different groups served by the school? Horace Mann was
no nearer a solution than we are today. Well-intentioned efforts to
minimize differences and to work out joint policy statements have
frequently exposed the schools to new criticisms. For a critic passes
judgment according to his own first principles or assumptions on the
success or failure of the school to meet its moral responsibility.

Fundamentally, the issue is not whether the public schools are
"godless," or whether they are teaching the right kind of moral and
spiritual values, but whether the public schools, *as they are presently
constituted,* can teach what many millions of parents believe in
conscience should be taught their children. Disagreement over the
function of any common moral and spiritual values program is the
inevitable result of the irreconcilable differences among conflicting
religions or philosophies or schemes of ultimate values, so that *after
many decades of experimenting, the problem of moral education in
the common public school is more defiant of solution than ever—is,
in fact, insoluble.* This is our first conclusion.

✦

The most recurrent criticism of the public school's shortcomings
relative to character education has come from those who argue that
religion cannot be separated from morality, that character training
must be rooted in religious values or related to religious sanctions.
Harris disagreed with this position. Mann and Dewey accepted it,
though their understanding of religion and religious values differed
from prevailing contemporary opinion.

Horace Mann faced the objection in a modified form which argued
that character training could not be effectively taught apart from
certain Christian dogmas, championed by the Orthodox Congregationalist churches. His own position, it will be recalled, very much approved of the union in the classroom of morality and what he called
"true" religion. He promoted a policy for the Massachusetts Common-

wealth, widely adopted elsewhere, that insisted upon instruction in the great *common* truths in the Christian religion but in such a way that no particular sect would be favored over another. The Bible, without note or interpreter, was to be the chief means for teaching these generally agreed upon ethical and religious truths of Christianity. Mann's compromise solution—a "nonsectarian," biblically based, liberal Protestant Christianity for the common schools—was an uneasy and temporary truce.

His policy was bitterly assailed by spokesmen for religious groups who charged that he was slyly introducing Unitarianism, deism, transcendentalism, and rationalism into the schools. Nonetheless, without Mann's compromise it is doubtful if the common school system could even have been established, much less have prospered. Mann's solution of the problem of religious pluralism lasted, despite Catholic and Protestant opposition, as long as most of the Protestant sects felt that a Christian influence, albeit a neutral nonsectarian one, did permeate the common school, and that no particular church group enjoyed an advantage over the others. Mann did the cause of religious freedom a service by refusing to accept the argument that the religion of the majority should be taught. This could have devolved into as intolerable abuse of the rights of conscience as the "Cujus regio ejus religio" principle of a supposedly less enlightened period in history.[7]

What Horace Mann did not see, however, was that there is no such thing as a "nonsectarian" Christianity or an undenominational religion. The reasons for this have been discussed in detail in Chapter IV. Here we might add one point. Even if there were an inoffensive nonsectarian religion, from the family's point of view what has been gained? What parent is satisfied when his children are merely *not* being educated in a belief contrary to his own? Ordinarily we assume that he wants them brought up to believe that what he holds is important truth. And as Brownson long ago said: "I always hold that to be important truth, wherein I differ from others." His meaning of course is that if differences were inconsequential, there would be no

[7] The Peace of Augsburg, 1555, proposed as a principle for settling the religious wars in the Holy Roman Empire that the religion of the prince should determine the religion of the territory, or at least the dictum came to be applied in this checkerboard fashion.

point in being different. It is precisely the conviction that a doctrinal difference is important that keeps the sincere churchgoer in a Lutheran rather than a Baptist or Catholic pew.

Advocates of the "common denominator" approach, moreover, have been continually frustrated by the courts, which are under the necessity of defending the religious freedom and the rights of conscience of all citizens in the State's common schools. Nearly all State Constitutions specifically forbid the teaching of any doctrine favorable to a single sect or distinctive of a single religious group. This makes the law a convenient weapon for a small minority or, at times, for even a single individual to challenge traditional school activities related to the religious beliefs of the community.[8] In court test after court test, the decision handed down has been in favor of the dissident group—to save them from real or fancied invasions of their religious liberty.

The Mann compromise contained the principle of its own dissolution. The precious little common ground among Unitarians, Methodists, Congregationalists, Jews, Catholics, and Deists gradually eroded away and again set the problem full adrift. Over the years the positive doctrinal elements regarding church organization, sacraments, and the mission of Christ had to be strained out of the common school religion piece by piece to avoid offending dissenters. Such a process inevitably worked to the advantage of groups holding a minimum of positive doctrine. A blandly Christian flavor that contented Unitarians and Universalists could only dismay Congregationalists and Episcopalians. The soup in time got so thin that it pleased no palate. Belief in God, the Golden Rule, and the Bible were about all that long survived this disintegrating process. The Bible in the classroom later became an object of contention between Protestants and Catholics with the result that the courts have banned Bible-reading in many states. Belief in God has until recent years fared better, but a number of communities have had to impose silence even on this point upon their schools. In 1956 New York City public school officials and their lay advisers found considerable opposition to a value policy statement that contained preferential references to God and belief in God.[9]

---

[8] The *McCollum* case is a clear example.

[9] In order to mollify critics the revised New York statement eliminated from

The principle that religious freedom in a religiously divided community requires the elimination of any teaching or practice from the common school not acceptable to everyone makes it impossible to preserve any kind of traditional religion in the school.[10] This is our second conclusion.

✦

In his turn, Harris argued, as we have seen, that the school by its nature is completely secular and hence has no competence to teach religious truth. He did indeed favor religious education but assigned it exclusively to the province of the Church. For he believed that the method, spirit, and content of secular truth are necessarily antagonistic to the acquisition of religious truth: the two cannot be taught together. Moreover, Harris held for the absolute separation of religion from moral training in the school. He dismissed the nonsectarian approach to religion, pointing out what had escaped Horace Mann, that to promote a "nonsectarian" religion is really to establish one more sect. The 1951 statement parallels Harris's thought here, insisting that "in view of differing religious faiths, a common education . . . must be derived, not from some synthetic patchwork of many religious

---

the original passages like these: "The public schools encourage the belief in God"; and "The public schools reinforce the program of the home and church in strengthening the belief in God." (See *America* [Sept. 29, 1956], p. 620.)

[10] And yet in many places religion remains. The discrepancy between policy statements on a national level (including the NEA's of 1951 on moral and spiritual values) and what actually occurs on the local level is often remarkable. In the final analysis it is usually strong local control that determines school policy. Hence, one finds "Baptist" public schools in Mississippi towns, "Mormon" public schools in Utah, "Lutheran" public schools in Minnesota, and "Catholic" public schools in New Mexico. At the 1957 Arden House conference on religion and public education, sponsored by the American Council on Education, Professor Arthur E. Sutherland of the Harvard Law School said: "The Federal Constitution, as interpreted in the McCollum case, and the State constitutions in all their variety, impose on public teaching limits more formidable in theory than they may be in practice. The great multitude of comparatively minor religious manifestations which obtain in many grade and high schools probably thrive on local approval. . . . The practical impossibility of consistent and doctrinaire constitutional literalism in matters of Church and State throughout our Federal nation may be one of the curious benefits of the system." (Neil G. McCluskey, S.J., "Educators Go to Arden House," *America* [March 30, 1957], p. 722.)

views, but rather from the moral and spiritual values which are shared by the members of all religious faiths." [11]

Fundamental to the Harris position was his principle that the development of moral habits in the school laid the groundwork for religious education: by inculcating moral discipline the school prepared the child to receive a superstructure of religious training from the Church.[12] Harris was convinced that only the Church, because of its authoritative methods and sacred surroundings, could properly communicate religious truth. Even Bible-reading in the schools came under his ban. This exercise too, he insisted, was a religious one requiring an atmosphere of authority and ceremonial rites.

It is important to keep in mind that the religion Harris was contrasting with moral education was *revealed* or supernatural religion. For he assumed general agreement in American society over the existence of a Creator who was the source of justice and its sanctions, and who had endowed men with equal rights. It was the most natural thing in the world then for Harris to base moral training upon the existence of God and other closely related theistic concepts of the natural law. He held that moral and intellectual education depended directly upon an acknowledgment of God's existence and man's immortal destiny. As a consequence Harris included in the moral training he advocated for the public schools many concepts of natural law theism that would not find universal acceptance today. Yet, in arguing elsewhere against religion in the schools, Harris had himself made the point that "even the doctrine of the existence of God implies a specific conception of Him." [13]

[11] *Moral and Spiritual Values in the Public Schools,* p. 6.

[12] Confronted with the claim that the home and the Church can handle the child's religious formation after school hours, most modern parents throw up hands in protest. During an earlier, simpler period this might have been possible. The changed patterns of mid-twentieth-century life in America have altered the relation of the child to the house and the Church. The school world *is* where the child passes the bulk of his waking hours, especially during the adolescent years. To the regular hours devoted to class and supervised study at the school itself is now added a continually increasing number of hours absorbed by a complex program of extracurricular activities to an extent undreamed of by Mann or Harris. Athletic events, socials, group projects, and trips sponsored by school and school clubs occupy many evenings and even weekends.

[13] "And the conception of the divine varies from that of the finite deities of animism to the infinite deity of East Indian pantheism and the Holy Bible. It

Both Mann and Harris urged the point that the teaching of sectarian religion in the common school infringes upon the rights of conscience and the constitutional freedom of some pupils. Neither, however, considered the theistically based natural law as sectarian. Horace Mann actually promoted the teaching of "general" Christianity in the school, leaving the home and the Church to fill in what he called sectarian doctrines. Harris opposed on principle the teaching of any kind of revealed religion in the common school. This was to remain the prerogative and responsibility of other educational agencies in society. The 1951 Educational Policies Commission statement follows both men in its awareness of the religious freedom issue and follows Harris's conception of the division of responsibility for character education:

The teaching of moral and spiritual values in the public schools of the United States must be done without endangering religious freedom and without circumventing the policy of separation of church and state. Our society leaves to the home and the church the responsibility for instruction designed to secure the acceptance of a religious faith. Thus the home, the church, and the school each share in moral and spiritual development, while each may make the contribution to that development for which it is peculiarly fitted.[14]

For his part John Dewey rejected the Harris dichotomy between moral training in the school and religious instruction in the Church —a logical result of his rejection of all dualisms. He viewed education as above all the handmaiden of democracy—democracy considered, not as a form of government, but as a "spiritual community." As one observer of the American scene has phrased it: "Thus every child is a potential member of the democratic church, and it is the function of education to actualize his membership and to widen his powers of participation." [15]

---

varies from the pantheistic Brahma, whose concept is that of negation of all attributes, to the Jehovah of the Bible, who is self-determined and personal, but elevated entirely above nature." (See p. 167.)

[14] *Moral and Spiritual Values in the Public Schools,* p. 6. Also: "Young people acquire their moral and spiritual values in many ways. The school is an important source of such values, but the school must always be a partner of the home, the church, and the community." (*Ibid.,* p. 83.)

[15] British historian Christopher Dawson, "Education and the State," *Commonweal,* LXV (Jan. 25, 1957), 424.

For Dewey religion was an evolving social construct whose values and beliefs are relative to the culture from which they rise. Religion and morality were to be tested by science and the scientific method. The school is a mode of society, so that in the classroom no more than in society were ethical and religious values separable. Dewey, it will be recalled, opposed religion but staunchly defended religious values, and these he situated in the natural social process. He was one with Mann in opposing sectarian religion in the public school and one with Harris against any form of supernatural religion in its classrooms, though he went beyond Harris in his total rejection of the *idea* of the supernatural. Dewey placed his ultimate faith in values verifiable in experience, but since the supernatural signified precisely that which lies beyond experience, he renounced the extra-empirical. This has been treated in Chapters IX and X.

The current absence of religion from the public schools is mainly attributable to the historical working out of the "nonsectarian" principle first championed by Horace Mann. This compromise was originally intended to safeguard the rights of conscience and the constitutional exercise of religious freedom by individuals, as well as to protect the equal position of the sects in the common schools. There was no question of a philosophy of education hostile to religious teaching as such. This process of exclusion was reinforced and hastened by William Torrey Harris. His Hegelian understanding of the nature of religion and social institutions led him to oppose religious teaching in the classroom, although he did not oppose it in what he considered its proper place, the Church. The naturalist philosophy propounded by John Dewey has had much to do with completing the process of exclusion. Dewey proposed a "scientific" substitute for the traditional concept of religion which he thought would be more in keeping with the exigencies of modern democratic society. His experimentalist philosophy of education left no place for supernatural religion either in or outside the school. Our third conclusion is that *the value philosophies espoused by these three men have led to the widespread elimination of religion from today's public schools.*

✦

Mann and Harris both assumed that the common school could lay a foundation for character—either general Christianity with Mann or basic natural law morality with Harris—upon which other educative agencies in society could build. This assumption is still recognizable throughout the 1951 NEA document. Underlying this assumption, however, is a theory of religion and religious commitment which is not entirely compatible with at least the usual Catholic and Jewish understanding of these things. This makes it impossible for these groups to give full allegiance to common statements of moral and spiritual values.

What have come to be known popularly as the three great American faiths are not simply variations of one basic theistic philosophy. The prophetic and individualistic genius of Protestantism runs athwart the authoritative and institutional character of Catholicism, while the ritualistic and communal spirit of Judaism sets it apart from either Catholic or Protestant Christianity. If there is some theoretical common denominator among these three faiths which the public schools might present as a basis for a common value philosophy, it is not universally acknowledged. Adherents of Judaism find a peculiar difficulty here. The Jewish position insists that the family and synagogue must assume exclusive responsibility for the foundation, superstructure, and complete furnishings of the religious edifice. This is understandable because the Jewish faith is above all a particular commitment centering in a complexus of traditional observances of a particular law given to a particular community. Even the natural law theism proposed as a common basis presents the religious Jew with a problem. Historically "theism" in a predominantly Christian community has taken on meanings and been given interpretations that do violence to his own religious beliefs. The Jewish experience merits sympathetic consideration. In addition to the Jewish demur there has been highly articulate opposition to such a proposal by groups whose ultimates do not derive from any form of theism.

Nonetheless, a large number of educators have argued that, since natural law theism has been the basis of our political consensus and is still commonly accepted, it should be reaffirmed as the basis for a program of moral and spiritual values in the public school. Many Catholics support this position, not because it satisfies the Catholic ideal, but because they judge this minimum better than nothing at all. Moreover, the symbolism in the school even of natural law theism is not without its values. It does testify to our continuity with the tradition of the founding fathers. It does reaffirm the basis of the American public philosophy. It does remind the impressionable child of some fundamental natural truths. It does throw up a barrier against the constant pressure of the minorities who seek to complete the secularization, *in fact,* of the public schools.

The 1951 NEA document in any event attempted to steer a neutral course between theism and nontheism. Subsequent criticism derived mainly from two objections: By taking a "neutral" position, the NEA statement (1) equivalently denies that religion is the starting point of education; (2) necessarily gives ultimate value to the purely secular world. Let us briefly consider these objections from a Catholic point of view.

A Catholic educator starts with an assumption (shared by many non-Catholics) that God and religion are the central concern of human existence. Religion for a Catholic answers the questions: What is man? What is man's chief end? Whence did he come? Whither is he going? How did he come here? Quite patently the character of education will depend to a large extent on the answer to these questions. A Catholic believes that his first purpose in life is to learn to live in such a way as to prepare himself for an immortal supernatural destiny. This precise purpose—not some vague humanitarianism, no matter how naturally noble—will accordingly be the foundation of moral education or character training in the school and will equip the Catholic child with a "sense of values which will lend dignity and direction to whatever else he may learn." [16]

Today, for reasons explained at length in the study, any philosophy of education presenting such a goal is constrained to operate outside the public schools. Faced with the ultimate question of whether or not religion is the starting point and essence of true education, the public school has had to adopt a theoretical neutrality. Yet the public

[16] *Moral and Spiritual Values in the Public Schools,* p. 13.

school, in a Catholic analysis, gives an equivalent denial to the question by actually taking another starting point and aiming at another goal.[17] What is worse, this attempt at neutrality has facilitated the entry of a new religion into the vacuum. These words are much to the point:

It seems unfortunately to be the case that what has been presented as a means for preserving religious peace and freedom through secularization has to some extent become a method of propagating a particular dogmatic faith, namely, scientific naturalism or, to give it another name, naturalistic humanism.[18]

To the point also are the words of the 1951 NEA document which define moral and spiritual values as "those values, which, when applied in human behavior, exalt and refine life and bring it into accord with the standards of conduct that are approved in our democratic culture." [19] All citizens agree that such values are vitally necessary for American society and, as far as they go, an appropriate charge for its common school. Mann, Harris, and Dewey would have approved this definition of values—but attached different meanings to it. All three, as we have seen, had to cope with the problem of conflicting sanctions, or the "whys" and "wherefores" of these common values. Mann did not exclude all religious sanctions but only those of extreme orthodoxy. Harris did not exclude from the school religious sanctions based upon natural law theism. Dewey, however, totally rejected sanctions outside the natural process.

The 1951 document lists only sanctions of the natural order and expressly warns that religious sanctions "may not be explicitly invoked in the public school classroom," adding that "of course they may play a powerful role in the moral and spiritual instruction of home and church." [20] Once more, from a Catholic point of view, this attempt

[17] This analysis, needless to add, is not intended to question in any way the sincerity of other religious groups whose theological convictions present them with no problem on this score.

[18] Philip H. Phenix, "Religion in American Public Education," *Teachers College Record*, LVII (Oct., 1955), 30.

[19] *Moral and Spiritual Values in the Public Schools*, p. 3.

[20] *Ibid.*, p. 16. This secularist atmosphere is one in which only the pupil coming to the school from a secularist family can feel completely at home. As one critic has pointed out: "Pupils from theist families live with one image

at compromise puts the public school on the side of the ethical scientists and scientific humanists. *Because sanctions are limited to a secular order and cannot be normally related to religious values, natural or supernatural, character education in the public schools is necessarily circumscribed by the purely secular order.* This is another conclusion of the study.

By default civic or political virtue must be the primary goal of common school education. In other words the schools exist primarily to produce good citizens. Those who believe the perfection of the temporal social order to be the supreme and ultimate aim of life will have no quarrel with this interpretation of the public school's responsibility for character education. Those who, while believing in a supernatural dimension to education and life, see here no irresolvable conflict of value systems can continue to give full allegiance to the public school value program. Those believers in a supernatural who do see an irresolvable conflict can not. The conclusion is inescapable: for millions of American families the public school system as presently constituted is simply incapable of caring for the moral side of education.

✦

The foregoing has indicated why many religious educators, Catholic, Protestant, and Jewish, are dissatisfied with the ability of the American public school, as it currently exists, to fulfill what they consider the primary purpose of education. For Catholics particularly this is a matter of conscience. The Archbishop of Boston, the Most Reverend Richard J. Cushing, has stated:

Catholics are not opposed to public schools. We will always have a great interest in them. More than half of our children are being educated in public schools and we pay taxes for their support. . . . At the same time, we believe that religious and moral training is essential in the formation of

---

of man at home and with another at school. The wall of separation between Church and State, thus interpreted, can easily become a wall of separation between the State school and the community it serves and, more dangerously, a wall of separation between home values and school values in the person of the child." (Charles Donohue, "Education and the Image of Man," *Religious Education*, LIII [March–April, 1958], 122.)

character. Since this cannot be given in the public schools because of the diversity of religious beliefs, we build our own schools at tremendous sacrifices while joining whenever possible with our non-Catholic friends and neighbors in a released time program of religious instruction outside the school buildings.[21]

The same thought has been put on the public record by the late Samuel Cardinal Stritch, who while Archbishop of Chicago publicly said:

We shall conduct our Catholic schools and we shall conduct them in full recognition of the rights and interests of public authority in the education of children. We shall conduct them because our conscience demands our doing this religious work. We shall conduct them because we know the place which religion has and must have in the education of children and youths. We recognize the problem which confronts those engaged in education in our tax-supported schools. We realize this problem is grave. We are hoping for a happy solution of it.[22]

An even more authoritative source has said:

Let it be loudly proclaimed and well understood and recognized by all that Catholics, no matter what their nationality, in agitating for Catholic schools for their children, are not mixing in party politics, but are engaged in a religious enterprise demanded by conscience. They do not intend to separate their children either from the body of the nation or its spirit, but to educate them in a perfect manner most conducive to the prosperity of the nation.[23]

✦

There are those who are troubled over the growth of the Catholic school population in the United States. In 1957 there were an estimated 4,415,691 primary and secondary school pupils, or 11.9 percent of the total school population, in Catholic parochial and private schools.[24] This percentage has doubled in fifty years.[25] In the face of a trend

[21] "The Function of the Parochial School," an address delivered at the laying of the cornerstone of the Rose Hawthorne School, Concord, Mass., April 19, 1952.

[22] National Catholic Educational Association, *Proceedings and Addresses,* 51st Annual Meeting, p. 49.

[23] "The Christian Education of Youth," an Encyclical Letter of Pope Pius XI, p. 29.

[24] Some 550,000 students, representing 1.5 percent of the entire elementary and secondary school populace, currently attend non-Catholic privately sponsored schools.

[25] The increase is shown in the following table:

which gives every indication of continuing, these people voice misgivings that "the common public school system as we know it, with its indispensable contribution to unity and common loyalties," might disappear from the American scene.[26] These people might also consider the dilemma confronting their Catholic fellow citizens who are not unmindful of the values to be gained in the civic and social order by having their children in the common public school. Catholics want to share in everything American that is good. But they likewise appreciate the importance of a religiously centered education which their children simply can not obtain in a secularized school. Their problem is rooted in conflicting value systems, as this study has shown. Their problem, moreover, is not just a "Catholic" problem but one, since it affects the whole nation, whose solution must ultimately come from the whole of American society.

Reasonable discussion of these points has been largely precluded by the absence of patience, understanding, and logic. The trading in public of epithets like "divisive" and "un-American" for "godless" and "secularist" is hardly conducive to rational debate.

It is true that the Catholic educational ideal frankly envisages every Catholic child in a Catholic school, and though this ideal was at least

Catholic and Public (Elementary-Secondary) School Enrollments in U.S., 1900–1957

Year	Catholic School Enrollment	Percentage of Total	Public School Enrollment	Percentage of Total	Total Catholic-Public School Enrollments
1900	854,523	5.2	15,503,110	94.8	16,357,633
1910	1,236,946	6.4	17,813,852	93.6	19,050,798
1920	1,826,213	7.8	21,578,316	92.8	23,404,529
1930	2,469,032	8.8	25,678,015	91.2	28,147,047
1940	2,581,596	9.2	25,434,542	90.8	28,016,138
1950	3,080,166	10.9	25,111,427	89.1	28,191,593
1955	3,973,224	11.5	30,673,800	88.5	34,647,024
1957	4,415,691	11.9	32,734,000	88.1	37,149,691

Sources: *Official Catholic Directory* (New York: P. J. Kenedy and Sons); *Biennial Survey of Education and School Life* (October, 1955 and 1956), U.S. Office of Education. John P. Sullivan, "The Growth of Catholic Schools," *America* (Nov. 16, 1957), p. 204.

[26] *Moral and Spiritual Values in the Public Schools*, p. 5.

in its origin a defense thrown up against the "Protestant" public schools of the nineteenth century, it nevertheless remains operative.[27] The problem has rarely reached the stage where possible modifications of this ideal could be calmly discussed.[28] A profitable avenue of conversation, for example, could explore what modifications the present public school might undergo to make broader Catholic participation both possible and desirable. However, in view of the practical impossibility of ever realizing this ideal and the growing recognition among Catholic leaders that there is some danger of "parochialism" in a completely separatist education, such discussions could be profitably undertaken.

On the other hand, in view of the findings of this study, it is legitimate to inquire whether society has not expected the impossible from the common school. The present book has tried to shed light on the reasons why the common school, as it has developed historically, has been unable to inculcate a unifying philosophy and at the same time provide for a religiously based character education satisfactory to everyone in our religiously fragmentized society. American society gazes fondly into the mirror of its common schools but the image reflected there is not the true one. For the *public* school, as presently constituted, is one *public* institution that does not reflect American society as it is. The State faces the problem of religious pluralism in the armed forces by cooperating with the different religious groups in caring for the spiritual needs of the uniformed personnel. Yet the

---

[27] See p. 50, footnote 55, and pp. 91–92. The American bishops in the Fifth Provincial Council of Baltimore in 1843 wrote: "We have seen with serious alarm, efforts made to poison the fountains of public education, by giving it a sectarian hue, and accustoming children to the use of a version of the Bible made under sectarian bias, and placing in their hands books of various kinds replete with offensive and dangerous matter." *The National Pastorals of the American Hierarchy (1792–1919)*, ed. by Peter Guilday (Washington: National Catholic Welfare Council, 1923), p. 152.

[28] One noteworthy attempt was that of Archbishop John Ireland of St. Paul. In his address at the 1890 NEA convention in St. Paul he said: "I am the friend and advocate of the state school. In the circumstances of the present time I uphold the parish school. I do sincerely wish that the need of it did not exist. I would have all schools for the children of the people state schools. "State Schools and Parish Schools: Is Union between Them Impossible?" *Journal of Proceedings and Addresses of the NEA*, p. 179.

same basic problem of religious pluralism is now officially treated in the schools as something nonexistent, irrelevant, or alien.

The precise form the American common school will take in the second half of the twentieth century will depend upon an enlightened citizenry. The author hopes that the present book has provided some material for fresh examination of the problem of values in public education. The final conclusion of the study is more correctly a prediction. *Unless serious efforts toward compromise succeed in modifying present patterns, the American public school will of necessity become increasingly secular. This in turn will continue to augment the percentage of children in non-public schools placed there by parents who desire some religious orientation in the formal education of their children.*

·A SELECTIVE BIBLIOGRAPHY

I. HORACE MANN

Manuscripts
The Collected Mann Papers, including Horace Mann's Journal and several
thousand letters and papers classified chronologically, are in the archives
of the Massachusetts Historical Society, Boston. Robert L. Straker has prepared a 14,000-page typescript which includes copies of many Mann documents in the archives of the Massachusetts Historical Society. The Straker
typescript is in the Antioch College Library.
The Minutes of the Meetings of the Massachusetts Board of Education,
1837–48, are in the records of the Department of Education, the State
House, Boston.

Books and Articles
1891   Life and Works of Horace Mann, ed. by Mary Peabody Mann and
        George Combe Mann. 5 vols. Boston: Lee and Shepard. (Vol-
        ume I: the *Life* by Mary Peabody Mann; Volume II: First and
        Second Annual Reports and education lectures; Volume III:
        Third to Eighth Annual Reports; Volume IV: Ninth to
        Twelfth Annual Reports and orations; Volume V: educational
        writings. The *Life* was first published in 1865 by Walker,
        Fuller and Company of Boston. The 1891 edition was printed

four years after Mrs. Mann's death and contains some new material.)

1838–48   Twelve Annual Reports of the Board of Education together with the Twelve Annual Reports of the Secretary of the Board. Boston: Dutton and Wentworth, State Printers. (The National Education Association issued facsimile editions of the following reports: *Seventh Annual Report Covering the Year 1843* [Washington, 1950]; *Tenth Annual Report Covering the Year 1846* [Washington, 1952]; and *Twelfth Annual Report Covering the Year 1848* [Washington, 1952].)

1839–52   Editor, with W. B. Fowle, *The Common School Journal.* 15 vols. Boston: March, Capen, Lyon and Webb. (Vols. I–XI, 1838–48; n.s. Vols. I–IV, January, 1849–December, 1852.)

1840   Lecture on Education. Boston: March, Capen, Lyon and Webb.

1844   The Common School Controversy: Consisting of Three Letters of the Secretary of the Board of Education of the State of Massachusetts in Reply to Charges Preferred against the Board by the Editor of the *Christian Witness* and by Edward A. Newton Esq. Boston: J. N. Bradley and Co.

Reply to the "Remarks" of Thirty-one Boston Schoolmasters on the Seventh Annual Report of the Secretary of the Massachusetts Board of Education. Boston: William B. Fowle and Nahum Capen.

1845   Answer to the "Rejoinder" of Twenty-nine Boston Schoolmasters, Part of the "Thirty-one" Who Published "Remarks" on the Seventh Annual Report (of the Secretary of the Massachusetts School Board). Boston: William B. Fowle and Nahum Capen.

1846   The Ground of the Free School System. From the Tenth Annual Report of the Secretary of the Massachusetts State Board of Education, 1846. Reprinted as Old South Leaflets No. 109. Boston: Directors of the Old South Work, 1902.

1847   Letter to the Rev. Matthew Hale Smith, in Answer to His "Reply" or "Supplement." Boston: William B. Fowle.

Sequel to the So Called Correspondence between the Rev. M. H. Smith and Horace Mann, Surreptitiously Published by Mr. Smith; containing a Letter from Mr. Mann, Suppressed by Mr. Smith, with the Reply Therein Promised. Boston: William B. Fowle.

1850   A Few Thoughts for a Young Man. Boston.

1861   Twelve Sermons Delivered at Antioch College. Boston: Ticknor and Fields.

II. WILLIAM TORREY HARRIS

Manuscripts
The Collected Harris Papers, approximately 13,475 items, are in the Library of Congress, Washington, D.C.
Source material relating to the St. Louis Movement is in the archives of the Missouri Historical Society, St. Louis.

Books and Articles

1868–79 The Twelve Annual Reports of the St. Louis Public Schools for the Years 1868–79. (Harris also prepared the Superintendent's Report for 1867.)

1889–1906 Reports of the U.S. Commissioner of Education for the Years 1889–1906.

1867 "Herbert Spencer," *Journal of Speculative Philosophy*, I, 6–22 (preface dated December, 1867).

1869 Hegel's First Principle: An Exposition of Comprehension and Idea (Begriff und Idee). St. Louis: George Knapp and Co.

1870 "The Immortality of the Soul," *Journal of Speculative Philosophy*, IV, 97–111.
"Why Patronize the Public Schools," *American Journal of Education* (St. Louis), II (February), 103–4.

1871 "The Theory of American Education," *American Journal of Education* (St. Louis), IV (January), 3.
"Nature versus Human Nature, or the Spiritual" (unsigned), *American Journal of Education* (St. Louis), III (January), 4–5.
How Far May the State Provide for the Education of Her Children at Public Cost? (Reprint of address to the National Education Association Meeting in St. Louis, August 23, 1871.)

1872 "Nature and Importance of Moral Training," in the Seventeenth Annual Report of the Board of Directors of the St. Louis Public Schools for the Year Ending August 1, 1871, pp. 21–37. St. Louis: Plate, Oldhausen and Co.

1874 "On Hegel's Philosophic Method," *Journal of Speculative Philosophy*, VIII (January), 35–48.
"Participation, the Essence of Spiritual Life," *American Journal of Education* (St. Louis), VII (February), 3–4.
"Church and State," *The Western* (St. Louis), I (March), 113–36.
"The Study of Evolution in Education," *American Journal of Education* (St. Louis), VII (July), 1.
Edited with Duane Doty. A Statement of the Theory of Education

in the United States of America. Washington: U.S. Bureau of Education.

1875 "On the Relation of the Will to the Intellect, or the Regulative Principle in Human Life," *The Western* (St. Louis), n.s. I (February), 102–9.

"Moral Education, I," *American Journal of Education* (St. Louis), VIII (October), 4–5.

"Moral Education, II," *American Journal of Education* (St. Louis), VIII (November), 4–5.

1876 "Moral Education, III," *American Journal of Education* (St. Louis), IX (January), 4.

"The Relation of Religion to Art," *Journal of Speculative Philosophy,* X (April), 204–15.

"The Division of School Funds for Religious Purposes," *Atlantic Monthly,* XXXVIII (August), 171–84.

1877 "The Idea of the State and Its Necessity," *The Western* (St. Louis), n.s. III (March), 206–15.

Moral Education in the Public Schools. New York: E. Steiger.

1881 "Thoughts on the Basis of Agnosticism," *Journal of Speculative Philosophy,* XV (April), 113–20.

"The Philosophy of Religion," *Journal of Speculative Philosophy,* XV (April), 207–15.

"Kant and Hegel in the History of Philosophy," *Journal of Speculative Philosophy,* XV (July), 241–52.

"The Church, the State, and the School," *North American Review,* CXXXIII (September), 215–27.

1882 "The Education of the Family and the Education of the School," *Journal of Social Science,* XV (February), 1–5.

"The History and Philosophy of Education," *Chautauquan,* III (October), 28–30.

"On the Crime of Educating the People in Free Common Schools," *Journal of Education* (New England and National), XVI (November 2), 227–28.

1883 "Other Institutions besides the School as Instrumentalities of Culture," *Journal of Social Science,* XVII (May), 133–55.

"Philosophy in Outline," *Journal of Speculative Philosophy,* XVII (July), 296–316; (October), 337–356.

With W. A. Mowry, J. H. Hoose, H. S. Tarbell, and G. S. Hall. "Moral Education in Schools"—Report of the Committee on Moral Education to the National Council of Education, *Education,* III (September), 1–14.

1884 "Moral Education in the Common Schools," *Journal of Social Science,* XVIII (May), 122–34.

"On the Relation of the College to the Common School," in

American Institute of Instruction Lectures, 1883, pp. 139–71. Boston: American Institute of Instruction.

1885   "Immortality of the Individual," *Journal of Speculative Philosophy,* XIX (April), 189–219.

"Is Pantheism the Legitimate Outcome of Modern Science?" *Journal of Speculative Philosophy,* XIX (October), 407–28.

"Psychological Inquiry," *Education,* VI (November), 156–68.

Compulsory Education in Relation to Crime and Social Morals. Washington.

"Emerson's Philosophy of Nature," in F. B. Sanborn, ed., The Genius and Character of Emerson: Lectures Delivered at the Concord School, pp. 339–63. Boston: James R. Osgood and Co.

"Emerson's Relation to Goethe and Carlyle," in F. B. Sanborn, ed., The Genius and Character of Emerson: Lectures Delivered at the Concord School, pp. 386–419. Boston: James R. Osgood and Co.

1886   "Religion in Art, 1," *Chautauquan,* VI (January), 190–93.

"Religion in Art, 2," *Chautauquan,* VI (February), 255–58.

"Religion in Art, 3," *Chautauquan,* VI (March), 314–16.

"How I Was Educated," *Forum,* I (August), 552–61.

"Goethe's Faust," in F. B. Sanborn, ed., The Life and Genius of Goethe: Lectures at the Concord School of Philosophy, pp. 368–445. Boston: Ticknor and Co.

1887   "Books That Have Helped Me," *Forum,* III (April), 142–51.

1888   "What Shall the Public Schools Teach?" *Forum,* IV (February), 573–81.

"The Present Need of Moral Training in the Public Schools," *Journal of Education* (New England and National), XXVII (March 1), 131–32.

"The Church and the State," *True Educator,* IV (April, 122–23.

1889   "Our Public Schools: Can Morality Be Taught without Sectarianism?" (Symposium), *Journal of Education* (New England and National), XXIX (February 14), 1.

"Windows of the Soul," *Indian School Journal,* XXXIV (February), 85–86.

"On the Normal School Course of Study," in Report of the Alumnae Association, State Normal School, Framingham, Mass. (July 2), pp. 10–33. Boston.

Art Education: The True Industrial Education. Papers on School Issues of the Day, III. Syracuse: C. W. Bardeen.

Morality in the Schools. Register Tract #12. Boston: Christian Register Association.

1889   The Psychology of Manual Training. (Reprint from *Education,*
        May, 1888 [hand corrected to 1889].)

1890   "Value of School Discipline," *Pennsylvania School Journal,*
        XXXIX (July), 27–28.

        Hegel's Logic. A Book on the Genesis of the Categories of the
        Mind. A Critical Exposition. (German Philosophical Classics,
        under the editorship of G. S. Morris.) Chicago: S. C. Griggs.

        The Philosophy of Crime and Punishment. (Reprint of paper
        read before the National Prison Association.) Cincinnati.

        Thoughts on Educational Psychology. (Reprint of a series of pa-
        pers in the *Illinois School Journal.*) Bloomington, Illinois: The
        Public School Publishing Co.

1891   "The Best Works on Pedagogy for Young Teachers," *Journal of
        Education* (New England and National), XXXIII (February
        26), 131.

        "Dante's Doctrine of Sin," in Year-Book of the American Dante
        Society, 1890–91, pp. 69–81. New York: American Dante So-
        ciety.

        "Vocation versus Culture; or the Two Aspects of Education," in
        American Institute of Instruction Lectures, 1891, pp. 1–20.
        Boston: American Institute of Instruction.

1892   "Our Educational System: What It Is; Why It Is; What It Accom-
        plishes," *Chautauquan,* XV (April), 16–20.

        Public Schools in the District of Columbia. Report made in com-
        pliance with a requirement of the Act of Congress, July 14,
        1892: Letter from the Secretary of the Interior. Senate Execu-
        tive Document No. 12, 52d Congress, 2d Session. Washington:
        Government Printing Office.

1893   "Herbart and Pestalozzi Compared," *Educational Review,* V
        (May), 417–23.

        With F. B. Sanborn. A. Bronson Alcott: His Life and Philosophy.
        2 vols. Boston: Roberts Brothers.

        "In Memoriam: Brother Azarias" (holograph in Harris collec-
        tion, #320, Library of Congress).

        "School Statistics and Morals." (Reprint from the Journal of Pro-
        ceedings and Addresses of the National Education Association,
        1893.)

1895   "The Old Psychology vs. the New," *Journal of Education* (New
        England and National), XLI (May 2), 295.

        "Herbart's Doctrine of Interest," *Educational Review,* X (June),
        71–80.

        "Herbart's Unmoral Education," *Education,* XVI (November),
        178–81.

"The Necessity of Five Co-ordinate Groups in a Complete Course of Study," *Education,* XVI (November), 129–34. (This is a reply to a criticism of the Report of the Committee of Fifteen, and is not the same as the similar title in 1896.)

1896   "Is Education Possible without Freedom of the Will?" *Education,* XVII (January), 301–5.

"In What Does Spiritual Evolution Consist?" *Education,* XVII (March), 413–21.

"Horace Mann," *Educational Review,* XII (September), 105–19.

The Necessity for Five Co-ordinate Groups of Studies in the School. (Reprint from *Educational Review,* April, 1896.)

Professor John Dewey's Doctrine of Interest as Related to Will. (Reprint from *Educational Review,* May, 1896.)

The Psychological Revival. (Chapters from the Report of the U.S. Commissioner of Education for the Year 1893–94.) Washington: Government Printing Office.

1897   The Aesthetic Element in Education. (Address read before the National Council of Education at Milwaukee, July, 1897.)

"George William Frederick Hegel," in Charles Dudley Warner, ed., A Library of the World's Best Literature, XII, 7174–83. New York: R. S. Peale and A. J. Hill.

"Relation of School Discipline to Moral Education," in National Herbart Society, Third Yearbook, 1897, pp. 58–72. Chicago.

The Science of Ethics as Based on the Science of Knowledge. Translated by A. E. Kroeger and edited by the Honorable Dr. W. T. Harris. New York: D. Appleton and Co.

1898   Psychologic Foundations of Education: An Attempt to Show the Genesis of the Higher Faculties of the Mind. New York: D. Appleton and Co.

1899   "Beauty in Art vs. Beauty in Nature," in the Report of the U.S. Commissioner of Education for the Year 1898–99. Washington: Government Printing Office.

1901   "Educative Work at Missions," *School and Home Education,* XX (May), 427–30.

"Isolation in the School—How It Hinders and How It Helps," in the Journal of Proceedings and Addresses of the National Education Association, 1901, pp. 357–63. Washington.

1902   "Herbert Spencer and What to Study," *Educational Review,* XXIV (September), 135–49.

"How the School Strengthens the Individuality of the Pupil," *Educational Review,* XXIV (October), 228–37.

"Moral Education in the Common School," *Educational Foundations,* XIV (October), 68–83.

1902   "The Danger of Using Biological Analogies in Reasoning on Educational Subjects." (Reprint from the Journal of Proceedings and Addresses of the National Education Association, 1902, pp. 215–21.)

1903   "Religious Instruction in Public Schools," *Independent*, LV (August), 1841–43.

"The Separation of the Church from the Tax-supported School," *Educational Review*, XXVI (October), 222–35.

1904   "A Definition of Civilization," in the Report of the U.S. Commissioner of Education for the Year 1903–4, I, 1129–33. Washington: Government Printing Office.

"Herbert Spencer and His Influence on Education," in the Journal of Proceedings and Addresses of the National Education Association, 1904, pp. 214–23. Washington.

"Primary and Secondary Phases of Causality: Natural Science Founded on the Latter and Theology on the Former." (Reprint of an address to the American Philosophical Association, Philadelphia, December 29.)

1905   "Social Culture in the Form of Education and Religion," *Educational Review*, XXIX (January), 18–37.

III. JOHN DEWEY

1882   "The Metaphysical Assumptions of Materialism," *Journal of Speculative Philosophy*, XVI (April), 208–13.

1884   "Kant and Philosophic Method," *Journal of Speculative Philosophy*, XVIII (April), 162–74.

"The New Psychology," *Andover Review*, II (September), 278–89.

1886   "The Psychological Standpoint," *Mind*, XI (January), 1–19.

"Psychology as Philosophic Method," *Mind*, XI (April), 153–73.

Psychology. New York: Harper and Brothers.

1887   "Ethics and Physical Science," *Andover Review*, VII (June), 573–91.

1888   "The Ethics of Democracy," in University of Michigan Philosophical Papers, Second Series, No. 1. Ann Arbor: Andrews and Co.

1889   "Ethics in the University of Michigan," *Ethical Record*, II (October), 145–48.

1891   "Moral Theory and Practice," *International Journal of Ethics*, I (January), 186–203.

Outlines of a Critical Theory of Ethics. Ann Arbor: Register Publishing Co.

1892   "Green's Theory of the Moral Motive," *Philosophical Review*, I (November), 593–612.

"Two Phases of Renan's Life: The Faith of 1850 and the Doubt of 1890," *Open Court*, VI (December 29), 3505–6. (Reprinted in Characters and Events [1929], I, 18–23, "Ernest Renan.")

1893   "Renan's Loss of Faith in Science," *Open Court*, VII (January 5), 3512–15. (Reprinted in Characters and Events [1929], I, 23–30, "Ernest Renan.")

"Self-Realization as the Moral Ideal," *Philosophical Review*, II (November), 652–64.

"Teaching Ethics in the High School," *Educational Review*, VI (November), 313–21.

1894   "The Chaos in Moral Training," *Popular Science Monthly*, XLV (August), 433–43.

The Study of Ethics: A Syllabus. Ann Arbor: Register Publishing Co.

1896   "The Metaphysical Method in Ethics," *Psychological Review*, III (March), 181–88.

1897   "Ethical Principles Underlying Education," in National Herbart Society, Third Yearbook, 1897, pp. 7–34. Chicago: University of Chicago Press.

My Pedagogic Creed. New York: E. L. Kellogg and Co.

1898   "Evolution and Ethics," *Monist*, VIII (April), 321–41.

Review of William Torrey Harris, *Psychologic Foundations of Education, Educational Review*, XVI (June), 1–14.

1900   The School and Society. Chicago: University of Chicago Press.

1902   "The Evolutionary Method as Applied to Morality: I—Its Scientific Necessity," *Philosophical Review*, XI (March), 107–24.

"The Evolutionary Method as Applied to Morality: II—Its Significance for Conduct," *Philosophical Review*, XI (July), 353–71.

The Child and the Curriculum. Chicago: University of Chicago Press.

1903   "Psychological Method in Ethics," *Psychological Review*, X (March), 158–60.

"Emerson—the Philosopher of Democracy," *International Journal of Ethics*, XIII (July), 405–13. (Reprinted in Characters and Events [1929], I, 69–77.)

The Logical Conditions of a Scientific Treatment of Morality. University of Chicago Decennial Monograph, First Series, Vol. III, pp. 113–39. Chicago: University of Chicago Press.

"Religious Education as Conditioned by Modern Psychology and Pedagogy," in Proceedings of the First Annual Convention, pp. 60–66. Chicago: Religious Education Association.

Studies in Logical Theory. Chicago: University of Chicago Press.

1904 "The Philosophical Work of Herbert Spencer," *Philosophical Review*, XIII (March), 159–75.

1908 "Religion and Our Schools," *Hibbert Journal*, VI (July), 796–809. (Reprinted in Characters and Events [1929], II, 504–16.)
With James H. Tufts. Ethics. New York: Henry Holt and Co.

1909 "Is Nature Good? A Conversation," *Hibbert Journal*, VII (July), 827–43.
"The Dilemma of the Intellectualist Theory of Truth," *Journal of Philosophy*, VI (August 5), 433–34.
Moral Principles in Education. Boston: Houghton Mifflin.
"The Moral Significance of the Common School Studies," in Northern Illinois Teachers' Association, Program of Meeting, November 5th and 6th, 1909, pp. 21–27. Elgin, Illinois: N.I.T.A. (Eastern Section).

1910 "Some Implications of Anti-Intellectualism," *Journal of Philosophy*, VII (September 1), 477–81.
Educational Essays by John Dewey. Edited by J. J. Findlay. London: Blackie and Son, Ltd.
How We Think. Boston: D. C. Heath and Co.
The Influence of Darwin on Philosophy and Other Essays in Contemporary Thought. New York: Henry Holt and Co.

1913 "The Problem of Values," *Journal of Philosophy*, X (May 8), 268–69.
Interest and Effort in Education. Boston: Houghton Mifflin Co.

1915 German Philosophy and Politics. New York: Henry Holt and Co.

1916 Democracy and Education: An Introduction to the Philosophy of Education. New York: Macmillan.
Essays in Experimental Logic. Chicago: University of Chicago Press.

1917 "H. G. Wells, Theological Assembler," *Seven Arts Magazine*, II (July), 334–39. (Reprinted in Characters and Events [1929], I, 78–82.)
"Duality and Dualism," *Journal of Philosophy*, XIV (August 30), 491–93.

1918 "The Objects of Valuation," *Journal of Philosophy*, XV (May 9), 253–58.

1920 Reconstruction in Philosophy. New York: Henry Holt and Co.

1921 "Classicism as an Evangel," *Journal of Philosophy*, XVIII (November 24), 664–66.

1922 "The American Intellectual Frontier," *New Republic*, XXX (May 10), 303–5. (Reprinted in Characters and Events [1929], II, 447–52.)
"Education as a Religion," *New Republic*, XXXII (September 13), 63–65.

Human Nature and Conduct. New York: Henry Holt and Co.

1924 "Kant after Two Hundred Years," *New Republic,* XXXVIII (April 30), 255.

1925 Experience and Nature. Lectures on the Paul Carus Foundation, First Series. Chicago: Open Court Publishing Co.

1926 "Church and State in Mexico," *New Republic,* XLVIII (August 25), 9–10. (Reprinted in Characters and Events [1929], I, 352–57.)

"Bishop Brown: A Fundamental Modernist," *New Republic,* XLVIII (November 17), 371–72.

1927 "Half-hearted Naturalism," *Journal of Philosophy,* XXIV (February 3), 57–64.

"Anthropology and Ethics," in The Social Sciences and Their Interrelations, pp. 24–36. Edited by W. F. Ogburn and Alexander Goldenweiser. Boston: Houghton Mifflin Co.

1928 "Personal Immortality: What I Believe," New York *Times,* April 8.

"The Direction of Education," *Teachers College Record,* XXX (October), 7–12.

1929 With Albert C. Barnes, Laurence Buermeyer, and others. Art and Education. (Articles by Dewey: "Experience and Nature and Art," pp. 3–12; and "Individuality and Experience," pp. 175–83.) Merion, Pa.: Barnes Foundation Press.

Characters and Events: Popular Essays in Social and Political Philosophy. Edited by Joseph Ratner. 2 vols. New York: Henry Holt and Co.

The Quest for Certainty. New York: Minton, Balch and Co.

The Sources of a Science of Education. New York: Horace Liveright.

1930 "Credo," *Forum,* LXXXIII (March), 176–82.

"Religion in the Soviet Union," *Current History and Forum,* XXXII (April), 31–36.

"From Absolutism to Experimentalism," in Contemporary American Philosophy, II, 13–27. Edited by G. P. Adams and W. P. Montague. New York: Macmillan.

Individualism, Old and New. New York: Minton, Balch and Co.

1931 Philosophy and Civilization. New York: Minton, Balch and Co.

1932 "Education and Birth Control," *Nation,* CXXXIV (January 27), 112.

"Monastery, Bargain Counter, or Laboratory?" *Barnwell Bulletin,* IX (February), 51–62.

1933 "A God or THE God?" (review of *Is There a God?: A Conversation,* by Henry N. Wieman, Douglas C. Macintosh, and

Max C. Otto), *Christian Century,* L (February 8), 193–96; (March 22), 394–95.

1934   Art as Experience. New York: Minton, Balch and Co.
A Common Faith. New Haven: Yale University Press.
"Education for a Changing Social Order," in American Association of Teachers Colleges, Thirteenth Yearbook, pp. 60–68. New York.
"Liberation of Modern Religion," *Yale Review,* n.s. XXIII, 751–70.

1935   "Religions and the 'Religious' ": A Letter, *New Republic,* LXXXII (March 13), 132.
"Intimations of Mortality" (review of Corliss Lamont, *The Illusion of Immortality*), *New Republic,* LXXXII (April 24), 318.
"Bergson on Instinct" (review of Henri Bergson, *The Two Sources of Morality and Religion*), *New Republic,* LXXXIII (June 26), 200–1.

1936   "One Current Religious Problem," *Journal of Philosophy,* XXXIII (June 4), 324–26.
"Religion, Science and Philosophy," *Southern Review,* 2d Series, I (Summer), 53–62.
"Horace Mann Today," *Social Frontier,* III (November), 41–42.

1937   "Education, the Foundation for Social Organization," in Educating for Democracy, a Symposium, pp. 37–54. Yellow Springs, Ohio: Antioch Press.
With W. H. Kilpatrick and others. The Teacher and Society. First Yearbook of the John Dewey Society. New York: Appleton-Century Co.

1938   "Does Human Nature Change?" *Rotarian,* LII (February), 8–11, 58–59.
"The Relation of Science and Philosophy as the Basis of Education," *School and Society,* XLVII (April 9), 470–73.
"Determination of Ultimate Values or Aims Through Antecedent or A Priori Speculation or Through Pragmatic or Empirical Inquiry," in National Society for the Study of Education, Thirty-seventh Yearbook, Part 2, pp. 471–85. Chicago.
Experience and Education. New York: Macmillan.
Logic: The Theory of Inquiry. New York: Henry Holt and Co.

1939   "Experience, Knowledge and Value: A Rejoinder," in The Philosophy of John Dewey, pp. 517–608. Volume I of the Library of Living Philosophers. Edited by Paul A. Schilpp. Evanston, Illinois: Northwestern University.
Freedom and Culture. New York: G. P. Putnam's Sons.
Intelligence in the Modern World. Edited by Joseph Ratner. New York: The Modern Library.

1940   "Nature in Experience," *Philosophical Review,* XLIX (March), 244–58.

Education Today. Edited and with a foreword by Joseph Ratner. New York: G. P. Putnam's Sons.

1942   "Ambiguity of 'Intrinsic Good,'" *Journal of Philosophy,* XXXIX (June 4), 328–30.

1943   "Valuation Judgments and Immediate Quality," *Journal of Philosophy,* XL (June 10), 309–17.

"Further as to Valuation as Judgment," *Journal of Philosophy,* XL (September 30), 543–52.

1944   "Democratic Faith and Education," *Antioch Review,* IV (June), 274–83.

"Some Questions about Value," *Journal of Philosophy,* XLI (August 17), 449–55.

1945   "Ethical Subject-Matter and Language," *Journal of Philosophy,* XLII (December 20), 701–12.

"Democratic Faith and Education," in The Authoritarian Attempt to Capture Education: Papers from the Second Conference on the Scientific Spirit and the Democratic Faith, pp. 1–12. New York: King's Crown Press.

1946   Problems of Men. New York: Philosophical Library.

1948   "William James' Morals and Julien Benda's," *Commentary,* V (January), 46–50.

1949   "Philosophy's Future in Our Scientific Age," *Commentary,* VIII (October), 388–94.

"The Field of Value," in Ray Lepley, Value: A Cooperative Inquiry, pp. 64–77. New York: Columbia University Press.

With Arthur F. Bentley. Knowing and the Known. Boston: Beacon Press.

N.B. The most complete listing of Dewey titles is to be found in "Bibliography of the Writings of John Dewey (1882–1950)," in The Philosophy of John Dewey, pp. 609–87. Volume I of the Library of Living Philosophers. Edited by Paul A. Schilpp. Evanston, Illinois: Northwestern University, 1939.

IV. OTHER SOURCES

Adams, James Truslow. The Founding of New England. Boston: Atlantic Monthly Press, 1921.

Addams, Jane. The Second Twenty Years at Hull-House: September 1909 to September 1929. New York: Macmillan, 1930.

—— Twenty Years at Hull-House. New York. Macmillan, 1910.

American Council on Education. The Function of the Public Schools in Dealing with Religion. Washington: American Council on Education, 1953.

—— The Relation of Religion to Public Education. Washington: American Council on Education, 1947.

—— Religion and Public Education. Washington: American Council on Education, 1944.

—— "Reports and Papers of the Conference on Religion and Public Education Held at Arden House, New York, March 10–12, 1957" (unpublished).

Aydelol, B. P. Report on the Study of the Bible in Common Schools. Cincinnati: N. S. Johnson, 1837.

Baker, Melvin C. Foundations of John Dewey's Educational Theory. New York: King's Crown Press, 1956.

Bardeen, C. W. "William Torrey Harris," School Bulletin, XXXVI (1909), 65–68.

Barnard, Henry. Educational Biography: Memoirs of Teachers, Educators, and Promoters and Benefactors of Education, Literature and Science. 2d ed. New York: Brownell, 1861.

—— "Horace Mann," American Journal of Education, V (December, 1858), 611–45.

—— "William Torrey Harris and St. Louis Public Schools," American Journal of Education, XXX (n.s. V) (September, 1880), 625–40.

Barzun, Jacques. Darwin, Marx, Wagner: Critique of a Heritage. Boston: Little, Brown and Co., 1941.

—— Teacher in America. Boston: Little, Brown and Co. 1944.

Beard, Charles A., and Mary R. Beard. The Rise of American Civilization. 2 vols. New York: Macmillan, 1927.

Becelaere, L. van. La Philosophie en Amérique depuis les origines jusqu'à nos jours (1607–1900). New York: Eclectic Publishing Co., 1904.

Becker, Carl L. The Heavenly City of the Eighteenth Century Philosophers. New Haven: Yale University Press, 1932.

Belsham, Thomas. American Unitarianism; or a Brief History of "The Progress and Present State of the Unitarian Churches in America." Extracted from his "Memoirs of the Life of the Reverend Theophilus Lindsey," printed in London, 1812, and now published for the benefit of the Christian Churches in this Country, without note or alteration. 2d ed. Boston, 1815.

Bergson, Henri. The Two Sources of Morality and Religion. Translated by R. Ashley Audra and Cloudesley Brereton. New York: Henry Holt and Co. 1935.

Bertocci, Peter A. "Child's Education and Morals," Harvard Educational Review, XXI (Fall, 1951), 203–20.

Bestor, Arthur E., Jr. Horace Mann, Elizabeth Peabody and Orestes A. Brownson. An Unpublished Letter with Commentary. (Reprinted from the Proceedings of the Middle States Association of History and Social Science Teachers, 1940–41.) New York: Columbia Teachers College, 1941.

"A Bibliography of Horace Mann," in Report of the U.S. Commissioner of Education for the Year 1896–97. Washington: Government Printing Office, 1898.

Billington, Ray A. The Protestant Crusade, 1800–1860. New York: Macmillan, 1938.

Blanshard, Paul. American Freedom and Catholic Power. Boston: Beacon Press, 1950.

—— Communism, Democracy, and Catholic Power. Boston: Beacon Press, 1951.

Blau, Joseph L. American Philosophic Addresses, 1700–1900. New York: Columbia University Press, 1946.

Blow, Susan E. "In Memoriam, Dr. William T. Harris," *Kindergarten Review*, XX (1909), 259–60.

—— "The Service of Dr. W. T. Harris to the Kindergarten," *Kindergarten Review*, XX (June, 1910), 589–603.

Branch, E. D. The Sentimental Years, 1836–1860. New York: D. Appleton-Century Co., 1934.

Brokmeyer, H. C. A Mechanic's Diary. Washington: E. C. Brokmeyer (private printing), 1910.

Brooks, Van Wyck. The Flowering of New England, 1815–1865. New York: Dutton, 1938.

Brosnahan, Timothy. Dr. Harris and the Agnostic School House. New York: Messenger Press, 1903.

Brown, James N. Educational Implications of Four Conceptions of Human Nature. Washington: Catholic University of America Press, 1940.

Brown, Samuel W. The Secularization of American Education. New York: Columbia University Press, 1912.

Brownson, Orestes. "Paganism in Education," *Brownson's Quarterly Review*, n.s. VI (April, 1852), 227–47.

—— "The School Library," *Boston Quarterly Review*, III (April, 1840), 225–37.

—— "Second Annual Report of the Board of Education, together with the Second Annual Report of the Secretary of the Board" (a review), *Boston Quarterly Review*, II (October, 1839), 393–434.

Brubacher, John S. Modern Philosophies of Education. 2d ed. New York: McGraw-Hill Book Co., 1950.

Brubacher, John S., ed. The Public Schools and Spiritual Values. New York: Harper and Brothers, 1944.

Bryson, Lyman, Louis Finkelstein, and Robert MacIver, eds. Goals for American Education. New York: Harper and Brothers, 1950.

Burns, J. A. The Growth and Development of the Catholic School System in the United States. New York: Benziger Brothers, 1912.

—— The Principles, Origin and Establishment of the Catholic School System in the United States. New York: Benziger Brothers, 1912.

Burns, J. A., and Bernard Kohlbrenner. A History of Catholic Education in the United States. New York. Benziger Brothers, 1937.

Bushnell, Horace. "Christianity and Common Schools," *Common School Journal of Connecticut,* II (January 15, 1840), 102–3.

Butts, R. Freeman. The American Tradition in Religion and Education. Boston: Beacon Press, 1950.

—— A Cultural History of Education. New York: McGraw-Hill Book Co., 1947.

Butts, R. Freeman, and Lawrence A. Cremin. A History of Education in American Culture. New York: Henry Holt and Co., 1953.

Carter, James G. Essays upon Popular Education, Containing a Particular Examination of the Schools of Massachusetts, and an Outline of an Institution for the Education of Teachers. Boston: Bowles and Dearborn, 1826.

Chadbourne, Richard M. "Two Organizers of Divinity: Ernest Renan and John Dewey," *Thought,* XXIV (September, 1949), 430–48.

Cheever, George B. Right of the Bible in Our Public Schools. New York: Robert Carter and Brothers, 1854.

Childs, John L. American Pragmatism and Education. New York: Henry Holt and Co., 1956.

—— Education and Morals. New York: Appleton-Century-Crofts, Inc., 1950.

—— "Values," *Harvard Educational Review,* XXII (Fall, 1952), 219–28.

"The Christian Education of Youth," an Encyclical Letter of Pope Pius XI. New York: America Press Pamphlets, 1936.

Clare, Thomas H. "The Sociological Theories of William Torrey Harris." Unpublished Ph.D. dissertation, Department of Sociology, Washington University, St. Louis, 1934.

Clark, Joseph S. Historical Sketch of the Congregational Churches in Massachusetts, 1620–1858. Boston: Congregational Board of Publications, 1858.

Clinton, John L., ed. Ten Famous American Educators. Columbus, Ohio: R. G. Adams and Company, 1933.

Cohen, Morris R. "Some Difficulties with John Dewey's Anthropocentric Naturalism," in Studies in Philosophy and Science. New York: Henry Holt and Co., 1949.

Collins, James. A History of Modern European Philosophy. Milwaukee: Bruce Publishing Co., 1954.

Combe, George. The Constitution of Man Considered in Relation to External Objects. New, revised, and enlarged ed. New York: Fowler and Wells Co., 1888.

—— "Education in America, State of Massachusetts," *Edinburgh Review,* LXXIII (July, 1841), 486–502.

—— Lectures on Popular Education. Boston: Marsh, Capen, Lyon and Webb, 1839.

—— Moral Philosophy or the Duties of Man. 3d ed. Edinburgh: Mac-Lachlan, Stewart, and Co., 1846.

—— Notes on the United States of North America during a Phrenological Visit in 1838–39–40. 2 vols. Philadelphia: Carey and Hart, 1841.

Commager, Henry Steele. Theodore Parker. Boston: Little, Brown and Co., 1936.

Committee of Boston Schoolmasters. Penitential Tears; or, A Cry from the Dust, by "The Thirty-one," Prostrated and Pulverized by the Hand of Horace Mann, Secretary, &c. Boston: C. Stimpson, 1845.

—— Rejoinder to the "Reply" of Hon. Horace Mann, Secretary of the Massachusetts Board of Education to the "Remarks" of the Association of Boston Masters upon His Seventh Annual Report. Boston: Charles C. Little and James Brown, 1845.

—— Remarks on the Seventh Annual Report of the Hon. Horace Mann, Secretary of the Massachusetts Board of Education. Boston: Charles C. Little and James Brown, 1844.

—— Report of the Special Committee of the Primary School Board, on a Portion of the Remarks of the Grammar Masters. Boston: John H. Eastburn, City Printer, 1844.

Compayré, Gabriel. Horace Mann and the Public School in the United States. Translated by Mary D. Frost. New York: T. Y. Crowell and Co., 1907.

Confrey, Burton. Secularism in American Education. Washington: Catholic University of America Press, 1931.

Connors, Edward M. Church-State Relationships in Education in the State of New York. Washington: Catholic University of America Press, 1951.

Constitutions of the States and United States. Albany: New York State Constitutional Convention Committee, 1938.

Cook, Francis E. William Torrey Harris in the Saint Louis Public Schools. (Reprinted from Annual Report of the Superintendent of Instructions, 1909–10.) St. Louis, 1910.

Counts, George S. Dare the School Build a New Social Order? New York: John Day Co., 1932.

—— The Social Foundations of Education. New York: Charles Scribner's Sons, 1934.

Cremin, Lawrence A. The American Common School: An Historic Conception. New York: Bureau of Publications, Columbia Teachers College, 1951.

Cremin, Lawrence A. *(Continued)*
—— "Public School and Public Philosophy," *Teachers College Record,* LVII (March, 1956), 354–60.
—— The Republic and the School. New York: Bureau of Publications, Columbia Teachers College, 1957.
Crosser, Paul K. The Nihilism of John Dewey. New York: Philosophical Library, 1955.
Cubberley, Ellwood P. The History of Education. Boston: Houghton Mifflin Co., 1920.
—— Public Education in the United States. Revised and enlarged ed. Boston: Houghton Mifflin Co., 1934.
Culver, Raymond B. Horace Mann and Religion in the Massachusetts Public Schools. New Haven: Yale University Press, 1929.
Curran, Francis X. The Churches and the Schools. Chicago: Loyola University Press, 1954.
—— Major Trends in American Church History. New York: America Press, 1946.
Curti, Merle. The Great Mr. Locke, America's Philosopher: 1783–1861. Reprint from the Huntington Library Bulletin, No. 11, pp. 107–51. Los Angeles: Huntington Library, 1937.
—— The Roots of American Loyalty. New York: Columbia University Press, 1946.
—— Social Ideas of American Educators. New York: Charles Scribner's Sons, 1935.
Dame, John F. Naturalism in Education: Its Meaning and Influence. Philadelphia: Temple University Press, 1938.
Darling, Arthur B. Political Changes in Massachusetts, 1824–1848: A Study of Liberal Movements in Politics. New Haven: Yale University Press, 1925.
Davies, John D. Phrenology: Fad and Science, a 19th Century American Crusade. New Haven: Yale University Press, 1955.
Davis, Emerson. "The Common School Controversy in Massachusetts," *New Englander,* V (October, 1847), 513–22.
Dawson, Christopher. "Education and the State," *Commonweal,* LXV (January 25, 1957), 423–27.
Donahue, Charles. "Education and the Image of Man," *Religious Education,* LIII (March–April, 1958), 121–26.
—— "Freedom and Education: The Pluralist Background," *Thought,* XXVII (Winter, 1952–53), 542–60.
—— "Freedom and Education: The Sacral Problem," *Thought,* XXVIII (Summer, 1953), 209–33.
Duncan, Henry. The Sacred Philosophy of the Seasons. 5th ed., 4 vols. Edinburgh: William Oliphant and Sons, 1851.

Dunn, William K. "The Decline of the Teaching of Religion in the American Public Elementary School in the States Originally the Thirteen Colonies, 1776–1861." Unpublished Ph.D. dissertation, Johns Hopkins University, 1956.

Edman, Irwin. John Dewey: His Contribution to the American Tradition. Indianapolis: Bobbs-Merrill Co., 1955.

Emerson, G. B. "Moral Education," in Lectures Delivered before the American Institute of Instruction, 1835. Boston: William D. Ticknor, 1843.

Essays for John Dewey's Ninetieth Birthday. Urbana, Illinois: University of Illinois College of Education, 1950.

Evans, Henry R. A List of the Writings of W. T. Harris. A chapter from the Report of the U.S. Commissioner of Education for 1906–7. Washington: Government Printing Office, 1908.

Federal Writers Project. Selective and Critical Bibliography of Horace Mann. Roxbury, Massachusetts, 1937.

Feldman, W. T. The Philosophy of John Dewey. Baltimore: Johns Hopkins Press, 1934.

Fenner, Mildred S. Pioneer American Educators. Washington: Hugh Birch–Horace Mann Fund, 1944.

Fitzpatrick, F. A. "William Torrey Harris: An Appreciation," *Educational Review,* XL (1910), 1–12.

Fleckenstein, Norbert J. A Critique of John Dewey's Theory of the Nature and the Knowledge of Reality in the Light of the Principles of Thomism. Washington: Catholic University of America Press, 1954.

Fleming, William S. God in Our Public Schools. Pittsburgh: National Reform Association, 1950.

Fuller, Edmund, ed. The Christian Idea of Education: Papers and Discussions. New Haven: Yale University Press, 1957.

Gibbon, Charles. The Life of George Combe. 2 vols. London: Macmillan and Co., 1878.

Golden Anniversary Convention Program, *Religious Education,* XLIX (March–April 1954), 67–176.

Guilday, Peter. A History of the Councils of Baltimore (1791–1884). New York: Macmillan, 1932.

Guilday, Peter, ed. The National Pastorals of the American Hierarchy (1792–1919). Washington: National Catholic Welfare Council, 1923.

Gutzke, Manford G. John Dewey's Thought and Its Implications for Christian Education. New York: King's Crown Press, 1956.

Hall, G. Stanley. Book review of John Dewey's *Psychology, American Journal of Psychology,* I (November, 1887), 146–64.

—— "Philosophy in the United States," *Mind,* IV (January, 1879), 89–105.

Hall, Royal G. "The Significance of John Dewey for Religious Interpretation," *Open Court,* XLII (June, 1928), 331–40.

Haraszti, Zoltán. John Adams and the Prophets of Progress. Cambridge, Mass.: Harvard University Press, 1952.

Harmon, Frances B. The Social Philosophy of the St. Louis Hegelians. New York: Privately printed, 1943.

Harris, D. H. A Brief Report of the Meeting Commemorative of the Early St. Louis Movement in Philosophy, Psychology, Literature, Art and Education (In Honor of Dr. Denton J. Snider's Eightieth Birthday). St. Louis: Privately published by D. H. Harris, 1922.

Hartnett, Robert C. "Education—Or Is It?: Report on *Moral and Spiritual Values in the Public Schools,*" *America* (March 31, 1951), pp. 745–47.

Hauser, C. A. Latent Religious Sources in Public School Education. Philadelphia: Heidelberg Press, 1924.

Hegel, Georg Wilhelm Friedrich. The Ethics of Hegel: Selections from His "Rechtsphilosophie." Translated by J. M. Sterrett. Boston: Ginn and Co., 1893.

—— Lectures on the History of Philosophy. Translated by E. S. Haldane and Frances H. Simson. 3 vols. New York: Humanities Press, 1955.

—— The Philosophy of History. Translated by J. Sibree. New York: Dover Publications, Inc., 1956.

Henry, Virgil. The Place of Religion in Public Schools. New York: Harper and Brothers, 1950.

Herberg, Will. Protestant, Catholic, Jew. New York: Doubleday, 1955.

Hill, Henry H. "Public Schools Must Be Secular," *Atlantic Monthly,* CXC (October, 1952), 75–77.

Hinsdale, B. A. Horace Mann and the Common School Revival in the United States. New York: Charles Scribner's Sons, 1900.

Hook, Sidney. John Dewey: An Intellectual Portrait. New York: John Day Co., 1939.

—— John Dewey, Philosopher of Science and Freedom: Symposium. New York: Dial Press, 1950.

—— "Moral Values and/or Religion in Our Schools," *Progressive Education* (May, 1946).

Horne, Herman Harrell. The Democratic Philosophy of Education: Companion to Dewey's *Democracy and Education:* Exposition and Comment. New York: Macmillan, 1932.

Hovre, Franz de. Philosophy and Education. Translated by Edward B. Jordan. New York: Benziger Brothers, 1931.

Hubbell, George A. Horace Mann, Educator, Patriot and Reformer. Philadelphia: W. F. Fell Co., 1910.

Index Librorum Prohibitorum Ss. D. N. Pii Pp. XII Jussu Editus. Rome: Typis Polyglottis Vaticanis, 1940.

Internationale Zeitschrift für Erziehung: Studies in Honor of William Torrey Harris. Berlin: Weidmannsche Buchhandlung, 1935.

Ireland, John. "State Schools and Parish Schools: Is Union between Them Impossible?" in Journal of Proceedings and Addresses of the National Education Association, 1890. Washington: National Education Association, 1891.

Irving, Washington. The Life and Voyages of Christopher Columbus. Abridged by the author. 1st ed. New York: J. and J. Harper, 1833.

James, William. Pragmatism, a New Name for Old Ways of Thinking. New York: Longmans, 1907.

—— The Principles of Psychology. Chicago: Encyclopaedia Britannica, 1952.

John, Walton C., ed. "William Torrey Harris." Centenary Bulletin, 1936, No. 17, U.S. Office of Education. Washington: Government Printing Office, 1936.

Johnson, F. Ernest. American Education and Religion. New York: Harper and Brothers, 1952.

Jones, Howard Mumford. "The Influence of European Ideas in Nineteenth-Century America," American Literature, VII (November, 1935), 241–73.

Jones, Marc E. George Sylvester Morris: His Philosophical Career and Theistic Idealism. Philadelphia: David McKay Co., 1948.

Kandel, Isaac. Twenty-five Years of American Education. New York: Macmillan, 1929.

Kane, W. An Essay toward a History of Education. Chicago: Loyola University Press, 1938.

Kasson, Frank H. "William Torrey Harris, LL.D. His Intellectual Growth and His Educational and Philosophic Work," Education, VIII (June, 1888), 619–30.

Kies, Marietta, ed. W. T. Harris: Introduction to the Study of Philosophy. Comprising Passages from His Writings Selected and Arranged with Commentary and Illustrations by Marietta Kies. New York: D. Appleton and Co., 1889.

Kilpatrick, William H. "Apprentice Citizens," Saturday Review (October 22, 1949), p. 12.

—— Philosophy of Education. New York: Macmillan, 1951.

Knight, Edgar W. Education in the United States. 3d ed. Boston: Ginn and Co., 1951.

Labaree, Benjamin. "The Education Demanded by the Peculiar Character of Our Civil Institutions," in Lectures Delivered before the American Institute of Instruction, 1850, pp. 27–58. Boston: Ticknor, Reed & Fields, 1850.

Lang, Ossian H. Horace Mann: His Life and Educational Work. New York: E. L. Kellogg and Co., 1893.

Lang, Ossian H., ed. Educational Creeds of the 19th Century. New York: E. L. Kellogg and Co., 1898.

Leidecker, Kurt F. Yankee Teacher. New York: Philosophical Library, 1946.

Lippmann, Walter. The Public Philosophy. New York: Little, Brown and Co., 1955.

Lubac, Henri de. The Drama of Atheist Humanism. Translated by Edith M. Riley. New York: Sheed and Ward, 1950.

McCluskey, Neil G. "Educators Go to Arden House," America (March 30, 1957), p. 722.

—— "Spiritual Values in Public Schools," America (September 29, 1956), pp. 619–20.

McGiffert, A. C. Protestant Thought before Kant. New York: Charles Scribner's Sons, 1911.

Madden, Ward E. Religious Values in Education. New York: Harper and Brothers, 1951.

Marsh, James, ed. Aids to Reflection and the Confessions of an Inquiring Spirit by Samuel Taylor Coleridge. London: G. Bell and Sons, 1893.

Martin, George N. The Evolution of the Massachusetts Public School System. New York: D. Appleton and Co., 1908.

Martin, R. H. Our Public Schools: Christian or Secular. Pittsburgh: National Reform Association, 1952.

Martineau, Harriet. The Positive Philosophy of Auguste Comte. Translated and with an introduction by Harriet Martineau. 2 vols. London: G. Bell and Sons, 1853.

Mayo, A. D. "The American Common School in New England from 1790 to 1840," in Report of the U.S. Commissioner of Education for the Year 1894–95, II, 1551–1615. Washington: Government Printing Office, 1896.

—— "The American Common School in the Southern States during the First Half Century of the Republic," in Report of the U.S. Commissioner of Education for the Year 1895–96, II, 267–338. Washington: Government Printing Office, 1897.

—— "The Common School in the Southern States beyond the Mississippi River, from 1830 to 1860," in Report of the U.S. Commissioner of Education for the Year 1900–1, I, 357–401. Washington: Government Printing Office, 1902.

—— "The Development of the Common School in the Western States from 1830 to 1865," in Report of the U.S. Commissioner of Education for the Year 1898–99, I, 357–450. Washington: Government Printing Office, 1900.

—— "Horace Mann and the Great Revival of the American Common School, 1830–1850," in Report of the U.S. Commissioner of Education for the Year 1896–97, I, 715–67. Washington: Government Printing Office, 1898.

—— "The Organization and Reconstruction of State Systems of Common-School Education in the North Atlantic States from 1830 to 1865," in

Report of the U.S. Commissioner of Education for the Year 1897–98, I, 355–486. Washington: Government Printing Office, 1899.

Miller, Perry. The New England Mind. New York: Macmillan, 1939.

Monroe, Will S. History of the Pestalozzian Movement in the United States. Syracuse: C. W. Bardeen, 1907.

Morgan, Joy E. Horace Mann at Antioch. Centennial edition. Washington: National Education Association, 1938.

Morris, George S. British Thought and Thinkers: Introductory Studies, Critical, Biographical and Philosophical. Chicago: S. C. Griggs and Co., 1880.

—— Kant's Critique of Pure Reason: A Critical Exposition. Chicago: S. C. Griggs and Co., 1882.

—— "Philosophy and Its Specific Problems," *Princeton Review,* n.s. IX (1882), 208–52.

Morse, James K. Jedidiah Morse: A Champion of New England Orthodoxy. New York: Columbia University Press, 1939.

Muelder, Walter G., and Laurence Sears. The Development of American Philosophy. Boston: Houghton Mifflin Co., 1940.

Murray, John Courtney. "The Problem of Pluralism in America," *Thought,* XXIX (Summer, 1954), 165–208.

Nathanson, J. John Dewey: The Reconstruction of the Democratic Life. New York: Charles Scribner's Sons, 1951.

National Catholic Educational Association. Proceedings and Addresses, 51st Annual Meeting. Washington: National Catholic Educational Association, 1954.

National Education Association. Discussion at the NEA National Meeting in 1889 by Cardinal Gibbons, Bishop Keane, Edwin D. Meade and John Jay. Syracuse: C. W. Bardeen, 1889.

—— The Essential Place of Religion in Education. Washington: National Education Association, 1915.

National Education Association and American Association of School Administrators, Educational Policies Commission. Moral and Spiritual Values in the Public Schools. Washington: The Commission, 1951.

—— Public Education and the Future of America. Washington: The Commission, 1955.

—— The Purposes of Education in American Democracy. Washington: The Commission, 1938.

—— The State and Sectarian Education. Washington: The Commission, 1946.

Nietzsche, Friedrich Wilhelm. The Anti-Christ. Translated by H. L. Mencken. New York: A. A. Knopf, 1920.

—— The Birth of Tragedy and the Genealogy of Morals. Translated by F. Golffing. Garden City, New York: Doubleday Anchor, 1956.

Nietzsche, Friedrich Wilhelm. (*Continued*)
—— Thus Spake Zarathustra. Translated by Thomas Common; edited by M. Komroff. New York: Tudor Publishing Co., 1936.
O'Connell, Geoffrey. Naturalism in American Education. New York: Benziger Brothers, 1938.
O'Farrell, John J. "A Thomistic Evaluation of the Epistemological and Ontological Bases of John Dewey's Instrumentalist Philosophy." Unpublished Ph.D. dissertation, School of Education, Fordham University, 1951.
O'Hara, James Henry. The Limitations of the Educational Theory of John Dewey. Washington: Catholic University of America Press, 1929.
O'Neill, James M. Religion and Education under the Constitution. New York: Harper and Brothers, 1949.
Otto, Max. Science and the Moral Life. New York: Mentor Books, 1949.
Packard, Frederick Adolphus. The Question: Will the Christian Religion Be Recognized as the Basis of the System of Public Instruction in Massachusetts? Discussed in Four Letters to the Rev. Dr. Humphrey, President of Amherst College. Boston: Whipple and Damrell, 1839. (This was published anonymously.)
—— Thoughts on the Condition and Prospects of Popular Education in the United States. Philadelphia: A. Waldie, 1836.
Paley, William. The Works of William Paley, D.D.: His Life, Moral and Political Philosophy, Evidences of Christianity, Natural Theology, Tracts, Horae Paulinae, Clergyman's Companion, and Sermons. 1-volume edition. Philadelphia: Crissy and Markley, 1802.
The Palladium. Edited by College Fraternities at the University of Michigan, Volume XXI. Ann Arbor, 1889.
Park, R. "On Religious Education," in Lectures Delivered before the American Institute of Instruction, 1835. Boston: Charles J. Hendee, 1836.
Parker, Francis W. Centennial of the Birth of the Greatest American Educator, Horace Mann. Chicago: 1896.
—— Talks on Pedagogics. New York: E. L. Kellogg and Co., 1894.
Parrington, Vernon L. Main Currents in American Thought. 3 vols. New York: Harcourt, Brace and Co., 1930.
Peirce, Charles Sanders. Collected Papers of Charles Sanders Peirce. Edited by Charles Hartshorne and Paul Weiss. 6 vols. Cambridge: Harvard University Press, 1931–35.
Perry, Charles M., ed. The St. Louis Movement in Philosophy: Some Source Material. Norman, Oklahoma: University of Oklahoma Press, 1930.
Perry, Ralph Barton. Puritanism and Democracy. New York: Vanguard Press, 1944.
Peterson, F. E., and O. Williamson. Philosophies of Education Current in the Preparation of Teachers in the United States. New York: Bureau of Publications, Columbia Teachers College, 1933.
Pfeffer, Leo. Church, State, and Freedom. Boston: Beacon Press, 1953.

Phelps, William F. Horace Mann. Cincinnati: Hitchcock and Walden, 1879.

Phenix, Philip H. Intelligible Religion. New York: Harper and Brothers, 1954.

—— "Religion in American Public Education," *Teachers College Record,* LVII (October, 1955), 26–31.

Pochmann, Henry A. New England Transcendentalism and St. Louis Hegelianism. Philadelphia: Carl Schurz-Memorial Foundation, Inc., 1948.

Politella, Joseph. Religion in Education: An Annotated Bibliography. Oneonta, New York: American Association of Colleges for Teacher Education, 1956.

Randall, Henry S. Decision of the State Superintendent of Schools, on the Right to Compel Catholic Children to Attend Prayers, and to Read or Commit Portions of the Bible, as School Exercises, Oct. 27, 1853. New York: 1853.

Randall, John Herman, Jr. The Making of the Modern Mind. Rev. ed. Boston: Houghton Mifflin Co., 1940.

Raup, R. B. Educational Philosophies Held by Faculty Members in Schools for the Professional Education of Teachers. Washington: Office of Education, 1933.

Reilly, D. F. The School Controversy. Washington: Catholic University of America Press, 1943.

Religion in State Schools (collection of bound pamphlets in Library of the Department of Health, Education, and Welfare). 6 vols. Washington.

"Religious Instruction in Public Schools" (editorial comment on Harris's NEA Boston talk), *Literary Digest,* XXVII (August 29, 1903), 261.

Richardson, James D. A Compilation of the Messages and Papers of the Presidents. Washington: Bureau of National Literature and Art, 1910.

Riley, Isaac Woodbridge. American Thought: From Puritanism to Pragmatism and Beyond. 2d ed. New York: Henry Holt and Co., 1923.

Roberts, J. S. William T. Harris: A Critical Study of His Educational and Related Philosophical Views. Washington: National Education Association, 1924.

The Role of the Independent School in American Democracy. Milwaukee: Marquette University Press, 1956.

Rossiter, Clinton. Seedtime of the Republic. New York: Harcourt, Brace and Co., 1953.

Rusk, Ralph L., ed. The Letters of Ralph Waldo Emerson. 6 vols. New York: Columbia University Press, 1939.

Rust, R. S. Religion in Common Schools (#479), and Method of Introducing Religion into Common Schools (#480). (Pamphlets in the Library of the Department of Education Collection "Religion in State Schools.") New York: Tract Society.

Schaub, Edward L. William Torrey Harris, 1835–1935: A Collection of

Essays, Including Papers and Addresses Presented in Commemoration of Dr. Harris' Centennial at the St. Louis Meeting of the Western Division of the American Philosophical Society. Chicago: Open Court Publishing Co., 1936.

Schilpp, Paul A., ed. The Philosophy of John Dewey. 2d ed. (Contains the Dewey biography by Jane M. Dewey.) New York: Tudor Publishing Co., 1951.

Schneider, Herbert W. A History of American Philosophy. New York: Columbia University Press, 1946.

Sheldon, W. H. "Professor Dewey, the Protagonist of Democracy," *Journal of Philosophy*, XVIII (June, 1921), 309–20.

Smith, Martin. John Dewey and Moral Education. Washington: Guthrie Lithograph Co., 1939.

Smith, Matthew Hale. The Bible, the Rod, and Religion, in Common Schools. (A Sermon, by Rev. M. Hale Smith; a Review of the Sermon by Wm. B. Fowle; Strictures on the Sectarian Character of the Common School Journal; Correspondence between Mann and Hall.) Boston: Redding and Co., 1847.

—— Reply to the Sequel of Hon. Horace Mann, Being a Supplement to The Bible, the Rod, and Religion, in Common Schools. Boston: J. M. Whittemore, 1847.

Smith, Sherman M. The Relation of the State to Religious Education in Massachusetts. Syracuse: Syracuse University Book Store, 1926.

Smith, Payson, A. E. Winship, and W. T. Harris. Horace Mann and Our Schools: "Horace Mann, His Central Mission" (Smith); "Horace Mann, America's Greatest Educator" (Winship); "Horace Mann, Educational Missionary" (Harris). New York: American Book Co., 1937.

Snider, Denton J. The St. Louis Movement. St. Louis: Sigma Publishing Co., 1920.

—— A Writer of Books in His Genesis. St. Louis: Sigma Publishing Co., 1910.

Steiner, B. C. Life of Henry Barnard, the First United States Commissioner of Education, 1867–1870. Washington: Government Printing Office, 1919.

Stokes, Anson Phelps. Church and State in the United States. 3 vols. New York: Harper and Brothers, 1950.

Stowe, Calvin. The Prussian System of Public Instruction. Cincinnati: Truman and Smith, 1836.

—— Report on Elementary Public Instruction in Europe, Made to the Thirty-sixth General Assembly of the State of Ohio, December 19, 1837. Boston: Dutton and Wentworth, 1838.

Straker, Robert L. "A Gloss upon Glosses" (unpublished manuscript giving critical comments on two books by Louise H. Tharp: *The Peabody Sisters of Salem,* and *Until Victory: Horace Mann and Mary Peabody;* copy in New York Public Library). New York: 1956.

—— The Unseen Harvest: Horace Mann and Antioch College. Yellow Springs, Ohio: Antioch Press, 1955.

Sullivan, John P. "The Growth of Catholic Schools," *America* (November 16, 1957), p. 204.

Sutton, W. S. Problems in Modern Education. Boston: Sherman, French and Co., 1913.

Tenenbaum, Samuel. William Heard Kilpatrick: Trail Blazer in Education. New York: Harper and Brothers, 1951.

Tharp, Louise H. The Peabody Sisters of Salem. Boston: Little, Brown and Co., 1950.

—— Until Victory: Horace Mann and Mary Peabody. Boston: Little, Brown and Co., 1953.

Thayer, Vivian T. The Attack upon the American Secular School. Boston: Beacon Press, 1951.

Thomas, Milton H. A Bibliography of John Dewey, 1882–1939. New York: Columbia University Press, 1939.

Thursfield, Richard E. Henry Barnard's "American Journal of Education." Baltimore: Johns Hopkins Press, 1945.

Tocqueville, Alexis de. Democracy in America. Edited and with an Introduction by Phillips Bradley. 2 vols. New York: Alfred A. Knopf, 1946.

Turner, Frederick Jackson. The Frontier in American History. New York: Henry Holt and Co., 1921.

Ulich, Robert. History of Educational Thought. New York: American Book Co., 1945.

Van Dusen, Henry P. God in Education. New York: Charles Scribner's Sons, 1951.

Voltaire, François Marie Arouet de. Oeuvres Complètes. 52 vols. Paris: Garnier Frères, 1877–85.

Waterston, R. C. "On Moral and Spiritual Culture in Early Education," in Lectures Delivered before the American Institute of Instruction, 1835. Boston: Charles J. Hendee, 1836.

Weiss, John. Life and Correspondence of Theodore Parker. 2 vols. New York: D. Appleton and Co., 1864.

Wenley, R. M. The Life and Work of George Sylvester Morris. New York: Macmillan, 1917.

Wesley, Edgar B. NEA: The First Hundred Years. New York: Harper and Brothers, 1957.

White, Morton G. The Origin of Dewey's Instrumentalism. New York: Columbia University Press, 1943.

Williams, Edward I. F. Horace Mann, Educational Statesman. New York: Macmillan, 1937.

"William T. Harris" (a phrenological analysis), *Phrenological Journal,* XCII (September, 1891), 102–3.

"William T. Harris, His Early Life and His St. Louis Reports," *American Education*, XIII (1909), 308–11.

Winship, A. E. "Friends and Acquaintances: William Torrey Harris," *Journal of Education*, CI (May 28, 1925), 603–7.

Bound volumes of these journals and reports covering the periods of the study were also consulted:

Introductory Discourses and the Annual Lectures Delivered before the American Institute of Instruction.

Journals of the Proceedings and Addresses of the National Education Association.

Religious Education, Volumes I–LII (Official Publication of the Religious Education Association).

Reports of the U.S. Commissioner of Education.

INDEX